G000017594

Modern Classics

Also by Frances Bissell

West Country Kitchen

An A–Z of Food and Wine
(with Tom Bissell)

Frances Bissell's

MODERN CLASSICS

MACMILLAN

First published 2000 by Macmillan
an imprint of Macmillan Publishers Ltd
25 Eccleston Place, London SW1W 9NF
Basingstoke and Oxford
Associated companies throughout the world
www.macmillan.com

ISBN 0 333 74127 7

9 8 7 6 5 4 3 2 1

A CIP catalogue record for this book is available from
the British Library.

Designed by Macmillan General Books Design Department
Photographic reproduction by Aylesbury Studios, Bromley, Kent
Printed and bound in Italy by New Interlitho S.p.a., Milan

Modern Classics

For Tom

Contents

The kind of food I write about is the food I cook at home, often just for the two of us: my husband Tom and me. And because good food is something to be shared, I sometimes cook for three or four friends; only occasionally do I cook for more than six, as our home is a small one.

My cooking is based almost entirely on fresh ingredients because I like the taste of fresh food more than the taste of processed or 'value-added' food. I prefer to do the 'processing' in my own kitchen, using my own skill and experience to judge seasonings, composition and balance.

There are those who would wish me to write only about vegetarian food or to concentrate on what is currently viewed as 'healthy' and 'correct'. But I believe, and this is reflected in my recipes, that a varied diet is a healthy diet, and that an enjoyable diet is a healthy diet. The recognition that wine is inextricably linked to the enjoyment of good food has also given focus to my cooking, as well as my writing.

The time and money spent on food and its preparation are seen by some as an extravagance, as a luxury, a waste. They say there are better things to do with such precious commodities. I do not agree. Food is such an important thread in the fabric of society that it cannot be dismissed. The growing, nurturing, harvesting, selling, trading, preparation, cooking and consumption of food inform and relate to many parts of our lives and that of the community. It tells us who we are.

Landscape and climate, religion and tradition, economics and sociology, all dictate how and what we eat. Foodways are arguably the most accessible part of a nation's culture. I shall never forget visiting Shanghai. For the first time in many years, I was faced with a completely unfamiliar language; newspapers, radio, theatre, literature, politics, humour, all were truly a closed book to me. I could not begin to relate to the people who lived there. Until I went to the market. There I could see who was selling, who was buying, what was in season and how much it cost. I began to understand the economy and way of life of this vast, geographically disparate country. Then I went for lunch. Food, in the form of mealtimes, brings with it a shared common activity, and I began to feel even more at home, when, surrounded by noisy diners, I tucked into the dish of the day, a steaming bowl of spicy Shanghainese eels.

Food and cooking are important to me also because they are the source of great pleasure and enjoyment. I love to see pyramids of gleaming fruit in the covered market in Modena and heaps of glistening moist fish tumbling out of the nets on the quayside in Boulogne. I love the feel of the raw fish in my kitchen, as I fillet a sole or clean a squid. The smells and tastes, the crunch and crispness of food, further delight the senses.

I cook to give pleasure. It also pleases me to give my recipes to readers. Whenever I cook a new dish, or a familiar one for the umpteenth time, it will spark off ideas for other recipes. I like to pass on these other ideas too. Life is too short to hoard recipes.

Whatever is fresh and seasonal and appropriate is what I like to cook. If it is after Christmas, I shall be cooking leftovers and budget-conscious dishes. If it is early summer, I shall cook and eat asparagus for a week. Whatever recipes I am working on at the moment are my favourites.

Often I do not know what I am going to cook until I actually begin cooking. Whilst some of my recipes have been inspired by visits to markets, by the food I discover when I am invited as guest cook at hotels in different parts of the world, and by the cooking of chefs and cooks here and abroad, I can be just as inspired on a Tuesday evening by the contents of my refrigerator.

What do food writers really eat?

What do food writers eat at home? I'm sometimes asked. Do you ever eat just beans on toast? If I were to describe a week's menus, they would show the thinking behind my cooking, how I use mainly what is in season, how I make use of leftovers, and how I plan menus.

At some stage, almost all of my cooking finds its way into my writing. When I write cookery books, I write the recipes that I have cooked at home. I do not cook my way through the vegetable chapter, the pasta chapter, the fish chapter, and so on. If neither of us likes what I have cooked, I probably never cook it again, and I certainly never write about it.

I was very pleased to read that Marcella Hazan writes her cookery books in the same way.

Let me describe one week's cooking, which is as representative as any. On the Sunday, old friends, whom we had not seen for a long time, came for a late Sunday lunch. I made, the day before, a terrine of skate, smoked salmon and courgettes (p. 98), and chocolate pots (p. 209). Preparing these two dishes in advance meant that I needed to spend only minimal time away from our guests at lunch. The main course was zampone with lentils and mashed potatoes. Good-tempered vegetables like these, once cooked, can be kept warm for half an hour or more on heat-diffusers. The zampone simmered in its foil bag until cooked, and then I drained it, sliced it, and served it on a bed of lentils, with the potatoes served separately. Green salad and two excellent farmhouse Cheddars followed, the Montgomery and the Keene's, and, after the chocolate pots, which were simply made with dark chocolate and soya 'cream', there was dessert of fruit, nuts and marrons glacés.

Monday's dinner started with an avocado and waxy potato salad, with walnuts and an orange and walnut vinaigrette. The main course has been a Monday night fixture for many years, a pot-roasted chicken with vegetables, and, separately, basmati rice cooked in the oven. Blueberries stirred into yoghurt followed. Of all the berry fruit, blueberries keep best, and I had bought four cartons for half price because they had reached their sell-by date, although they went on to keep for another week in the refrigerator. I also find little difference in flavour and texture between northern and southern hemisphere blueberries available in the shops.

Fennel, tomato and chicory made a bright, crisp salad to start Tuesday's dinner, and I followed it with one of our favourite pasta dishes, spaghetti Genovese with small waxy potatoes, green beans, and a pesto that I had whizzed up from two packets of basil, a handful of pine nuts, a heel of Parmesan, and some extraordinarily good olive oil, which a neighbour of mine sells for her neighbour in Mani, in Greece: Kosta's olive oil is green, fruity and delicious.

When I walked past Steele's, our local butcher in Hampstead, on Wednesday morning, I saw they had lamb shanks. Irresistible. I bought two and made a slow-cooked casserole with olives, white wine, carrots and onions. We started dinner with the last slice of the skate terrine.

On Thursday, I made the second of our vegetable-based meals, of which I usually make three or four a week. I found very good fresh okra at Brian Lay's, my local greengrocer. This I cut up, dipped in a thick cornmeal batter, and deep-fried in olive oil. I was delighted with the result. The okra was very dry and crisp, and when I measured the strained oil, I saw I had not used much at all.

I made a vegetable gumbo with more okra, beans, courgettes, carrots, onions, fennel, small waxy potatoes and chilli, and served this with rice. The blueberries turned up again in a crumble, but before I put on the topping, I poached the berries in some homemade sloe gin (p. 217).

The pièce de résistance on Friday was fish, a fillet cut from a huge Gulf red snapper that I saw in the window of Hampstead Seafoods. It was a fine piece of fish, dense, sweet, and, it has to be said, quite chewy. I oiled an ovenproof dish, and put in a bulb of fennel, sliced, and a red pepper, which I peeled with a swivel-head potato peeler, seeded, and cut into strips. These I cooked, with a little olive oil, until they were soft, and then the seasoned fish went on top with more olive oil, a splash of fino, zest of a Seville orange and its juice, some shreds of chorizo, and a handful of stoned black olives (p. 98–9).

On Saturday, I made a vegetable lasagne. Potatoes, spread with pesto, and leeks made up one layer, grilled aubergine, fennel and red pepper, the second. I also used up all remaining raw vegetables and trimmings to make a stunning vegetable juice, whizzing it all through the Magimix juicer attachment. The fibrous residue made an excellent vegetable stock. This I used in Sunday's dish.

Coming full circle, I used the left-over red snapper, blended to a cream in the food processor, to stuff some pimentos del Piquillo, a can of which I bought on our last visit to Spain. The main course was a knuckle of free-range pork, one of the most inexpensive cuts of meat, braised slowly with fino, aromatics, the vegetable broth and rice. I thinned down the cornmeal batter with milk, added a little more flour, and made crêpes to serve with the rest of the blueberries and sloe gin.

Throughout the book, I have further illustrated my approach to cooking and menu-planning by interspersing the self-explanatory chapters with suggested menus and accompanying recipes. I have devised a set of six menus for different occasions.

The menus are complete in themselves, but with all six of them, you will be able to mix and match starters, main courses and puddings to create many more permutations. You will recognize, too, that the starters are substantial. Indeed, you may prefer to serve them as a main course, and do as I often do, serve crudités, salad or a simple vegetable soup first.

The menus include oysters, a rice pudding with a twist, traditional dishes such as cottage pie and Hindle Wakes in new guises, exciting vegetable dishes and some stunningly simple, yet sophisticated, desserts. And if you like the general look of the menu, but would prefer a different first course, a soup perhaps, you have only to look at the appropriate chapter.

Modern British cooking

The joy of developing a collection of 'modern classics' resides in the fact that I can cook what I like. As a cook, cooking in Britain today, with the ingredients available to me, how can I help but cook 'modern' British? The barriers are down. I can wood-roast, char-grill and stir-fry. I can serve a chilli and papaya salsa with my roast lamb, steam my smoked haddock with lemon grass, serve it with a wasabi mash, and add soy sauce to my risotto. Can't I? Well, actually, I can't. Not me, personally.

For me, cooking modern British classics means never having to cook mangetout and baby corn. It means using all the good vegetables that grow here. I do not mind clocking up air miles myself, but I hate buying vegetables that have flown halfway round the world.

Our own home-grown potatoes, leeks, root vegetables, cauliflowers, spinach, beans, salad stuffs and herbs are second to none. And, when one thing goes out of season, I choose something else. Our plums, apples and pears are hard to beat, and indeed with Apple Day, 21 October, now a well-established date in our culinary calendar, our apples are a cause for celebration. I shall be happy to use the late crop of Scottish raspberries which reaches us in October, and will then be content to do without until the following summer. Certainly, I can buy Chilean and South African soft fruit in winter, but it does not taste as good as our native fruit. By then, I shall be more than happy to buy those fruits that we have never grown, and which for hundreds of years have been exotic imports, the indispensable lemons and oranges, pineapples, mangoes, persimmons and pomegranates.

Lest all this sounds impossibly purist, let me readily admit to a cupboard full of spices, pulses, rices, noodles, dried orange peel, dried cranberries, tomatoes, mangoes, rice wrappers, and condiments of all varieties and from everywhere. But I would not necessarily use them in dishes that I would feel happy describing as modern British.

Each of us has a different view of what has become assimilated into British cooking. I recognize that I cannot avoid red peppers for ever, and, indeed, I have used them in a delicious terrine with potatoes and leeks (p. 75). Pasta has become part of a universal diet, but I abhor the notion of 'chicken tikka lasagne'.

The reason for disliking this particular concoction – I am loathe to call it a dish – and others like it, is that it dishonours both Indian and Italian cooking, and does nothing for the ingredients. To me, the key to good cooking, modern British or any other kind, is to use good, not necessarily expensive, ingredients and cook them in a way which shows them at their best, and enhances the other food with which they are served. Thus I love making pesto, the classical Genovese recipe with basil – and then all the other members of the family. Parsley pounded with walnuts and grated hard English goat's cheese is a fine accompaniment to grilled chicken or vegetables, as it is to pasta. Pesto has nothing to do with basil, and everything to do with the pestle, or *pestello*, which grinds the ingredients in the mortar. Similarly the use of herbs and other aromatics with mashed potatoes produces a singularly harmonious result. Juices extracted from vegetables put through the juicer make an unusual cooking medium, full of flavour, light and elegant, and this is a modern technique I like to deploy in the kitchen.

On the whole, I do not believe that modern British cooking should open the flood gates to every traditional dish that was ever cooked. I attended a seminar on forgotten dishes in France some time ago, and came to the conclusion that there is a good reason why some dishes have been forgotten. There are many, many more though which, although perhaps first cooked in Elizabethan times, have great appeal today. Oysters set in a savoury pale lemon jelly and garnished with pomegranate seeds appeals to me greatly as a recipe.

Fusion cooking

Fusion cooking is an area of great fascination for the cook. It is also fraught with pitfalls. Why put just two or three flavours on a plate when you can mix a palette of seven or eight? And why not visit three continents at the same time? A little tamarind paste, some *balsamico*, a few shards of lemon grass? Just what the best-dressed lamb shank is wearing these days.

Sometimes fusion cooking works well, sometimes it is spectacularly awful. On the whole it works best where there is a sound knowledge of the individual types of cooking being fused, as it were. It is important to be aware of the underlying cultures and the authentic use of the ingredients being deployed. Having spent a good deal of time in kitchens in the Far East, I feel comfortable using oriental flavours in my own kitchen, and am glad that all the ingredients I like to cook with are much more readily available than they used to be. Packets of ready-selected Thai herbs, for example, are most useful. And coconut milk is an excellent ingredient in soups. One of my tomato soups is a 'fusion' version of the tomato, lovage and garlic soup I often cook in the summer; Thai lime leaves and ginger replace the lovage and garlic, and coconut the milk or cream.

Fusion cooking has been around for longer than we might think. What I call 'organic' fusion cooking goes back several hundred years at least. Dutch, British and Indonesian fused long ago into the unique, subtle and spicy Cape Malay cooking to be found in Cape Town. The French in Kerala left their influence on the food, as did the British throughout the subcontinent.

In Colombo I once asked for a typical Sri Lankan meal, and I was given roast chicken and gravy, cabbage, cauliflower and roast potatoes, with a caramel custard for dessert. But I could as easily have been given dishes which reflected the Portuguese or Dutch influence in the kitchen.

Islands and other outposts are often a rich source of organic fusion cooking. In Malta one finds not only the British legacy of boiled vegetables, but Arabic influences in the sweet almond pastries. One of the most unusual examples of fusion cooking is that found in Macau. Portuguese until 1999, that colonial influence on the food is of course very strong, but so too is the Chinese. This in turn is spiced with a hint of Africa, as in Henri's famous African chicken, said to have been introduced from Portugal's African colonies by sailors who also brought with them the essential hot piri-piri sauce.

Ingredients

One of my greatest pleasures is to experience new tastes and introduce them to others. Thus, I find myself seeking out on my travels ingredients that are rare, unusual, seasonal, typical, regional, and, above all, not available in my local supermarket.

When pressed, I usually put down my hobbies as cooking and travelling, but a closer examination reveals that this includes a tendency to acquire and collect, which is every bit as absorbing and obsessive as other 'collecting' hobbies. Although I suppose, if I wanted to be grand, I could call my version culinary research.

Food shops, other people's kitchens, markets and hardware stores are my sources. The latter are important because I also like to know how people prepare and cook their food. In Oslo, for example, I found marvellous implements for scaling and cleaning fish and for slicing cheese. Sharp knives for cutting the dense coarse Galician maize bread, I found in the market in Santiago de Compostela; cooking pots from Malta, Ireland, Portugal, France and Morocco are stacked on my kitchen shelves. And a set of bamboo soup steamers from Hong Kong are stored at the rear of a cupboard.

Acquiring unusual ingredients is usually much easier on the luggage allowance than are cooking pots. Spices weigh next to nothing. *Ras el hanout* from Morocco, Kuwaiti fish spice, mastic from Turkey, vanilla pods, nutmeg and cloves from Sri Lanka, sachets of spice mixture for 'pork ribs tea' from Singapore, *epazote* from Mexico, *guascas* from

Colombia, and Texas ground green chilli powder, all add to a mélange of fragrances in my store cupboard.

Syrups, oils, vinegars, nuts and seeds are heavier, but I had a strong urge to acquire poppy seeds in Vienna, pumpkin seed oil in Slovenia, maple syrup in Vermont, pecans in Georgia, jaggery in Colombo, *dulce de leche* in Bogotá and coconut vinegar in the Philippines.

When I first started writing about food, supermarkets did not sell fresh basil. I used to bring it back home in bunches from Liguria to make into pesto. It was even difficult to find crème fraiche and unsalted French butter then. I used to dry tomatoes in the sun on the flat roof of my parents' house in Gozo, near Malta. Now I can find most ingredients here that I used to carry home from my travels; I no longer fill my bag with maple syrup, sherry vinegar and *dulce de leche*. We can buy the authentic *aceto balsamico tradizionale di Modena*, certified by the Consorzio, without having to travel to Emilia Romagna.

It is still, nevertheless, a great thrill to be given homemade produce that will never be available in the high-street supermarket, whether it is my mother's lemon curd, Mama Lancellotti's Lambrusco, or Miguel Valdespino's ancient sherry vinegar from the family cask.

Some years ago it was suggested that I was being elitist writing about hard-to-find ingredients, in that particular case wild boar. It might have seemed so at the time, but now wild boar is available by mail order, as, indeed, are kangaroo, alligator and ostrich, unimaginable a few years ago, and wild boar sausages are to be found in the supermarkets.

Not all of my acquisitions come from exotic places. I am just as delighted to find Arran Victor potatoes in a supermarket, and in due season, forced rhubarb from Yorkshire, asparagus from East Anglia, Kentish strawberries, cobnuts and Victoria plums in the local greengrocer. John Dory and seabass from Cornwall, Cromer crabs and Loch Fyne kippers are, at the appropriate time of year, the very high point of my cooking. And I love to buy my meat and poultry direct from the farm when possible.

Investigating ingredients abroad also leads to new ways of using familiar ingredients. In January, Seville oranges are sent to Britain for marmalade-making. But in Andalusia, I discovered that they are used in savoury dishes, as we might use lemons. I have, in fact, substituted Seville oranges for lemons and made an exquisite orange curd. The juice makes an excellent vinaigrette, or glaze for a roast duck or pork loin. I have used it to glaze small turnips and other root vegetables, and both juice and zest in a fine mayonnaise. Indeed the Seville orange is one of my favourite things and I have devoted a large part of the fruit chapter to it and other citrus fruit.

Other favourite ingredients are highlighted in boxes throughout the text. In fact, many of the chapters are ingredient-based, since I find this more useful than chapters for first courses and main courses and so on. We do not necessarily eat like that any more. Puddings and soups have their own chapters, however.

On a more practical note, rather than repeat myself throughout, when a recipe calls for eggs, I mean medium-size, unless otherwise stated. Pepper is freshly ground black pepper. Salt is sea salt. Chocolate is at least 70 per cent cocoa solids. I buy organically produced food when I can, fruit, vegetables, milk, eggs, cheese and dry goods. When I buy pork and poultry I look for meat from organically reared or truly free-range livestock, as I do for beef, veal and lamb.

I cook in metric, although I was 'brought up' in imperial. I find metric straightforward to use, but I realize that there are those who object to using metric, on practical grounds and on principle. I have, therefore, included imperial measurements as well. But do not look for symmetry. Some recipes will show 125g as 4oz, others will show 100g as 4oz. What is important is to follow one system of measurement in each recipe, and ignore the other, and you will find that the proportions of the ingredients in that system work in relation to each other. Quite often, the imperial version of a dish will be slightly smaller than the metric version, since I use logical measurements, 500g (1lb), when in fact 450 grams is closer to a pound in weight.

Where possible, I have dispensed with measurement altogether in favour of units, e.g. 4 carrots, rather than 8oz carrots. With the exception of baking, recipes do not need to be exact down to the last gram (or fraction of an ounce). And for baking, of course, the ingredients we use, flour, butter, sugar, are all sold by metric weight.

The first chapter contains more practical information, on cooking techniques, basic recipes and how to adapt them, a kitchen revision course if you like.

If it's true that 60 per cent of us serve supermarket ready-made meals at home, even when entertaining, that makes for a lot of people who are missing out on the pleasures of cooking. There is great enjoyment to be derived from cooking, first in the preparation and creation of appetizing food from a selection of prime raw materials, and then from the appreciation of those who eat it. Food and wine are one of society's more civilized and inclusive pleasures, and far from the most expensive. I find our puritanical distaste for them hard to understand.

Naturally, there are those who begrudge spending time on doing something they regard as an unpleasant chore and a burden. For them, ready-made meals are the answer; the supermarkets have done it all, choosing the quality, texture and taste of the food, where it comes from, how it looks, and how it is seasoned. Personally, I would rather do all that for myself. And I doubt whether the real reason for choosing ready meals is lack of time. I believe it is lack of confidence which in turn leads to lack of imagination.

Is it really so much easier and quicker shopping for ready meals? Instead of picking up a first course, some bread to go with it, a main course, an accompanying vegetable dish or two, a bag of salad and a dessert, try this exercise.

Buy a ciabatta loaf, a bag of prepared salad, a bag of prepared spinach, a carton of mixed wild mushrooms, two skinless free-range chicken breasts, a mozzarella cheese, a net of oranges and some flaked almonds. I'm assuming you have olive oil, salt, pepper, parsley, herbs and garlic, as well as the odd bottle of orange or almond liqueur. If not, put those in your basket too.

When you get home, peel and slice the oranges, squeezing in the juice from the end pieces. Flavour with a dash of liqueur and chill them in the fridge. In a dry frying pan, lightly toast the almond flakes and put to one side, to scatter over the oranges before serving. With a sharp knife, make a pocket in the chicken. Slice the mozzarella, season it and coat it lightly in chopped herbs before sliding the slices inside the chicken breasts. Brush the meat with olive oil, and grill, fry or bake in the oven at 200°C/400°F/gas mark 6 for 20 to 25 minutes.

While it is cooking, wipe the mushrooms, slice if necessary and fry them in olive oil with a little garlic and finely chopped parsley. When cooked, heap them on the toasted ciabatta, with more chopped

parsley on top, and serve with the salad. Do not wash out the frying pan, because when you are ready to serve the chicken, you can put the contents of the bag of spinach in the pan with a couple of tablespoons of water, and wilt it over a fairly high heat, stirring it well. Divide between two dinner plates, and serve the chicken breast on top, sliced across the middle to show the by now meltingly soft mozzarella, which is both stuffing and sauce. Follow with the chilled oranges, liberally scattered with the toasted almonds.

This is a simple strategy for everyday cooking, to be varied at will. I really believe anyone can cook and can enjoy cooking. And if you decide to give home cooking a try, rather than rely on food technicians to do it all for you, you could do worse than consider classic English cooking.

A simple roast, and I promise you, a roast is simple, with perhaps mashed potatoes and creamed leeks, is much easier to shop for than all the ingredients you need for a Thai meal, or a 'fusion' creation.

And with cooking like this, you reach a point where you do not need recipes. Once you have roasted a leg of lamb or loin of pork, a chicken or a fillet of beef, it is a matter of applying that experience to the next joint of meat, taking into account whether it has its own natural fat, or whether it needs lubricating as it cooks.

The same is true of grilling and frying. Once you have seen how a piece of fish or meat responds to contact with the hot pan or grill, how long it takes to cook, how it tastes and what its texture is once cooked, that experience can be applied again and again. As you vary the seasoning, and accompaniments, you gradually build up your own repertoire of methods and 'recipes'.

Having, for example, made your own sauces for pasta a couple of times, you will no longer be satisfied with the bland lowest common denominator flavours of ready-made sauces. You will very quickly appreciate how easy and enjoyable it is to create your own dishes, in your own style, with a degree of flavour and depth so often lacking in restaurant cooking.

Not long ago I was invited to dinner in a fashionable London haunt, where the main course was a tournedos (sic) of cod with a herb crust, served with roasted garlic, cherry tomatoes and potato stacks. It sounded delicious, it was not bad, but it could have been so much better. Everything had been cooked separately, and was assembled on the plate, so no garlicky juices or sweet tang of tomato had seeped into the fish.

To make the same dish at home, put a handful or more of unpeeled garlic cloves in an ovenproof dish, together with thinly sliced potatoes and onions, and the contents of a punnet of cherry or miniature plum tomatoes. Add a sprig or two of rosemary, and swirl plenty of olive oil around the vegetables. Cook these in a moderate oven, 180°C/350°F/gas mark 4, until the garlic and potatoes are soft, about 45 minutes. Remove from the oven, which you turn up to 200°C/400°F/gas mark 6. Season some cod cutlets, brush with tapenade or olive oil, and scatter on a handful of breadcrumbs mixed with chopped herbs. Put the fish on top of the vegetables and put back in the oven for 10 to 12 minutes to just cook the fish. Serve and enjoy the fragrant garlic purée which you squeeze out of the garlic skins onto the fish and potatoes.

In order to cook delicious food, you do not need a huge kitchen with vast gleaming restaurant-style ranges. My new kitchen is far removed from high tech or cosy rusticity. It is tomorrow's kitchen, in that it fits unobtrusively into our lives, with the dividing lines between kitchen, dining room, study and living room seamlessly overlapping. All you need is what I have, a gas hob and an accurate oven, some storage space and a worktop, and pots and pans that do the job for which they are intended.

Oils and vinegars

I would have a good deal more room on my worktop if I didn't have my bottles of oil and vinegar. I find new ones quite irresistible.

For every day, I use Cretan olive oil and, when I can get it, Portuguese. But then I also like to use the various Spanish olive oils, and any others that come my way. Hence the crowded worktop.

Hazelnut oil, walnut oil and pumpkin seed oil are excellent for salads, and to add to hot vegetable dishes. But they have a low smoke point and are not, therefore, suitable as a cooking medium. A low smoke point means that the oils burn at a lower temperature than, say, groundnut or sunflower or olive oil. When any oil is heated to smoking point, it is too hot, has burnt and will give off acrid and ultimately toxic fumes

When using sesame seed oil, take care to distinguish which one is required. Virgin sesame oil is a clear oil and can be used for cooking. Toasted sesame seed oil, used in oriental dishes, is not suitable for cooking with, as the seeds have already been 'cooked' or toasted, and this distinctive brown oil has a low smoke point.

And what vinegar to combine with the extra-virgin olive oil in the vinaigrette? Homemade lavender, or elderflower vinegar? Too delicate, perhaps. Cider vinegar, certainly. Rice vinegar too, although this is more for use in oriental dishes. Red and white wine vinegars are immensely versatile, and these are the ones to use for your custom-made vinegars; herbs or citrus zest in the white, and berry fruit in the red.

Sherry vinegar from Jerez is an excellent product, and not expensive considering the careful ageing process it undergoes; it is made by the same people who produce finos, amontillados and olorosos. A. R. Valdespino is a name to look for, as is Lustau. In Jerez I have found Gonzalez Byass' own *vinagre de Jerez*, but it is not yet available here. Sherry vinegar is full-flavoured and powerful, quite at the opposite end of the spectrum to cider vinegar and rice vinegar. It does wonders for fish and chips, as well as combining with some of the fruitier olive oils to make a fine vinaigrette. I like it too on red things, such as sliced tomatoes, roasted red peppers, and strawberries, but in modest quantity, as a little goes a long way.

Shopping

When I first set up home and went shopping in the local supermarket, I watched others in amazement as they confidently reached for a few cans of this and packets of that, swiftly filling their trolleys with their weekly shopping. How did they know what to buy? And how much of it to buy?

Fairly quickly I learned that a) you do not know, when you shop on Saturday morning, what you will feel like eating when you get home the following Friday, and b) it was no use putting in the basket items I thought I ought to buy, either because I saw other people buying them, or I remembered my parents buying them.

I developed my own shopping list to take account of our own tastes and way of life.

Even today, my shopping list reflects some of those early lessons. Carrots, onions, celery and root vegetables are near the top of the weekly list, because they have a good shelf life. Greens and salad stuffs are bought more frequently, as and when needed, which is much easier to do now with shops staying open longer and longer hours.

But why onions and carrots anyway? We like homemade soups and casseroles, and every recipe starts: 'Peel and slice the onion and fry until golden brown', then carrots, celery and leeks are added. I use the same basic practice to start a tomato sauce. Only now, instead of making it with one can, I'll use six, or in summer, kilos of fresh tomatoes. Once cooked, I divide the sauce into two-portion batches and freeze them. That way we will have something we know we like to eat on Friday night. My freezer is used for very little: broth made from chicken carcasses, homemade tomato sauce and pesto, egg whites left over from making mayonnaise, and occasionally homemade bread.

Techniques

Simple cooking techniques and ingredients that cook quickly are what we need to call on at the end of a busy day, or any other day when time is at a premium. My theme here, and indeed throughout my book, is not how to cope with cooking, which already induces negative feelings, but how to enjoy cooking. I have included some tried and tested short cuts that will help in producing good tasty dishes to meet these circumstances.

Raw food

The fastest cooking technique is, of course, not to cook at all but to serve the food raw. Such food, however, has to be the best, the freshest, the most impeccable. Carpaccio of beef, steak tartare and slivers of raw fish can be delicious, but need to come from the most reliable sources, and preferably on the same day you serve them. Instead, consider serving smoked salmon or *jamón serrano*, Spain's answer to Parma ham, and an exquisitely sweet and beautifully cured product. Charcuterie, smoked eels, gravad lax, hot smoked salmon and smoked mackerel are all speedy alternatives.

Naturally, raw food has its place in a meal, and it is particularly good as a complement to the one-pot cooking I describe on p. 12, providing a perfect balance of textures and nutritional elements. Salads of leaves and herbs and crisp vegetable crudités can be rapidly assembled from readily available ingredients, then given an elegant and unusual dressing to lift them out of the ordinary. Or choose to make an absolutely classic vinaigrette with the best extra-virgin olive oil, a fine vinegar such as an aged sherry vinegar, sea salt, freshly ground black pepper, and some snipped-up tarragon or chives.

At the other end of a meal, fresh fruit is always welcome. Try a green fruit salad of apples, piel de sapo melon, grapes and kiwi fruit, and flavour it with ginger wine or lime cordial. A golden fruit salad of mango, melon, papaya, physalis, pineapple and any other bright fruit you can find, is delicious liberally bathed in sweet muscat wine, or white grape juice. For autumn I like to make an 'imperial' fruit salad, using red and purple fruit, plums, blueberries, blackberries, tayberries and black and red grapes. These are perfect in a spiced red wine syrup, or simply dressed with red grape juice.

Quick cooking

Some suggestions and an example

Stir-frying, grilling or shallow-frying, sometimes called pan-frying, are the quickest cooking methods, and amongst the most flexible, allowing for endless permutations of seasonings, marinades and accompaniments with your chosen ingredients. They are also relatively economical of fuel, using just one or two burners on the hob.

Expect to spend less time but more money, because fast, hot cooking methods require tender prime cuts of meat. The meat, even if marinated, will not have time to 'improve' during cooking, as it might, marginally, if cooked slowly with lots of additional flavours and helpers. Choose a piece of mature, grass-fed English or Scottish beef, new season's Dorset lamb, organic pork and poultry. Fish and shellfish cook well by these methods, but are never inexpensive.

Meat and fish are not the only ingredients suitable for fast and hot treatment. Vegetables can be fried, stir-fried or grilled and served as accompaniments or can form the basis of a salad or main course. Particularly suitable vegetables for stir-frying include asparagus, broccoli, beans, bean-sprouts, cabbage, cauliflower, chard, Chinese greens, courgettes, kohlrabi, mushrooms, peas, sea-kale, spinach and spring greens. For grilling or frying, I would suggest aubergines, courgettes, mushrooms, peppers and tomatoes.

A ridged cast-iron griddle is a useful piece of equipment for cooking meat, fish and vegetables with the characteristic charred stripes. A good-quality, heavy frying pan, particularly a professional-grade stainless-steel one, the best you can afford, is a worthwhile investment, because it will last for ever if properly cared for. Cast-iron, which you season well, and anodized aluminium also make good frying pans. Non-stick and enamelled cast-iron have their place, but not for using on very high heat.

Marinate some skinned chicken breasts in olive oil, lemon juice, crushed garlic and thyme or tarragon for half an hour, pat them dry on paper towels and cook them on a greased ridged griddle or under the grill, until the juices run clear when you pierce the meat with a skewer.

Brush duck breasts with honey and soy sauce, having first scored the skin and fat with a sharp knife, and cook in the same way.

Brush a cod cutlet with olive oil and tapenade or black olive paste, and sweat it in its own juices in a lidded frying pan; a dish that will take a matter of minutes.

A quick pan sauce for small pieces of meat does not require stock. Sear the meat in a greased heavy stainless-steel frying pan, and once the meat is cooked, transfer it to a warm plate and deglaze the pan by pouring on a small amount of wine and water, scraping up any residues in the pan, and letting it boil for a few minutes before seasoning and serving with the meat. All of these are delicious on a bed of green salad, with the pan juices poured over everything, as in the recipe which follows.

Duck breasts with aromatic herb salad

Serves 4

4 duck breasts
freshly ground black pepper
sea salt
freshly grated nutmeg
rocket
lamb's lettuce
oak leaf lettuce
chervil
chives
tarragon
5–6 tablespoons of whatever wine you are
    serving with the duck

Season the meat with black pepper, a little salt and a hint of nutmeg.

Heat a heavy frying pan, and fry the duck breasts, skin side down, for 5 minutes, until much of the fat has been melted. Remove the pan from the heat and pour off most of the fat.

Take the skin off the duck breasts, and cut it into thin strips.

Arrange salad leaves and herbs on individual plates.

Reheat the frying pan, and fry the duck breasts on the uncooked side, until done to your liking. Transfer them to the dinner plates.

Raise the heat, and fry the duck skin until crisp. Scatter the pieces over the salad leaves. Pour the wine into the frying pan, heat, and scrape up any pan juices before pouring over the meat and salad.

How to make a good stir-fry

The best, freshest ingredients cooked at top speed is the essence of a stir-fry. There is not time to achieve a gentle amalgamation of flavours through slow cooking and judicious adding of seasonings; the flavours must be good and assertive from the word go. My rule of thumb is that if the food is good enough to eat raw, it's good enough to stir-fry.

Certainly borrow from the oriental kitchen, by having everything neatly sliced or chopped and all the ingredients to hand before you start, but do not be restricted to oriental flavourings. The wok is not far removed from the sauté pan of French cookery, and the old English tossing pan.

Stir-fried prawns and spinach

Serves 2

butter or olive oil
500g (1lb) raw shell-on prawns
teaspoon of crushed juniper berries
1 lemon
crushed garlic clove or two, if you like
gin
bag of baby spinach
salt
pepper
fresh dill, chopped

Heat the fat in a wok or sauté pan and when hot, drop in the prawns.

Toss and stir them until they turn pink.

Meanwhile, stir in the juniper and grate in plenty of lemon zest, and add the garlic if using it.

Splash on a measure or two of gin, stand back and light it.

When the flames have died down, stir in the spinach and seasoning.

Serve when the spinach is just wilted, and scatter on the dill and a sprinkling of lemon juice. Or hand the lemon round separately. This takes longer to type than to cook.

The recipe can be adapted to queen scallops, and other greenery such as rocket or watercress, and other spirits or flavouring. It is such a fast, hot dish that even if you cannot get raw prawns, the pink shell-on Greenland prawns, which are already cooked, can be given this treatment, and taste delicious. The shell protects from overcooking, and I would not use cooked, shelled prawns in this recipe.

How to dish up an easy dessert

Goat's cheese with figs and honey

Serves 2

2 large or 6 small slices of fresh goat's cheese 'log'
6 semi-dried figs
2 tablespoons clear honey
nutmeg, cinnamon or cardamom

Put the cheese and figs together on plates, trickle the honey over both, and dust lightly with freshly grated, ground or crushed spice. Quantities can simply be multiplied if more servings are required.

You can replace the soft goat's cheese, if you like, with a thick wedge of ricotta, for example. And if you plan in advance, poach the semi-dried figs in red wine, then boil down the juices and sweeten with honey. Alternatively poach them in orange or apple juice, or herb tea.

Or simply serve the figs with a dollop of crème fraiche, mascarpone or Greek yoghurt, topped with toasted flaked almonds or pine nuts. Maple syrup or *dulce de leche* (caramel spread), instead of honey, can be trickled over whatever you choose. And for an amazing sauce to pour over vanilla, or other, ice cream, heat two or three table-spoons of clear honey in a saucepan, remove from the heat and stir in a broken-up bar of 70 per cent chocolate. Use when the chocolate has melted and mingled with the honey.

And another one:

Flamed bananas

Peel a banana for each person and then add another one or two. Cut in half, and then halve each piece lengthways. Heat unsalted or clarified butter in a frying pan and fry the bananas for 3 or 4 minutes. Add two tablespoons orange or apple juice per person, a dash of lemon juice and a teaspoon of sugar. Pour on a measure or two of spirits or liqueur – rum or an orange liqueur are particularly good – stand back and light it. When the flames have died down, add cream if you want to make a caramel sauce, or serve without, and dust with icing sugar. An excellent accompaniment to nutmeg ice cream.

To make a hot fruit salad, follow the same principle, but use a mixture of fruit such as thinly sliced apple or pear, sliced bananas, soaked dried apricots, slivers of mango and grapes.

One-pot cooking

One-pot cooking is an excellent way of entertaining with ease. Into the pot go the protein, grain or pulse and vegetables, together with the seasoning. The pot goes into the oven, and the dish looks after itself. My recipe for lamb shanks with barley follows this pattern, and produces a succulent, full-flavoured casserole.

Enamelled cast-iron casseroles, tagines, clay pots or chicken bricks, Dutch ovens and electric slow cookers are the utensils to invest in if you like this kind of cooking, and its results. I must admit I do, and my shelves groan under sturdy pots and enamelled cast-iron. The beauty of so many casseroles and stews is that they are even better reheated the next day or so. Thus you can prepare one when you have the time, and use it when time is at a premium, when you get back from work and only have half an hour to get a meal on the table. A vegetable salad, a casserole reheated for 30 minutes, and one of my speedy dessert ideas will amply deal with the situation.

Pulses, too, are ideal candidates for one-pot cooking. Real baked beans, cassoulet, bean stews using the rich variety of pulses available, the borlotti, the pinto, the navy, the turtle, the flageolet to name but a few, are hard to beat on a cool spring day. I have included my favourite, and popular, black bean soup recipe which is almost a meal in itself, especially when served Cuban-style over a mound of cooked rice.

When cooking dried beans, an initial 15 min-utes' boiling is necessary to destroy toxins found on the surface, but not interior, of the bean. It is wise to apply this to all dried beans, rather than trying to remember which need it (red and black kidney beans, and black-eyed beans) and which do not. Canned beans are widely available and can also be used. These do not, of course, require an initial boiling. I have included the delicate, pale green flageolets in a spring vegetable casserole, which makes a perfect main course for a vegetarian meal.

Black bean soup

Serves 4

250g (½lb) turtle beans or black kidney beans
1 medium onion, peeled and finely chopped
1 tablespoon sunflower or olive oil
1 tablespoon each ground cumin and paprika
¼ teaspoon each cayenne pepper or chilli
    powder and ground cloves
1 tablespoon tomato purée
1 litre (1¾ pints) vegetable or chicken stock or
    water
salt

Boil the beans for 15 minutes, then rinse and drain and put them in a bowl. Pour fresh boiling water over them and leave for one hour. Rinse and drain them again.

In an enamelled casserole or other pot suitable for both stove top and oven, gently fry the onion in the oil until beginning to brown. Add the spices and cook for 2 to 3 minutes. Stir in the tomato purée, and cook until the mixture thickens and darkens, as the liquid evaporates.

Add the beans and stock, put the lid on and cook until the beans are tender. You can cook this in the oven at 180°C/350°F/gas mark 4, or on a low simmer on the hob. When the beans are soft, add salt to taste.

Allow the beans to cool slightly in their liquid before making a purée of them in a blender or food processor. It is best to do this in two batches, unless you have a large-capacity machine. Alternatively, you can rub the soup through a sieve, or leave it chunky.

If the consistency is too thick for you, gradually add a little more water or stock and appropriate seasoning, until the taste and consistency are as you want them.

I like to serve the soup very hot, pouring it when practically boiling into earthenware soup bowls containing a splash of sherry or rum so that the heat of the soup evaporates most of the alcohol, leaving the flavour behind. I then add to each bowl a very thin slice of lemon, a sprinkling of finely chopped parsley, and perhaps a tablespoonful of soured cream.

Courgettes, asparagus and new potatoes cooked in cider

Serves 4

about 500g (1lb) each new potatoes, green
    asparagus and small courgettes

50g (2oz) unsalted butter
3 shallots, peeled and finely chopped
150mls (¼ pint) each dry cider and vegetable
    stock or water
6 ripe tomatoes, seeded and chopped
8 basil leaves, torn into shreds
1 can flageolets
sea salt
freshly ground black pepper
fresh chervil or tarragon
50g (2oz) Parma ham pieces – optional
Parmesan

Scrub but do not peel the potatoes. Snap off the woody base of the asparagus, and slice off the stalk and base of the courgettes.

In a casserole melt the butter, and add the shallots and the potatoes, stirring to coat them, and fry gently until the shallots begin to turn golden brown.

Add the cider and stock. Bring to the boil, and cook until the potatoes are yielding but not soft.

Add the courgettes, whole if very small, or cut into chunks, and the asparagus broken into two or three pieces and simmer for 4 to 5 minutes.

Add the tomato, basil and flageolets, and season to taste after bringing back to the boil. Scatter on chervil or tarragon and shave large flakes of Parmesan on top before serving.

If you wish, you can strain the cooking liquid into another saucepan, and boil it down to reduce the volume and concentrate the flavour before serving.

For a non-vegetarian version, you can stir in some shreds of Parma ham, or other cured ham.

For a more substantial dish, add a poached or lightly boiled egg to each serving.

Lamb shanks with spring vegetables and pearl barley

Serves 4

1 large onion, peeled and sliced or chopped
1 tablespoon olive or sunflower oil
2 or 3 garlic cloves peeled and crushed
    – optional
4 lamb shanks
300mls (½ pint) red or white wine, lamb stock or
    water
1 teaspoon black peppercorns
2 bay leaves

sprig or 2 of thyme
175g (6oz) pearl barley
500g (1lb) vegetables, prepared weight
   – see recipe
salt

In a casserole fry the onion in the oil until golden brown, and add the garlic, if using it. Brown the lamb shanks all over, and then add the wine, peppercorns, bay leaves, thyme and barley.

Bring to the boil, cover, and simmer for 1 hour.

In the meantime, prepare the vegetables: baby leeks, courgettes, new carrots, small onions, green beans, a selection of what you like, but all cut to roughly the same thickness to ensure even cooking.

Add the vegetables after the lamb has cooked for an hour, stir to cover them with juice, and then continue cooking until the lamb, barley and vegetables are tender.

The casserole can also be cooked in the oven at 180°C/350°F/gas mark 4, for about 2 hours, or for longer at a lower temperature if more convenient. If cooking the casserole in advance, add the leeks when you reheat, especially if using young, tender leeks. Season to taste with salt.

The same basic method can be applied to other meats. If you cannot get shanks, use best-end-of-neck chops. Alternatively, try knuckle of pork or pork spare rib chops, or shin of veal. For variety, replace the barley with lentils or dried beans, or try chicken pieces cooked with wild rice instead of barley. Thighs produce a tastier dish than breasts, and the meat and rice will cook in the same time, about 1 hour.

Baking and roasting

Unlike the dry hot methods of grilling and stir-frying, the dry hot cooking of the oven is best suited to larger quantities and larger portions. Thus one grills a lamb chop, but roasts a leg of lamb. And one does not, for reasons of economy, use the oven to roast a red pepper and an aubergine, one roasts a whole tray of vegetables.

There are many benefits to using the oven. With the heat turned down, you can cook inexpensive cuts of meat which require longer, slower cooking than prime cuts. And there is the added benefit of flavours melding as several ingredients cook together. It is the ideal cooking method for home cooking, and one which many restaurants would love to emulate.

Vegetables suitable for roasting and baking include aubergines, peppers, courgettes and all the squash family, tomatoes, mushrooms and all root vegetables. As they cook, their juices caramelize to an appetizing golden brown, especially along the cut edges. The vegetables in the Catalan recipe, *escalivada,* can be cooked on an open fire, on a griddle, or, just as easily, in the oven. It makes a fine accompaniment to a slow-roasted lamb dish, or can be served cold as a first course. Alternatively, for a more substantial dish, pile the vegetables into a baked pastry case, and scatter in some diced goat's cheese; this version is especially good served just after the vegetables have come out of the oven, as they begin to melt the cheese.

Escalivada (Catalan roasted vegetables)

Serves 4 to 6, plus leftovers

2 large aubergines
2 or 3 large mild onions
4 red peppers
extra-virgin olive oil
seasoning

Slice the aubergines and onion about 1cm (1/3 inch) thick, leaving the skin. Quarter the peppers, and remove the seeds and white pith.

Brush the vegetables and the roasting tin with olive oil, and roast the vegetables until they are soft.

Skin the peppers, and remove the skin from the onion slices.

Put the vegetables in a shallow bowl, and pour on more olive oil. Season lightly, and let the flavours blend for at least an hour or so before serving. You can add a splash of sherry vinegar, if you like, but I prefer the wine-friendly mellowness of the vegetable juices as they are.

Cornbread

Rather than a yeast bread recipe, which I give in the Basic Recipes section (p. 27), I have included here a quick bread, cornbread. Once you have made cornbread, you will appreciate its versatility. It is the perfect accompaniment to spicy stews and gumbos, and it is excellent at breakfast with eggs any style and crisp bacon. You can add grated cheese to the mixture, or chopped chillies, crumbled bacon or fried onions.

Serves 8

275g (9oz) yellow cornmeal
125g (4oz) plain flour
1 tablespoon baking powder
1 tablespoon sugar
scant teaspoon bicarbonate of soda
½ teaspoon salt
350mls (12oz) buttermilk or soured milk
3 free-range medium eggs
50mls (2oz) melted butter, bacon fat, olive or
    groundnut oil

Sift the dry ingredients together, and beat the milk and eggs.

Use 15mls (½oz) of the fat to grease a 20cm (8 inch) cake tin, or cast-iron pan. Put this in a preheated oven at 200°C/400°F/gas mark 6.

Combine the wet and dry ingredients until just mixed, and stir in the remaining fat. The mixture will still be lumpy rather than smooth, and that is how it should be. Using a food processor tends to overwork the batter, and, for this reason, I prefer to make the mixture by hand.

Pour the batter into the hot greased pan, and bake for 30 minutes, or until golden brown with the bread shrinking from the edge of the pan. A skewer poked into the centre will come out clean when the cornbread is cooked.

Break into wedges with a non-metal spatula and serve hot.

Roast stuffed shoulder of lamb with olive sauce

My recipe for roast lamb, perfect for a lazy Sunday lunch, is easy and inexpensive, using the tasty shoulder which lends itself to slow roasting. I love this method of cooking lamb, which results in sweet, tender meat, almost falling from the bone. This is not one of your temperamental roasts that has to be brought out and served just so, at the point of perfect pinkness. You can vary the stuffing and accompanying sauce next time you make it, perhaps using mushrooms in the stuffing and capers in the sauce.

Ask your butcher to remove the blade and thigh bones from a shoulder of lamb, but to leave in the leg bone. This makes for much easier carving. Remove as much visible fat as possible.

Serves 4 to 6

1 shoulder of lamb, boned as above, weighing
    about 1.35–1.8kg (3–4lbs), boned weight
100g (3oz) fresh soft breadcrumbs
2 tablespoons extra-virgin olive oil
1 small onion, peeled and chopped
2 tablespoons toasted pine nuts
2 tablespoons sultanas or chopped dried
    apricots
2–3 cloves of crushed garlic
grated zest and rind of 1 lemon and 1 orange
1 tablespoon finely chopped chervil, basil or
    parsley
1 teaspoon thyme
½ teaspoon rosemary, chopped

Mix all the stuffing ingredients together, and place in the centre of the opened-out shoulder. Fold the edges of the meat over, tie it round three times to form a rosette shape, and place in a roasting tin.

Roast for 20 minutes in a preheated oven at 220°C/450°F/gas mark 7, then turn the heat down to 150°C/300°F/gas mark 2, and roast slowly for about 2 to 2½ hours. Allow the meat to rest for at least 15 minutes in a warm place before carving.

At the same time as you put the lamb in the oven, you can put in a dish of potatoes and onions. Peel and thinly slice both, and layer them in an oiled ovenproof dish, lightly seasoning each layer with a little salt and pepper and a trickle of olive oil. This is even better if you put the lamb on top of the vegetables for the last hour of cooking, together with any cooking juices, from which you have skimmed the fat.

Olive sauce

2 tablespoons plain flour
2 tablespoons olive oil
300mls (½ pint) lamb stock
4 tablespoons black olives, stoned and chopped
½ teaspoon fresh thyme
zest and juice of half a lemon
salt
pepper

In a saucepan on a low heat, stir the flour into the oil, and cook for 5 minutes, making a roux.

Gradually blend in the stock, and cook until smooth and the flour is no longer raw-tasting. Stir in the olives, thyme, lemon zest, and juice to taste, bring to the boil, and season to taste with salt and pepper.

This is very good using Seville orange zest and juice in place of the lemon.

Use the oven not just for cooking your Sunday lunch, but for baking all manner of breads and cakes. Baking is not as daunting as it might at first appear, and to demonstrate this, I have developed a recipe for a luscious cake.

If you are going to take the trouble to bake a cake, it may as well be a spectacular one, which your friends will hardly believe you made. Chocolate cakes are universally popular, look impressive, and are in fact so simple a child can make them, especially this version, which uses the all-in-one food processor method of mixing, rather than separately creaming the fat and sugar, then adding the eggs, then the flour. It is based on a recipe my mother taught me when I was eight, only then we used soured milk, not yoghurt, and had never heard of crème fraiche.

The ingredients list and method look long and complicated, but do not be put off. Cakes do require precision and attention to detail. With all baking, whether pastry, biscuits or cakes, I always check quantities and proportions. Just as when I make batter I always check my recipe to see whether it is an equal volume of flour to liquid, or just half. But even if you have never baked a cake before, you can make this one. Serve it as a 'gateau' for dessert, or a centrepiece for Sunday tea. I suggest you bake it in

the morning, and that way the oven will be heated ready for you to put in the lamb roast.

Rich chocolate cake

Serves 12

100g (4oz) bar of 70 per cent chocolate
125mls (generous 4oz) chocolate or coffee
    liqueur, espresso or other strong black coffee
    left over from breakfast; or use a mixture of
    these liquids
100g (4oz) unsalted butter, softened
225g (8oz) light muscovado or caster sugar
½ teaspoon pure vanilla essence
200g (7oz) self-raising flour sifted with 25g (1oz)
    cocoa, 1 teaspoon ground mixed spice and
    ½ teaspoon bicarbonate of soda
125mls (generous 4oz) plain yoghurt, crème
    fraiche, sour cream or soured milk
3 free-range eggs, separated

filling

100g (4oz) bar of chocolate
200mls (7oz) double cream

Grease and flour two 18–20cm (7–8 inch) sponge tins, or line with Bakewell paper.

Put the broken-up chocolate in a bowl over hot water, and add the liquid. Leave until the chocolate has melted, and stir.

Put the rest of the ingredients, except the egg whites, in the food processor and process for 25 seconds, stopping and scraping down the sides with a spatula halfway through.

Add the chocolate mixture, and process for a couple of seconds more.

Whisk the egg whites until firm and snowy, and fold lightly into the cake mixture with a metal spoon, having first removed the bowl from the processor and taken out the blade.

Spoon the mixture equally into the two prepared tins, smooth the surface, and bake in the middle of a preheated oven at 180°C/350°F/gas mark 4 for about 25 minutes.

Allow to cool in the tins for a few minutes, then turn out onto a wire rack.

When cool, sandwich with a filling made by melting the chocolate in the double cream, which you then beat as it cools, to thicken it.

Dust the top with icing sugar, or glaze with sieved,

warmed apricot jam and sift over it chips of drinking chocolate (not powder), such as that from Charbonnel & Walker and the Chocolate Society.

If you sandwich the cake with black cherry jam and plenty of whipped cream, and spread or pipe whipped cream all over the top and sides, you will have something not far removed from Black Forest gateau.

Alternatively, to make this into a golden cake, melt a 100g (4oz) bar of good white chocolate in 100mls (4oz) orange or almond liqueur, and infuse a good pinch of saffron in 25mls (1oz) hot skimmed milk. Use 225g (8oz) self-raising flour and leave out the cocoa, then proceed to mix as described in the above recipe. Sandwich with a white chocolate and cream filling, whipped cream flavoured with orange or almond liqueur, or almond-flavoured butter cream. Dust with icing sugar.

Steaming and poaching

These are the wet methods of cooking – steaming, poaching and cooking by absorption, of which the paella and risotto are the best examples.

No special equipment is required, although naturally there is much specialist equipment on offer, from electric steamers to couscoussiéres. All you need is a large saucepan for poaching and steaming; and for cooking pasta, and for the rice dishes, a much shallower pan to encourage faster absorption. You do not even need a steamer basket. One of the best steamed dishes I ever had was a piece of fish seasoned with oriental aromatics, placed in a soup plate over a saucepan of boiling water, covered with foil and steamed in its own juices.

However, if you are likely to use it a lot, a fish kettle is worth buying, as is a large saucepan with steamer insert, or a simple collapsible steamer basket, which will fit most sizes of saucepan.

Eggs too should be considered for poaching and boiling. Poached eggs are at the heart of some delightfully sophisticated dishes like eggs Florentine (on a bed of spinach and masked with hollandaise sauce), Benedict (on a toasted muffin, between a slice of ham and a blanket of hollandaise), and variously served in hollowed-out potatoes, on artichoke *fonds* and in thick red-wine sauces.

I recently came across a nice idea from France, for serving boiled eggs as a first course – not the one with caviar. Two eggs per person are boiled for 4 minutes, cooled under running cold water long enough to shell them. Plenty of butter is melted in a frying pan, the eggs put in together with a couple of handfuls of soft breadcrumbs. The eggs are gently, but quickly, turned so that they are coated with a crisp golden crust of breadcrumbs before serving. I would serve them on a bed of watercress and lamb's lettuce salad. An appealing version can also be made with quail eggs; allow in this case three eggs per person.

Suitable vegetables for steaming include asparagus, broccoli, beans, bean-sprouts, cabbage, cauliflower, chard, Chinese cabbage and all the oriental brassicas, as well as courgettes, kohlrabi, peas, seakale, spinach and spring greens. And it really is best, even though some of the green vegetables lose some of their brightness, to steam them, to avoid all the flavour and vitamins leaching into the water if you boil them.

Fish particularly lends itself to these gentler techniques, as meat lends itself to hot and fast cooking. One does not have to cook fish to tenderize it, but simply to set the protein, thus making it palatable. Shellfish, too, is good steamed, both molluscs like mussels and clams, and prawns and other crustacea.

Generally, I prefer not to tamper with classic dishes, but the mussel recipe, it will be very evident, is based on moules marinière, and a very good version it is too, served either with grilled polenta slices or cornbread.

The dish is best cooked à la minute, with the freshest mussels you can buy. If they are freshly harvested, they will also be plump. Once they are out of the water, they are no longer feeding, and get skinnier and skinnier.

It astonishes me that something so delicious and so beautiful should still be inexpensive, relative to other fish and shellfish. They are well worth the small amount of effort it takes to scrub and de-beard them under the cold tap. And you can feel quite secure about those you buy in your fish-monger, as they will have come from certified puri-fied sources. I would not gather them in the wild.

Chilli mussels with cornbread

Serves 4 as a first course, 2 as a main course

2kg (about 4lbs) mussels, well scrubbed and
    rinsed
freshly ground black pepper
4 spring onions, trimmed, rinsed and finely
    sliced
1 tablespoon fresh coriander, chopped
1 or 2 red or green chillies, split, seeded and
    finely sliced – use more or less, to taste
3 or 4 pieces dried tomato, soaked and cut into
    narrow strips
glass of dry white wine, cider or beer, about
    200mls (7oz)
4 sticks of cornbread or 4 slices pre-cooked
    polenta
extra-virgin olive oil – optional

As the mussels cook so quickly, first bake the cornbread, or heat it through. If using the polenta instead, heat the grill or a well-seasoned frying pan and sear it on both sides, until hot all the way through.

Discard any mussels that remain open after scrubbing and rinsing – they are dead – put the rest in a large lidded saucepan with the flavourings and liquid and cover with the lid.

Cook the mussels until they open, shaking the pan for the heat to reach all of them. This should take about five minutes.

Put the cornbread or polenta in large soup plates, with a splash or two of olive oil if using it, and ladle the mussels and juice on top. Serve very hot.

Quantities can simply be multiplied if more servings are required.

As an alternative, flavour the mussels with oriental aro-matics – lemon grass, lime leaves, garlic chives, ginger, perhaps a spoonful or two of Thai green curry paste – then cook the mussels in coconut milk. Serve them not with cornbread, but over rice, rice noodles or wheat noodles, cooked according to the directions on the packet. Because all versions cook very quickly, it is as well to have your starch accompaniment and any garnishes ready before you start cooking the mussels.

Steamed sole fillets in lettuce leaves

Serves 4

1 or 2 star anise
thumb of fresh ginger, the outer part peeled,
    the remaining part cut into slivers
dried tangerine peel or a sliver of orange
    zest
½ teaspoon fennel seeds
1 cinnamon stick
250g (½lb) Thai fragrant or basmati rice
½ teaspoon salt
6 tablespoons rice vinegar
500g (1lb) prepared vegetables, such as
    shredded Chinese leaves, slivers of celery,
    bok choy (white Chinese cabbage), shreds of
    carrot, bean sprouts
2 lemon or Dover soles, filleted and skinned
3 cloves garlic
4 spring onions
4 tablespoons soy sauce

This recipe uses three steamer baskets, either an electric steamer or a wok with three bamboo baskets. At a pinch, you can steam the fish directly on top of the vegetables.

Put the star anise, ginger peelings, orange, fennel and cinnamon in the pan or wok which is going to be the base of the steamer, and add water, but not enough to submerge the first steamer basket.

In a saucepan bring the rice to the boil in twice its volume of water, and add half a teaspoon of salt. Simmer with the lid on for 5 minutes.

Drain the rice, rinse and strain again, and place it in a steamer basket, lined with muslin if it has large holes. Steam the rice for 5 minutes, over the aromatics.

While the rice is steaming, prepare the vegetables, and place them in the second steamer basket which you fit on top of the rice. Steam the vegetables for 5 to 8 minutes while you prepare the fish.

Cut each fillet lengthways so that you now have 8 pieces of fish. Season lightly and roll up each piece.

Put the fish in the third steamer basket, and on top scatter the thinnest slivers of garlic and fresh ginger, with shreds of spring onions. Sprinkle on a few drops of soy sauce and rice vinegar. Place the third steamer basket over the vegetables, cover with a lid, and steam for 3 minutes only.

If you are using bamboo baskets, these can be brought to the table, and everyone can help themselves using Chinese soupspoons, chopsticks and bowls. A dipping sauce can be made by adding a little chilli sauce and grated ginger to the remaining soy sauce and rice vinegar. Warm sake or rice wine would accompany this dish very well.

An old-fashioned yet very effective method of cooking, the pressure cooker, also relies on the absorption method. This is now being given a new lease of life in America where it is known as 'infusion cooking' – a good description, since whatever is being cooked infuses in its own juices. The other distinctive feature of the pressure cooker is that cooking time is dramatically reduced. I started using one again about three years ago, and I am utterly converted. So much so that I use a pressure frying pan as well. I was deeply sceptical of the promotional leaflet, which suggested I could cook a risotto in 10 minutes. Indeed, I doubted that a passable risotto could be produced by this method. It can. The creaminess induced by the constant stirring and breaking down of the rice grain by the manual method is produced by the application of pressure to the grain, and the results are very good indeed. I include a recipe below to demonstrate this, as well as the standard stirred risotto recipe.

Carrot and celery risotto

(using the Duromatic pressure frying pan)

Serves 4 to 6

25mls (1oz) extra-virgin olive oil
1 large onion, peeled and finely chopped
2 celery stalks and 2 carrots, peeled, trimmed
    and finely chopped
250g (½lb) Arborio or Carnaroli rice
salt
pepper
nutmeg
1 bay leaf
150mls (5oz) dry white wine
450mls (16oz) vegetable or chicken stock
25g (1oz) each butter and freshly grated
    Parmesan

Heat the oil in the pressure cooker, and in it cook the vegetables until the onions are soft. Stir in the rice, light seasoning, including a little nutmeg and bay leaf, and then add the wine and stock.

Close the lid, and let the pressure rise until the first red ring appears. Cook thus for 5 to 7 minutes.

Lift the frying pan to the sink, and cool the lid under cold running water.

Open the lid. Remove the bay leaf, and stir in the butter and Parmesan. Let the risotto stand, with the lid half covering the pan for a minute, and then spoon the risotto into heated soup plates. Grind on a little more nutmeg, and hand round a hunk of Parmesan and a grater.

Champagne risotto with caramelized scallops and coral butter

Serves 2

6 scallops, with roe
75g (3oz) unsalted butter
1 scant tablespoon chervil, finely chopped
150g (5oz) risotto rice
up to 450mls (¾ pint) fish or vegetable stock,
    simmering
about 150mls (¼ pint) champagne
seasoning

Rinse the scallops, discard the pad of muscle and put the roe and scallops to one side.

Poach the roe in water or a little of the measured fish stock for 3 to 4 minutes, and put aside until cool. Keep the liquid to add to the risotto. When cool, pound the roe with half the butter, and then stir in the chervil. Chill until required.

Melt the rest of the butter in a heavy pan, and stir in the rice. Pour on a quarter of the stock, and cook, stirring until the liquid has been absorbed before adding a bit more, a little at a time. You may need to add more or less liquid, depending on how creamy you like your risotto.

Halfway through cooking, add the champagne.

Just before you are ready to serve the risotto, season to taste, then quickly grill or fry the scallops, on both sides, using a high heat to lightly caramelize, and arrange three for each serving on the risotto, which is best served in heated soup plates.

Spoon the coral butter on top, and it will melt into the risotto, adding to the creamy unctuousness. Serve immediately.

Cook's note

You can prepare the risotto an hour or so in advance to the point where you have about 150mls (½ pint) stock left to add. Cool the risotto quickly so that it stops cooking. Then when ready to proceed, carefully reheat, and commence adding the remaining stock, which should be brought to the boil once more.

Note that quantities can be increased to provide more servings, but even a large risotto does not need more than about 200–250mls (7–9oz) champagne; make up the rest of the required liquid in stock.

Poached pears with cinnamon and orange zest

Fruit poached in syrup, wine or other flavoured liquid makes an easy and versatile dessert. In autumn use pears and plums, in spring rhubarb and gooseberries, and in summer apricots, peaches and nectarines. When good fresh fruit is not available, try dried apricots, prunes and pears poached in a fragrant tea such as jasmine or rose congou.

Serves 6

6 large Conference or firm Williams pears
50g (2oz) sugar
2 cinnamon sticks
grating of nutmeg
6 cloves
1 bay leaf
thinly pared zest of orange and its juice
300mls (½ pint) white wine

Peel the pears carefully, leaving the stalks, if possible.

Put all the ingredients in a large saucepan, sticking the cloves in the base of each pear. Bring to the boil, and then simmer gently until the pears are tender.

Transfer the pears to wine glasses or serving dishes, and then strain the cooking juice, and boil it down to a syrup to pour over the pears.

These are very good served with custard, crème fraiche, or thick plain yoghurt.

Sandwiches

The British sandwich, *le sandwich anglais*, has taken Paris by storm. As fast as they fill the shelves at Marks and Spencer in Boulevard Haussmann with chicken tikka, reduced-fat chicken salad, and egg and Cheddar sandwiches, they sell out. That particular store is the biggest seller of sandwiches in the whole chain. And the medium-sliced loaf is the third-largest seller (muffins are the top seller). Is this, perhaps, a comment on the falling standards of French bread-making, or rather an indication that the French are becoming more broad-minded about their food habits? Certainly sandwich shops abound in Paris now, and with rather more exotic fillings than ours. I have not yet seen foie gras sandwiches in Pret A Manger here, but they have them on the room service menu at Le Bristol in Paris.

Philadelphia is a paradox. Home of some of the finest restaurants in the United States, including Le Bec Fin, which has regularly been voted number one in America, the city's main claim to gastronomic fame is, according to Mayor Edward Rendell, its junk food. So I was looking forward to my first taste of Philadelphia, wondering whether it would be a cheesesteak or a hoagie, or perhaps a soft pretzel with the appetizer and a Tastykake and a water-ice to finish.

At Jim's Steaks on 4th and South Street we ordered, after a long wait, a cheesesteak 'with'. Just one, because they were huge, but we should have known better. It was so good that we had to queue up all over again for another. Thinly sliced steak is quickly cooked on the griddle, and slapped between an Italian roll 'with' fried onions and Cheez Whiz, and extras such as peppers and mushrooms, for those who like a sophisticated sandwich. And, to be authentic, the 'cheese' has to be Cheez Whiz, a 'cheese food', slices of processed cheese, although at Jim's you can substitute provolone (an Italian smoked cheese) or American cheese.

The cheesesteak-makers of Philly almost fell out with their mayor, when he declared the hoagie the official sandwich of Philadelphia. Quick thinking on the part of this consummate politician provided the solution. He declared the hoagie to be

Philadelphia's official cold sandwich, and the noble cheesesteak its hot sandwich. The half-hour that I spent with him ended with the exhortation from my host to take me for lunch at Salumeria's – 'even if you just have a bite, you should try it with the hot peppers, it's the filet mignon of hoagies'. He also talked me through the recipe for the quintessential hoagie, upon which I base my recipe below.

In my own repertoire there are two entirely different sandwiches. There is the sandwich as meal replacement. This includes the burger, the barbecue, the lobster club, the baguette stuffed full of cured ham, the thick layer of Roquefort between grilled slices of *pain Poilâne*, the Louisiana po' boy stuffed full of oysters, the hero, the sub, the hoagie, the Reuben, the Philly cheesesteak and many others.

Comforting and satisfying, whilst not reaching the gastronomic heights, a sandwich like this is sometimes just what you want to eat. A generous, highly flavoured filling, combined with fairly sturdy bread, makes an excellent lunch or supper, easy on the washing-up.

However, you can also build a sandwich such as this into a suitable centrepiece for casual entertaining. Have all the ingredients on the table, and let your guests make up their own sandwiches, adding toppings and accompaniments to taste. Breaded fried fillets of fish, or hamburgers, will need buns, pickles, some onions, thinly sliced and marinated in rice vinegar, some relishes, hot sauce, tartare sauce and coleslaw.

Once when we visited friends in Auburn, Alabama, our first meal was delicious and casual in the extreme, barbecue and 'fixin's'. The barbecue was tender thin slices of pork shoulder, which had been slow-smoked and cooked for hours in the best local barbecue pit, which does a brisk takeaway trade. You can cook barbecue in the oven, but the smoky flavour is missing. Soft rolls, pickles, coleslaw and beer were the other essential accompaniments.

The most luxurious sandwich I have ever tasted is Ann Rosenzweig's 'lobster club', at her restaurant, The Lobster Club, on New York's upper east side. This is indeed a whole meal on a large platter, a two-hander of a sandwich, and absolutely delicious. I have always liked crab as much as lobster, and I give below my 'crab club' recipe.

The crab club sandwich

Serves 1

1 generous portion white crab meat
1 teaspoon Jalapeño Tabasco (green Tabasco)
1 tablespoon crème fraiche or mayonnaise
salted butter, softened
freshly ground pepper
1 tablespoon fresh coriander or chervil, finely
    chopped
3 slices of bread, lightly toasted if you wish
½ ripe avocado, peeled and thinly sliced
1 ripe tomato, seeded and thinly sliced
seasoning
iceberg or other lettuce, shredded

Mix the crab, Tabasco and crème fraiche or mayonnaise. Mix the butter, sufficient to spread on 3 slices of bread, with the pepper and herbs. Butter the bread, then build up the first layer of avocado and tomato; season lightly. Place the middle slice of bread on top, and spread the crab on it. Top with shredded lettuce, then the final slice of bread. Spear with cocktail sticks in strategic positions, then cut the sandwich in quarters, or otherwise as appropriate.

The famous Philly cheesesteak

Serves 1

1 long soft fresh bread roll
1 generous portion of steak, very thinly sliced
3 or 4 thin slices of cheese
Tabasco, sliced or whole chillies, fried onions
    – all optional

Halve the roll without cutting all the way through, and discard some of the filling. Warm the roll in the oven or on the griddle. On an oiled griddle or frying pan, fry the steak, flipping it and chopping it until done. Cram it into the bun, add the cheese slices, and any extras. Clamp together and serve.

Very thinly sliced 'sandwich steak' is available in supermarkets, or slice your own from a tail-end of fillet steak. Cheese can be thinly sliced Cheddar, provolone or what you will.

The perfect steak sandwich

Here is a substantial meal in a bun for those who take their racing or other outdoor pursuits far too seriously to stop for a fancy hamper lunch.

YOU NEED, for 2 people, 2 thick, well-hung Aberdeen Angus sirloin steaks or pieces of rump steak, unsalted butter, 1 ciabatta or other small crusty loaf, salt and freshly ground black pepper.

METHOD Grill the steak until done to your liking. Remove it from the heat, and allow to cool. Soften the butter, split the ciabatta in half, and butter both sides. When the steak is cool, remove all the fat, and thinly cut the steak into small, thin rectangular slices. Fill the ciabatta with the meat, cut the loaf in two and wrap tightly. By the time the sandwiches are eaten, the meat juices will have been absorbed by the bread.

NOTE It is not a good idea to put lettuce in the sandwich between the bread and the meat, as it will act as a moisture-proof barrier.

The Reuben sandwich

Serves 1

2 slices light rye bread
2 or 3 forkfuls sauerkraut from jar, can or
    vacuum pack
American mustard, or other, to taste
1 generous portion pastrami or US-style
    corned beef, sliced
dill pickle
crisps

Toast or grill the bread on one side only. The centre of the sandwich needs to be soft rather than crisp in order to grip the filling. Meanwhile, heat up the sauerkraut. Spread the untoasted side of the bread with the mustard. Arrange the meat slices on top, and heap on the sauerkraut. Clamp on the top slice of rye. Cut in half, and spear with cocktail sticks. Serve with pickle and crisps on the side.

The Hoagie

Serves 1

1 long bread roll or half-baguette
extra-virgin olive oil
oregano, chopped
iceberg lettuce, finely shredded
1 or 2 ripe, sweet tomatoes, thinly sliced
generous portion of salami, mortadella and other
    Italian *salumi*, thinly sliced
mayonnaise
sliced artichoke hearts, sliced hot or medium-hot
    peppers – all optional

Split the roll down the middle, but leave a 'hinge'. Take out some of the soft crumb, and brush the roll with olive oil and sprinkle with herbs. Layer the lettuce, tomatoes and meat, and finish with a squiggle of mayonnaise. Clamp together, and eat in both hands.

Ciabatta sandwiches with grilled vegetables and spinach

Serves 2

extra-virgin olive oil
4 flat mushrooms, wiped and peeled,
    if necessary
2 red peppers, quartered and seeded
250g (½lb) cooked and drained spinach
75g (3oz) goat's cheese – optional
1 ciabatta loaf
2 tablespoons black olive paste
1 teaspoon sun-dried tomato or some
    chilli paste

Use the olive oil to brush over the mushrooms and pepper and to oil the grill or a baking sheet. Grill or bake the vegetables until tender, and skin the peppers. Warm the spinach.

Split the loaf in half, and, if you are using it, slice the goat's cheese. Mix the olive and tomato paste, and spread on the bread. Put the cheese on top, and then the spinach, the peppers and the mushrooms. Clamp on the top half of the loaf, and cut in half. Spear with cocktail sticks to hold it all together.

Any combination of these vegetables can be layered with a flattened grilled chicken breast, in which case I would leave out the goat's cheese. One chicken breast, split horizontally, will be sufficient for two people.

More superior sandwiches

The Sybarite – diced chicken mixed with finely chopped, cooked spinach and chunks of avocado, delicately seasoned and bound in a creamy lemon dressing, with choice of breads.

The Viking – cured salmon, dill cucumber, dill and mustard butter.

The Tiffinwallah – a club sandwich with a difference: curried lamb, devilled egg, curried chicken or ham, layered with bread, spread with spicy mango chutney and butter.

The Breakfast Special – bacon rashers, thick grilled tomato slices, cooked sausage or black pudding and scrambled eggs.

The Country Cousin – sliced roast pork, gherkins, pickled onions, mixed salad leaves and fruit butter.

The Tsar – pickled herring, marinated mushrooms, sliced gherkins, raw onion and hard-boiled egg, served on rye bread.

The Sultan – pitta or olive bread, spread with hummus and filled with pink roast lamb, chopped dried apricots, cucumber, yoghurt and garlic salad.

The Fisherman's Friend – a soft, large bun spread with tartare sauce, holding a deep-fried fillet of fish, sprinkled with hot sauce.

The Gondolier – Italian bread, split and filled with shredded lettuce and seafood salad, mixed with a well-flavoured lemon, garlic and herb mayonnaise.

The Mediterranean – pink slices of tender roast lamb, sandwiched in slices of olive and herb bread, spread with ratatouille.

The Tex Mex – beef fajitas and salsa; marinated roast beef with a subtle, fruity but not too hot salsa, wrapped in a floury tortilla.

The Oriental – sliced chicken breast marinated in oriental spices, sandwiched in bread, spread with an unusual peanut and ginger butter and served with a pineapple chutney.

The Don – served in a split ciabatta bun, sliced mozzarella, avocado and ripe tomatoes with fresh basil leaves and sun-dried tomato butter; this is suitable for vegetarians.

The Laird – several layers of thinly sliced smoked salmon on multigrain brown bread, spread with a dill, lemon and green peppercorn butter.

The perfect hamburger

Unlike much of the junk masquerading under the name of hamburger, a real hamburger, made with good-quality, lean, flavoursome beef, is a treat. It may not qualify as a 'serious' meal, with a beginning, middle and end, but, set against the realities of modern life, it makes a perfect snack, a lunchtime sandwich, something at the end of a busy day, especially for just one or two people.

YOU NEED, for each hamburger, about 150–200g (5–7oz) trimmed lean beef, which might be sirloin, rump, tail-end of fillet or feather steak. One to 2 teaspoons finely chopped and trimmed shallots are optional, as is a teaspoon of finely chopped fresh herbs. A pinch of freshly ground black pepper and a little salt are important. Instead of a pappy bun, I prefer a chunk of ciabatta or focaccia split in two, or a decent bap, but for many the sesame-topped soft bun will be de rigueur.

METHOD Mince or finely chop the beef. Mix with the shallots, herbs and pepper, and shape it into a firm, neat patty, roughly the size of the bun. Have the grill hot, or use a well-seasoned cast-iron, or a non-stick frying pan. Cook the hamburger on both sides until done to your liking. Lightly salt it, and serve hot on the bread of your choice, lightly toasted if you wish.

TO SERVE Any accompaniments should be got ready before you start. These might include lettuce, a slice or two of tomato, onion, sweet pickle, relish, ketchup, mayonnaise and cheese. The cheeseburger version is best with a thin slice of mild cheese placed on top of the meat, before you top it with the second half of bread or bun. Roquefort does *nothing* for a hamburger and vice versa.

Comfort food

After a long flight and a few weeks travelling away from home, our bodies quickly tell us what they want for nourishment and repair. Mine wants raw food, vegetables and starches for a few days.

The juicer then becomes my most used kitchen gadget. Fruit and vegetable juices replenish moisture lost in heated hotels and air-conditioned aircraft cabins. In addition they give an immediate and powerful infusion of minerals and vitamins. There is no limit to the juices you can make up from fresh ingredients. I like the recipe below, red, sweet, full-flavoured and peppery. The leftovers make a very good vegetable broth, which in turn makes a perfect lunch when accompanied by some good bread. But experiment with the juicer. Try a green juice with apples, celery, green peppers, spinach and watercress. Carrots and pineapple, together with yellow pepper, a small swede and some fresh ginger produce a power-packing zinger of a golden cocktail. This is an area of food preparation in which the organic vegetable box schemes really come into their own. And there are plenty of books on juicing and on the beneficial properties of individual fruit, vegetables and herbs, so that you can make up your own combinations.

Vegetables are also excellent combined in rice and pasta dishes, of which I have included two very simple recipes, Beetroot Risotto and Pasta Primavera. That particular risotto developed from the broth I was using, rich garnet-red from the beetroot juice. Use a green broth, from green juice, to make a celery or broccoli risotto, an orange or yellow broth to make a carrot or pumpkin risotto.

Delicate and subtle in flavour, a simple vegetable risotto is every bit as good as a risotto full of rich ingredients – truffle, shellfish, wild mushrooms. One of the best I ever tasted was in Florence; the rice was combined with nothing more than celery and carrot, very finely diced, and flavoured with a little rosemary.

Similarly, pasta dishes can range from the simple to the sumptuous, but as an antidote to jet-lag I favour the former. Pasta is most definitely a mood food. Eating it, as with other carbohydrates, induces the amino acid, tryptophan, to enter the brain more easily, where serotonin is produced, the chemical which helps calm anxiety, depression and irritability.

So if you feel down, eat a bowl of steaming pasta and within 90 minutes or so, you can expect to feel a noticeable improvement in your mood. This will be most effective if the pasta is dressed with a non-fat or low-fat sauce, since fat slows down the digestion of carbohydrates. Use a tomato or mushroom sauce rather than a cheese or meat sauce. A few vegetables, dropped into the pasta water at appropriate intervals, are, indeed, all you need to make a complete dish, exceedingly simple to prepare and needing no more than one saucepan.

Vegetable soups will also appeal to the jaded or jet-lagged palate, even at the same meal as a bowl of pasta, if you wish. I had always been brought up to think that one did not eat soup and pasta at the same meal. In a little Roman trattoria one night, I scolded Tom for wanting to order soup, and pointed out that it was not done. He immediately told me to look over at the party of elegant Romans on the other side of the room. Pasta followed soup, then the main course, cheese and pudding, and then, for everyone, the chef brought in a steaming bowl of spaghetti carbonara. When in Rome . . .

For pudding, when I am feeling tired and not very adventurous, after a surfeit of pastry chefs' creations, I am happy with apple purée, whether mixed with yoghurt, served with poached dried apricots or used in a soufflé flavoured with plenty of cinnamon or nutmeg. Rice pudding and fruit fools are similarly comforting.

Jet-lag tonic

Makes about 1 litre (1³/₄ pints)

2 beetroots
1 small swede
4 celery stalks
6 large carrots
½ bunch watercress
bunch of parsley stalks
1 cooking apple
1 or 2 red peppers

Scrub and rinse the vegetables as necessary. Cut into pieces, and feed through the juicer, a few pieces at a time.
Serve immediately. You may need to stop halfway

through the process to remove the build-up of fibrous residue. Use this for the next simple recipe.

Vegetable soup

Serves 4 to 6

2 tablespoons extra-virgin olive oil
2 onions, peeled and finely chopped
1 celery stalk, peeled and finely chopped
2 carrots, peeled and finely chopped
3 cloves garlic, peeled and finely chopped
1 x 400g (14oz) can chopped tomatoes
1.75 litres (3 pints) vegetable stock
2 leeks
¼ lb Savoy cabbage
2 courgettes
handful of green beans
fresh herbs, such as basil, chives, parsley

Heat the oil in a large saucepan or casserole, and in it gently fry the onions, celery, carrots and garlic until soft; this will take 20 to 30 minutes and is what gives the soup its underlying depth of flavour. Stir in the chopped tomatoes, and cook until most of the liquid from them has evaporated. Add the stock, bring to the boil, and simmer while you prepare the green vegetables.

Shred the cabbage, slice or dice the courgettes, and break up the beans. Add to the simmering stock and cook until the vegetables are tender. Stir in the chopped herbs, season at this point, and ladle into hot soup bowls, with a little more olive oil floated on top. Pasta can be added to the soup when you put in the green vegetables, and canned beans added towards the end for a one-pot meal.

Vegetable broth

Makes about 1.75 litres (3 pints)

Take the residue from the above juice mix, put in a large saucepan, add 2 litres (3½ pints) of water, and simmer for an hour or so.

Strain into a jug, pressing to remove as much extract as possible. This will make a deep red broth, which you can use for borscht, or in a rich red risotto.

Beetroot risotto

Serves 2 as a main course, 4 as a first course

1 onion, peeled and finely chopped
1 celery stalk, trimmed and finely sliced
2 tablespoons extra-virgin olive oil
300g (10oz) Arborio rice
salt
pepper
about 1 litre (1¾ pints) vegetable broth, boiling
½ beetroot, grated
Parmesan cheese

Gently fry the onion and celery in the olive oil until translucent and golden, and then stir in the rice, a little seasoning, and a ladle or two of broth.

Stir and cook until the rice has absorbed the liquid. Add the beetroot and a little more broth, and continue cooking, adding more hot liquid until the rice is cooked to your liking.

Stir in a little cheese, and serve in heated soup plates with extra cheese handed round separately.

Pasta primavera

Serves 2

about 200g (7oz) spaghetti, or other pasta
handful of slim green beans, topped and tailed
1 small fennel bulb, trimmed, and cut into thin
    wedges
6 pieces of dried tomato, cut into strips
½ bunch of watercress, rinsed and chopped
extra-virgin olive oil
several sprigs flat-leaf parsley, rinsed and
    chopped
salt
pepper
Parmesan cheese

Bring a large pot of water to the boil, lightly salted if you wish, and add the pasta. After 5 minutes, add the beans, fennel and tomato, and continue cooking until the pasta is cooked al dente.

Drain, using the boiling water to heat the serving bowl. Tip the pasta back into the saucepan with some olive oil, the watercress and parsley, and plenty of freshly ground black pepper.

Stir and transfer to the hot serving bowl, from which you have emptied the water. Serve with a chunk of Parmesan for grating.

Basic recipes and how to adapt them

Wherever possible I indicate how, with a few minor alterations, the recipes can be adapted, thus providing a useful collection of blueprint recipes which will carry you through numerous enjoyable occasions.

The basic batter

Pancakes, crêpes, hot-cakes, galettes, griddle cakes, drop scones, even very passable blini can all be made from a simple batter mixture.

Makes 8 pancakes

125g (4oz) plain flour
a pinch of salt
a large free-range egg
300mls (½ pint) semi-skimmed milk
a little butter to lightly grease a well-seasoned,
    heavy-based frying pan, about 20cm (8 inch)
    diameter for preference

Grease and heat the pan while you beat all the ingredients together for a smooth, lump-free batter. When the pan is really hot, pour in just enough batter to coat the base of the pan, tilting it to spread the batter evenly. Cook the pancake until golden on the underside, and matt on the top, about a minute, then turn it over and cook the other side. Slide onto a plate set over a pan of hot water to keep it warm while you cook the rest of the pancakes in the same way.

Thicker hot-cakes, blini and drop scones can be made by adding a teaspoon or so of baking powder to a batter using equal quantities of liquid and flour. For a Breton galette, wheat flour can be mixed with buckwheat. Cornmeal, and even corn kernels, can be added to the thick version to make cornmeal griddle cakes. Even a little cocoa can be added for chocolate pancakes – a novel twist for Shrove Tuesday, unless you want to serve them plain in the classic way, a dab of butter, a squeeze of lemon and a sprinkling of sugar. (See also pp. 87–9.)

The basic béchamel

Serves 6 to 8

50g (2oz) unsalted butter
50g (2oz) plain flour
600mls (1 pint) milk, hot
seasoning – see recipe

In a heavy saucepan, melt the butter, stir in the flour, and cook for a few minutes.

Remove from the heat, and stir in about a quarter of the milk until smooth. Put on the heat again, stirring continuously, and, as the mixture begins to thicken, remove again from the heat.

Gradually add another quarter of the milk, stirring until smooth, thickening it again over the heat, and so on, until you have a smooth thick sauce. Season lightly with salt and white pepper, if making a savoury sauce. If you do not mind the darker flecks, a grating of nutmeg is good too.

Cook it gently for 10 minutes. This is important. Even though the sauce looks finished before then, it is important to fully cook the flour.

To make cheese sauce, to the above quantity of sauce, stir in about 100g (4oz) of your chosen grated cheese. To make parsley sauce, remove the stalks and any damaged parts from a generous bunch of parsley. Rinse well, roughly chop and put in a blender with about 200mls (⅓ pint) boiling water. Blitz until smooth. Stir as much of this purée as you need into the béchamel sauce. To make egg sauce, add two or three finely chopped hard-boiled eggs.

For a richer or sweet sauce, substitute single cream for the milk. Sweet sauces can be flavoured with grated lemon or orange zest, and sweetened with sugar or honey.

The basic bread

Makes a 1kg (2lb) loaf

500g (1lb) stoneground flour
2 teaspoons salt
2 teaspoons fast-action easy-blend yeast
    granules
2 tablespoons olive oil
generous 300mls (½ pint) warm water

In a bowl mix the dry ingredients. Make a well in the centre, and pour in the liquid ingredients. Draw the flour into the centre and mix well, until the dough leaves the sides of the bowl. You can, of course, make the dough in a food processor.

Turn onto a floured surface, and knead for five minutes. Shape the dough, and put it into a lightly greased 1kg (2lb) loaf tin. Cover loosely with lightly oiled clingfilm, and let it rise in a moderately warm place for about an hour until doubled in size.

Bake in a preheated oven at 200°C/400°F/gas mark 6 for about 30 minutes. Turn the loaf onto a wire rack, and cool completely before slicing.

Mix wholemeal and white flour for a different loaf, and experiment with additions of other grains and seeds, such as sunflower and sesame. If you make an entirely wholemeal loaf, you will find you need to add a little more water. Herbs, chopped olives, grated cheese and nuts can also be added for variety.

Cook's note

In making your own recipes, remember the proportions:
*   1 teaspoon salt to approx. 250g (½lb) flour
*   approximately half liquid to flour
*   500g (1lb) flour will make 12 to 18 bread rolls; these will bake at the same temperature in about 15 minutes.

The basic custard

Serves 4 to 6

600mls (1 pint) cream
125g (generous 4oz) caster sugar
8 free-range egg yolks
flavourings – see recipe

Put the cream in a saucepan. Bring gently to the boil. In a bowl mix the sugar and egg yolks, and pour on the scalded cream, stirring well. Pour back into the saucepan, add any flavourings and simmer gently for a couple of minutes, stirring continuously. Do not let the custard boil or it will curdle. Remove from the heat, and allow to cool before refrigerating. This will also allow any flavourings, such as vanilla pods, cinnamon sticks, liquorice root, to infuse. Cover the surface with a butter paper or clingfilm to stop a skin from forming. Remove any extraneous flavourings before using in a trifle or making ice cream.

To flavour the custard, add spices, flower petals, citrus zest, etc. when you scald the cream. Liqueurs and essences should be added just before you take the cream off the heat. Three or four cloves, the zest of a lemon or 2–3 tablespoons of liqueur are sufficient to flavour this amount of custard. A quarter teaspoon of essence will be sufficient.

To make ice cream simply freeze the cooled custard in an ice-cream maker or sorbetière.

The basic hollandaise

Makes 300mls (¹/₂ pint)

3 tablespoons white wine vinegar
1 tablespoon water
1 blade of mace
4 peppercorns
3 free-range egg yolks
175g (6oz) unsalted butter, very soft
salt
pepper

Put the vinegar, water, mace and peppercorns in a saucepan and boil to reduce to 1 tablespoon. Put the egg yolks in a bowl set over a pan of simmering water and beat them with a teaspoon of butter, pinch of salt and grind of pepper. Strain in the vinegar, remove the pan from the heat but keep the bowl over hot water. Gradually whisk in the butter, a small amount at a time, rather like making mayonnaise, until you have a smooth, glossy sauce.

You can change the flavour of the sauce by using different vinegars. Chopped shallots cooked with the vinegar and water, but using an extra tablespoon tarragon vinegar, will give you béarnaise sauce, which is wonderful with grills. Finely chopped mint added to the hollandaise will give you sauce paloise, a classic French sauce from Pau.

Cook's note

As with mayonnaise, you can make this in the blender, first blending the eggs, vinegar and seasoning, and then adding the butter, piece by piece. The blender is particularly useful if you are making double quantities or more.

The basic mayonnaise

Makes 300mls (½ pint)

1 large free-range egg yolk
salt
pepper
300mls (½ pint) sunflower or grapeseed oil
lemon juice or wine vinegar

Put the egg yolk in a bowl and season lightly. Add the oil to the egg in the initial stages with a very sparing hand, literally drop by drop, and beating in each addition of oil before adding the next. Once the mixture starts to thicken, the oil can be added more liberally, but no more than a thin stream, about a tablespoon at a time. This too should be beaten until the mixture looks thick and glossy, but with no surface film of oil, before you add the next stream of oil. When all the oil has been taken up, add more seasoning to taste, the lemon juice or vinegar, or add an extra flavouring. If the mayonnaise seems very stiff and oily-looking, you can beat in a tablespoon of boiling water, which will emulsify and give a smooth, velvety texture.

Mustard, chopped herbs, horseradish, tomato purée, chopped *cornichons* and spring onions are just some of the many ingredients you can use to flavour mayonnaise. Seville orange juice can be used to sharpen it, as can the juice of a blood orange, when it becomes mayonnaise maltaise. To make mayonnaise mousseline, which is the classic accompaniment to asparagus, season the mayonnaise with tarragon vinegar, and fold in whipped cream. (See also p. 77.) To make a lighter version, I often simply fold in a stiffly beaten egg white. Sauce maltaise and sauce

mousseline are made in the same way, but with a base of hollandaise sauce, not mayonnaise.

Cook's note

The risk of curdling can be minimized if you use all ingredients at room temperature.

The basic meringue

Makes 4

1 large free-range egg white
100g (scant 4oz) caster sugar

Put the egg white in a scrupulously clean bowl – any film of grease will prevent it attaining its full volume. Sprinkle on a tablespoon of sugar and begin whisking. When the egg white is foamy and increased in volume, add half the remaining sugar and continue whisking. The meringue will begin to take shape, becoming glossy and with smaller bubbles. Continue whisking until you have added all the sugar and the meringue is now a firm mass of glossy foam, with tiny bubbles. When you trail the whisk through it the mixture will peak and hold its shape.

Line a baking sheet with non-stick baking parchment or a special baking mat. Spoon or pipe the meringue into four nests or baskets, with a depression in the middle. Bake, or rather, dry, in a preheated oven at 125–150°C/300°F/gas mark 1–2 for about 45 minutes. Cool on a wire rack and store in an airtight tin until required.

Quantities can be increased by simple multiplication. For filled meringues, pipe or spoon into heaps on the baking sheet, and when cooked and cooled, sandwich with whipped cream. Ivory-coloured meringues can be achieved by using light muscovado sugar. A little cocoa powder can be whisked in with the final addition of sugar to make chocolate meringues. Fill them with coffee- or chocolate-flavoured cream.

The basic muffin

Makes 6 large or 12 smaller ones

175g (6oz) plain flour
1 tablespoon baking powder
50g (2oz) sugar
75g (3oz) butter, melted
2 free-range eggs, lightly beaten

Mix the dry ingredients, then stir in the wet ingredients until just combined. The mixture remains somewhat lumpy and should not be overmixed. Spoon into double paper cases set on a baking sheet, and bake in a preheated oven at 180°C/350°F/gas mark 4 for 15 to 20 minutes, until well risen and golden brown.

Two tablespoons ground almonds can be substituted for 25g (1oz) of the flour. For fruit and nut muffins, add 2 tablespoons raisins or other dried fruit, chopped if necessary, and 2 tablespoons chopped nuts.

The basic pastry

Shortcrust pastry

250g (8oz) plain flour
1 scant teaspoon salt
125g (4oz) unsalted butter, chilled and diced
approx. 6 tablespoons chilled water

Sift the flour and salt together in a bowl. Cut in the butter and then, with your fingertips, rub the mixture lightly together, lifting it to incorporate plenty of air, until it resembles breadcrumbs. With a palette knife mix in enough water to bind the mixture to a dough. Work it into a ball. Cover and chill the pastry for 30 minutes. Flour the worktop and lightly roll out the pastry as required.

Note

Concentrated butter, part of the EU butter mountain, can sometimes be found in supermarkets. This is excellent for baking, but because it is concentrated, it will require a little more liquid than conventional butter.

Flaky pastry

250g (8oz) plain flour
scant teaspoon salt
125g (4oz) unsalted butter, chilled and diced
approx. 6 tablespoons chilled water

Make the pastry as for short pastry above, using only half the butter.

After it has been chilled for 30 minutes, roll the dough into a rectangle, with the short sides top and bottom. Dot half the remaining butter over the bottom two-thirds of the dough. Fold the top third down and the bottom third over it. Press to seal the sides. Give a quarter turn and roll out again to the same rectangular shape you started with. Fold it into three as before, without the butter, give it another quarter turn, and roll out into another rectangle. Dot with the rest of the butter, fold the dough as before, give it a turn, roll it and continue with two more turns.

If the kitchen or your hands are getting too warm, chill the dough in the refrigerator before continuing. After the last turn, roll the dough as required.

Sweet shortcrust pastry

250g (8oz) plain flour
125g (4oz) unsalted butter, chilled and diced
pinch of salt
50g (2oz) caster sugar
1 small free-range egg, lightly beaten
iced water

Rub the flour and butter together until well combined and crumbly, but do not overwork. Stir in the salt and sugar, and then the egg and enough iced water to bind. Wrap and cool in the refrigerator for 20 minutes before using.

To bake blind

Roll out the pastry, and line a greased tart tin 20–25cm (8–10 inches) in diameter. Prick the pastry all over, line with greaseproof paper, weight down with ceramic baking beans (dried beans will do, and can be stored and re-used for the same purpose), and bake blind for 8 to 10 minutes in a preheated oven at 200°C/400°F/gas mark 6.

Remove from the oven, take out the beans and paper, and let the pastry case cool.

The basic choux pastry

150mls (¼ pint) water
50g (2oz) butter
pinch of salt
65g (2½oz) sifted plain flour
2 medium free-range eggs

Put the water, butter and salt in a saucepan. Bring to the boil, and add the flour all at once, beating vigorously and continuously as you cook the mixture, for 2 or 3 minutes to obtain a thick firm paste. When it leaves the sides of the pan and has a shiny appearance, remove from the heat. Beat in the eggs, one at a time, making sure the first is fully incorporated before adding the second.

Because the absorbent quality of flour can change from batch to batch and can vary with the day's humidity, it is a good idea not to add the whole of the second egg, as you may not need it all to give you a soft, pliable but not liquid dough. On the other hand, if the flour is very dry, you may need to add a little more beaten egg.

At this point add cheese if using it, or other flavourings. Spoon or pipe the pastry into a ring on a greased baking sheet. To make it rise even more, create a steam-oven effect by inverting a deep roasting tin or cake tin over the pastry, and bake it in a hot oven, 220°C/450°F/gas mark 7 for 15 minutes, and then turn the heat down to 180°C/350°F/gas mark 4 for another 12 to 15 minutes. Remove from the oven, and serve while still warm.

Alternatively, make small heaps of the choux paste on the prepared baking sheet, and these will make excellent small bites to hand round with drinks, when split and stuffed with a savoury mixture. Or fill with sweetened whipped cream and dip in melted chocolate for profiteroles.

The basic rice

Serves 4

1 tablespoon olive oil or butter
250–300g (8–10oz) basmati rice
1 bay leaf
½ teaspoon salt
grinding of fresh pepper
450–550mls (15–18oz) water

Heat the fat in a heavy, lidded saucepan and stir in the rice. Cook for a couple of minutes until the rice is well coated, then add the seasoning and water. Bring to the boil, reduce the heat as low as possible and put on the lid. Cook for 18 minutes or so, by which time all the water will have been absorbed by the rice.

Instead of water, you can cook the rice in suitable stock. If it is to accompany a meal of curry, you might like to cook some crushed cardamom pods, cloves and a cinnamon stick with the rice. Or lemon grass and star anise if it is to accompany an oriental meal.

Cook's note

The rice does not need rinsing before cooking, nor does it need draining afterwards. It can also be cooked in the oven, which is useful if you want the rice as an accompaniment to a roast chicken.

The basic salsa

Serves 4

1 ripe mango
3 shallots
1 green or red chilli
lime juice
sugar
mint
coriander
salt and pepper

The ingredients are simply chopped very small, and mixed together in whichever proportions you prefer, more fruit, more chilli or more onion according to taste. The thick, viscous juice of the mango holds everything together without any thickening agent, and it has a most pleasing texture.

The essentials for a salsa are hot, sour, sweet, not unlike punch, to which are added onion and luscious fruit, which might, instead of mango, be pineapple, papaya, melon or tomatoes. Mint and coriander seem absolutely the right herbs, but if you have access to them you might try more exotic herbs such as *hoja santa*, Mexican tarragon, and epazote.

The basic scone

Makes 10 to 12

250g (½lb) self-raising flour
50g (2oz) butter, chilled and diced
1 tablespoon golden caster sugar
150–175mls (5–6oz) soured milk or
    buttermilk

With your fingertips, rub flour and butter together, until it resembles coarse breadcrumbs. Stir in the sugar and enough liquid to make a soft, pliable dough. Transfer to a floured worktop, and knead lightly and briefly until smooth.

Roll and cut out scones. Bake at 200°C/400°F/gas mark 6 in a preheated oven for about 15 minutes, until well risen and golden.

To this quantity you can add 3 or 4 tablespoons of sultanas or chopped mixed peel for fancy scones. Make cheese scones by leaving out the sugar and adding 50g (2oz) grated Parmesan or Cheddar.

Cook's note

My mother taught me to put the scones on the baking sheet close together, to encourage them to rise well and evenly. It never fails, and gives a nice tender edge to the scone.

The basic sponge

Makes 1 cake

175g (6oz) unsalted butter, room temperature
175g (6oz) caster sugar
4 medium-size free-range eggs
175g (6oz) self-raising flour, sifted

Cream the butter and sugar thoroughly until pale, light and fluffy. Beat the eggs, and gradually beat, a little at a time, into the creamed mixture. Once the eggs have been incorporated, gently fold in the flour.

Spoon the batter into 2 x 20cm (8 inch) greased and floured sandwich tins, smooth the top, and bake in a preheated oven at 180°C/350°F/gas mark 4 for 20–25 minutes.

Allow to cool in the tin for a few minutes, and then ease the sponges out onto wire racks to cool.

To serve, sandwich with raspberry jam and whipped cream or with lemon curd. Sift icing sugar over the top before serving.

To make a chocolate cake, substitute 25–40g (1–2oz) flour for 25–40g (1–2oz) cocoa, and use a filling of melted chocolate folded into whipped cream. For a coffee cake, add to the original mixture two tablespoons espresso coffee, and use more coffee to flavour butter cream, a mixture of softened unsalted butter and icing sugar. Chopped walnuts can be added to the coffee cake batter for yet another version.

The basic stock

Makes 1 litre (1¾ pints)

400g (14oz) cheaper cuts of meat
bones
celery leaves
bay leaf
slice of ginger
1 litre (1¾ pints) water

Brown the meat and bones first in a heavy saucepan, then add the flavourings and water. Simmer for two to three hours and strain into a bowl. Once cool it can be refrigerated. And once chilled, the layer of fat can be lifted off. Browning the meat first gives a good colour to the stock.

A cheaper way of acquiring stock, for a casserole for example, is to buy your meat in a whole piece, trim it, dice it and use the trimmings to make a little stock while you fry the meat, onions and vegetables.

To make fish stock, use uncooked fish bones, which your fishmonger will give you for nothing, and the same flavourings, but simmer for no more than 20 to 30 minutes before straining and rapidly cooling.

Cook's note

If you are really in a hurry, there are a number of ingredients which can add flavour to your cooking without your having to make or buy stock. Wine, vermouth, soy sauce, miso (fermented soy bean paste, sometimes with rice and other cereals added), and dried mushrooms, especially ceps and shiitake, are invaluable for their flavouring and savoury qualities.

To add colour as well as flavour, halve an onion and let it caramelize slowly, cut side down, in a small heavy frying pan, and then add water, bring to the boil, simmer for 5 minutes and strain, to produce a rich brown juice. This is, to my mind, rather more effective than adding a piece of onion skin to the stock pot, which can bring about a bitter taste.

Another type of flavouring, which, at first, might seem bizarre when added to meat, is that of cured or dried fish. This technique is much used in oriental cooking with, for example, dashi, Japanese stock ingredients of dried tuna flakes and seaweed, Chinese and Vietnamese fish sauce, or nuoc mam; and in Sri Lankan cooking, Maldive fish, pounded dried tuna or other oily fish. But a dash of anchovy essence will do just as well, adding a surprising, yet subtle, depth of flavour.

One summer I spent a morning high up in the Swiss Alps near Villars, making cheese and butter with a young cheese-maker, Denis Champs, at La Ferme de Frience. He patiently milked his family's small herd of beautiful blonde milch cows, and then took the milk through all its processes. First, he added to it the starter from the previous day's cheese-making, gently heated it in the large three-legged copper cauldron, adding the rennet, waiting for the milk to coagulate, cutting it and draining it, and once in its *forme* or mould, pressing it into a 24 kilo *fromage de montagne* made to a Gruyère recipe. The cheese, once it had been transferred to the *cave*, would undergo a process of *affinage* or maturing, being washed and turned every day for a year.

Making cheese is hard work. It is an agricul-tural product, born of the soil, the pasture and the climate, as well as the skill of the cheese-maker and the breed of dairy cow, goat or sheep. Once described as 'milk's leap to immortality', cheese-making goes back thousands of years to the first livestock farmers, who almost certainly discovered the process by accident.

Silvano Bergianti has been making Parmesan cheese for over fifty years, at the Caseificio San Giovanni in the heart of the Modenese country-side, having taken over from his father. There is no one to take over from him. His sons, whilst respecting their parents for their hard work, their seven-day week, do not want it for themselves. And I think their parents do not want it for them either, although they don't want the cheese-making to end.

Parmesan cheese has been made in the region since the 11th or 12th century. The local version of its origins recounts that it was one of the Lucio Friars who had milked his goats, set the pail under a lemon tree and nature did the rest, introducing the coagulating acid of the windfall lemon into the waiting milk.

Watching the birth of a Parmesan cheese in the Bergianti dairy was no less dramatic. Far from removing the mystery, being able to watch food being created from the raw material and attend every stage of the process is a curiously moving and exhausting experience. I eat the cheese now with a deep respect for the people who make it; those who rise before dawn to milk the cows and those like Silvano Bergianti, the *casero*, who is at the dairy before 7 a.m. to receive the milk.

Although cheese-making has become more sophisticated since its simple beginnings, the pro-cess remains essentially the same in all cheese-making areas of the world. The moist, warm, appetizing smell at the Caseificio San Giovanni is not unlike that of the cheese dairy at Sharpham Barton in Devon where Robin Congdon makes his range of fine West Country cheeses, using milk from local farmers who raise sheep, goats and cows on the rich Devon pasture. I visited him one spring when I was making a TV series on West Country food, and then visited the Ticklemore cheese shop in Totnes, run by his partner Sari Cooper. More than anything else I was impressed by her descrip-tions of these marvellous English cheeses, blue cheeses, goat's cheeses, soft cheeses, and not once did she compare them to, for example, Roquefort or Gorgonzola. 'These are unique cheeses, with their own distinctive flavour and texture, and not made to resemble other cheeses.'

Some of the foodstuff which now masquerades as cheese is an insult to these gifted and hard-working craftsmen and women. I once tasted some-thing truly nasty at a London tasting of top-class gift hampers. After the judges had waded through indifferent smoked salmon and worse than indif-ferent pâtés, we came to the cheese, some of which could barely be described as such. Imagine, if you will, 'fruit-cake Cheddar'. The two disparate ingre-dients had been mashed together, rolled into a cylinder, and coated with burgundy wax. Cheese, it now seems, is the province of the men in grey suits. After ruining good Cheddar, they turned their attention to Lancashire, in its natural state buttery, crumbly, rich-tasting, a mellow yet piquant delight from the northwest of England. Here it was pre-sented as 'Lancashire with apple and blackcurrant', cheese mashed up with fruit.

With luck, these travesties will sink without a trace, and others like them that combine cheese with chutney, with apricots, or layer together fac-tory versions of fine British regional cheeses like a multicoloured sandwich.

The world of cheese is wonderful and varied, from the well-known classics of the international cheeseboard, such as Roquefort, Camembert, Blue Stilton, Parmigiano and Cheddar, to the lesser known regional treasures of Europe. All are dis-tinctive and exquisite. Portugal's Queso da Serra, Spain's Manchego and Cabrales, France's Cantal and Laguiole, Italy's Taleggio are a few of my favourites.

I would be hard put, in fact, to select my ideal cheeseboard. One thing, I do know: it would consist of no more than five cheeses, would include a blue cheese, a soft bloomy cheese, perhaps a washed rind cheese, a hard cheese and a goat's cheese. And I would take them out of the refrigerator a couple of hours before serving them.

At certain times of year, cold November, blustery March, for example, I like to cook with cheese, and a fondue or raclette makes a lovely casual supper for friends. Swiss food was possibly the first 'foreign' food to enter my consciousness; Johanna Spyri's *Heidi* was a much loved book, and I became very familiar with the description of Heidi's grandfather toasting cheese in front of the fire, which is exactly what raclette is, melting cheese which is scraped (*raclé*) on to a waiting plate. It was many years before I tasted my first raclette, in a small restaurant somewhere in the back streets of Geneva where I much enjoyed the ceremony attached to the making of the raclette. A half-moon of cheese was set on a rack in front of the fire. Plates were stacked nearby to keep warm, and one was fed in relays, one single scraping of melted cheese at a time, which was eaten with small potatoes boiled in their skins, *cornichons* and silver-skinned pickled onions. A carafe of local white wine was what we drank with this agreeable, sociable meal.

Since then, once I set up home with my husband Tom, we went on to enjoy many a fondue evening and raclette supper, cooking and eating from the communal pot. This kind of cooking and entertaining is fun, and I'm not surprised that it is becoming popular again. Kitchenware manufacturers continue to produce fondue sets and have also devised methods of cooking raclette at the table for those of us who do not have open fires and hearth stones.

What sort of cheese to use for raclette and fondues? Traditionally, a semi-hard cheese is used for the raclette and which one would probably depend on which Swiss valley or canton you live in. There are many creamery raclette cheeses, some simply labelled Raclette, but there are those from the Valais which have their own appellation, such as Gomser, Bagnes and Simplon, all mild sweet cheeses.

For fondues, there is no hard-and-fast rule about the cheese to use. Amongst the hard cheeses, Emmental and Gruyère are the most commonly available. The semi-hard cheese Appenzell has a rich, strong fruitiness which combines well with some of the milder cheeses, and the very hard Sbrinz can also be used in combination with other cheeses. Swiss Tilsit, the French Beaufort and Comté, the Norwegian Jarlsberg, other Scandinavian lookalikes as well as the Italian Fontina, all have similar cooking qualities which make them suitable alternatives for fondue, either alone or in combination.

The basic recipe is simple and starts with the ceremonial rubbing of a cut garlic clove over the inside of the cooking pot.

Fondue

Serves 8

600mls (1 pint) good dry white wine
1kg (2¼ lbs) hard or semi-hard cheese, grated
2 tablespoons potato flour or arrowroot
freshly ground pepper
freshly grated nutmeg
2 miniatures or 70mls (⅛ pint) kirsch

Reserve a couple of tablespoons of the wine and pour the rest into the pot, the proportions generally being one part wine to two parts cheese, and heat gently. Gradually add the grated cheese, stirring all the while. Bind the mixture with a little potato flour or arrowroot mixed with the remaining 2 tablespoons of the white wine. Season the cheese dish with ground pepper and nutmeg. Stir in the kirsch, and transfer the fondue from the stove, while bubbling, to a spirit lamp on the table.

There are, of course, many variations on the above. The genevoise fondue contains finely chopped dried morels, which add a delicious flavour to the cheese, that of the eastern cantons of Switzerland uses dry cider instead of wine. I have even come across a recipe for pink fondue in which a dry rosé wine is used instead of white.

Not far from the alpine farm I visited is the Refuge de Frience, a simple chalet restaurant where I tasted a very good fondue that I was curious to try when I returned to England. This was the *fondue de tomate*, which I made to the traditional fondue recipe above, and added a homemade tomato sauce. Instead of bread, I served the fondue with small potatoes boiled in their skins. The main feature about the tomato sauce is that you use very ripe, sweet tomatoes, and char them, either under the grill, on a griddle, in the oven, or whatever is most convenient.

Tomato sauce

Enough to flavour a fondue for 8

1 onion, peeled and sliced
25g (1oz) unsalted butter
6 tomatoes, halved, seeded and charred
75mls (⅛ pint) white wine
seasoning

Gently cook the onion in the butter until translucent and soft. Add the charred tomatoes and white wine. Bring to the boil, and simmer for 10 to 15 minutes. Rub through a sieve, season lightly, and stir into the hot fondue just before serving.

Potato and cheese purée

Serves 4 to 6

1kg (2lbs) potato
4–8 tablespoons warm milk
300g (10oz) Fontina cheese, sliced
1–2 tablespoons softened butter
salt
pepper

Peel and boil the potatoes until soft, and then push through a ricer or mouli-légumes. Otherwise, mash thoroughly with the warm milk. Stir in the cheese and the butter, and beat until thoroughly incorporated. Season to taste with salt and pepper. Serve with *cotechino*, zampone, pork chops or roast pork, or on its own as a soothing first course.

It is particularly good with a shower of white truffles shaved over it.

Green salad with Stilton dressing

Serves 6

100g (4oz) each (approximately) lamb's lettuce, trimmed watercress or rocket and baby spinach leaves

75g (3oz) Stilton
1 tablespoon crème fraiche or soured cream
3 tablespoons milk
lemon juice to taste
freshly ground black pepper to taste

Rinse, drain and carefully dry the salad leaves, and place in a bowl. Crumble the Stilton, and then blend with the cream and milk, adding the lemon juice and black pepper. If you prefer a stronger dressing, add more cheese; if a creamier dressing is required, add more cream, and if a thinner dressing, then add more milk. Pour the dressing over the salad, turn it carefully, and serve immediately.

Three starters

Here are three of my favourite recipes for a first course that is neither fish- nor meat-based. Blue cheese such as Lanark or Yorkshire Blue, Harbourne, Devon or Beenleigh Blue can replace the soft goat's cheese, as, indeed, can slices of hard goat's or sheep's milk cheese.

At different times of the year, I replace the leeks in the second recipe with asparagus, broad beans, green beans, seakale, even beetroot.

Light mousse of three cheeses

Note: this recipe contains raw eggs.

Serves 4

1½ leaves or teaspoons gelatine, or vegetarian equivalent
100mls (4oz) vegetable or chicken stock
100g (4oz) soft fresh goat's cheese
100g (4oz) blue cheese
250g (8oz) fromage frais
2 free-range or organic egg whites

Put the gelatine in a jug, and soften it in the cold stock. Then stand the jug in a pan of hot water, and leave until the gelatine has dissolved.

Blend the cheeses until smooth, and then blend in the gelatine liquid. Whisk the whites until firm, and fold into the cheese. Spoon into wet ramekins or dariole moulds, cover, and refrigerate until set, or overnight.

When ready to serve, run a sharp knife between mousse and mould, and turn out onto plates garnished with salad.

Goat's cheese, walnut and leek salad

Serves 6

1 x 250g (8oz) English goat's cheese, such as
   Golden Cross
2 or 3 garlic cloves, peeled and sliced
1 teaspoon black peppercorns
200mls (7oz) walnut oil
18 baby leeks
3 tablespoons walnuts, chopped
1 teaspoon fresh thyme leaves,
   finely chopped
1–2 tablespoons cider vinegar

Slice the cheese into 6 pieces. Put in a bowl with the garlic, pepper and walnut oil, and marinate for 24 hours at least. When ready to assemble the salad, drop the trimmed leeks into boiling water, and boil them for 3 or 4 minutes, slightly more if the leeks are quite tough and mature. Drain, and rinse under cold water. Put three on each plate with a slice of goat's cheese on top. Mix the walnuts and herbs with 4 tablespoons of the oil marinade and the vinegar. Spoon over the cheese and leeks, and serve.

Goat's cheese with sweet and sour salad

Serves 4 to 6

1 radicchio
4 or 5 blood oranges
1 or 2 fennel bulbs, depending on size, trimmed
   and sliced, or cut into wedges
2 sweet white onions, if available, peeled and
   thinly sliced
2 small fresh goat's cheeses
1 teaspoon grain mustard
4 tablespoons extra-virgin olive oil
seasoning to taste

Separate the radicchio leaves, and arrange on a large platter or individual plates. Slice the blood oranges, and peel the middle slices. Squeeze the end slices into a small jug. Arrange the orange on the radicchio, and then top with the fennel and onion, and finally the goat's cheese, sliced into rounds. Mix the orange juice with the mustard, olive oil and seasoning, and pour over the salad.

For other variations on the theme, keep the radicchio and blood oranges, but substitute red onion for the white, and thinly sliced, freshly cooked beetroot for the fennel. Use the same dressing, and enliven the rich colours with sprigs of watercress.

The savoury

When our Edwardian and Victorian forebears entertained, they did so on a lavish scale; a twelve-course dinner was not unusual. It was during this period that the savoury enjoyed its heyday. And how necessary it was, performing the same function at the end of the meal that the hors d'oeuvre performed at the beginning. The latter stimulated the gastric juices to enable all that followed to be digested. At the end of a long, and copious, meal the system would have slowed down somewhat. This was the point at which a small, intensely savoury mouthful would drive the digestive juices into action once more.

Cookery books of the era invariably have a chapter of savoury recipes, and even up to the 1960s these were to be found in magazines. But no longer. Our meals are not as elaborate, or as lengthy, as they once were. But whenever I have been served a savoury, or made one at home, it has been enjoyed.

Many classic savouries, such as cheese aigrettes, cheese puffs, cheese ramekins, cheese soufflés and the various rarebits or rabbits can well replace the cheese course as an agreeable way of finishing off the red wine. And if you served white wine with a fish main course, a cheese savoury is as good an excuse as any to open a bottle of claret.

And if you choose not to serve the savoury in its proper place at the end of the meal, consider serving them as hot appetizers with drinks. The more substantial ones make excellent light lunch or supper dishes.

Classic rarebit

Many variations on the rarebit theme can be developed. Use Cheddar, apple and cider for a West Country rarebit. For a Welsh rarebit, use Caerphilly and a dash of mead or white wine, and try a Lancashire rarebit made with Lancashire cheese and ale, a Yorkshire rarebit made with Wensleydale cheese and Theakestone's Old Peculiar, and the Hunter's rarebit made with blue and white Stilton and a good measure of tawny port. This is an old favourite.

Serves 1

3 tablespoons cider, wine or beer
50–75g (2–3oz) hard cheese, diced or grated

1 thick slice bread, toasted on one side, buttered on the other, and spread with a little English grain mustard

Put the liquid in a saucepan, and heat gently but do not boil. Stir in the cheese, and when melted, spoon over the bread, butter side up, which you have placed in an ovenproof dish.

Finish off under the grill or in the top of a hot oven, until the top is bubbling and golden brown. You can also make several of these, placing the toast in a large ovenproof dish.

Hot potted cheese

Serves 6 to 8

4 tablespoons soft white breadcrumbs
4 tablespoons port or sweet Oloroso sherry
250g (8oz) grated hard cheese
75g (3oz) softened butter
4 free-range eggs, separated
freshly ground pepper

Soak the breadcrumbs in the port for a few minutes. Drain them and mix with the cheese and softened butter. Mix in the egg yolks, season, and then fold in the stiffly whipped egg whites. Spoon into buttered ramekins and bake in a preheated oven at 180°C/350°F/gas mark 4 for about 15 to 20 minutes. Smaller versions can be baked in paper cases for serving as finger food.

Glamorgan sausages

Makes 20

250g (8oz) fresh breadcrumbs
250g (8oz) grated cheese, Caerphilly or other semi-hard cheese
1 leek or 4 spring onions, trimmed and finely chopped
1 tablespoon chopped fresh chives
1 tablespoon chopped fresh parsley
1 teaspoon mustard powder
salt
pepper
nutmeg
2 free-range eggs plus one egg white
milk
flour or breadcrumbs for coating
25g (1oz) butter
1 tablespoon olive oil

The perfect croque-monsieur

You sip a *vin blanc cassis*, or *demi pression*, watching the world go by your Paris café table. You have just ordered a croque-monsieur.

Sadly, the anticipation proves more enjoyable than the reality. More often than should be the case, this long-time favourite Parisian bar snack is a travesty of the real thing.

YOU NEED, for each person, two slices of buttered bread, crusts removed, a slice of cheese and a slice of ham. With only three main ingredients, there is not much leeway for failure. Use the best ingredients you can find. Choose real ham, not pressed shoulder, good cheese – Gruyère is traditional, but Comté is even better – and use bread with some substance.

METHOD For each 'croque', place the ham and cheese between the slices of bread, trimmed to fit. Grill or fry on both sides, until the bread is crisp and browned, and the cheese is melting.

ALTERNATIVES A fried egg on top turns this into a 'croque-madame'. Another version involves spreading the filled sandwich with a thick cheese-flavoured béchamel, before baking in the oven. This makes a tasty supper or lunch. Cut into squares, it can be served with drinks.

Mix together the crumbs, cheese, onion, herbs and seasoning. Stir 1 whole egg and an egg yolk into the mixture and as much milk as is needed to bind it together. Whisk the egg whites to a froth on a plate, and put the flour or breadcrumbs on another. Divide the cheese mixture into twenty, and roll each portion into a small sausage shape. Coat each one in the egg white and then in flour or breadcrumbs. Heat the butter and oil in a frying pan, and fry for about 10 minutes until golden brown.

Serve hot, warm or cold. They are good with homemade tomato sauce, chutney or pickles. Larger versions can be served as a first course.

Celery and Stilton

Serves 8

1 or 2 heads of crisp celery
150g (5oz) Stilton
75g (3oz) unsalted butter
3 tablespoons cream
pinch of powdered saffron
125g (generous 4oz) smoked streaky bacon,
    diced and fried until crisp

Using the inner, crisper stalks only (the outer stalks can be saved for soup or juicing), cut the celery into 7.5cm (3 inch) lengths. Cream the cheese and butter, and then mix in the cream, saffron and bacon pieces. Spoon or pipe into the celery stalks, and serve as an appetizer with drinks or as the cheese-savoury course.

Stilton mousse pancakes

Serves 4

175g (6oz) Stilton
75mls (3oz) cream
1 tablespoon clear mild honey
4 freshly made pancakes

Cream the Stilton with a fork or in a food processor, and blend in the cream and honey. Divide the mixture amongst the pancakes, and fold into parcels, or tie into bundles with chives. Serve cold, or heat through in the oven for a few minutes.

The perfect cheese biscuit

Homemade cheese biscuits could not be simpler, and your guests will be very impressed that you have made them yourself. Using the same proportions, you can make up a much larger batch of mixture and freeze several cylinders of dough for use when needed.

YOU NEED 100g (4oz) each butter, plain flour, and grated hard, well-flavoured cheese. If you like, add a generous pinch of cayenne, some dried, rubbed sage or some cumin seeds.

METHOD Rub the butter and flour together, stir in the cheese and add a little water to bind to a firm dough. Roll out, and stamp out 5cm (2 inch) discs. Place on baking sheets, and bake for 8 to 10 minutes. Cool on wire racks before storing in an air-tight container.

ALTERNATIVE To prepare in advance, roll the raw mixture into a cylinder, wrap well and freeze and cut off thin slices to bake as you need them.

Cheddar scones

Makes 12

250g (8oz) self-raising flour
50g (2oz) butter, chilled and diced
50g (2oz) mature farmhouse Cheddar, grated
about 100mls (3½oz) buttermilk, or fresh milk
    soured with lemon juice. Or use 75mls (3oz)
    water with 25mls (1oz) yoghurt

Rub the flour and butter together in a bowl. Stir in the cheese and add enough liquid to make a soft, pliable dough. Transfer to a floured board, and knead it lightly.

Roll and cut out scones. Bake at 200°C/400°F/gas mark 6 in a preheated oven for about 15 minutes. Cool on a wire rack before serving warm.

Cheese

SUNDAY LUNCH
FOR FOUR

**Mint-cured mackerel with
potato farls**

**Slow-cooked lamb shanks with
potato and cauliflower mash**

Steamed quince pudding

This menu, which would be perfect for Sunday lunch, includes an inexpensive cut of lamb, slowly cooked to a deeply flavourful tenderness, and that quintessentially British dessert, a steamed pudding. The starter, cured mackerel, in the style of gravad lax, using mint instead of dill, can be prepared two or three days in advance. The accompanying potato farls, like thick griddle cakes, can be bought or made. In all, this is a meal which will not require you to spend a great deal of time in the kitchen, as the lamb and the pudding will look after themselves once you have got them under way.

All depends on successful shopping, however, for the lamb shanks, the quinces, and really fresh mackerel.

For those who enjoy cooking, it is a deeply pleasurable and satisfying activity. Satisfactory in the production of the end result, and the pleasure in getting there. There are many facets to cooking – thinking about the meal, thinking about who it is for, planning it, perhaps while you are attending to unavoidable chores, shopping, and then fine-tuning, once you see what is available.

I find that it is never a good idea fully to plan a meal before I return home from shopping. Not only will I discover things I hadn't really intended to buy, and that I have forgotten to buy others, but I will probably have had to substitute something else for my planned main course. This situation is stimulating, rather than frustrating. Adapting recipes to new ingredients is creative, and it is immensely satisfying to produce in turn new recipes.

In a sense my mackerel recipe originated in such adaptations. To begin with, I used dill with it, then coriander leaves and crushed coriander seeds with some soy sauce and toasted sesame oil, and over a ten-year period I have used various permutations. You can follow the principles of my recipe, but adapt it to your own taste.

With the lamb, the key features are that it is an inexpensive cut of meat, with lots of sinews in it, which means that slow cooking will bring out the best in it. Shin of beef, knuckle of veal, or pork, can be cooked in the same way, with your own choice of aromatics.

If you cannot buy quinces, or get them from a neighbour, the pudding works very well with pears, apples or plums. None of these will need the longer pre-cooking of the quince, and you can vary the spices to match the fruit; try cardamom with pears, cloves with apple, and cinnamon with plums.

The lamb recipe is, in a sense, a work in progress. Complete in itself at this stage, it works very well, but I have an idea for a further stage, which I pass on for those who would like to try it. The initial preparation, the seasoning and light curing, is exactly the same as for preparing confit of duck or goose. The object of making confit is to preserve the meat, sealed under its own fat, so that it provides a ready meal in a hurry. You remove the piece of meat from its fat, scraping off any excess, and reheat it gently, to serve with potatoes and vegetables or green salad. Since lamb shanks have little fat, they will need to be cooked and sealed, either under olive oil or under the goose fat that you might have saved from Christmas. And wine will not be used in this cooking, as it is in the recipe that follows. Because temperatures in our centrally heated houses are high, I keep all my confits in the refrigerator.

Of course, lamb is such an important, readily available and everyday part of the British culinary repertoire, and always has been, that you might argue that there is little point in preserving it. But do try the recipe below, even if you are not going to make a confit of lamb shanks. This is a lovely plain, homely dish, which acts as a perfect foil for good red wines, a claret especially. A substantial Chardonnay will accompany the mackerel very well, and to finish, a liquorous sweet wine, such as the Portuguese Moscatel de Setubal. An *eau de vie de coing* served ice-cold with the quince pudding is a marriage made in heaven, however.

the rest of the seasoning, and put the rest of the mint on top. Cover with foil, and weigh down with tins. Refrigerate and keep for up to 3 or 4 days, although the mackerel is good to eat after just 8 hours or so, and can be prepared in the morning to serve at night. To serve it, wipe off the herbs and seasoning, and slice into oblique or vertical slices. A sweet mustard mayonnaise is the traditional accompaniment.

Potato farls

Makes about a dozen

75g (3oz) potato flour
75g (3oz) plain flour
pinch of salt
1 free-range egg
100mls (4oz) water or skimmed milk
100g (4oz) sieved cooked potato

Sift the flours and salt together, add the egg, lightly beaten, and gradually beat in the liquid until smooth. Stir in the potato.

Pour into a greased square cake tin or roasting pan, and bake at about 190°C/375°F/gas mark 5 for 20 minutes or so, until the mixture is brown on top.

Turn out, allow to cool a little, and cut into squares to serve.

Slow-cooked lamb shanks

The shoulder shanks are smaller than the leg shanks, and less expensive. Generally, as they are not that easy to come by, I take what I can get. With leg shanks, an accompanying potato dish is sufficient, or some green salad. With shoulder shanks, you might like to serve another vegetable.

Serves 4

4 lamb shanks
1 teaspoon freshly ground black pepper
1 tablespoon coarse sea salt
1 tablespoon chopped thyme and marjoram, mixed
½ teaspoon cinnamon
2 tablespoons extra-virgin olive oil
1 tablespoon plain flour
200mls (7oz) dry red wine

Mint-cured mackerel

Serves 8

About 1kg (2lbs) large mackerel fillets
bunch of fresh mint
2 tablespoons coarse sea salt
1 tablespoon golden granulated sugar
1 tablespoon coarsely ground black or white pepper
1 tablespoon cognac – optional

Remove all the pin bones from the mackerel. Spread a third of the mint on the bottom of the dish. Mix the salt, sugar and pepper, and sprinkle a third of it over the mint. Place one layer of fillets on top, skin side down. Sprinkle half the remaining seasoning over the fillets, and lay half the mint on top. Sprinkle on the cognac, if using it.

Place the other fillets on top, skin side up. Sprinkle with

Remove any excess fat from the shanks, and rub them all over with the pepper, salt, herbs and cinnamon. Cover and refrigerate overnight.

Heat the oil in a heavy casserole, brown the lamb all over, sift on the flour, and mix it with the oil. Pour on the wine, bring to the boil, cover, and then cook on the lowest heat or in a low oven until the lamb is tender and begins to fall away from the bone. I generally give it 2 to 2½ hours.

Serve with jacket potatoes, a potato gratin, or this potato and cauliflower mash.

Potato and cauliflower mash

Serves 4

1 medium cauliflower
500g (1lb) potatoes
salt
pepper
milk, butter or olive oil
pinch of nutmeg

Break off the cauliflower florets, and boil until tender.

Drain, peel, and boil the potatoes. Drain and season, and then mash with the oil, butter or milk to a smooth purée, or simply use some of the cooking water.

Using an electric beater or food processor, and a little lubrication, make a purée with the cauliflower; fold into the potatoes, add more salt and pepper if necessary, and some freshly grated nutmeg.

Steamed quince pudding

Serves 4

1 large quince
150g (5oz) light muscovado sugar
150g (5oz) unsalted butter
125g (4oz) self-raising flour
3 free-range eggs, lightly beaten

Parboil the quince until it feels yielding. When cool enough to handle, peel and thinly slice, and put in the bottom of individual buttered pudding bowls or tins. Melt 50g (2oz) of the butter and stir in 50g (2oz) of the sugar. When this has dissolved, pour it over the quince. Cream the remaining sugar and butter, and stir in the flour and eggs alternately.

Spoon the mixture into the pudding bowls, cover with foil and cook in a roasting tin with water halfway up the bowls, for about 40 minutes in a preheated oven at 180°C/350°F/gas mark 4. Turn out and serve. Whilst the ubiquitous crème fraiche is a good accompaniment, real custard is even better – see p. 27.

You can also cook the pudding in a single, larger pudding basin, allowing about 1¼ hours. No one imagines that these are puddings for everyday eating, as they once were. We simply do not need the pile of calories that our great-grandparents required in the days of much harder physical work and unheated houses. Nevertheless, as a once-in-a-while treat, I believe they do no harm. Yes, they contain sugar and butter, but at least you know exactly, down to the last teaspoon, how much of each has been used, rather than having some manufacturer decide for you.

Chicken and poultry

Chicken

When I was growing up in the fifties, chicken was a rare treat for high days and holidays. My mother used to roast it to an appetizing golden brown, a combination of crispness and succulence, and she would serve it with roast potatoes and cauliflower cheese. Then in the sixties and seventies we saw the nadir of factory farming. During those years, one would not dream of cooking a chicken for a treat. They were stuffed full of fish meal and growth promoters, tasted awful, with a woolly texture.

Factory farming is, regrettably, still with us, witness the 80p a kilo broiler in the supermarket. But it is now possible to buy real free-range chickens and organic chickens from small producers. Many farmers are going back to the traditional breeds of poultry and livestock, which are slower-growing than the broiler, are adapted to our climate and conditions and develop a deep, full flavour and good texture. These are the birds to look for, whether chicken, duck or turkey, and it is well worth paying more for them. These are the birds I have used in the following recipes.

Prune, leek and walnut stuffing

Serves 4 to 6

4–6 slices day-old bread, left out to dry
2 or 3 celery stalks, trimmed and chopped
2 leeks, trimmed, sliced and thoroughly rinsed
1 clove
1 piece of cinnamon
1 bay leaf
150mls (¼ pint) milk
100g (4oz) walnut pieces
100g (4oz) ready-to-eat prunes, stoned and
    finely chopped
salt
pepper
grated zest of a lemon
1 free-range organic egg, lightly beaten

Tear the bread into small pieces, with or without the crusts, as you prefer. Simmer the celery, leeks and spices in the milk for 5 minutes. Discard the spices, and strain the vegetables. You can keep the milk if you wish to make a cream gravy for the chicken.

Mix the bread, vegetables, walnuts, prunes, seasoning and lemon zest, and bind with the egg. Spoon into a greased ovenproof container, such as a soufflé dish. Smooth the surface, and bake the stuffing in the bottom half of the oven, for about an hour.

Other dried fruits and nuts can be used in place of the prunes and walnuts, but I like the way this stuffing picks up some of the flavours of the traditional cock-a-leekie.

I like to serve the chicken just with its gravy and stuffing, and follow it with a green salad. If you prefer to serve vegetables with the chicken, I suggest beans, broccoli or cabbage, together with a baked or roasted root vegetable such as parsnip or celeriac.

This is not, of course, the end of the chicken. The carcass, while it will not produce a sparkling, restaurant-clear stock, will make a very good base for a soup. Simmer it gently with a celery top, a slice of ginger, if you wish, the outer layer of a small onion and a few peppercorns. After a couple of hours, strain, cool and chill the broth, or reduce it, chill it, and freeze it for later use. If you want to use it the next day, also use any left-over scraps of chicken to make this lovely soup, creamy, intriguingly spicy, and deeply satisfying.

Cream of chicken and barley soup

Serves 4 to 6

1 onion, peeled and finely chopped
1 celery stalk, trimmed and sliced
1 tablespoon butter or olive oil
75g (3oz) pearl barley
1.25 litres (2 pints) chicken broth – see above
150mls (¼ pint) milk or cream
seasoning
diced chicken meat
grated nutmeg – optional

If you prefer, you can simmer the vegetables in a few tablespoons of stock until soft, and leave out the fat. Or sweat the vegetables in butter or oil until soft, and just lightly golden. Stir in the pearl barley, add half the broth, and simmer until the barley is tender, about 1½ to 2 hours. Stir in the remaining broth and milk or cream. Add salt and pepper to taste, and a little grating of nutmeg, if you like. Add the chicken meat, bring to the boil, simmer for 5 minutes, and serve.

Chicken giblet and potato salad

If you are lucky enough to buy chickens with giblets, here is a very good recipe for a first course.

Serves 2

250g (½lb) small waxy potatoes, such as Pink
    Fir Apple, Charlotte, Francine or La Ratte
4 tablespoons olive oil
1 chicken liver
1 chicken heart, sliced
1 chicken gizzard, skinned and sliced
salad leaves
1 tablespoon sherry vinegar, cider vinegar or
    fruit vinegar
chives, finely chopped

Scrub the potatoes, boil, and slice when cool enough to handle. Heat a tablespoon of the oil, and in it fry the giblets until done to your liking. Remove them from the pan. Put salad leaves on two plates, with the potatoes and giblets on top. Deglaze the pan with the vinegar, scraping up all the residues. Add the remaining oil, stir together, and pour over the salad. Scatter chives on top.

A more substantial dish, a main course, can be made by adding strips of fried pancetta or bacon, fried quail eggs and slices of grilled black pudding.

Chicken giblets chopped small, fried with chopped onion and garlic, and simmered with chopped tomatoes, marjoram and good red wine make an excellent sauce for pasta. Or, indeed, chopped even smaller or blended, this can make a good filling for ravioli to serve in chicken broth.

Roast chicken stuffed with cheese

In the following recipe, the stuffing is not placed in the cavity, but under the skin, which keeps the bird beautifully moist. It is also a recipe that can be adapted by using turkey instead of chicken.

Serves 4

1.5kg (about 3lb) traditional free-range or
    organic chicken
sprigs of fresh herbs such as chervil, parsley or
    tarragon, finely chopped
bunch of chives, finely chopped
150g (5oz) curd or cream cheese
150g (5oz) mild Lancashire, crumbled

freshly ground black pepper
1 lemon

Remove any visible fat from the bird. Ease the skin away from the flesh by gradually inserting your fingers between the skin and the breasts. Continue working your way round the bird until the skin is loose around the legs and back. Mix the herbs and cheese, and spread the mixture over the flesh,

The perfect roast chicken

Choose the most expensive bird you can afford; an organic chicken will give a thick crisp skin, flavourful meat which does not fall apart when you bite into it, and very good stock when you boil up the carcass.

YOU NEED, for 3 to 4 people, a 1.5kg (3lb) chicken, 1 bay leaf, 2 cloves, ½ lemon, salt and pepper.

METHOD Remove any excess fat from the body cavity. Spike the bay leaf with the cloves, and tuck this into the cavity. Rub the bird all over with the cut lemon, squeezing the juice over the bird, and then put the half-lemon inside. Lightly season inside and out, and place the chicken on its side on a rack in the roasting tin.

Roast on its side for 20 minutes in a preheated oven at 200°C/400°F/gas mark 6. Turn onto its other side, and roast at the same temperature for 20 minutes. Finally, turn the chicken on its back, and roast for about 15 minutes to brown it nicely. Juices, which are released when you pierce the inner thigh with a skewer, should be clear and not pink. A real free-range chicken may take up to an hour and a quarter to cook. Transfer the chicken to a serving platter.

TO SERVE with a simple gravy, skim and discard the fat from the pan juices, and transfer them to a saucepan. Add a splash or two of the wine you will serve with the chicken, simmer for 5 minutes and, if you wish, thicken with a little potato flour or cornflour.

For a cream gravy, add the milk in which the stuffing ingredients are cooked. While the bird is roasting, the stuffing can also be cooking in the oven.

under the skin, then ease the skin back into place. This is all much easier than it sounds.

Rub the pepper over the chicken and season inside. Prick the lemon all over with a skewer and put it into the cavity. Cover the bird loosely, but carefully, with foil and roast in a preheated oven at 200°C/400°F/gas mark 6 for about 1¼ hours.

Chicken breasts stuffed with oysters

Supposedly aphrodisiac oysters appear in the following recipe, which I developed for a Valentine's Day dinner, and thereafter used it on a number of occasions, as it tastes so good and is easy to cook.

This use of oysters with meat, particularly poultry, has very long traditions in English cookery, dating back to a time when oysters were part of the everyday diet, and not a luxury. The practice still survives in the traditional American kitchen, where oysters are used to stuff turkey. For this recipe, four or six oysters will be sufficient. It is a very useful recipe, as quantities can be multiplied to serve six or a dozen guests.

For up to six, I cook the chicken breasts in a frying pan. More than that I cook in the oven, with generous bastings of buttery, oystery juices to stop the meat drying. Chicken liver and/or mushrooms can be used in the stuffing for those not able to eat oysters.

Serves 2

2 free-range or organic chicken breasts
freshly ground pepper
salt
ground mace or freshly grated nutmeg
½ shallot, peeled and finely chopped
½ celery stalk, trimmed and finely chopped
50mls (2oz) milk
2 slices white bread, crust removed
generous sprig of tarragon, finely chopped
4 or 6 fresh oysters, shucked, and the liquor
    reserved
seasoned flour
1 free-range egg – optional
breadcrumbs for coating – optional
25g (1oz) butter
3–4 tablespoons dry white wine or champagne
lemon slices – for garnish

Remove the arrow-shaped fillet from under the breast and use in another dish – I find it the perfect amount of meat for chicken risotto.

Cut a pocket in each chicken breast with the point of a sharp knife, and season the meat lightly. Cover and refrigerate while you prepare the stuffing. Simmer the shallot and celery in the milk until soft, then put to one side. Crumble the bread and put in a bowl with the drained vegetables, the chopped tarragon and enough milk to bind together.

Divide the stuffing in four, and fill each breast with first some stuffing, then the oysters, then the remaining stuffing. Secure closed with cocktail sticks. Dust with seasoned flour, dipping in beaten egg, and coating with breadcrumbs if you wish. Fry in the butter until the chicken is cooked through, and the outside golden brown.

Make a gravy with the pan juices, wine or champagne and the reserved oyster liquid. Pour around the chicken, and garnish with lemon slices. My favourite thing to serve with the oyster-stuffed chicken, apart from mashed potatoes, is wilted spinach or cooked cucumber.

Chicken yakitori

The following dish does not require lengthy marinating, just the time it takes you to lay the table and make a salad for the first course, making this a good standby for last-minute entertaining.

Serves 6

6 skinless free-range or organic chicken breasts,
    trimmed and cut into chunks
12 spring onions, cut into 3 or 4 pieces
12 wooden skewers, soaked in water
6 tablespoons fermented soy sauce, or tamari
3 tablespoons toasted sesame oil
4 tablespoons mirin, or pale cream sherry
1–2 teaspoons freshly grated ginger
2 tablespoons rice vinegar or sherry vinegar

Thread the chicken pieces on the skewers, alternating with the spring onions.

Make a teriyaki sauce with the remaining ingredients, and marinate the skewers in it.

Cook on a barbecue or under the grill, for 8 to 10 minutes, and serve with the rest of the sauce, briefly boiled, and a bowl of steamed rice.

Prawns, scallops or small pieces of pork can be cooked in the same away.

Cajun seared chicken

Care needs to be taken with this next recipe. This popular style of cooking, originally from Louisiana and now spread far and wide, entails heating a sturdy well-seasoned cast-iron griddle, or frying pan, to as high a heat as possible. A piece of fish or meat, which has been dipped in melted butter and a seasoning mixture, is then cooked by fast searing. More suited to the professional restaurant than the domestic kitchen though it may be, I include this recipe because good results can be obtained, either with a heavy frying pan or on the barbecue. Flat cuts, which cook evenly and relatively quickly, are best done over such fierce heat, so choose chicken breasts in preference to thighs and drumsticks.

You can make up your own seasoning mix, and store it in a jar in your spice cupboard. Many variations can be made on the theme.

Serves 2

2 free-range or organic chicken breasts, off the bone, and with the skin and small fillet removed
50g (2oz) butter, melted
3–4 tablespoons Cajun seasoning:
    50g (2oz) cayenne pepper
    25g (1oz) fine sea-salt
    25g (1oz) freshly ground black pepper
    25g (1oz) freshly ground white pepper
    25g (1oz) ground coriander seeds
    25g (1oz) ground cumin
    25g (1oz) ground celery seeds
    25g (1oz) dried oregano or marjoram

Heat the frying pan or griddle. Thoroughly dry the chicken breasts, flatten them, and dip them in the butter. Sprinkle liberally on both sides with the seasoning, pressing it in well.

When the frying pan or barbecue coals are as hot as you can get them, put on the chicken pieces. Cook for 4 to 5 minutes on each side, and serve.

A crisp, cooling salad, and a baked potato with soured cream, or mashed potatoes are good accompaniments.

Moroccan-style chicken parcels

Based on the famous *pastilla* (see p. 142), individual filo parcels are filled with a mixture of cooked chicken, eggs, dried fruit, sugar and spices in an intriguing and subtle combination. Miniature versions make excellent hors d'oeuvres.

Serves 6 to 8

750g (1½lbs) cooked free-range or organic chicken, off the bone, diced very small or shredded
6 free-range eggs
200mls (7oz) strong chicken stock
150g (5oz) butter, melted
18 sheets of filo pastry, about 15cms (6 inches) square
75–100g (3–4oz) golden granulated sugar
100g (4oz) flaked almonds, fried gently in butter
1 teaspoon powdered cinnamon
150g (5oz) chopped dried fruit, such as apricots, prunes, peaches or pears, or a mixture
50g (2oz) pickled lemons, chopped – optional
2 teaspoons each cardamom, cumin and coriander seeds, crushed
toasted almonds, black olives, fresh mint leaves – for garnish

Beat the eggs with the stock, and cook gently in a non-stick frying pan, as if you were making scrambled eggs. When the mixture has thickened slightly, remove the pan from the heat, and let it cool. Stir in the chicken and add the rest of the ingredients.

Stack up the filo squares, brushing each of them with melted butter. To make one parcel, take three squares, laying one on top of the other at an angle. Spoon some of the filling into the middle, and dampen the pastry around the edges. Draw into the centre and pinch together to make a bundle. Alternatively, fold the filo into envelope or cigar shapes.

Bake for 20 to 25 minutes, and serve hot, warm or cold, decorated with the olives, almonds and mint leaves.

Chicken and melon salad with warm coriander dressing

Substantial enough to serve as a light lunch or supper dish, this sweet and savoury salad has a mellow oriental flavour.

Serves 6

3 skinless, boneless free-range or organic
   chicken breasts
1 small honeydew melon
1 tablespoon coriander seeds, lightly crushed
2 tablespoons sesame seeds
2 tablespoons virgin sesame or groundnut oil
1 tablespoon rice vinegar
2 teaspoons fresh ginger, peeled and finely
   chopped
2 cloves garlic, peeled and crushed
1–2 tablespoons fresh coriander, chopped
1 or 2 teaspoons toasted sesame oil

Poach or steam the chicken for 8 minutes. When cool enough to handle, slice, and arrange the slices on plates, alternating with slices of melon, or put a fan of chicken slices to one side of the plate and a fan of melon slices on the other.

In a small heavy frying pan, toast the coriander and sesame seeds until golden brown. Scatter them over the chicken and melon. In the same pan mix all the other ingredients except the fresh coriander and toasted sesame oil; bring to the boil, remove from the heat, stir in the coriander and toasted sesame oil, and spoon over the salad. Serve immediately. Fresh basil or mint can replace coriander for those who do not like it.

Forty-cloves-of-garlic chicken

Only a mere hint of mild, creamy garlic is evident in this classic French dish. I like to cook it as soon as we get the first of the new season's garlic from Lautrec in the Languedoc, usually in July.

Serves 4 to 6

about 5 heads new season's garlic, cloves
   separated and peeled
2kg (4lb) free-range or organic chicken
½ lemon
salt

pepper
couple of sprigs tarragon, sage or rosemary
2 tablespoons cognac
75mls (⅛ pint) good dry white wine

Remove excess fat from the chicken cavity and neck. Rub all over with lemon juice, and put the rest of the lemon inside the chicken. Season lightly, inside and out, and put the herbs inside the bird.

Brown the bird all over in a non-stick frying pan. Pour on the cognac, and light it. Transfer the bird and juices to an ovenproof casserole. Add the garlic and wine. Cover, and cook in a preheated oven at 180°C/350°F/gas mark 4 for about 1½ hours. Serve hot, warm, or cold.

Poached chicken

Many cuisines have a poached chicken dish, often served on festive occasions. I have included four of my favourites, including the classic French *poule au pot*, and *riso e gallina* from Piedmont. This is based on the dish Signora Beppina Bava serves to her family for special Sunday lunches. When we were there, white truffles, found nearby, were grated over the dish just before it was served, but nutmeg also provides a good seasoning. I asked Signora Bava how much rice she allowed per person. '*Una manciata*,' she replied, a handful, and one for the pot. The recipe goes back to Beppo Stefano and Stefano Borello, who established the culinary reputation of the town of Cocconato, where the Bava family have lived for several generations.

The third recipe is the festive chicken dish so popular for Sunday lunch in Bogotá, Colombia. It is one of the best dishes I have ever come across in my travels. Delicious, convivial and fun to eat.

And finally, from my brother's Hong Kong household, Hainan chicken, as cooked by my sister-in-law, Bettina, a fine Cantonese cook. Popular all over Southeast Asia, wherever there are Chinese cooks, it originated on Hainan, the large tropical island off the southwest coast of China, but you are as likely to be served it in Singapore as in Shanghai.

All these make excellent party dishes, which is why I have included so many.

La poule au pot

Serves 4 to 6

1 large oven-ready free-range or organic
 chicken, about 2kg (4lbs), with giblets
1 veal shin bone, chopped (ask your butcher to
 do this for you), or pig's trotter
large sprig of lemon thyme or plain thyme
1 celery stalk
1 onion stuck with four cloves
salt, pepper
parsley stalks
bay leaf
12 young carrots, peeled or scrubbed
12 small turnips, peeled
12 pickling onions or shallots, peeled
1 small cabbage, cut into wedges

stuffing (optional)

200g (7oz) belly pork, rind removed, and minced
2–3 garlic cloves, peeled and crushed
1 onion or shallot, peeled and finely chopped
handful of parsley, finely chopped
6 heaped tablespoons fresh breadcrumbs
2 free-range egg yolks
freshly grated nutmeg
salt
pepper

Mix all the stuffing ingredients together with the finely chopped heart, liver and gizzard.

If the chicken is trussed, remove the string if you wish to stuff the bird. Spoon the stuffing into the cavity, having first removed any excess fat, and either sew up the vent or secure it closed with cocktail sticks.

Put the chicken, veal bone or pig's trotter, thyme, celery stalk and onion in a large stockpot, and cover with water. Add a little seasoning, the bay leaf, parsley stalks, neck and wing tips and other trimmings.

Bring the water just to the boil, skim any foam from the surface, lower the heat as far as possible, and poach the chicken very gently for an hour. The water should not boil.

After an hour, remove the herbs, celery and onion, and add the prepared vegetables. Bring back to the boil, lower the heat, and poach until the vegetables are just cooked. Throughout the cooking, the surface should be skimmed occasionally to remove any impurities.

Transfer the chicken to a carving board, and the vegetables to a serving platter. Cut up the chicken, and arrange with the vegetables, moistening with a little of the broth.

Serve the broth first with a slice of stuffing in each bowl and then the meat and vegetables together with rice, noodles or new potatoes. Whichever starchy accompaniment you have chosen will already have been cooked, of course, and for the cooking liquid, you can use some of the broth from the pot of chicken.

The veal or pig's trotter will provide enough gelatine in the broth for you to serve a cold *poule au pot*, if you wish. Make this by arranging the vegetables, chicken and stuffing in a deep platter, and pour over it the strained, reduced stock. Cool, then chill until just set.

Riso e gallina (Italian rice and chicken)

Serves 6 to 8

1.5–2kg (3–4lbs) free-range or organic mature
 chicken
1 celery stalk, finely chopped
1 shallot, peeled and chopped
2 cloves garlic, peeled and finely chopped
50g (2oz) butter or extra-virgin olive oil
150mls (¼ pint) dry white wine, preferably
 sparkling
500g (1lb) risotto rice
4 free-range egg yolks
250mls (scant ½ pint) whipping or double cream
salt
pepper
nutmeg

Remove any excess fat from the bird's cavity, and put the bird in a large stockpot, together with aromatics such as a slice or two of fresh ginger, a bay leaf or two, a sliver of lemon zest, a celery stalk. Cover with water, and bring slowly to the boil. Turn down the heat to the merest simmer, and cook until the chicken is tender, about 50 to 60 minutes, somewhat longer if you are using a boiling fowl.

Meanwhile, gently fry the celery, shallot and garlic in the butter or oil until soft. Stir in the wine, and cook until evaporated. Stir in the rice, and when it is well coated, add a ladleful of boiling chicken stock, poured from the chicken pot into a smaller saucepan. When it has been absorbed, add another ladleful, continuing in this way until the rice is almost cooked.

Meanwhile, beat the egg yolks and cream, and cook gently over a low heat until thickened, but take care not to curdle it. Take the chicken out of the pot, and take off the meat in large slivers. Finish cooking the rice, and season it; it should be quite tender but not sloppy. Remove it from the heat. Stir in half the cream sauce, and heap the rice into a hot bowl, serving platter or tureen. Arrange the pieces of chicken around the edges, and trickle the rest of the sauce over the rice. A grating of white truffles turns this into a feast.

Colombian *ajiaco*

Serves 6 to 8

approx. 2kg (4lb) free-range or organic chicken
2 large onions, peeled and quartered
a handful of coriander sprigs
3 litres (5 pints) water
1kg (2lbs) soft-cooking potatoes, peeled and thickly sliced
1kg (2lbs) firm potatoes, peeled and sliced
500g (1lb) small waxy salad potatoes, scrubbed and halved, or left whole if small
bunch of watercress, leaves only
3 or 4 ears of sweetcorn
fresh green or red chilli, or crushed dried chillies to taste
salt to taste
fresh coriander

Rinse and dry the chicken, and remove any cavity fat. Put the bird in a large saucepan with the onion, coriander stalks and water. Add more water if necessary, to cover the chicken. Bring to the boil, remove any scum from the surface, cover, and simmer gently for 15 minutes. Add the soft-cooking potatoes, and cook for a further 25 to 30 minutes. Remove the coriander and onion and discard. Take out the chicken, and put to one side.

Put in the rest of the potatoes, and cook for 15 to 20 minutes until the first batch is quite soft enough for you to break up with a fork and the other two kinds of potato are still firm but cooked. Meanwhile, remove the meat from the chicken carcass. Add the chilli and watercress to the pan with the corn cobs, each cut into three or four pieces, plus the salt, and bring to the boil. Put in the chicken meat, and simmer for about 5 minutes until the corn is tender. Stir in the fresh coriander, ladle into deep soup bowls, and serve very hot.

The traditional accompaniments for *ajiaco*, served in separate bowls for each to help themselves, are: thick yoghurt or cream, capers, chopped parsley and *aji* (a hot sauce of finely chopped spring onion or leek, tomato, fresh chillies and fresh coriander leaves, mixed with lime juice or vinegar). Each person is also served half an avocado, peeled and sliced on to a side plate.

Hainan chicken

Serves 6

2kg (4lb) free-range or organic chicken
1 teaspoon five-spice powder
6 star-anise pods, plus extra for garnish
12 peppercorns, roughly crushed
1 medium onion, stuck with 6 cloves
6 fresh coriander stalks, and then use the leaves for garnish
6 thin slices fresh ginger root
7.5cm (3 inch) piece cinnamon stick
2 tablespoons rice wine, or Amontillado sherry
2 tablespoons soy sauce

Rinse the chicken thoroughly, inside and out, remove any fat, and cut off the wing pinions. If it has been trussed, remove the string to allow it to cook through more evenly.

Place the chicken in a large saucepan, cover it with water, and add the rest of the ingredients. Bring to the boil over medium heat, skim off, and then poach very gently – that is, with the occasional bubble just breaking on the surface, for 35 minutes.

Remove the pan from the heat, and allow the chicken to cool in the stock. The initial residual heat will easily complete the cooking of the chicken. After 1½ hours, remove the chicken from the stock, reserving the stock, and plunge it into a large bowl full of water and ice cubes for 10 minutes. This will set the juices in the chicken to a clear jelly.

Remove the chicken from the ice, and then chop, cut or cleave it into neat pieces, of a size to be picked up by chopsticks. Arrange on a dish, and garnish with coriander and extra star anise.

The accompanying dishes can be prepared while the chicken is cooking. Cook some long-grain rice in twice its volume of stock or water.

Garnish the rice with thinly sliced and fried onion. Grate a 7.5cm (3 inch) piece of fresh ginger, mix with a teaspoon of sea salt, and serve in a small bowl. Another condiment can be made by mixing some chilli sauce, or chopped chillies with garlic, oil and rice vinegar. In a third bowl mix equal quantities of soy sauce and rice vinegar with a teaspoon of toasted sesame oil.

The stock, once you have removed the chicken, can be boiled, strained, and served in bowls with some shredded spring onion as a first course.

Gumbo

The next recipe, a gumbo, is really a main course rather than a soup, and it makes good use of seasonal vegetables. I sometimes thicken the gumbo with *filé* powder, bought in America, which is the powdered dry leaf of the sassafras tree. One or two teaspoons of powder are mixed with a little water and stirred into the soup right at the end of cooking time and after the final seasoning. The soup should not be boiled after adding the *filé*, as it becomes stringy. Otherwise use okra, which thickens the broth to a silky rich texture. You can adapt the gumbo recipe for vegetarians quite easily, by leaving out the chicken and replacing the chicken stock with vegetable stock.

Serves 6 to 8

1kg (2 lbs) free-range or organic chicken joints
1 large onion, peeled and chopped
500g (1lb) ripe tomatoes, seeded and chopped,
    or canned will do
3 celery stalks, trimmed and thinly sliced
2 tablespoons olive oil
125g (¼lb) okra, or more
1 red or green pepper
1.75 litres (3 pints) chicken stock
250g (½lb) green beans
250g (½lb) courgettes
kernels of 2 or 3 corn cobs
200g (7oz) chick-peas or black-eyed beans,
    soaked and cooked, as well as the cooking
    liquid from them. Or use canned pulses
sprigs of coriander, thyme, parsley and bay
    leaves, tied together
salt
pepper
chopped parsley or coriander

Fry the chicken pieces, onion, tomato and celery in the oil until the vegetables are translucent and the tomatoes collapsed. Trim and slice the okra. Quarter the pepper, remove the pith and seeds and slice. Add to the pot together with the stock. Bring to the boil, and simmer for 20 minutes. Add the rest of the vegetables, the cooking liquid from the pulses and the bundle of herbs. Continue cooking until the vegetables are done to your liking. Remove the bundle of herbs, season the gumbo and stir in the fresh herbs. You might like to add a dash of hot pepper sauce, and certainly serve hot sauce and bowls of rice as accompaniments.

Poulet à la basquaise

Serves 4 to 6

2kg (4 lbs) organic or free-range chicken, jointed
2 tablespoons plain flour
salt
pepper
piment d'Espelette – see recipe
olive oil, chicken fat or butter
1 onion, peeled and sliced
300mls (½ pint) dry white wine
3 or 4 sweet red peppers
1 sweet green pepper
1 bay leaf
50g (2oz) Bayonne or other cured ham, diced or
    shredded

Dust the chicken joints with the flour, season with the salt, pepper and *piment d'Espelette* (the small dried peppers from Espelette in the Basque country), for which you can, if necessary, substitute a mildly piquant paprika or pimento. Heat a little fat in a casserole, gently fry the onions, then brown the chicken all over. Pour on the wine, bring to the boil, cover, and simmer for an hour or so.

Meanwhile, quarter, seed, and roast or grill the peppers. Skin them, and cut into strips. Add to the casserole, together with the bay leaf and ham, and continue cooking until the chicken is tender. Remove the bay leaf before serving.

Rice, cooked in the oven, is an excellent accompaniment to this well-sauced dish.

Chicken livers with pine nuts, spinach and watercress

Serves 2 to 3

25g (1oz) pine nuts
200g (7oz) chicken livers
olive oil
75g (3oz) young spinach and watercress
1 tablespoon fruit vinegar, or blackcurrant jelly
    and dash of lemon juice
salt
pepper

Lightly toast the pine nuts in a dry frying pan, and put to one side. Trim the chicken livers, and discard any threads and bile-stained parts. Fry the livers in olive oil, and remove from the frying pan.

Arrange the salad leaves on plates, put the chicken livers on top, and scatter on the pine nuts. Put a couple of tablespoons of water in the frying pan, and deglaze it. Add the fruit vinegar or jelly, and bring to the boil. Season lightly, and pour over the salad.

Using similar ingredients, you can readily make a main course; fried chicken livers and pine nuts in a sweet-sour sauce on a bed of cooked rice and accompanied by a little spinach and watercress are very good.

The chicken livers, cooked in this way, are also delicious stirred into a bowl of freshly cooked penne, rigatoni or pappardelle.

Warm salad of chicken livers, leeks and black pudding

Serves 6

12 young leeks
250g (8oz) chicken livers
2 tablespoons sunflower oil
mixed small salad leaves
250g (8oz) black pudding
1–2 tablespoons English grain mustard
5 tablespoons walnut oil
2 tablespoons cider vinegar
salt
pepper
1 tablespoon finely chopped chives

Trim the leeks, split lengthways, cut off the coarse green tops and discard, and rinse the rest thoroughly. Steam or boil until tender. Clean up the chicken livers and fry them in the sunflower oil until just pink inside, about 5 to 6 minutes. Put to one side. Arrange the salad leaves on plates. Slice the black pudding and fry on both sides for a couple of minutes.

Put the chicken livers, leeks and black pudding on the salad leaves. Whisk the remaining ingredients and spoon over the salad. Serve immediately.

You can turn this into a more substantial dish, suitable for a casual lunch or supper main course, by adding diced and fried potatoes, parboiled first, with even a poached egg on top.

Duck

Fragrant smoked duck breasts

This next recipe shows how to improvise a home smoker. The same method can be used for chicken, turkey breasts, fish, shellfish, what you will.

Serves 6 to 8

4 duck breasts
1 tablespoon coarse sea salt
1 tablespoon juniper berries
1 tablespoon black peppercorns
100g (¼lb) uncooked rice
100g (¼lb) sugar
1 cinnamon stick
2 sprigs of rosemary

Crush the salt and spices, toast them lightly in the wok, and when cool, rub them all over the meat. Put a few inches of water in the wok; put the duck breasts on a rack in the wok, cover, and steam for about 20 minutes. Remove the meat and the rack.

Rinse and dry the wok, and line it with a double thickness of foil. Put the rice, sugar, cinnamon and rosemary in the bottom of the wok. Place the rack on top, and arrange the duck breasts on it. Put the lid on, and seal the edge with foil or damp paper towels rolled up.

Place the wok on medium-high heat, and once the contents – that is, the rice and sugar – have begun to smoke, which you will smell rather than see, resist the temptation to lift the lid, and leave it for 10 to 15 minutes. Remove from the heat, and with the lid still on, leave for a further 15 minutes. Transfer the meat to a carving board, slice thinly, and serve warm or cold.

Fruit sauces were particularly popular in the Edwardian era, and Cumberland sauce, made with redcurrants, is probably the best known. Cherry sauce was popular too, and made, and indeed still makes, an ideal accompaniment to duck as well as ham, tongue and pork. Made with orange juice, port and red wine, it is a fairly heavyweight sauce, eminently suitable for roasts. But for when fresh cherries are available, I have adapted the recipe to make a lighter, vinaigrette-style sauce, to serve with a cold duck or ham. Either dish would be excellent for a summer luncheon in the garden. I have opted for duck breasts, as they are so quick and easy to cook, but if you were feeling more adventurous, you could ask your butcher to bone a duck for you so that you could turn it into a ballotine, stuffing it with minced duck and pork, pistachios, herbs and seasoning, the breasts left whole, all wrapped in the duck skin, roasted, allowed to go cold and then sliced.

Duckling and new potato salad with cherry vinaigrette

Serves 6

6 duck breasts
½ teaspoon each cinnamon, ground ginger, black pepper
1.5kg (about 3lbs) new potatoes, scrubbed
250mls (9oz) red wine
2 tablespoons red wine vinegar
sliver of fresh ginger
1 cinnamon stick
1 bay leaf
1 teaspoon black peppercorns
2 shallots, peeled and finely chopped
2 or 3 sprigs tarragon, plus extra for garnish
coarse sea salt
250g (9oz) cherries, Dukes or sours (see p.117), stoned
75mls (3oz) extra-virgin olive oil

Rub the duck breasts all over with the first lot of spices, having first scored the skin and put them in a heavy frying pan, skin side down, over a moderate heat. When all the fat has melted, pour it off, and continue cooking the duck breasts, on both sides, until done to your liking. Put to one side. Meanwhile, boil the potatoes and when cooked, toss them in a little of the oil, chopped tarragon and coarse sea salt. While the potatoes and duck are cooking, you can also start the vinaigrette. Simmer the wine, vinegar, the second lot of spices, herbs and shallots for 30 minutes or so, reducing by about half. Strain into a clean saucepan, add the cherries and simmer for 5 to 8 minutes. Remove from the heat and whisk in the rest of the olive oil, together with any further seasoning you wish to add.

To serve, place a heap of salad leaves on a platter, and the sliced duck breasts on top. Put the potatoes around the edge of the heap, and pour the hot vinaigrette over the duck. This dish is best freshly cooked, rather than served from the refrigerator.

Cured spring duckling

This next recipe might sound like a French confit, but is in fact a traditional Welsh way with duck, curing it for a few days in salt. The whole duck used to be prepared this way, and served hot with onion sauce. This is a fabulous dish for winter, but generally now I use the legs for another dish, the carcasses for stock, and cure the breasts. The meat is delicious hot or cold. If I plan to serve it hot, I cook the breasts slowly, just in their own fat and juices, like a confit. For a cold dish, I poach the meat, cool it and then slice it thinly. A fruit chutney makes a most perfect accompaniment if served as a first course.

Serves 6

6 duck breasts
1 tablespoon freshly ground pepper
5 tablespoons coarse sea salt
2 teaspoons light muscovado sugar

Score the skin in lozenges, and rub all over with the pepper, salt and sugar mixed together. Put the meat in a covered container, and keep for one or two days, rubbing the mixture into the duck every 12 hours or so.

When ready to cook, rinse the duck under cold water and dry it very thoroughly with kitchen paper.

Gently heat a heavy pan with a lid, and place the duck, skin side down, in a single layer. When some of the fat has been rendered, turn up the heat and sear the meat on the other side for three minutes. Turn the duck breasts skin side down once more, turn down the heat, partially cover and cook for about 30 minutes, or until the duck is done to your liking.

Serve the meat in wide, shallow soup plates on top of asparagus, small onions, quartered trimmed artichokes, fresh peas and new potatoes, all cooked in duck stock. Garnish with fresh chervil or watercress.

Duck casserole with damsons

The casserole is a very easy recipe, which can be adapted to chicken, guinea fowl or pheasant. Rabbit, too, is delicious with damsons; farmed rabbit will cook in the same time as the duck, wild rabbit will take about twice as long. If you cannot get damsons, use mirabelles, greengages or small plums, all on the under-ripe side.

Serves 4

2 x 2.5kg (5lb) ducklings – but see below
2 onions, peeled and sliced
piece of cinnamon
1 bay leaf
1 sprig of thyme
300mls (½ pint) full-bodied red wine
500g (1lb) celeriac, peeled and diced
250g (8oz) damsons, rinsed
2–3 tablespoons damson or sloe gin – optional

You can, of course, make the casserole with duck portions, but if you buy the whole birds, this is what to do with them.

Remove the wishbone from each duckling, then with a sharp knife, remove each breast. These are for another meal, for four, and can be marinated and refrigerated. Cut off the wings and the legs. Divide the leg joints into thigh and drumstick, and cut the wings into the three obvious joints. The smallest wing joints and the carcasses chopped up go into a large pan of water with a piece of celery stalk, a slice of ginger, if you have it, and a bay leaf, to make stock. But first, remove as much of the skin and fat as possible from carcasses and leg joints. Put this in a casserole or ovenproof dish, cover and place in the bottom of the oven to melt. This will take at least as long as the casserole takes to cook.

When all the fat has been rendered, strain into a container, and refrigerate when cool. This is excellent in bread-making and for frying potatoes.

The remaining bits of skin and meat in the pan can be chopped, transferred to a frying pan and crisped up to serve as lardons with a warm salad. Thus, nothing is wasted. If you have got giblets with the ducklings, put the necks in the stockpot, and the hearts, gizzards and livers with the casserole.

To make this, fry the onions in a spoonful of duck fat, and then brown the meat. Add the cinnamon, herbs and wine. Bring to simmering point, add the celeriac and damsons, cover and cook in the middle of a preheated oven at 180°C/350°F/gas mark 4 until the meat is tender, about 45 to 60 minutes.

With a slotted spoon, remove the damsons, and any loose stones, from the casserole, and rub the damson flesh through a sieve. Stir as much of the purée as you want back into the casserole, together with the sloe or damson gin. Bring back to the boil and serve. This is very good with mashed potatoes, or potatoes sliced and baked in the oven in a layer, well seasoned and flavoured with stock or cream. The casserole is also very good with diced small turnips instead of, or as well as, celeriac.

Turkey

The reason that I avoided turkey for so long is that it is only in recent years that one has been able to find real turkeys with taste. Norfolk Black, Cambridge Bronze, organic, truly free-range, we now have a wider choice than ever. Once I started cooking these birds, we soon realized we were eating the best turkey ever, and at the same time had the easiest Christmas Day for a long time.

There is no doubt that it is much easier to cook a turkey than a goose, or a haunch of wild boar and the other things I have cooked in my efforts to avoid turkey over the years. Several cooks of my acquaintance have reported that they cook turkey for just those reasons.

There was a small hiatus one year, nevertheless, at an almost impossibly last moment. At 5.30 p.m. one Christmas Eve, my husband Tom decided he did not want me to cook the turkey next day, as I had planned, Lebanese style, with spices and a rice stuffing. He wanted ours to be traditional Anglo-American, with stuffing, gravy and cranberry sauce. Change of plan, then.

I baked some of the stuffing in a dish, and stuffed the neck end of the bird. The neck, gizzard and heart made stock, with a sliver of ginger and a piece of celery. I dusted the roasting tin with flour before putting the turkey on a rack in the tin. The flour browns, the drippings mix with it, and once the bird is done, removed and resting, the stock is strained on to it, stirred in, well mixed and poured into a saucepan, making sure that all the cooking residues are loosened and scraped up from the roasting tin.

Let the juices boil down to a tasty gravy, season lightly and pour into a heated jug. You can add a splash of wine to the roasting tin before you add the stock, if you wish. We found ours quite tasty without it, as no one was going to part with a drop of their 1966 Château Pape Clément for gravy.

Cooking a full-size turkey just for two makes one something of an authority on the subject of left-over turkey, and I have included several recipes which will see you over the holiday season in fine style, one based on an excellent eighteenth-century recipe for pulled turkey. Left-over turkey makes the most fabulous sandwiches. These are best as simple as possible. Thick, spongy slices of chewy white bread, turkey slices, brown and white meat, thin slices of stuffing, a dab of cranberry sauce, iceberg lettuce, and some mayonnaise. Squash this all down, and eat with two hands.

To roast a turkey

Weigh the stuffed bird. Calculate about 35 to 40 minutes' cooking time per kilo in all, for a bird weighing up to 4 kilos, and 30 to 35 minutes per kilo for larger birds.

Season the bird lightly inside and out. Rub it with lemon juice and a little spice, if you wish – mixed spice, or cinnamon and cardamom. Place the bird breast down on the roasting rack, and put in a preheated oven at 200°C/400°F/gas mark 6.

After 20 minutes, turn down to 180°C/350°F/gas mark 4. Halfway through cooking, turn the oven up to 200°C/400°F/gas mark 6, remove the bird from the oven, turn it breast up, and return it to the oven. Turn down to 180°C/350°F/gas mark 4 after 20 minutes, and cover loosely with foil. Continue cooking until the juices run clear when you prick the bird in the inner thigh. The drumstick will also feel loose when you 'shake hands' with it. Remove from the oven, transfer to a serving platter or carving board, cover loosely with foil, and let it stand for 15 to 20 minutes while you make the gravy.

At Tom's suggestion, we had no potatoes, no vegetables, and certainly no sprouts and chestnuts, only turkey, gravy and stuffing, and some of my homemade cranberry sauce. And with it I served a big bowl of salad, sweet fennel, bitter chicory and peppery watercress. This is truly delicious with turkey gravy instead of the more usual vinaigrette.

If you want to vary the flavourings and accompaniments, here is my 'turkey à la carte' guide:

American

Glaze with maple syrup, orange juice and mustard

Bread stuffing with dried cranberries and pecans

Accompaniments of wild rice, wild mushrooms and roasted sweet potatoes

Oriental

Glaze with soy sauce, honey and rice vinegar

Minced pork, ginger and garlic stuffing

Accompaniments of steamed rice, steamed bok choy, stir-fried shredded Brussels sprouts with ginger, Mosimann-style

Lebanese

Glaze with honey or pomegranate syrup and spices

Stuff with minced lamb mixed with spiced rice or bulgar wheat

Accompaniments of extra bulgar wheat, parsley salad, mint and cucumber salad, hummus and spiced vegetable stew

French

Truffle or herbs under skin

Minced veal, herb and turkey liver stuffing

Accompaniments of mashed or sauté potatoes, glazed chestnuts and green salad.

Pulled turkey

Remove the meat from the carcass, white in one pile, brown in the other. Pull into pieces, little-finger width, or less, and somewhat shorter than that. The white meat is reheated in a creamy white sauce, the brown meat frizzled.

Hannah Glasse, upon whose recipe this is based, has no recommendations for accompaniments. You might cook some basmati rice, toss it in butter, pack it into a ring mould, and then turn out onto a large serving dish. Or simply spoon the rice into a ring. Fill the centre with the creamed turkey, and garnish the outside with the frizzled, spicy turkey. Or you might like to serve a portion of each with a piece of cornbread.

Creamed turkey

Serves 4

8 dried morels, or other flavoursome wild
   mushrooms, soaked in boiling water
1 onion, peeled and quartered
6 cloves

1 bay leaf
300mls (½ pint) milk
25g (1oz) butter
1 tablespoon plain flour
150mls (¼ pint) double cream
400g (14oz) pulled white turkey meat

When the morels are soft, rinse, and cut in half if necessary.

Stick the cloves in the onion, and with the bay leaf, simmer in the milk for 10 minutes, and then infuse for 20 to 30 minutes.

Melt the butter, stir in the flour, and gradually add the still warm milk, to make a béchamel. Cook gently for 5 minutes or so, add the cream and the morels. Bring to the boil, stir in the turkey, and allow to simmer for a few minutes, until the turkey is thoroughly heated through.

Frizzled turkey

Serves 4

400g (14oz) pulled dark turkey meat
1 teaspoon each freshly ground black pepper, paprika, allspice and cumin
½ teaspoon each salt, cayenne, or chilli and mustard powder

Mix the dry ingredients, and roll the turkey pieces in this spice mixture.

Heat about 5cm (2 inches) olive oil in a wok, and when very hot, briefly fry the turkey, until heated through and nicely browned and frizzled. Drain on kitchen paper before serving.

Festive chilli

Traditionally made with beef or with venison, chilli is a good dish to serve around Christmas time when you might have more turkey than you know what to do with. And a spicy dish makes a welcome change from rich holiday food. This is a perfect recipe for a New Year's Eve party and was devised by Ron Miller of Pittsburgh.

Serves 6

2 tablespoons sunflower or olive oil
1 onion, peeled and finely chopped
250g (8oz) blade, feather or rump steak, diced very small rather than minced
750g (1½lbs) boneless turkey meat, raw, diced very small
1–2 tablespoons paprika
1–2 tablespoons ground cumin
1–2 teaspoons cayenne or dried chilli
1 can – about 150g (5oz) – tomato purée
equal amount of American whiskey
1 can American beer – 450mls (16oz)
300mls (½ pint) beef stock, or another can of beer
salt to taste
beans – see recipe

Heat the oil in a large, heavy casserole or sauté pan, and in it brown the onion and meat. Then stir in the spices and the tomato purée, whiskey and beer. Bring to the boil, cover partially, and simmer for about 1½ to 2 hours. Add soaked, cooked beans, if using them, about 400g (14oz), and simmer for a further 20 minutes or so. Add stock or more beer from time to time, if necessary, to prevent the mixture from burning.

For almost a century, the Spaniards kept the secret of the 'food of the gods' to themselves, having, in turn, discovered it in Mexico a century earlier. It gradually crept over the Spanish border into France, to St Jean de Luz, Biarritz and Bayonne, and this is still where some of the best *chocolatiers* in the world are to be found. But it was the Spanish Infanta, Anne of Austria, wife of Louis XIII of France who popularized chocolate amongst the French aristocracy. Soon there were *chocolatiers* in Paris making chocolate drinks and confectionery. It caught on in England soon after that, particularly after Samuel Pepys had given his approval.

By the end of the seventeenth century in France, there were many small factories producing fine chocolate from the raw materials, and it is probably true to say that the French dominated chocolate production during the next century too. By the beginning of the nineteenth century, Van Houten was founded in Amsterdam, and the Menier chocolate factory near Paris soon after that. The firms of Suchard, Kohler, Lindt and Tobler were founded in Switzerland, where milk chocolate was perfected, and, at about the same time, Cadbury and Rowntree in England. By then, the chocolate industry was well established worldwide. But it was not until 1913 that filled chocolates were invented in Switzerland.

The search for the ultimate chocolate reached extremes in recent years, with chocolate bars of 99 per cent and even 100 per cent cocoa solids, deep, dark, and as austere and elegant as the little black dress. But these are, in effect, pure cocoa, not chocolate. A small amount of fat and sugar is needed to 'season' chocolate, to enhance its aroma, flavour and texture. Too high a concentration of cocoa solids in chocolate is like putting too much chilli in a curry, so many nuances of flavour are lost. A 70–75 per cent cocoa solids content is about right for dark chocolate, though I still like a 'fix' of 85 per cent occasionally.

This, of course, is one of the keys to chocolate's quality. Look at the ingredients list on a bar of chocolate. The best contains nothing more than cocoa paste, cane sugar, cocoa butter, and natural vanilla for flavouring. And with a cocoa content of, say, 70 per cent there is little room for other ingredients, such as sugar. Too much sugar and a low cocoa content means that any chocolate flavour will be masked by sweetness.

There are three types of cocoa bean, criollo, forastero and trinitario, which is a hybrid of the first two. Criollo is grown chiefly in Central and Latin America, as well as in Sri Lanka, Madagascar, the Comoros and Java. It is expensive because it is rare, producing only 5 per cent of the world's crop, and it will only be found in the most expensive chocolate. It can be likened perhaps to Arabica coffee, whereas the forastero cocoa is more like robusta coffee, more widely grown, in West Africa, South East Asia, and Brazil, producing 85 per cent of the world's crop of cocoa.

Now *grand cru* chocolate, made from cocoa from each of the world's cocoa-growing regions, is all the rage. It only makes sense – it's rare, it's special, it's expensive and it's elitist.

The first taste of a *grand cru* chocolate is a revelation comparable to that of tasting a *grand cru* wine against a lesser wine. It is made with the same care, blending the criollo bean with its fine, fruity perfumed characteristic and the robust forastero, which adds weight and strength. Good chocolate can be recognized by its uniform, dark, glossy surface, silky smooth to the touch, making a clean break in your fingers. In your mouth, it will break with a crisp snap. As you eat the chocolate, it will melt in your mouth and you will be aware of its silky, uncloying texture, smooth, but not fatty, and its intense, deep, rich flavour, with a pleasant bitterness and a lingering fruity finish, which I can only describe as winey. It contains small amounts of caffeine, and theobromine, which induce a feeling of well-being, comforting at the same time as being stimulating. When it is this good, I like to eat it just as it is, a small square at the end of a meal.

There have also been great improvements in the manufacture of milk chocolate. There had to be. Much of it was far too fatty, sweet and cloying. The best *chocolatiers* now make superb milk chocolate, with a cocoa butter content of around 50 per cent. Milk chocolate made by Cluizel, the Lait Java Pur, Valrhona's Jivara Lactée and Lindt's Excellence Milk are very good examples. The first, particularly, has a deceptively mild flavour as it melts in the mouth, silkily, not cloyingly, but the finish is long, deep and definitely chocolate.

Chocolate is a very rewarding ingredient to work with in the kitchen. Its use as a spice or seasoning passed from Mexican into Spanish, and then into

Italian cooking, and survives to this day in a few rich, savoury, somewhat baroque dishes.

But it is only relatively recently that chocolate has become widely used as an ingredient in baking and desserts. There is, for example, a Victorian recipe for a chocolate bread pudding, on which I have based one of my recipes, which can be made to taste very good using the best chocolate and cream. There is also a seventeenth-century recipe for chocolate meringues. From those early beginnings, chocolate has been used in desserts of all varieties, hot and cold, tarts, ices, mousses, cakes, gateaux, puddings, parfaits, madeleines. Certain types of desserts have become very fashionable, such as the chocolate sorbet, the warm flourless chocolate cake, the chocolate truffle tart, not forgetting the chocolate mousse in its heyday.

For all of these recipes, use a plain, or dark, chocolate of 70 per cent cocoa solids, unless, for example, white chocolate is specified.

Drinking chocolate

This is a very rich hot drink to be served in small cups.

Serves 6

600mls (1 pint) full-cream milk
3 tablespoons whipping or single cream
1 vanilla pod, or 7.5cm (3 inch) stick of
    cinnamon, or 2 blades of mace
pinch of salt
pinch of freshly ground black pepper
150g (5oz) chocolate

Put the milk and cream with the spice, salt and pepper in a saucepan, and scald it; that is, bring to the point where tiny bubbles appear around the edge of the pan.

Break up the chocolate, put it in a bowl standing in very hot water. Pour the milk over the chocolate and stir until the chocolate has melted. Let it stand for a few minutes for the flavours to infuse.

Strain it into a heated jug, whisk to a froth, if you like, and serve very hot.

Chocolate and almond biscuits

Makes 20 to 24

125g (generous 4oz) unsalted butter
125g (generous 4oz) unrefined caster sugar
1 free-range egg, beaten with 2 tablespoons
    Amaretto
175g (6oz) self-raising flour
85g (3½oz) chocolate
85g (3½oz) flaked or chopped almonds

Cream the butter and sugar, and beat in the egg, liquid and flour. Chop the chocolate and stir it and the almonds into the mixture.

Scoop up balls, about 1 tablespoonful, with floured hands, and place on two prepared baking sheets, well spaced. Press down with fingers, or spatula, to a diameter of about 7.5cm (3 inches), and bake for 12 to 15 minutes in a preheated oven at 180°C/350°F/gas mark 4. Remove from the oven, leave for a minute or two, and then cool the biscuits on a wire rack to crisp them up. These are perfect with the chocolate drink.

Frozen chocolate Jonathan

Serves 10

3 free-range eggs, separated
100g (3½oz) light muscovado or golden caster
    sugar
25g (1oz) cocoa powder
75g (3oz) self-raising flour
1 tablespoon strong coffee, rum or Tia Maria

filling
200g (7oz) chocolate
1 tablespoon strong coffee, rum or Tia Maria
50g (2oz) unsalted butter, softened
2 free-range eggs, separated
25g (1oz) golden caster sugar
pinch of salt

Preheat the oven to 180°C/350°F/gas mark 4. Line a Swiss roll tin, approx. 25 x 35cm (10 x 14 inches), with buttered greaseproof paper. Put the egg yolks and three-quarters of the sugar into a pudding basin, set over a saucepan of barely simmering water. Whisk together until pale, foamy and much increased in volume.

Sift the cocoa powder and flour together, and fold gently into the egg and sugar mixture. Stir in the coffee or liqueur.

Whisk the egg whites with the remaining sugar and fold into the cake mix. Pour into the Swiss roll tin, level it off, and bake in the top half of the oven for about 10 minutes. Remove, and turn out onto a wire rack. Peel off the paper, and leave to cool.

To prepare the filling, put the chocolate and liqueur in a clean pudding basin over hot water, and melt the chocolate. Remove from the heat, cool slightly, and mix in the softened butter. Whisk the egg yolks and sugar until pale and ribbony. Whisk the egg whites with a pinch of salt until stiff, and fold both into the chocolate.

Line a 500g (1lb) loaf tin with clingfilm. Cut the sponge into pieces and use to line the tin, except for the short sides, leaving a piece of cake to fit over the top. Line the tin with the shiny surface of the cake towards the centre. Pour the filling in, and cover with the final slice of sponge.

Cover with clingfilm, and freeze for several hours until set. Turn out onto a board, slice, and serve on individual plates with a spoonful of crème fraiche or a dash of coffee liqueur, and a dusting of icing sugar.

Chocolate and almond pudding

Serves 4 to 6

75g (3oz) butter
300mls (½ pint) single cream
150g (5oz) chocolate, broken into pieces
50g (2oz) ground almonds
50g (2oz) fresh white breadcrumbs
100g (4oz) vanilla sugar
3 free-range eggs, separated

Heat the butter and cream to boiling point, remove from the heat, and stir in the chocolate. When this has melted, stir in the almonds, breadcrumbs and sugar.

Let the mixture stand until cool, and then beat in the egg yolks. Whisk the whites to firm peaks, fold into the chocolate mixture, and spoon into a well-buttered pudding basin.

Cover with a double thickness of foil, pleated down the middle, and steam the pudding for about 2 hours, putting it in a saucepan with boiling water coming halfway up the basin. The water should be kept boiling.

When cooked, turn out, and serve with hot chocolate sauce, or cream.

Serious chocolate pots

Serves 4

150mls (¼ pint) double cream
1 free-range egg yolk, lightly beaten
100g (4oz) bar of chocolate

Scald the cream, and pour it over the egg, beating continuously. Break up the chocolate, and stir it into the cream.

Spoon into 50ml (2oz) ramekins (Apilco size 3), or into espresso coffee cups. Cover and refrigerate until set, which should take about 2 hours.

Double chocolate tarts

Makes 4

Pastry

50g (2oz) unsalted butter
75g (3oz) plain flour, sifted with 25g (1oz) cocoa
1 tablespoon caster sugar
1 free-range egg yolk
iced water

Rub the butter into the flour and cocoa, and then stir in the sugar and egg yolk. Add iced water, if necessary, to bind to a pastry. Leave it to rest for half an hour, and then roll out, and line 4 pastry cases.

Bake blind for 6 to 8 minutes at 180°C/350°F/gas mark 4, remove from the oven, and leave to cool. You can make these a day or so in advance, if you wish.

Filling

2 free-range egg yolks, and 1 whole egg
caster sugar
50g (2oz) unsalted butter
150g (5oz) chocolate, broken into pieces

Whisk the eggs and sugar until pale and much increased in volume. In a bowl set over a pan of hot water, melt the chocolate and butter.

Remove from the heat, and fold into the egg mixture.

Leave to cool, and then spoon into the pastry cases, and bake at 150°C/300°F/gas mark 2 in a preheated oven for 5 minutes.

Serve, dusted with icing sugar, or decorated with a small piece of gold leaf or thinly cut crystallized orange peel.

Bitter chocolate sorbet

Serves 2 to 4

200mls (7oz) hot water
1 tablespoon cocoa powder
4 tablespoons golden syrup

Blend the ingredients until well mixed. Allow to cool, and then freeze in a sorbetière, ice-cream maker, or in a container in the freezer. If using the latter method, stir from time to time to soften the mixture.

Chocolate and red wine sorbet

Serves 4

100g (4oz) chocolate
200mls (7oz) good full-bodied red wine
1 cinnamon stick
200g (7oz) caster sugar

Break up the chocolate, and put it in a bowl. Bring the wine, cinnamon, and sugar to the boil, and simmer for 5 minutes.

Remove the cinnamon stick, and pour the wine over the chocolate. Stir until melted and well mixed.

Allow to cool, and then freeze in a sorbetière, or ice-cream maker, following the manufacturer's instructions.

Warm chocolate cakes

Serves 6

150g (5oz) chocolate
3 free-range eggs, plus 2 egg whites
5 scant dessertspoons, plus 2 teaspoons, caster sugar

Butter and dust with cocoa 6 ramekins, which hold about 100mls (4oz). Break up the chocolate, and melt in a bowl set over hot water. Remove from the heat.

In another bowl set over hot water, beat the whole eggs with the larger quantity of sugar until pale and the mixture leaves ribbons when trailed from the whisk. With a clean whisk, whisk the egg whites with the remaining caster sugar until firm.

Carefully, and gradually, fold the melted chocolate, the egg yolk and egg white mixtures together.

Spoon into the ramekins, place them in a roasting tin with a little water, and place in a preheated oven at 160°C/310°F/gas mark 3 for 15 to 20 minutes, or one notch up for 12 to 15 minutes.

Remove from the oven, and allow the cakes to cool in the ramekins for a few minutes until they begin to shrink from the edge. The mixture will have risen during cooking but will now begin to sink.

With a knife, ease round the cakes, and gently turn them out onto serving plates, dusting them with icing sugar or cocoa beforehand, if you wish.

A crème anglaise, custard, almond, orange or mint sauce will go well with these light moist cakes, which ideally should still be creamy right in the centre.

As an alternative, try the recipe below, as saffron goes unusually well with chocolate.

Saffron and almond sauce

200mls (7oz) skimmed milk
good pinch of saffron
150g (5oz) marzipan
4 tablespoons skimmed milk powder

Scald the milk with the saffron, and remove from the heat.

Break up the marzipan. Whisk the milk powder into the milk and saffron, and then stir in the marzipan.

When the marzipan has dissolved, stir once more, and cool the sauce. Serve it warm, or cold.

Chocolate meringues

Note: this recipe contains raw eggs.

Makes about 6 to 8

Meringue

50g (2oz) icing sugar
1 tablespoon cocoa powder
2 free-range egg whites
50g (2oz) caster sugar

Sift the icing sugar and cocoa. Whisk the egg whites to firm peaks, adding a tablespoon of caster sugar after a minute or two. When the whites are firm, gently whisk in the remaining sugar, and then carefully fold in the cocoa mixture. Butter and dust with flour two baking trays. Spoon on the meringue mixture in neat ovals, using two tablespoons to shape them. Bake in a preheated oven at 150°C/300°F/gas mark 2 for about an hour. Take care that the meringues do not brown. Turn the baking sheets to ensure regular baking. When the meringues are cooked, remove them from the oven, and allow to cool and dry out.

Mousse

150g (5oz) chocolate
25g (1oz) unsalted butter, softened and at room
    temperature
2 free-range eggs, separated

Melt the chocolate in a bowl set over hot water. Remove from the heat, and when cooled slightly, beat in the butter until smoothly incorporated. Thoroughly mix in the egg yolks, and when the mixture is cool, whisk the egg whites, and gently fold in the chocolate mixture. Use this mousse to sandwich two meringues together.

Light white chocolate mousse

Note: this recipe contains raw eggs.

Serves 6

150g (5oz) bar of white Swiss chocolate
1 teaspoon powdered gelatine
2 tablespoons rum
6 generous tablespoons plain thick Greek
    yoghurt or crème fraiche, at room
    temperature
2 free-range egg whites

Break up the chocolate, and melt it in a bowl set over hot water. Sprinkle the gelatine over the rum in a small heat-proof container. When the chocolate has melted, remove the bowl from the hot water, and allow the chocolate to cool slightly. Stand the container in the hot water until the gelatine has completely dissolved. Stir into the melted chocolate, and then add the yoghurt gradually, beating it to keep it smooth.

If you put very cold yoghurt into very hot chocolate, the chocolate will 'seize up' and become hard; instead, combine them at similar tepid temperatures.

Whisk the egg whites, and gradually combine with the chocolate. Spoon into ramekins, or simply into a container which you can store in the refrigerator.

To serve, scoop out quenelles, and shape them with two dessert spoons. This mixture also makes an excellent filling for sponge cakes.

White chocolate-dipped fruit

This could not be simpler. Melt the white chocolate, and in it dip dried mango slices, Agen prunes and Medjool dates. Let any excess chocolate drip into the bowl, and place the fruit on waxed paper. Allow to set in the refrigerator.

In these next, savoury, recipes, the chocolate adds a richness and a subtle flavour, but not detectable as chocolate.

Hare casserole

Serves 6 to 8

1kg (2lbs) hare, off the bone and cubed
1 tablespoon seasoned plain flour
1 tablespoon olive oil
2 onions, peeled and sliced
250mls (8oz) game or beef stock
2 tablespoons red wine vinegar, balsamic or
    sherry vinegar
50g (2oz) raisins or sultanas
50g (2oz) pine kernels or walnuts
10g (⅓oz) chocolate

Toss the meat in the seasoned flour and brown it in the olive oil. Put it in a heavy ovenproof casserole.

Fry the onions until brown, and pour the stock over them. Bubble until it is slightly reduced, scraping up any bits stuck to the pan. Add the wine vinegar, raisins or sultanas, nuts and chocolate. Stir until the chocolate has melted, and pour over the meat.

Cook in a low oven at 170°C/325°F/gas mark 3 for about an hour or so until the meat is tender. Season to taste.

Braised red cabbage is delicious with game, and so too are sliced Jerusalem artichokes or celeriac, baked in the oven in a little stock.

Pappardelle with guinea fowl

I often use hare in the following recipe, but when this is not sold, between March and July, guinea fowl is a good substitute. This is an ideal recipe for using up the legs if you have made a dish for two with the breasts. Pappardelle are broad flat noodles which when cooked wind and fold themselves around a chunky meat sauce, as in this dish, based loosely on a traditional Tuscan one. If you cannot get or make pappardelle, tagliatelle or fettuccine can be substituted.

Serves 2 to 4

2 guinea fowl legs
1 onion, peeled and chopped
1 celery stalk, trimmed and finely chopped
2–3 cloves of garlic, peeled and finely chopped
1 tablespoon extra-virgin olive oil
150mls (¼ pint) red wine or chicken stock
25–40g (1–1½oz) dark chocolate
sprig or two of fresh marjoram or pinch of dried
    oregano
50g (2oz) seedless raisins
50g (2oz) pine nuts – optional
1 tablespoon balsamic vinegar

Strip the meat from the bones, and dice it. Fry the vegetables in the olive oil until wilted. Raise the heat, add the meat, and brown it briefly. Add the wine or stock, the chocolate and the herbs. Simmer for about 40 minutes, uncovered, until the meat is tender and the sauce reduced. Stir in the raisins and pine nuts and cook for a few minutes to let the flavours mingle, and finally add the dash of balsamic vinegar. Stir the sauce into the freshly cooked and drained pasta. It is this last ingredient which leads me to describe the dish as being loosely based on a Tuscan classic. In Tuscany a red wine vinegar would be used; balsamic vinegar comes from over the Apennines in Emilia Romagna. The deep, fruity complexity is a perfect counterpoint to the chocolate, however.

Caponata (Sweet and sour Sicilian aubergine stew)

Serves 6

2 large aubergines
1 tablespoon salt
olive oil for frying
1 large onion, peeled and thinly sliced
5 celery stalks, trimmed and thinly sliced
4–5 cloves garlic, peeled and crushed
200g (7oz) fresh or canned plum tomatoes
half a dozen olives
2 tablespoons capers, well rinsed
2–3 tablespoons red wine vinegar
1 tablespoon light muscovado sugar
1 tablespoon cocoa
salt and pepper
2 tablespoons flaked almonds, lightly toasted

Remove the stalks from the aubergines. Dice, put in a colander, and sprinkle with the salt. Leave to drain for an hour or so. Rinse, and rub dry in a clean tea towel. Fry until golden brown, remove from the oil, drain, and put to one side.

In the remaining oil, gently fry the onion, celery and garlic until soft, and then add the tomatoes, olives and capers, and simmer for 20 to 30 minutes.

Stir in the vinegar, sugar and cocoa, bring to the boil, simmer for 5 minutes, remove from the heat, and allow to cool.

Season to taste, cover, and keep in a cool place or refrigerator for 24 hours to allow the flavours to develop. Serve garnished with the almonds, and perhaps some flat parsley leaves. I like this best cold, but it can be served hot, and is very good with rice, pasta or good bread.

An invitation to cook in Sri Lanka some years ago consolidated all my previous experience of curries and subcontinental food. Curry remains a favourite today, and I often find myself cooking curries at home to try to capture a little bit of those fragrant tropical nights.

A wide range of authentic spice mixtures, pastes, chutneys, sambals and breads is now made here. These are available far beyond the specialist Asian shops, even in the high-street supermarket. Fresh-produce shelves and the greengrocers are stocked with small aubergines, okra, drumsticks, dudi, kantola, karela, tindoor and all manner of squashes and chillies. Choose amongst them to make into flavoursome masalas, kormas, chaats, bhajias and curries, combined with meat or fish, or simply combinations of vegetables.

To round out the meal with breads, dhal and rice, look to the dry-goods section for red and green lentils, mung, or moong, beans, basmati and Patna rice, and flours made from chick-peas, millet and wholemeal.

It is well worth exploring some of the more unusual spices and flavourings that you might come across. Ajowan, for example, is a greenish-brown seed a little larger than celery seed, with a pronounced aroma of rather coarse thyme. The herb can, in fact, be used as a thyme substitute. Asafoetida, in its natural state, is a hard brown resin from a large fennel-like plant. As it is so hard, I advise buying it in its powdered form and keeping it in an airtight jar or tin. The smell is not pleasant, and you might wonder what this curiously sulphurous resinous spice could do for any dish, but in minute quantities it works wonders.

Tamarind is the pulp from the pods of the tamarind tree. Sometimes it is sold in blocks with the seeds, sometimes ready-prepared as a paste. It is mixed with water, and the resulting liquid used as a delicate souring agent. It makes delicious chutneys and dips. Kalonji, or nigella, is a small black seed, mildly spicy, mildly peppery, and is good in vegetable dishes.

I have always found it difficult to cope with the amount of oil and ghee that is used, both in Indian restaurants and in Indian recipes. This gives every dish a bright, burnished look, but also a greasy overlay which diminishes the taste of the ingredients underneath. And it is not necessary. It is quite possible to cook Indian food placing more emphasis on achieving flavours from spices, herbs and marinades rather than heavy oily preparations.

Keep cooking times short so that vegetables will still retain their texture. Start the dish by dry-toasting the spices in a frying pan, beginning with the hardest ones first, such as peppercorns. Cumin and coriander, having a softer outer coating, can be added to the pan later. This initial toasting is to release the flavours before the other ingredients are added. Stocks can be used, as they are in the Western kitchen, and the result will be a new brightness and vibrancy, with no loss of authenticity.

The recipes in this chapter provide a feast of South Asian snacks, side dishes and main courses.

Potato raita

Serves 6

350mls (12oz) low-fat yoghurt
750g (1½lbs) new potatoes, boiled and diced
¼ teaspoon each salt and freshly ground black
    pepper
½ teaspoon dry-roasted cumin seeds
2–3 tablespoons onion, spring onion or shallot,
    finely chopped
1 tablespoon fresh coriander, finely chopped
½ teaspoon green chilli, seeded and finely
    chopped – optional
½ teaspoon dry-roasted ground cumin
½ teaspoon red chilli, seeded and finely
    chopped – optional

This is best prepared while the potatoes are still warm. Beat the yoghurt until smooth, and then put it in a bowl with the potatoes, salt, pepper, cumin seeds, onion and half the coriander, as well as the green chilli, if using it. Scatter the remaining coriander, the ground cumin and the red chilli on top before serving.

Fresh yellow chutney

Serves 6 to 8

1 yellow pepper, quartered and seeded
1 or 2 red chillies, seeded
1 mango, peeled, and the stone removed
2 bananas, peeled
1 teaspoon or so of fresh lime juice
1 mild onion, peeled and grated

2 or 3 sprigs of mint, leaves only
1 teaspoon salt
1 teaspoon ground cumin
½ teaspoon each ground coriander and
    cardamom

Put all the ingredients in the food processor, and 'pulse' until you have the texture you prefer, chunky or smooth. Red and green versions can be made with appropriate fruit and vegetables.

Date and tamarind chutney

Serves 6 to 8

100g (4oz) block of tamarind
200mls (7oz) water
1 medium onion, peeled and grated
12 Medjool dates, stoned and finely chopped
½ teaspoon ground cardamom
ground chilli, to taste
salt, to taste

Boil the tamarind in the water for a few minutes. Cool, and rub through a sieve into a bowl with the onion, dates and seasoning. With its many seeds and fibres, this is a somewhat lengthy process. Tamarind paste, available in jars, is a good shortcut.

Vegetable bhajias

Serves 6 to 8

250g (½lb) gram flour
1 tablespoon lemon juice
2–3 tablespoons yoghurt
1 teaspoon salt
½ teaspoon each turmeric, freshly ground black
    pepper, ground cumin, cumin seeds, ajowan
    seeds
pinch of asafoetida
1 large potato, peeled and grated
1 onion, peeled and grated
1 carrot, peeled and grated
100g (4oz) fresh or frozen peas
2 tablespoons fresh coriander, finely chopped
1 green chilli, seeded and finely chopped

Make a thick batter with the flour, lemon juice, yoghurt, salt and spices, adding a little water. Stir in the vegetables, coriander and chilli, and mix well.

Drop tablespoons of the mixture on a heated non-stick griddle, or frying pan, and cook until browned all over, turning as necessary.

I am also told that spoonfuls of bhajia mixture can be cooked inside sandwich toasters.

Spiced carrot and mint soup

Serves 4 to 6

1 small onion, peeled and sliced
1 tablespoon sunflower or groundnut oil
1 teaspoon each, ground cumin, coriander and
    cardamom
500g (1lb) organic carrots, scrubbed and sliced
7.5cm (3 inches) orange or tangerine zest
1.25 litres (2 pints) vegetable stock, or water in
    which you have cooked pasta or potatoes
2 ripe tomatoes
several sprigs of fresh mint
salt
pepper

Fry the onion in the oil until golden, and then stir in the spices. Fry for a few minutes, and then add the carrots, zest and stock. Simmer until the carrots are tender.

Roughly chop the tomatoes, and strip the leaves from the mint sprigs. Put both in a blender or food processor, and pour the cooked vegetables and stock on top.

When cool enough, process until smooth. Sieve, or not, as you wish. You can enrich the soup with crème fraiche or yoghurt, if you wish, or swirl in some buttermilk or smetana (sour cream), when you serve it. The soup can also be served chilled.

Kichri

This is the original dish on which the familiar kedgeree is based, with its addition of chopped, hard-boiled eggs and flaked fish. Rice and lentils alone are a very good combination, one that provides complete protein, and the dish is suitable for both vegetarians and vegans.

Serves 6

½ teaspoon crushed black peppercorns
3 cloves
1 teaspoon each whole cumin and ground
    coriander
seeds of 4 cardamom pods

½ teaspoon mustard seed
½ teaspoon ground turmeric
1 large onion, peeled and thinly sliced
350g (12oz) basmati rice
125g (generous 4oz) red lentils
2 or 3 curry leaves, if available, or a bay leaf
1 teaspoon salt

Heat a heavy-based well-seasoned, or non-stick saucepan, and in it toast first the pepper and cloves, then add the cumin and coriander after a couple of minutes, and then the cardamom and mustard seeds. Stir in the turmeric, and then add the onion to the spices, and coat it well.

Add the rice and lentils, and when well coated with the spice mixture, add the leaves, the salt and about 600mls (1 pint) water. Bring to the boil, cover tightly with the lid, and cook on the lowest possible heat for 15 to 18 minutes, without removing the lid. Fork the ingredients together, turn off the heat, replace the lid and let the mixture dry off for a few minutes before serving.

Baked curry pasties

Makes 1½ to 2 dozen

1 medium onion, peeled and finely chopped
1 tablespoon sunflower or groundnut oil
250g (½lb) minced lamb
2 teaspoons, or more to taste, mild curry paste
½ teaspoon freshly ground black pepper
½ teaspoon ground allspice
grated zest of a lime, and 1–2 teaspoons juice
1 or 2 green chillies, seeded and finely chopped
1 tablespoon fresh mint, finely chopped
3 tablespoons soya milk, or skimmed milk
salt to taste
500g (1lb) puff pastry
1 free-range egg, lightly beaten with a
    tablespoon or so of water

Fry the onion in the oil in a non-stick pan until half wilted, and then add the lamb, and cook until it loses its raw appearance.

Stir in the curry paste, spices, lime zest and juice, chillies and mint, and cook for a few minutes.

Add the milk, and cook over a low heat until the mixture is almost dry. Add salt, if necessary, and allow to cool. You can prepare to this point the day before required, and refrigerate the mixture, if you prefer.

Roll out the puff pastry on a floured work surface, and cut into 7–8cm (3 inch) rounds. Wet the edges with the egg wash, and put a teaspoon or so of filling in the middle.

Fold over into a half-circle and seal. You can either crimp the pastry like a Cornish pasty, or simply press a fork all the way around to seal. Any remaining egg wash can be used to glaze the pasties.

Place on damp baking trays, and bake in a preheated oven at 180°C/350°F/gas mark 4 for 20 to 25 minutes, or until golden brown.

Roasted tandoori-style aubergine

Serves 4

2 long aubergines, about 350g (12oz) each
2–3 tablespoons Greek yoghurt
2 tablespoons each of grated, or finely chopped,
    onion and tandoori spice mix
1 teaspoon freshly grated ginger
½ teaspoon each ground cardamom and black
    pepper

Halve the aubergines, and prick all over with a sharp knife point. Mix the remaining ingredients, and spread the paste all over the aubergines. Place on a non-stick baking sheet, and roast in a preheated oven at 200°C/400°F/gas mark 6 for 15 minutes, and then turn down the heat and cook until the aubergines are soft when pierced with a knife.

Serve on a platter with sliced mild onions, wedges of lime, fresh mint, some fruit chutney, and some lime or mango pickle.

Mild potato and mustard seed curry

Serves 4 to 6

1 large mild onion
1 tablespoon sunflower or groundnut oil
1kg (2lbs) potatoes, peeled and diced
1 tablespoon mustard seeds
1 teaspoon each ground turmeric, cardamom
    and cumin
1 teaspoon cumin seeds
100g (4oz) creamed coconut
pinch of salt

Peel and chop the onion, and fry gently in the oil until soft and golden. Add the potatoes and spices, and fry for a few minutes before adding the creamed coconut, a pinch of salt, and about 150mls (¼ pint) water. Bring to the boil, cover, and simmer on a very low heat until the potatoes are cooked.

Potato curry

Serves 6

500g (1lb) onions
1 tablespoon sunflower or groundnut oil
500g (1lb) potatoes
½ teaspoon hot curry paste
½ teaspoon each ground ginger, cinnamon and
   cardamom seeds
1 teaspoon each ground turmeric, cumin and
   coriander
150mls (¼ pint) coconut cream

Peel and finely chop the onions, and cook in the oil until soft. Speed up the process, if you like, by adding about 150mls (¼ pint) water and cooking over a high heat. When the onions are soft, stir in the peeled, diced potatoes, together with the spices and coconut cream. Cook until the potatoes are tender. Add, if you like, a dash of lime or lemon juice.

An excellent accompaniment to this dish is Gram Flour and Coriander Pancakes (see p. 88). If you are making these as an accompaniment, fry them now and serve heaped with the potato curry. Garnish with toasted coconut and fresh coriander leaves, if you wish.

Spiced lentils

Serves 4 to 6

1 onion, peeled and thinly sliced
1 tablespoon sunflower or groundnut oil
1 tablespoon each ground cumin and coriander
½ teaspoon ground turmeric
250g (½lb) red/orange lentils
water
salt

Fry the onions until soft, and then brown them, but do not let them burn. Remove, and put to one side.

Add the spices and lentils to the pan, and fry for a minute or two. Cover with twice their volume of water, add a pinch of salt, and simmer until the lentils are soft. Serve topped with the fried onions.

If you like a soupy mixture, add more water as the lentils cook.

Fragrant lemon rice

Serves 4 to 6

1 tablespoon sunflower or groundnut oil, or
   clarified butter
4 cardamom pods, lightly crushed
4 cloves
2 or 3 shavings of a nutmeg
6 peppercorns
1 bay leaf
1 or 2 curry leaves – optional
1 lemon grass stalk, cut in 2 or 3 pieces
piece of cinnamon
350g (12oz) basmati rice
2 tablespoons each of toasted flaked almonds
   and sultanas
about 600mls (1 pint) water
salt
grated zest and juice of a lemon
fresh coriander or mint – for garnish

Heat the oil in a heavy saucepan, and in it fry all the spices and leaves until fragrant. Stir in the rice, the lemon zest and juice, and then add the water and a pinch of salt. Bring to the boil, cover, and reduce to the lowest possible heat.

Leave for 15 minutes or so until the rice has absorbed the water. Remove the leaves and lemon grass. Fork in the nuts and sultanas, and heap the rice in a serving bowl. Decorate with fresh herbs, such as coriander.

To slice nutmeg, I use a truffle grater, or the slicing side of a grater. It can also be grated, and this is probably safer for the knuckles.

Dry prawn curry

Serves 4

4 green chillies, seeded
3 cloves garlic, peeled and crushed
½ thumb-size piece of ginger
½ teaspoon ground cinnamon
½ tablespoon freshly ground black pepper
1 teaspoon chilli powder – optional
½ teaspoon salt
1 tablespoon tamarind paste or lime juice
500g (generous 1lb) raw prawns, shelled weight

Grind the chillies, garlic and ginger and mix with the remaining seasoning ingredients. Stir in about 125mls (generous 4oz) water and transfer to a saucepan. Add the prawns and stir to coat them with the mixture. Simmer uncovered until the prawns are done and the liquid almost evaporated. Transfer to a serving plate and accompany with steamed rice.

Unorthodox, but very appealing, is to serve the prawns with rice as a cold dish, garnished with chopped coriander leaves.

Broccoli, cauliflower and cashew nut curry

Serves 4 to 6

3 heaped tablespoons medium or hot curry
    paste, or 1 tablespoon each ground
    coriander, cumin and cardamom
2 teaspoons each ground ginger and mixed
    spices
1 teaspoon each ground cinnamon, cayenne,
    turmeric and cloves
1 teaspoon each cumin and coriander seeds
1 onion, peeled and sliced
2 celery stalks, trimmed and sliced
3 carrots, peeled and cut into batons
250g (½lb) each broccoli and cauliflower florets
125g (4½oz) unsalted cashew nuts
75g (3oz) creamed coconut

Fry the spices in a large non-stick pan until fragrant, and then stir in the vegetables and nuts, the coconut, and about 250mls (9oz) water.

Bring to the boil and simmer, uncovered, until the vegetables are cooked and the sauce thickened.

Simple curried chicken with spinach and chick-peas

Serves 4 to 6

1.5–2kg (3–4lbs) organic or free-range chicken,
    jointed
2 or 3 tablespoons medium curry paste
olive oil or chicken fat
1 onion, peeled and sliced
300mls (½ pint) chicken stock or water

1 bay leaf
bag of young spinach leaves, ready to use
can of chick-peas, drained of most of their liquid

Rub the chicken joints with the curry paste. Heat a little fat in a casserole, gently fry the onion, then brown the chicken all over. Pour on the liquid, add the bay leaf, bring to the boil, cover, and simmer for three-quarters of an hour or so.

When the chicken is ready, transfer the casserole to the stove top and bring to the boil. Stir in the chick-peas and spinach, and serve once the curry is heated through and the spinach wilted.

The same recipe can be adapted to beef and lamb.

The perfect kulfi

One of my favourite desserts in Indian restaurants is kulfi, that richly flavoured, intense concoction of frozen evaporated milk. In fact, it is not nearly as rich as cream and egg-based ice creams. It can be frozen in an ice-cream maker, but that will produce a soft freeze, whereas freezing it in a box or mould will give the characteristic concrete-like texture.

YOU NEED, for 2 or 3 servings, 1 can (400ml) evaporated milk, 2 tablespoons Amaretto or ½ teaspoon pure almond essence and 100g (4oz) ground almonds.

METHOD Whisk the milk and flavouring until foamy. Stir in the almonds, pour into small, clean yoghurt cartons or a plastic container, cover and freeze overnight, or at least 4 hours. Turn out, slice if necessary, and garnish, if you like, with toasted flaked almonds.

ALTERNATIVES For passion-fruit kulfi, replace half the ground almonds with the sieved pulp of two or three passion-fruit. For mango kulfi, replace the ground almonds with thick mango purée. You may need to sweeten the mixture to taste. Whisk in some icing sugar in this case.

Spices

A bachelor cousin, Walt, asked me to solve a culinary problem for him. He likes to cook, but not regularly, and it occurs to me the problem is a common one.

Each time one turns to a recipe, one is told to buy half a dozen spices, which one duly does, and produces an excellent dish. The spices languish in the cupboard. Weeks, months, later, you come across another recipe you'd like to try. It calls for six or seven spices. Different spices from those you have already bought. Are there any that can double up? Can I do without them? Is it possible to make do with a few basic spices?

In a sense, there are families of flavours within the spice world as there are with herbs. Cloves and cinnamon are the sweet spices. Nutmeg and mace have similar flavours. Cumin and coriander, while not really the same, do share some similarities. Anis or fennel seeds can stand in for star anis, but lack the almost overwhelming flavour. Cardamom is an extremely useful spice, in that it can move between the sweet and the savoury, as at home in chocolate cake as it is in curry.

Undoubtedly, there are spices and spice mixtures which you cannot do without if you aim to cook authentic dishes. These are the real signatures of cooking, and to do without them, or to use a substitute, is to miss the flavour of the authentic kitchen. It depends on how important authenticity is to you.

Turmeric cannot stand in for saffron in a Spanish paella. Nutmeg is a vital flavouring in Italian cooking, especially for pasta fillings combining ricotta and Parmesan, almonds and pumpkin. Fenugreek is indispensable for an authentic Indian flavour, just as galangal is necessary in Thai cooking, and five-spice in Chinese cooking.

In many cases the solution is to buy the ready-made curry pastes and wet spice mixtures, available in jars, sachets and vacuum packs. They are usually measured out to contain enough for one recipe dish, and I am impressed by their quality and authenticity, for they include all the 'signature' flavours. These mixtures are in a different class altogether from the 'cook-in' sauces. I particularly like Patak's curry pastes, and the Thai curry pastes from Merchant Gourmet. An added benefit of curry pastes is that the spices have already been slowly cooked. It is essential that spices are thoroughly cooked into a dish from the beginning, as the flavour of raw spices is bitter, unformed and unpleasant. The exception is those spices and spice mixtures dusted on at the end, such as nutmeg on a rice pudding, or garam masala on an Indian dish.

If you like to cook Chinese, I suggest buying the five-spice mix as whole mixed spices and grinding yourself; star anis, cassia, cloves, fennel seeds and Szechuan pepper, or *far chiew*. You can also add the whole spices to aromatize rice or stir-fries, and retrieve the larger pieces before serving.

Not counting good pepper and salt, my list of indispensable spices comprises cardamom, nutmeg or mace, allspice (Jamaica pepper), coriander, cumin and saffron, with anis, fennel seeds or star anis. With the exception of coriander and cumin, perhaps, the spices can be used in both sweet and savoury cooking. Allspice is a particularly useful spice, pleasingly versatile, and owing its name to the fact that, when ground, it tastes like a mixture of cinnamon, cloves, nutmeg and perhaps ginger and pepper. Like cardamom, it can play in the sweet or savoury team. It adds a warm and subtle spiciness to cakes, biscuits and pies. Coarsely ground and added to a wine and garlic marinade, it is excellent with beef, pork and game. Use it also to flavour cheese sauces. I like to keep a few of the berries in my pepper-grinder along with the black peppercorns.

If I want ginger or chillies in my cooking, I buy fresh. Any left-over chillies dry nicely, and fresh ginger can be grated and kept in a jar of sherry, which makes it doubly useful – in stir-fry dishes and in cakes, ice creams and desserts.

SPECIAL DINNER FOR TWO

Oyster fritters

Oysters in sea-water jelly

Veal skirt with lovage sauce

Potato, red pepper and leek terrine

Espresso coffee jellies

Special birthdays in our house, as well as anniversaries and holiday celebrations, are often spent at home, opening a very nice bottle or two of claret or champagne to accompany a meal that I enjoy cooking just for the two of us. This menu fits the bill.

Opening oysters for more than two people is tedious. I speak from experience, having spent some Christmas mornings helping to open a hundred or so of these tough-shelled molluscs. But I do not mind opening a dozen, or persuading my husband Tom to open them. Plain on the half-shell is, without doubt, the best and easiest way to eat them, but here are a couple of different ways of preparing them.

The contrast of hot and cold oysters is appealing, and the idea was suggested to me by the way of preparing them in Bordeaux, where raw oysters are often served with small sizzling sausages. If you prefer not to deep-fry the oysters, bake them instead. Having opened them, discard the flat top shell, dip the oysters in beaten egg yolk, roll them in soft white breadcrumbs or oatmeal, and place back in the shells, which you have first buttered. Bake in the top of a hot oven for 4 to 5 minutes, and serve in the shells, with wedges of lemon and a bottle of Tabasco on the table.

Veal has never been a mainstream traditional British meat, and there are far fewer recipes for it than for beef, pork and lamb. Nevertheless, as long as we have a dairy industry, there will be veal from those animals not needed as replacements for the dairy herd.

Efforts have been made in recent years to rear these young animals with care and respect, rather than in cruel, confined conditions, and it is possible to buy organic veal now, reared in humane conditions, from one of the country's most successful and respected organic farmers, Helen Browning, at Eastbrook Farm (tel: 01793 790 460).

If you can find a source of veal that you are happy to eat, it is worth looking for veal skirt. This is a cut of veal that you rarely come across. I have never seen it for sale in Britain, because the skirt usually gets diced for pie veal. However, if you can persuade your butcher or farmer to keep you a piece, you will be well rewarded. It is, by far and away, the tastiest piece of the animal. You can, of course, substitute the more expensive veal fillet or escalope.

If you cannot get free-range or organic veal, or do not like veal, the same method can be used for a piece of good beef skirt. Fast, high cooking is required for this lean meat, which will keep it tender.

The veal skirt is the ideal size for two people. It will weigh about 280–450g (10–16oz.) The meat lends itself to a delicate herby sauce, perhaps

Oyster fritters

Makes 6

1 small free-range egg, separated
1 tablespoon olive oil
pinch of salt
2 tablespoons plain flour
3 tablespoons cold water
6 oysters
olive oil for frying

Mix together until you have a smooth batter the egg yolk, oil, salt, flour and water. Leave for the flour to expand for 20 minutes, and fold in the stiffly beaten egg white and the oysters.

Pour the oil into a frying pan to a depth of about 1cm (⅓ inch), and heat. Drop heaped spoonfuls of the batter into the oil, making sure there is an oyster in each spoon, and fry until golden brown. Drain on crumpled kitchen paper. Serve hot.

Oysters in sea-water jelly

Makes 6

1 sheet or 1 teaspoon gelatine
6 oysters
small bunch of watercress, fresh dill or chervil

Soften the gelatine in 2 tablespoons of cold water. Open the oysters carefully, and strain the liquid into a jug.

Loosen the oysters from their shells, and put in a bowl. Scrub the oyster shells to use as containers. Heat the gelatine gently until it dissolves, and stir it into the oyster liquid. Make it up to about 125mls (4oz), adding a little sea salt if necessary to keep the 'sea-water' flavour.

Arrange the shells on a bed of salt or crumpled foil to keep them stable, and spoon a little liquid into each. Refrigerate to set it, and then place an oyster on each with a small sprig of watercress or herbs, and cover with more liquid. Chill until set and ready to serve.

An alternative presentation is to set the oyster jelly in small moulds or ramekins, 3 oysters to each, and then turn out onto serving plates. Accompany with a spoonful of crème fraiche mixed with finely chopped shallots and chives and a wedge of lemon or lime.

tarragon or chives. Lovage, a truly English flavour, with its pronounced celery notes, is as good with veal as it is with beef. We should encourage greengrocers and supermarkets to stock it, for it is an exceptionally good herb in the kitchen, with egg, cheese and potato dishes. I make a creamy potato and lovage soup, which is intriguing, subtle, and deeply satisfying.

And, on the subject of potatoes, I highly recommend the potato, red pepper and leek terrine. It would also be a good addition to the vegetarian menu that I describe on p. 206. A slice of it looks very attractive, and it accompanies fish as well as meat. Try it, for example, with a piece of poached or steamed smoked haddock, or with medallions of monkfish, wrapped in bacon and grilled. Whilst the terrine could not be described as fast food, it is not at all difficult to prepare, and the various components can be prepared in advance.

Make the dessert, too, the day before required. Dark and intense, this will appeal to those who love real coffee. And if you do not like coffee-flavoured desserts, why not make a jelly, or granita, with your favourite herbal tisane?

Veal skirt with lovage sauce

Serves 2

300–400g (10–14oz) veal skirt in a piece
1–2 teaspoons unsalted butter
2–3 tablespoons dry white wine
100mls (4oz) chicken, veal or vegetable stock
2–3 sprigs of lovage, finely chopped
seasoning

Cut the piece of meat in two, trimming off any fat and skin.
Heat the butter in a heavy pan, and, when nut-brown, fry the
meat on both sides and cook it for 5 to 6 minutes in all, a
little more if the meat is especially thick.

Transfer it to warm dinner plates, and quickly make a
sauce with the pan juices, deglazing with the wine, and then
adding the stock, lovage and seasoning to taste.

Cook it down until you have 3 to 4 tablespoons, and
spoon it around the veal before serving.

This is very good with some mixed, fried mushrooms
on a round of toast. I have also served it with saffron
mashed potatoes and wilted spinach, and with this delicious
potato terrine. It is worth making more than you need,
because a slice of it cold makes an excellent accompaniment to smoked or cured salmon, mackerel or trout, as in
the recipe for marinated mackerel on p. 42.

Potato, red pepper and leek terrine

Serves 6

2 or 3 large waxy potatoes, peeled and thinly
    sliced
8 baby leeks, or 3 large ones, carefully rinsed
2 or 3 red peppers, quartered, roasted and
    skinned
salt
pepper

Boil the potatoes and leeks for 2 to 3 minutes, and drain
them. If using large leeks, quarter them, and use mainly the
white part.

Oil a loaf tin or terrine, and layer the potatoes, leeks and
peppers, trying to catch and use as much of the juice from
the peppers as possible.

Lightly season the terrine at intervals. Fill to within 2cm
(a scant inch) from the top, cover with foil, and bake the
terrine for about ¾ of an hour at 180°C/350°F/gas mark 4.

Once out of the oven, weight it down very heavily, which
will make for easier slicing, and leave it for 15 to 20 minutes before you do so.

Espresso coffee jellies

Serves 2

1 sheet or 1 teaspoon gelatine
2 tablespoons water
150mls (5oz) freshly made hot espresso
sugar to taste
2 curls of lemon zest
double cream – optional

Soften the gelatine in the water, and then stir it into the hot
coffee. Sweeten to taste.

Pour into coffee cups, and allow to set. Garnish with a
curl of lemon zest, and serve.

If you wish, you can run a thin layer of cream on top of
the jelly, once it has set, and then place the lemon zest
on top.

If anyone were to call on Tom and me, late on a Saturday morning, they might think we had regressed to the nursery. Not for us bagels or pain au chocolat from the nearby deli. First breakfast with the early-morning coffee remains toast with marmalade or lemon curd, but the second breakfast, or early lunch, is a boiled egg with soldiers of granary toast, sea salt and coarsely ground black pepper. It is an uncommonly good egg too, a tough shell, with a creamy white and sunshine-yellow yolk.

This passion for eggs outlasts any 'salmonella in a sandwich' story. I came home one evening to find some eggs had been delivered for me to try, and Tom had already used several of them to make scrambled eggs for his lunch. Not the way I make scrambled eggs; he likes them with a little milk. 'I'm never going to eat another egg,' he proclaimed, 'unless I can eat these.'

'These' were the ideal egg, from a farmer in Wiltshire. The hens had been fed on rations rich in vitamins and minerals from seaweed and oyster shells. The feed was not bought in, but made up at the farm and supplemented with the layers' own feeding and scratching outside on acres of organic grassland, which they share with the rest of the farm animals. This varied feed (which contains no additives such as the colourant betacarotene) produced the tough shell and rich, yellow yolk.

Living in small flocks, chickens lead a stress-free life, which, in turn, gives them a good immunity to diseases. Routine pre-emptive drugs and antibiotics are not needed. There is also no need to debeak the birds, as it is only in stressful conditions that they become aggressive and peck each other. These particular chickens, their eggs and their feed are tested regularly and frequently, which is said to ensure freedom from salmonella.

These really are free-range eggs, the ones I wish we could all use when I refer to 'free-range' in my recipes. Fortunately, there is an increasing number of farmers who produce eggs to high standards of quality, purity and welfare, and who are establishing excellent reputations in their local area. Unfortunately, we cannot assume that an egg described as 'free-range', which comes in a box with an appealingly rustic label, has been laid by a happy chicken scratching around in a farmyard.

Why does it have to be all so complicated for the consumer? Should we care? We can buy cheap eggs, and perpetuate factory farming, or we can pay more for our eggs, use them less often, and endorse sustainable systems of agriculture, which produce healthy food, and, at the same time, protect the environment. When in doubt, buy eggs labelled 'organic'.

Really delicious eggs such as these are best used as the main focus of a dish, although they do, of course, make wonderful cakes and sauces. I feel quite happy to use real free-range organic eggs for making mayonnaise, although I would add the usual warning for any recipes containing raw or lightly cooked eggs: those people who are susceptible, such as the elderly, the sick, the very young, pregnant women and anyone with a compromised immune system, should only eat well-cooked eggs.

Mayonnaise

Although the basic mayonnaise recipe (p. 28) requires only egg yolk and oil, there is a surprising range of methods and additions. Some like to add the seasonings with the egg yolk at the beginning, before starting to add the oil. Some make it in a food processor, some with whisk and bowl, some with fork and bowl, and yet others with a wooden spoon. You can also make it in a pestle and mortar. The oil you use can be olive, grapeseed, sunflower or groundnut. I would not use an anonymous vegetable oil, since there are many better oils available. One medium-size egg yolk will absorb 150–200mls (¼–⅓ pint) of oil quite easily.

Curdling can be minimized if you use all ingredients at room temperature, and add the oil to the egg in the initial stages with a very sparing hand, literally drop by drop, and beating in each addition of oil before adding the next. Once the mixture starts to thicken, the oil can be added more liberally, but no more than a thin stream, about a tablespoon at a time. This too should be beaten until the mixture looks thick and glossy, but with no surface film of oil, before you add the next stream of oil.

Once all the oil has been absorbed, you can then begin to play with the flavours. For a simple, classic version, season with salt and pepper, and sharpen with lemon juice. But you can also sharpen it with flavoured vinegars such as tarragon or shallot, lime juice, Seville orange or blood orange juice, tamarind water, rice vinegar and sherry vinegar.

The last addition of oil might be extra-virgin olive oil, walnut or hazelnut oil, all of which change the final flavour, which can be enhanced yet further. For example, to serve with cold chicken or fish, consider sharpening your mayonnaise with orange juice, adding walnut oil, and stirring in a tablespoon or so of crushed or finely chopped walnuts. Mustard, herbs, garlic, tomato purée, Tabasco sauce are other additions to consider. Folding in a stiffly beaten egg white produces sauce mousseline.

Mayonnaise is best made for immediate use, although it will keep a day or two in the refrigerator.

Salad cream

As an alternative to mayonnaise, you might consider a very traditional English salad dressing which Eliza Acton wrote about in the middle of the nineteenth century. As with homemade mayonnaise, it is much better than anything you will buy off the shelf.

For this, you need the yolks of two hard-boiled eggs, really quite hard-boiled so that the yolks can be pounded to a smooth paste with a little salt, pepper, sugar, mustard and wine vinegar or cider. Then, simply work in about 150mls (¼ pint) cream, single, whipping or double, depending on how rich a dressing you want.

Plain eggs

With bread, toast, pastry, pasta, potatoes and other staples, eggs combine to make the most satisfying inexpensive and easy-to-cook dishes. Think of poached egg on toast. Think again, and top it with a little cream mixed with grated cheese, or place it on top of a few fried mushrooms. Beat some eggs, and stir them into freshly cooked spaghetti with some crisply fried crumbled ham or bacon or shredded prosciutto, and you have spaghetti carbonara. Argument continues over whether cream is beaten with the eggs, or not. Do as it pleases you.

If you have a certain amount of nerve and manual dexterity, make the Tunisian *brik à l'oeuf*. Take a piece about 20–25cm (8–10 inches) square of soft filo dough, open it out, and on it place a very fresh egg, just out of its shell; moisten the pastry edges, fold into a triangle, fold over the edges to seal, and twist the corners. Fry in hot oil for a few minutes, leaving the egg still lightly cooked, and the pastry crisp and golden. It is important that the egg is very fresh. If it is not, the white will be runny and loose and escape over the dough. Not quite as elegant or exotic, but less nerve-wracking, is to warm a pitta bread, open it, and slide in a fried egg.

My favourite egg sandwiches use boiled eggs which are processed to a smooth paste with seasoning and a nut of butter, spread on granary bread, and covered with shredded lettuce. If you mix in herbs such as chervil or tarragon, or the pepperiness of rocket or watercress, the sandwiches will be even better.

For a very good supper dish, you can hardly do better than a large baked potato and an egg. Baking the egg in the partly cooked, partly hollowed-out potato is one way, but it is very easy to overcook the egg. Instead, fully bake a large potato for each person. Take off a horizontal slice, not too deep. Hollow out the potato, scooping the flesh into a bowl. Mash it with butter or olive oil, seasoning with chopped herbs, what you will. Spoon a layer into the potato, and on top, place a freshly poached egg. Cover with another layer of potato. Add grated cheese or a sauce, and finish off in the top of a hot oven, or under the grill for a few minutes. The eggs can be poached while the potatoes are baking, and then trimmed and kept in warm water.

Fancy eggs

Just as eggs combine well with plain ingredients, so do they partner exotic ingredients very well. For a few years, one of the classic *amuse-gueules* served in elegant French restaurants has been what looks like a boiled egg, at a distance. A cap is carefully cut from the raw egg, and the egg carefully poured out and separated. The shell is rinsed and kept warm. The egg white is used for another dish, and the egg yolk beaten with a spoonful of cream and a little seasoning. Heat it, but do not scramble it, in a bowl set over hot water. Spoon the creamed egg into the shell, and top with a spoonful of caviar.

Why eggs for Easter?

Not long ago I came across details of a medieval practice, which perhaps explains not only why children are given Easter eggs, but why sugared almonds are distributed at christenings. Apparently, when infants were baptized at Easter, to compensate for the privations they had endured during the previous forty days of Lent, they were given eggs and almond milk as extra-special nourishment.

Egg recipes for breakfast, brunch, supper and any time

Breakfast tortilla

Serves 2

2 flour tortillas
½ a mild onion, peeled and finely chopped
1 tablespoon olive oil
2 small green tomatoes, or tomatillos, chopped
2 yellow tomatoes, seeded and chopped
2 red tomatoes, seeded and chopped
1 green chilli, seeded and sliced
pinch of salt
chilli powder – optional
2 tablespoons grated Bramley apple, or jicama
2 tablespoons chopped fresh coriander, or basil
100g (4oz) cooked left-over chicken, ham, salmon, smoked haddock or other fish
2 or 3 large free-range eggs, lightly beaten
2 tablespoons cream cheese – optional

Wrap the tortillas in foil, and warm in the oven.

Fry the onion until soft, and then stir in the tomatoes and chilli, and cook until soft. Add salt, and a little chilli powder, if you like. Then stir in the apple and herbs.

Remove 2 tablespoons of the mixture, and put to one side to be served as a salsa with the tortilla.

Stir in the meat or fish, and then the eggs, and stir until just set. Spread the tortillas with the cream cheese, if using it, and spoon on the egg mixture.

Roll up, and serve on heated plates with the salsa, and, if you like, a little crisp fruit salad, sprinkled with lime juice. Plain red tomatoes can be used in place of the green and yellow ones.

Scrambled egg tortillas with lime and avocado sauce

Serves 2

4 flour tortillas
1 or 2 chorizo sausages, crumbled or diced
4 spring onions, chopped
1 red and 1 green pepper, grilled or roasted and skinned, and cut into strips
4 free-range eggs, beaten
knob of butter
handful of rocket leaves, chopped
'light' cream cheese
1 ripe avocado
1 lime
salt
pepper
Tabasco sauce to taste, red or green
a few coriander leaves

Wrap the tortillas in foil, and put them in the oven to warm.

Fry the chorizo, onions and peppers in oil in a frying pan until cooked, and then gently scramble the eggs in the butter with the vegetables and sausage, stirring in the rocket.

Spread the tortillas with the cheese, roll round a filling of scrambled eggs, and serve with a sauce made from the avocado, blended with a little lime juice, zest, seasoning and coriander.

Hangtown fry

Many years ago in a Chiu Chow restaurant in Hong Kong I tasted a wonderful oyster dish, which I asked my Hong Kong sister-in-law about recently. She said it was *ho jai daan*, or 'oyster egg', and made by blanching oysters, putting them in a shallow,

Oysters

In Britain we consume thirty million oysters, some way from the 1,200 million which the Victorians used to get through. Even that is far from the 2,000 million oysters, which the French eat every year. There are many things one can do with an oyster, including stews, chowders, omelettes, fritters, and gratins. You can even barbecue them.

Cooked oysters were a great favourite according to early cookery books. Eliza Acton lists 13 recipes using oysters, Hannah Glasse lists 8, and Mrs Beeton lists 37. Oysters can also be used as an ingredient in stuffing for turkeys or chicken, in a carpet-bag steak, or in a steamed steak and kidney pudding. Purists will always prefer oysters raw on the half-shell, with or without a seasoning of lemon juice, hot sauce, or finely chopped shallots in red wine vinegar or sherry vinegar.

There are two main types of oyster, the flat, or native oyster, and the pacific, or gigas oyster. Natives are known by their provenance, such as Helford, Whitstable and Colchester. These are best eaten raw, to appreciate their intense and unique flavour. The pacific oyster, because it is more prolific, tends to be less expensive than the native and is the one to use in cooking.

Fresh unopened oysters will keep well for a few days in a cold place. Damp sacking, or newspaper, can cover them. Before opening oysters, it is a good idea to scrub them first to remove any sand or mud. An oyster knife, with a shield, protects the knuckles, and the hand used to steady the oyster should be wrapped in a folded tea towel, in case the oyster knife should slip. Butchers chain mail gloves are much to be coveted for this task. As soon as the oyster is open, lift it carefully so as not to lose the juice, and sniff it. A bad oyster will be immediately recognizable, and should be thrown away.

greased pan over low heat, beating eggs, perhaps with a little ginger and wine, and pouring this over the oysters. When cooked on one side, the omelette is flipped over until just set.

Chiu Chow, or Chaozhou, has the Han river, or Han Jiang, running through it, and I have often wondered if this dish is the basis of Hangtown Fry. Made of eggs and oysters, this dish is said to have originated in Hangtown, California.

The easiest way to make Hangtown Fry is to lightly dust the raw oysters in seasoned flour; then fry in butter, and pour over the eggs beaten with a little chopped parsley, chervil or chives, and a tablespoon of melted butter. Cook very lightly indeed, and serve with hot buttered toast. Thinly sliced, crisply fried streaky bacon sometimes accompanies the dish.

Duelos y quebrantos

Duelos y quebrantos was Don Quixote's Saturday meal, after lentils on Fridays and to be followed by 'perhaps a pigeon on Sundays'. It is still a popular dish today, and they serve an excellent version at El Molino del Conde on the Jimena to San Roque road in Cadiz province. This recipe uses not only bacon and chorizo, but diced potatoes and black pudding with the scrambled eggs. It is an extremely simple and tasty dish for lunch or supper on a cold day.

Serves 2

2 tablespoons olive oil
2 slices streaky bacon, rind removed
75g (3oz) chorizo, sliced or diced
1 potato, diced and parboiled
75g (3oz) black pudding, diced
4–5 free range eggs, lightly beaten

In the oil gently fry the bacon, dicing it first, and then the chorizo and potato.

When the potato is browning nicely, add the black pudding. When this is almost cooked, pour off most of the fat. Stir in the eggs, and cook gently until just lightly set. Serve immediately with crusty bread.

Cream of lettuce with poached eggs

This next dish is more of a purée than a soup. If you can only get iceberg lettuce, add a little flat-leaf parsley or spinach when you cook it, to enhance both colour and flavour.

Serves 4

2 large green lettuces, not lollo, or oak-leaf;
    Cos or Webb would be excellent
50g (2oz) unsalted butter
750mls (1¼ pints) vegetable stock, or
    500mls (18oz) water and
    250mls (9oz) dry white wine
salt
pepper
freshly grated nutmeg
200g (7oz) crème fraiche
4 free-range eggs

Remove any damaged part of the lettuces, cut off the root end, and rinse and drain thoroughly. Take off all the leaves, and wilt them in the butter in a saucepan. Add the liquid and a little seasoning, and simmer for 15 minutes. Add the nutmeg and cream, and cook for 5 minutes more.

Meanwhile, carefully poach the eggs in a large saucepan of water, salted or not, acidulated or not, as you prefer, for 3 minutes. Remove them with a slotted spoon, and drain on paper towels.

Blend the soup until smooth. Reheat, and serve in heated soup plates with a poached egg in each. You can garnish with shreds of cured ham or smoked salmon if you wish.

Bouillabaisse of spring vegetables and eggs

This makes a light meal in a soup bowl; you can vary the vegetables according to the season, but the soup is particularly good with *primeurs,* or the first of the spring vegetables.

Serves 4 to 6

2 leeks, trimmed and sliced
2 small onions, peeled and diced
4 garlic cloves, new season's if possible, and
    peeled and crushed
6 waxy potatoes, scrubbed and diced
1 medium fennel bulb, diced
2 tomatoes, halved, seeded and chopped
75mls (3oz) extra-virgin olive oil
sprig each of parsley, thyme and sage or
    rosemary, tied together
good pinch of saffron
salt
pepper
1.5 litres (2½ pints) water or vegetable stock
4 or 6 free-range eggs
4 or 6 slices bread

In a large saucepan, gently fry all the vegetables in the olive oil for 5 to 10 minutes. Add the herbs, saffron and a little seasoning, together with the water. Boil for 30 to 40 minutes, the boiling of the oil and water being the bouillabaisse of the title, then lower the heat to barely simmering, and poach the eggs in the soup for 3 minutes.

Meanwhile, toast the bread, and put one slice in each heated soup bowl. Place a poached egg on top, check the seasonings of the vegetable broth, remove the herbs, and pour the broth and vegetables over the eggs. Serve immediately. A hot piquant rouille will go very well with this, but that might be over-egging the dish.

Tomatoes and eggs

This makes a lovely simple, casual starter, or light lunch or supper dish. Crusty bread and a watercress salad accompany it very well.

Serves 4

2 tablespoons extra-virgin olive oil
500g (1lb) peeled and seeded tomatoes, roughly
    chopped
2 garlic cloves, peeled and crushed
1 shallot or small onion, peeled and finely
    chopped
salt
pepper
shredded basil, chopped tarragon or chives to
    taste
4 free-range eggs

Heat the olive oil in a sauté pan, or in an earthenware dish set on a heat-diffusing mat. Put in the tomatoes, garlic and shallot, cover, and cook for about 15 minutes. Uncover, and let much of the liquid evaporate for about 5 minutes.

Having cracked each egg into a saucer, slide them, one by one, into the tomato mixture. Cook for 3 to 4 minutes more, until the eggs are set.

Tomato soufflés

Here is another variation on the egg-and-tomato theme, this time with the eggs cooked soufflé-style in the tomato. Plum tomatoes work very well in this recipe because you can set them in ovenproof egg cups for baking. Otherwise, use whatever good-sized and well-flavoured tomatoes you can find, and bake them in ramekins. Alternatively, save this recipe for the summer and your own home-grown tomatoes.

Serves 2 as a starter, or 4 as an appetizer

4 tomatoes
2 tablespoons double cream, crème fraiche,
    sieved cottage cheese, or ricotta cheese
salt
cayenne pepper
2 free-range eggs

Cut a slice from the top of each tomato, and squeeze the seeds into a sieve, set over a bowl. Rub the liquid through the sieve and use for a tomato vinaigrette. Scoop the central part of the flesh out of the tomatoes, chop it, mix with cream, salt, a little cayenne pepper and with the well-beaten eggs.

Fill the hollow tomatoes with the mixture, and bake them in a preheated oven at 190°C/375°F/gas mark 5 for 10 minutes or so. These are very good served with toast fingers spread with anchovy butter.

Cheese soufflé

Serves 6

600mls (1 pint) milk
salt
freshly ground black pepper
freshly grated nutmeg
50g (2oz) butter
7 free-range eggs, 5 of them separated
50g (2oz) plain flour, sifted
75g (3oz) cheese, grated

Butter a soufflé dish, or dishes, and dust with a little grated Parmesan.

Put three-quarters of the milk in a saucepan with the seasoning and butter. Bring to the boil.

Beat the two whole eggs with the 5 egg yolks, the flour and the remaining milk, and stir slowly into the boiling milk over a low heat. Stir continuously until the mixture thickens but does not curdle.

The perfect Spanish omelette

Eggs and potatoes are all you need for this sub-stantial dish.

YOU NEED, to make a six-egg omelette, as well as the eggs, one large potato, peeled and diced, and a little olive oil for frying; the oil adds flavour even if you use a non-stick pan. Use a small, heavy frying pan, non-stick or well seasoned, and no more than 20cm (8 inches) in diameter, to give the characteristic thick cake shape.

METHOD You can cook the potatoes completely in the frying pan, which requires more attention to ensure that they cook through but do not burn. Or you can parboil them first. Fry the potatoes until tender and golden brown. Beat, but do not over-beat, the eggs and pour them onto the potatoes. As the eggs begin to set, draw the edges of the omelette to the centre, letting the uncooked egg slide underneath. Do not have the heat too high, or the underside will burn before the eggs set. Once the omelette is beginning to firm up, draw the edges again towards the middle, as this will give a neat finish to the tortilla once you turn it. Put a plate over the pan, tip it upside down and catch the omelette on the plate.

Wipe out the pan if there are any dribbles and put it back on the heat with a little more oil. Slide the omelette back in the pan, cooked side upper-most, and finish cooking for a minute or two more. The omelette should be well set when you slide it out onto a serving plate.

SERVE as a starter, as part of a buffet, or best of all, cut into squares, spiked with a cocktail stick, as a tapa to accompany a *copita* of chilled fino sherry. It tastes best served warm and freshly cooked, or at room temperature.

Remove from the heat. Whisk the egg whites until stiff. Stir the cheese into the sauce, and then fold in the egg whites.

Pour into the prepared dish, or dishes, and bake in a preheated oven at 200°C/400°F/gas mark 6 for 12 to 22 minutes, depending on the size of the dishes.

The perfect scrambled egg

A few years ago a court case hinged on, amongst other things, the correct way to cook scrambled eggs. Celebrities and experts, living and dead, were consulted. I had to admit to having a husband who scrambles his eggs with milk, whereas any fule kno that butter, and at a pinch, a little water, are the only other admissible ingredients, apart from seasoning, of course.

YOU NEED, for 2 people, 4–6 large free-range eggs, salt, pepper, 1–2 tablespoons water and 50g (2oz) unsalted butter, chilled and diced.

METHOD Lightly beat the eggs with the salt, pepper and a tablespoon of water. Stir in half the diced butter, and pour the eggs into a non-stick frying pan, set over a very gentle heat.

Stir the eggs continuously, adding the remaining cold butter gradually. This lowers the temperature of the eggs, preventing them setting too hard. The eggs should be creamy and rich, not grainy and firm. You may, or may not, need to add the extra spoonful of water.

TO SERVE Hot buttered toast, with or without a spoonful of caviar on top. You can, for a very elegant starter, spoon the egg into clean egg shells, and top with a sliver of smoked salmon or teaspoon of salmon roe.

Pipérade

Pipérade is the classic Basque dish of pimentos, tomatoes and onions. Eggs were added as a later development, to produce a nice dish for tourists.

Serves 2 to 4

2 red peppers
1 green pepper
1 onion, peeled and finely chopped
2 tablespoons olive oil, or 30g (generous 1oz)
    butter
6 ripe tomatoes, peeled, deseeded and chopped
6 free-range eggs

sea salt
freshly ground black pepper
cayenne pepper or chilli powder, to taste

Char and skin the peppers, and then seed and chop them. Cook the onion in the olive oil or butter, until soft.

Add the tomatoes, and continue cooking until you have a thick purée. Lightly beat the eggs. Lower the heat under the pan, and once the mixture is no longer boiling, stir in the eggs.

Season with salt and pepper, and cayenne or chilli powder, and continue stirring over a low heat until the eggs are cooked to a cream. They should not be lumpy but should have amalgamated with the purée and thickened it. Serve immediately with toast or fried bread.

Poached eggs

Use very fresh free-range eggs at room temperature and a wide shallow pan. A frying pan is quite deep enough, a sauté pan is perfect.

Fill the pan three-quarters full with water, bring to a full rolling boil, and then turn it down to a simmer. Break the eggs, one at a time, into a cup, and slide them into the simmering water, holding the cup over the egg for a few seconds to stop it from spreading too much. With a large spoon, immediately draw the white back towards, and over, the yolk to envelope.

Add more eggs, and treat in the same way. Simmer for 3 minutes, and transfer to a bowl of warm water until needed. Remove with a slotted spoon, blot with kitchen paper, and trim off any ragged edges.

Serve on hot buttered toast, use to make Eggs Benedict or *Oeufs en Meurette*, or combine them with a savoury soufflé (p. 82), in a spectacular soufflé enclosing poached eggs. You make this by spooning half the soufflé mixture into the prepared dish, arranging the poached egg or eggs on top, and covering with the remaining mixture. The soufflé is then cooked in the usual way.

Eggs

'Poached' eggs with truffle oil and mushrooms

Arzak in San Sebastian in Spain's Basque country is one of the world's best restaurants. Juan Mari Arzak has been joined in the kitchen, for the last five years, by his daughter Elena. They are, he says, highly compatible, he being, in his own words, 'an old rocker', and she a heavy-metal aficionado. She is an outstanding chef, and I predict that she will be one of the leading chefs of this new century. I have never eaten better food than the lunch the two of them cooked for us. Hugely imaginative, experimental even, but not off the wall, exquisite in its freshness, flavour and presentation, it was truly inspirational, witness this next recipe.

Here is a poached egg with a difference. At the restaurant it was served with a line of fried bread-crumbs to soak up the yolk, a line of sauce made of *txistorra* (Basque sausage) and dates, and topped with finely chopped and sautéed ceps. It is not a difficult technique to master, and adapts perfectly to a domestic kitchen, I can assure you. I'm not sure, though, that I would want to prepare them single-handedly for more than six people. Also, because of worries about fats and molecules migrating from food-wrap to food, it is not a technique that I would employ in my kitchen every day, but am happy to do so occasionally.

Serves 6

2 shallots, peeled and finely chopped
2 tablespoons grapeseed, sunflower or
    groundnut oil
150g (5oz) mushrooms, wiped and finely
    chopped
salt
pepper
generous pinch of *pimentón* or paprika
6 teaspoons truffoil
6 large organic or real free-range eggs

Gently fry the shallots in the grapeseed oil until wilted, then stir in the mushrooms and cook on a moderately high heat until their juices have evaporated. Season with salt, pepper and *pimentón* and put to one side.

Although I use olive oil and extra-virgin olive oil for most of my cooking, here I use a more neutral oil, as I do not want anything to interfere with the truffle oil. White truffle oil is more expensive than black, and a less intense 'truffoil'

is also available. I have used the latter in this recipe, and it works well, the cooking method retaining all the perfume.

To shape and wrap each egg, you need small, fairly shallow dishes, of at least 60mls (⅛ pint) volume, which is that of a large egg. Use perforated clingfilm and drape a sheet of it over each dish, making a depression in it, but in no sense lining the dish. Crack an egg and gently slide it into the clingfilmed dish. Gather up the edges of film and twist into a bundle, but not too tightly and allowing the egg to fall freely in a neat oval. Lower each parcel gently into simmering water and poach for 3 to 4 minutes until the white has set and the yolk is runny.

Remove from the pan and allow to cool for a minute before carefully opening each parcel one at a time and sliding it onto the waiting plate. Spoon the mushroom mixture on top and serve immediately.

Oeufs en meurette

Serves 2

75g (3oz) streaky bacon, rind discarded, cut into
    small pieces
8 small onions, peeled
25g (1oz) butter
10 button mushrooms, wiped and sliced or
    quartered
½ bottle good dry red wine
2 free-range eggs
sea salt
freshly ground black pepper

Heat the bacon gently in a small frying pan, and when the fat runs, add the onions. Cook on a low heat until the onions are almost tender. Add the butter, raise the heat slightly, and fry the mushrooms.

Remove from the heat while you poach the eggs. Pour the wine into a shallow pan (another frying pan, or a sauté pan is ideal), and bring to the boil.

Crack the eggs, and slide them into the wine from opposite sides of the pan. Let them cook until the white has just set, completely enclosing the yolk.

Carefully remove with a slotted spoon, and drain on kitchen paper. Boil the wine fiercely to reduce it by at least half, and pour it into the pan with the onions, bacon and mushrooms, and season to taste. Cook for a few minutes more.

Meanwhile, neaten up the eggs by trimming off any ragged portions of white. Place on pieces of toast or fried bread, in heated soup plates, and spoon the hot sauce over.

Spring vegetables and eggs

Serves 4

4 new potatoes, or other small waxy potatoes,
    scrubbed
8 small carrots, scrubbed or peeled
bunch of spring onions
150g (5oz) mushrooms
2 or 3 courgettes
25g (1oz) unsalted butter, or extra-virgin olive oil
salt
pepper
4 free-range eggs
chives or flat-leaf parsley – for garnish

Steam or boil the potatoes and carrots until tender. Trim the onions down to the bulbs, using the green for another dish, a salad perhaps. Wipe and slice the mushrooms, which could be plain cultivated button mushrooms, oyster, shiitake, or wild mushrooms.

Dice the courgettes. Heat half the fat in a frying pan, and in it sauté the spring onions, mushrooms and courgettes. Partially cover, lower the heat, and cook for 8 to 10 minutes.

Add the potatoes and carrots, sliced and cut into short batons respectively, and cook for a few minutes more. Season the vegetables, and divide them between four shallow dishes. Add the rest of the fat to the pan, and in it fry the eggs carefully, without breaking them, and then serve on top of the vegetables, garnished with the chives.

You can also use this idea in miniature, with finely diced cooked vegetables in pastry tartlets, topped with fried quail eggs.

Exotic Eggs

Did you make lunch? I asked. 'Yes, I had an omelette,' replied my husband, Tom. But there were no eggs left, I said. 'I used the quail eggs.' One of the dafter recipes to emerge from my kitchen, a twelve-quail-egg omelette. Especially as I was saving them for another recipe, quail eggs baked in potatoes, for a supper party the next day.

If you have the time and inclination, these delicate small eggs can be turned into all manner of dainties – fried and served with tiny young asparagus spears; poached and served on miniature muffins as Eggs Benedict; boiled, shelled and served in a sauce in a nest of green tagliolini, not to mention as salad garnishes, or even individual quail-egg omelettes. But quail eggs are not a good idea for large numbers, unless you pile them, hard-boiled, in a basket, hand round seasoned salt, and let your guests help themselves and shell their own eggs. Quail eggs for 2 to 4 is a manageable plan; for 6 or more, it is asking for trouble, unless you have someone to help you. They are devilishly fiddly and difficult to shell.

Baked quail eggs in potatoes

Makes 12

12 small potatoes, weighing about 50–75g
    (2–3oz) each
salt and freshly ground black pepper
50g (2oz) unsalted butter, melted
12 quail eggs

Wash and scrub the potatoes. If new, they should not need peeling. With a melon-baller, scoop out a hollow in each potato large enough to hold the quail egg, and remove a very thin slice from the bottom to allow it to stand flat. Put the hollowed-out potatoes in a pan of salted water, bring to the boil, and boil briskly until just cooked. Drain.

Preheat your oven to 180°C/350°F/gas mark 4.

Brush the potatoes inside and out with the melted butter, season lightly, and stand them on an oiled baking tray. Carefully crack a quail's egg into each potato. Place in the top half of the oven, and bake for 8 to 10 minutes. Serve immediately.

Right at the other end of the scale is the ostrich egg, about which, and ostriches in general, André Simon in his *Concise Encyclopaedia of Gastronomy* was somewhat unenthusiastic: 'their contribution to the gastronomic requirements of the people of other continents is restricted to their dehydrated eggs'.

But now with so much big-business investment in ostrich farming, ostrich eggs must be at a premium, although one might hesitate to eat the nest eggs.

If anyone can afford to eat ostrich eggs today, by the way, I have it on good authority that they are best boiled for at least an hour, brought to the table sliced, and eaten mashed with butter, salt and pepper.

Turkeys' eggs, too, are at a premium, quite delicious, but too expensive to be made available commercially, so chat up your local turkey farmer if you want to enjoy this richly flavoured egg.

When we were living in Cornwall one spring, our neighbour's geese would occasionally lay an egg on our side of the hedge, and it would find its way into golden-yellow, airy sponge cakes. On the whole, I prefer to use goose eggs in dishes where they will be well cooked. Like ducks, geese have a tendency to lay in surroundings so unsavoury that the thought of making mayonnaise, or lightly poached eggs, is far from appealing.

Little fresh bantam eggs are, on the other hand, quite exquisite for breakfast; as are all the other varieties of hens' eggs, if you can get them from specialist hen breeders, who sometimes have surplus eggs for sale. Look for pale blue Aracana, not unlike a small duck egg, the Black Peking, a small creamy-grey egg, the similar Buff Plymouth Rock, and the Wellsummer, a relatively large, dark brown egg.

Occasionally, dealers also dispose of guinea fowl, red-legged partridge and pheasant eggs, all well worth having for their excellent rich flavour.

Pigeon eggs, white and slightly larger than quail eggs, are most often found on French or Chinese menus, usually served lightly poached in a rich consommé of pigeon.

Gulls' eggs

For a special springtime delicacy, we always look out for the first of the gulls' eggs, which our game-dealer sells. These pale blue-grey eggs, heavily speckled in dark brown, have a very short season, and are at other times of the year protected by law. We eat them hard-boiled, shelling them and dipping them into celery salt. They are delicious with fine old white burgundy or a champagne with some bottle age.

Because of EU regulations, butchers and game-dealers, who sell gulls' eggs in the short late-spring season, are not allowed to cook them on the same premises where meat is being prepared. This means you cannot always get them freshly cooked but unrefrigerated. Like most things, gulls' eggs taste best freshly cooked. I therefore decided to order and cook them myself, under the expert guidance of Allens of Mount Street (tel: 020 7499 5831), suppliers of fine meat and game to the top hotels and restaurants in London.

To cook up to a dozen gulls' eggs, put in cold water, bring to the boil, and boil for 7 to 8 minutes. Drain the eggs, run them under cold water, and, when cold, examine them and serve. To examine the cooked egg, pierce, and slightly open the shell at each end with a skewer. In a good gull's egg, when cooked the egg white will show an opalescent blue-white. In a bad egg the yolk will simply not cook, and remains runny. It will smell 'off'.

Eggs also mean pancakes

I like pancakes because I enjoy eating food in my fingers. It is a pleasure to be indulged in many places, since it reflects a form of cooking used in a variety of kitchens.

Walk through the cobbled streets of Rennes, eating a galette made of *sarrasin,* or buckwheat flour. Sit by the Seine having just bought a lacy crêpe doused in Grand Marnier from one of the small crêperies on the rue de Rivoli. Enjoy the tender wrappers of rice flour enveloping the fragrant herbs and succulent meats which fill Vietnamese spring rolls. Dip the crisp edges of a Sri Lankan *hoppa* into the softly fried egg nestling in the middle. Or go to any vegetarian Indian restaurant, and eat your way through a masala dosai with its flavoursome coconut sambal.

Closer to home, for tea-time, spread a Scottish drop scone or Welsh griddle cake with unsalted butter, roll, and eat while still warm, the trick being to put it in your mouth before the butter melts and trickles down to your elbow. Or stand in the kitchen and eat Shrove Tuesday pancakes as they come out of the pan, simply sprinkled with lemon juice and sugar and folded or rolled.

A whole lunch or dinner built around pancakes is perhaps not the best idea, but they are versatile enough to appear at the beginning, middle, or end of a meal. Try, for starters, small griddle cakes in which grated courgettes are mixed into the batter. These are based on a Greek recipe and are not unlike the modern version found in many restaurants where corn kernels and cornmeal are mixed into the batter. These make a very pleasing accompaniment to a vegetable soup, or they can be eaten on their own. The gram flour and coriander pancakes (p.88) are very moreish, and are especially good with a potato curry (see p. 69), which is best served, not steaming hot, just very warm. In Germany plain pancakes are rolled up, cut into very thin strips, and used as garnish for a clear beef broth. I like to do this occasionally as a change from consommé with rice or pasta. Vegetable or chicken broth can replace the beef broth.

As a main course, consider the Italian *crespelle,* thin pancakes rolled around a meat or cheese filling, packed into a shallow earthenware dish, covered with a cheese or tomato sauce, and baked in the oven. Or stack the crêpes one on top of the other, sandwiched with, for example, spinach purée, crumbled cheese, ragout or meat sauce, cooked chicken livers, or a thick leek or fennel purée. Top with a spreading of cheese sauce, grated cheese and breadcrumbs, and brown in the top of the oven. Cut into wedges like a cake, and serve with salad or grilled vegetables.

To finish your meal, try my unusual chocolate crêpes, or best of all, the classic and flamboyant crêpes Suzette, a fitting way to use up all the sumptuous food in your larder before the rigours of Lent.

With the standard pancake recipe, you can devise many variations, in the flours and liquids used, any added flavourings, and, of course, the fillings. On a practical note, even with sweet crêpes I prefer not to use sugar in the batter, as they have a tendency to stick.

Standard pancake recipe

Serves 4 to 6

100g (4oz) plain flour
pinch of salt
1 size 3 free-range egg, lightly beaten
300mls (½ pint) milk or water

Sift the flour and salt together, and mix with the egg and liquid in a blender or food processor. Or mix by hand: put the dry ingredients in a bowl, make a well in the centre, and add the egg and half the liquid. Gradually draw in and beat the flour into the liquid until you have a thick, smooth batter. Then stir in the remaining liquid, and beat until smooth.

If it is more convenient to do so, you can let the batter stand for an hour or so, or even keep it refrigerated for twenty-four hours. It will thicken eventually and can be thinned down, if you wish, with a little fizzy water. Adding extra eggs to the mixture makes for a tougher batter, in my view.

If I am making pancakes for a sweet filling, I will probably use milk, which can be skimmed, semi-skimmed or whole milk. Water is what I usually use for savoury pancakes, occasionally with the addition of beer or cider. Batter for coating fritters is made in the same way, but you use exactly half the quantity of liquid as for pancake batter.

Kolokytha krokettes
(Greek courgette pancakes)

Serves 6 to 8

500g (1lb) courgettes
1 teaspoon salt
3 free-range eggs
1 teaspoon finely chopped fresh mint
4 heaped tablespoons plain flour, sifted
pepper
100g (4oz) feta cheese, crumbled
oil for frying

Wash and trim the courgettes, and grate them into a colander. Sprinkle with the salt, and leave for an hour. Squeeze out the moisture. Beat the eggs, mint and flour to a batter, and then season with a little pepper, and stir in the feta and courgettes.

Heat a heavy frying pan, pour in a little oil, and fry table-spoons of the mixture, 3 or 4 at a time, depending on the size of your pan. When the top of each pancake is dry, flip it over to cook the other side while you are cooking the remaining mixture. The pancakes can be kept warm on a plate, set over a pan of simmering water. These are very good eaten with a spoonful of yoghurt on top as an appetizer, or serve them as an unusual accompaniment to grilled lamb cutlets or roast lamb.

Gram flour and coriander pancakes

Serves 4 as a starter or side dish, or 2 as a main course

125g (generous 4oz) gram flour
1 tablespoon self-raising flour
pinch of salt
1 medium free-range egg, lightly beaten
200mls (7oz) water
2 tablespoons finely chopped coriander
sunflower or groundnut oil for frying

Sift the flours into a bowl. Add the salt, egg and water, and beat to a smooth lump-free batter (see previous page for batter method). Stir in the chopped coriander. If you wish to serve this with the potato curry, the batter can be put to one side while you make the curry now. Or you can make the curry the day before. It is delicious cold and reheats well.

The pancakes can be made small or large. Small, and served two or three together, they make an unusual accom-paniment to fish; try them with a piece of poached smoked haddock, or with grilled salmon, which you have first brushed with oil and dusted with some of the spices used in the curry. The pancakes are also very good served with a heap of kedgeree on top.

If you replace the self-raising flour with extra gram flour, you can serve these pancakes to someone on a gluten-free diet.

If the batter thickens too much on standing, thin it down with 2 to 3 tablespoons of chilled soda water, or sparkling mineral water.

Chocolate crêpes with chocolate and honey sauce

Serves 6

crêpes

75g (3oz) plain flour
25g (1oz) cocoa powder
1 medium-size free-range egg and 1 egg yolk,
    lightly beaten
200mls (7oz) semi-skimmed or skimmed milk

sauce

2 tablespoons clear, runny honey
100g (3½oz) bar dark chocolate with at least
    70 per cent cocoa solids

For the crêpes, sift the dry ingredients together, and beat in the eggs and milk to make a smooth lump-free batter. Put it to one side while you make the sauce.

Put the honey in a bowl, set over a pan of simmering water. When the honey is hot, break the chocolate into small pieces, and stir into the honey, together with any flavouring such as a pinch of ground cardamon, 1 tablespoon orange liqueur, or 1 tablespoon rum. Remove the pan from the heat. The water will be hot enough to keep the sauce warm and runny while you make the crêpes.

Use a non-stick pan or butter a heavy frying pan. Pour on a thin layer of batter, just sufficient to cover the bottom of the pan. When the top is dry, turn each crêpe to cook the other side. Stack the crêpes on a plate, set on another pan of hot water until you have used up all the batter.

To serve, fold each crêpe twice, into a triangular pocket. In this pocket spoon some crème fraiche, crème Chantilly or ice cream and arrange them on plates with the sauce poured over the point of each crêpe. Serve immediately.

The perfect crêpes Suzette

This is the way they used to make them at the Café Royal Grill Room in London.

YOU NEED pancakes made from the ingredients given in the standard pancake recipe (p. 87), 3–4 tablespoons caster sugar, 3 oranges, about 100g (4oz) unsalted butter, half a lemon, orange liqueur and brandy or cognac. Curaçao is highly recommended, and I like the Mandarine liqueur, but you can also use Grand Marnier or Cointreau.

METHOD In a heavy frying pan over a moderately high heat, put in the sugar with the thinly peeled orange zest. Add the butter and the juice of the squeezed oranges. Keep the zest moving with a fork until the sugar has dissolved and the butter melted. Squeeze in the lemon juice, adjust for taste, and then add the orange liqueur.

Then put in the crêpes, one at a time, making sure they are well coated with the syrup before folding them in half, and then again, and pushing to one side. Once all the crêpes are in the pan and thoroughly bathed in syrup, pour on some warmed brandy, and, standing well back, light it, and serve. This is far too good to need any accompaniment in the way of fruit or ice cream.

Apricot soufflé omelette

Serves 4

200g (7oz) dried apricots, soaked in tea or wine
6 free-range eggs, separated
pinch of salt
100mls (4oz) crème fraiche
100g (4oz) light muscovado sugar or golden
    caster sugar
2 tablespoons almond liqueur or rum
25g (1oz) unsalted butter

Poach the apricots until soft. Whisk the egg whites with the salt until stiff. Fold in the beaten egg yolks, the cream, half the sugar, and the liqueur.

Heat the butter in an omelette pan, and pour in the mixture, cooking the omelette in the usual way for a soufflé omelette.

Place the drained apricots on one half of the omelette, fold it over, and slide it onto an ovenproof plate. Dust with the remaining sugar, and place the omelette in a preheated oven at 220°C/425°F/gas mark 7 for 3 minutes, or under the grill. Serve hot with chilled yoghurt, or crème fraiche.

Eggs

The celebrated eighteenth-century diarist Parson James Woodforde was a keen coarse fisherman. On 16 May 1781, he and his friends had 'the best day fishing we ever had', landing with nets, not rods, a yard-long pike weighing over 13 pounds, 15 brace of trout, the largest not more than 1½ pounds, three brace of perch, 'one tolerable Tench and I dare say near or not quite five hundred brace of Roach and Dace'.

We do not have details of his dinner, as he 'was rather fatigued this evening by fishing'. Next day, however, he treated his company to a fine dinner: 'My great Pike which was roasted and a Pudding in his Belly, some boiled Trout, Perch and Tench, Eel and Gudgeon fryed, a neck of Mutton boiled and a Plain Pudding for Mrs Howes'. The fish was so large that it had to be presented on part of the kitchen window shutters, covered with a tablecloth. Despite its size, the pike 'was declared by all the company to be prodigious fine eating, being so moist'. Parson Woodforde closes his entry for that day with, 'I put a large Pike into the boot of Mr Howes's chaise before they went back.'

Izaak Walton in *The Compleat Angler*, written a century earlier, describes a lovely stuffing for a large pike, which includes herbs, oysters and butter. Rather less ambitious, I generally settle on a sea trout or small salmon for stuffing and baking.

With the remaining fish, Woodforde could have made a water souchet, or souchy. This is none other than the Flemish *waterzooi* or *waterzootjie*, introduced to Britain in the late seventeenth century with the court of William III of the House of Nassau/Orange. It is a very good recipe, in which the fish is poached in a flavoured court bouillon and eaten with its broth with a spoon and fork. There are those who maintain that it should be made with freshwater fish.

Francatelli, chef in the royal kitchens in Queen Victoria's day, reckoned char to be the finest fish for water souchy. Aeneas Sweeting Dallas, who wrote book reviews and obituaries in *The Times* in the mid-1800s, as well as *Kettner's Book of the Table* in 1877, firmly recommends the large perch, or zander, but also comments that at Greenwich, Thames flounders or dabs were the choice fish for this dish. Lady Jekyll, my predecessor on *The Times* cookery page by some seventy years, recommended Dover slips in her recipe.

Sometimes I use salmon or salmon trout or firm-fleshed sea fish such as cod or monkfish, for my water souchy. When I ate the dish in Brussels, it was a fairly rich dish, including vegetables and cream. The version in this chapter is closer to the original, very plain and simple, using wild salmon. Mr Dallas' suggested accompaniment of brown bread and butter is most appropriate.

I have also included another salmon dish, not unlike a fishy version of toad-in-the-hole. This solid salmon custard is called a sefton, after the nineteenth-century earl, who was fond of his tummy and gave his name to a number of recipes.

Baked stuffed sea trout

Serves 4 to 6

1.25kg (3lb) sea trout, scaled, cleaned, gutted
    and boned
1 lemon
salt
pepper
4 slices white bread, crusts removed and
    soaked in milk and then squeezed
6 canned anchovies, chopped
175g (6oz) shelled prawns, chopped
100g (4oz) unsalted butter, softened
2 free-range hard-boiled eggs, chopped
¼ teaspoon mace
2 tablespoons chopped chives or spring onions
150mls (¼ pint) good dry white wine

Season the fish, inside and out, with lemon juice, salt and pepper. Mix the remaining ingredients except the wine, and using only half the butter, stuff the fish with the mixture, and secure with cocktail sticks. Place the fish in a buttered dish (using the remaining butter), pour on the wine, cover with foil, and cook for 50 to 60 minutes in a preheated oven at 170°C/325°F/gas mark 3. Transfer the fish to a serving platter, reduce the cooking juices, and hand around separately. (Salmon and rainbow trout can be cooked in the same way.)

This baked sea trout can be served with new potatoes and a dish of lightly cooked cucumber, a perfect accompaniment to this and the following salmon dishes.

Sefton of salmon

Serves 6

500g (1lb) cooked wild salmon fillet, boneless
    and skinless
25g (1oz) unsalted butter
6 free-range eggs
600mls (1 pint) milk
1 tablespoon white wine
salt
pepper
mace
1 tablespoon each finely chopped tarragon and
    parsley

Break the salmon into chunks or flakes. Generously butter
an ovenproof dish, and lay the salmon in the bottom. Beat
the remaining ingredients, and pour over the fish. Dot with
any remaining butter. Bake in a preheated oven at 180°C/
350°F/gas mark 4 for about 30 minutes, or until the custard
has set. Serve hot, warm or cold. The mixture can, of
course, also be baked in a pastry case as a salmon tart
or quiche.

Salmon burgers

Serves 2

400g (14oz) wild salmon fillet, or trimmings,
    skinned
2 or 3 spring onions, trimmed and finely
    chopped – optional
freshly ground black pepper
sea salt
dash of Worcester sauce and Angostura Bitters
2 focaccia or ciabatta buns
50g (2oz) unsalted butter, softened
1 teaspoon grated lemon zest
1–2 teaspoons lemon juice
1 tablespoon *mostarda di Cremona*, sold as
    'mustard fruit chutney', finely chopped

Remove any bones from the salmon, dice it, and then finely
chop it. Mix in the onion, if using it. Season lightly and
shape into cakes.

Warm and split the buns, and mix the butter, lemon and
mostarda, then butter the buns. In a non-stick frying pan,
sear the burgers on both sides and place on the buns. Serve
immediately. A fresh cucumber salad or salsa goes very well
with this.

Souchy of wild salmon

Serves 4

500–750g (1–1½lbs) wild salmon fillet
salt
pepper
salmon bones and head
celery stalk
parsley stalks
chives
tarragon stalks or lovage
850mls (1½ pints) full dry white wine
tarragon or lovage leaves – for garnish

Slice the salmon very thinly, season, and put to one side.
Make a broth with the remaining ingredients, and simmer
for 30 to 40 minutes. Have the soup plates very hot, and lay
the salmon pieces in them with the parsley, chives and
tarragon on top. Strain the boiling broth over the salmon,
and serve immediately, garnished with tarragon or lovage.

Salmon cured with Irish whiskey

Serves 8, plus leftovers

1 tail of wild salmon, when available, weighing
    about 1kg (2lbs)
5 tablespoons coarse sea salt
2 tablespoons light muscovado sugar
2 tablespoons freshly ground black pepper
2–3 tablespoons Irish whiskey
small bunch fresh dill

Have the fish scaled before dividing into two neat fillets.
Remove as many bones from the fillets as possible.

Mix the salt, sugar, pepper and whiskey.

Spread a few fronds of dill in the bottom of a rectangular dish, large enough to take the piece of fish. Spoon 3
tablespoons of the marinade over the dill, and lay one piece
of fish on top, skin side down.

Spread a further half of the remaining mixture on the
flesh side of each fillet of salmon, and sandwich the two
together with plenty of dill between.

The last of the salt mixture should be spread on the skin
side of the top fillet, covered with dill, then the whole thing
covered with film and weighted down for 2 to 3 days.

To serve, scrape off the dill and salt, drain off the liquid,
and slice thinly.

To cook a whole salmon

Wild salmon or sea trout will make an excellent main course for a special occasion, and you have a variety of ways to serve the fish. Leave it whole if you want to poach or bake it, perhaps en croûte or even in a bed of salt. Or you might want to serve it cold and garnished. Whichever way you choose, and even if you prefer it filleted, have the fish scaled first. Also measure its thickness, at the thickest point.

To poach a salmon, if you have a fish kettle large enough, put the salmon on the rack, lower it into the kettle, and just cover with water. Next remove the fish and rack, and put to one side. Into the water put half a bottle or so of white wine, some aromatics such as lemon zest, a sliver of ginger, a piece of celery, one of onion, a few handfuls of parsley and watercress stalks, some peppercorns and a bayleaf. Bring the water to the boil and simmer for 45 minutes or so. Bring it to a full boil, and lower in the fish on its rack. The water temperature will drop immediately. Allow the water to come back to simmering point, which will take longer for a larger fish than for a smaller one. For a salmon 5cm (2 inches) thick, allow about 17 minutes' poaching time. Three, 4 and 6cm respectively, require 6, 11 and 25 minutes' poaching. I am indebted to Alan Davidson for this technical information.

The fish should be carefully lifted out of the kettle, for serving hot, warm or cold. A sauce can be made by reducing some of the cooking liquid, adding some chopped herbs, a little cream and seasoning. New potatoes and hollandaise sauce (see p. 27–8) are the perfect accompaniments to poached salmon. If a whole fish is too daunting to cook, have it filleted and divided into neat serving portions, and use something like the recipe below. I have included a recipe for left-over cooked salmon.

Potted salmon

An excellent way of using up cooked salmon, this is better not made in a food processor, which turns it into salmon paste. I prefer the slightly uneven texture achieved when making it by hand.

Use equal quantities of softened unsalted butter and cooked salmon, or slightly more fish, depending on your taste.

Season the fish lightly, and pull it apart with two forks until you have a pile of shreds. Either clarified or very soft butter can be used. Stir it into the salmon until well mixed. Season to taste, adding mace or nutmeg if liked, and pot in a jar or ramekins. Top with clarified butter if planning to keep it for a few days in the refrigerator. Cooked undyed smoked haddock is very good prepared in the same way.

Seared wild salmon with mashed potatoes and stewed corn and tomatoes

Serves 4 to 6

2 or 3 corn cobs
4 or 6 ripe tomatoes of a good size
4 or 6 x 175g (6oz) pieces of wild salmon, skin
    on, but scaled
salt
pepper
about 750g (1½lb) potatoes
butter, milk or olive oil
fresh basil

Discard the husks and silk from the corn. Stand each one upright in a shallow bowl or plate, and cut off the kernels with a sharp knife; put to one side.

Halve the tomatoes, and squeeze out the seeds. Chop or dice the tomato flesh. When tomatoes are going to be cooked only briefly, as in this recipe, the skins do not need to be removed; they will not have time to become detached, and roll up into tight, disagreeable little spikes.

Lightly season the tomatoes and the salmon fillets, and put these to one side. Peel, cut up and boil the potatoes until tender, and then drain and mash them with whatever additions you choose, keeping them warm.

Put the corn and tomato in a saucepan with a nut of unsalted butter or a little extra-virgin olive oil, and some shredded basil. Allow this to simmer on the gentlest pos-sible heat, while you cook the salmon.

Have a non-stick or well-seasoned pan very hot, and in it put the salmon, flesh side down, for 30 seconds or so. Turn the fish over, and let it cook on the skin side until done to your liking.

Spoon the vegetables onto heated plates, the mashed potatoes on top, and then place the piece of salmon on top of each heap. Extra basil can be used for garnish.

Lime and tequila grilled salmon

Serves 4

4 x 170g (6oz) wild salmon cutlets
4 tablespoons olive oil
2–3 tablespoons tequila, in a teacup
1 lime, grated zest and juice separate
fresh, coarsely ground black pepper
fresh coriander leaves and lime wedges
   – for garnish

Brush the fish all over, first with olive oil and then tequila, and let the flavours mingle for 20 minutes or so. Then brush with the lime juice, sprinkle on the pepper and lime zest, and cook under a hot grill, or on a griddle, until cooked to your liking. Serve with a salsa, sliced avocado, and mashed potatoes into which you have mixed a little finely chopped green chilli, coriander and chives.

Some of the marinade ingredients make a drink not unlike margarita. It is called Border Buttermilk, a mixture of frozen lime juice and tequila, and a little syrup, if you like, or salt.

Aromatic steamed salmon trout

One evening, I cooked dinner for my brother and sister-in-law, visiting from Hong Kong. I showed them the silver, gleaming salmon trout that I had bought that morning from Emi at Hampstead Seafoods, my local fishmonger. How long are you going to steam it? Bettina asked. About 12 minutes, I told her. She approved, as 14 minutes would have been much too long. She was concerned lest I overcooked the fish head, which she delicately dismantles and elegantly consumes with chopsticks.

Serves 4 to 6

approx. 1.25kg (2½lbs) salmon or sea trout
seasoning
large thumb of ginger
1 medium onion
2 celery stalks
parsley stalks
1 lemon grass stalk or lemon zest

Have the fish scaled and cleaned and cut off the fins. Season the fish lightly. Lightly oil the tray which fits inside the fish kettle, and place the fish on it. Put it in a cool place. Put about 1.15 litres (2 pints) water in the fish kettle, and place the aromatics in the kettle in such a way that the rack will fit on top and you can still get the lid on. Cutting a narrow slice off the top and bottom of the onion before halving it gives a firm base. Put the lid on, and bring the water to the boil. Put the fish, on its tray, inside the kettle, put the lid back on, and steam for 12 minutes. Remove from the heat, and lift the tray out of the kettle to prevent the fish cooking more. Transfer to a serving platter, and serve hot, warm or cold.

When salmon trout is in season, in early summer, Jersey potatoes and samphire are perfect accompaniments. The samphire, after picking over and rinsing, I simply blanch for about 2 to 3 minutes, drain, and toss in a little butter. If you can get enough of it, it makes a marvellous first course to a fish dinner, eaten like asparagus in the fingers and dripping with melted butter.

Steamed fish needs no sauce, but on the other hand, a white wine and butter sauce would not be out of place. Such a sauce can also be flavoured with soy sauce, crushed lemon grass, fresh ginger or other aromatics, if you wish to heighten the oriental overtones. I like to eat steamed fish with extra-virgin olive oil over it and the potatoes.

Red wine, mint and olive sauce

Rich fish, such as salmon and salmon trout, can be accompanied by red wine quite happily.

Here is the red wine sauce I made to accompany the steamed salmon trout and a delicious bottle of 1979 Chateau Trotanoy. It is a dark, glossy sauce. Whilst fish stock is the usual ingredient for fish sauces, it is by no means de rigueur, and I have often used chicken stock; for this sauce, I used a pale sticky stock made with pig's trotters. With a meat or vegetable stock, this is also a good sauce for grilled lamb or chicken. Fish stock is not as versatile; it does not taste good in a sauce made to accompany meat, except in one or two very specific recipes such as the crayfish sauce Nantua, which in classical French cookery is served with chicken. Tapenade can replace the olive paste, but will, with its capers and anchovies, give a different flavour.

Serves 4 to 6

300mls (½ pint) good red wine
300mls (½ pint) stock

leaves of 3 or 4 mint sprigs

pinch of coarse sea salt

2 teaspoons black olive paste

freshly ground black pepper

50g (2oz) unsalted butter, chilled and diced

Boil the wine and stock until reduced to about 150–200mls (¼–⅓ pint). Tear up the mint leaves, and crush with the salt in a mortar. Stir it and the olive paste into the sauce. Bring to the boil, and season with the pepper. If the wine is somewhat acidic, you may, at this point, need to add a pinch of sugar to balance the sauce. Then whisk in the chilled cubes of butter, one or two at a time, until it has all been absorbed by the liquid and you have a quite thick, glossy, emulsified sauce.

Fideuada with allioli and salmon

The next recipe is based on a classic dish of Catalunya, *fideuada*, in which pasta is cooked in broth and served with allioli. The method, however, is more like that for a risotto, and sounds very bizarre. It is an extremely unusual and delicious dish, and I highly recommend it. In Catalunya it is more usually served with shellfish, but I have discovered that it and salmon go surprisingly well together. The crudités are to be dipped in the mayonnaise and eaten in the fingers, adding to the communality of the pot.

I am aware that authentic Catalan allioli requires nothing more than garlic, crushed in sea salt in a mortar, to which is added, drop by drop, olive oil, until the two cohere into an unctuous, opaque, golden-green mass. Impressive if you get it right, frustrating if the mixture splits. I suggest a compromise of good-quality mayonnaise, preferably homemade, into which you stir plenty of crushed garlic.

Serves 8

1kg (2lbs) salmon fillet, scaled

sea salt

freshly ground black pepper

2 tablespoons olive oil

500g (1lb) spaghettini or other thin dried pasta, broken into short pieces

fish or shellfish stock – for quantity, see recipe

homemade garlic mayonnaise

raw fennel, carrots, small tomatoes, cucumber batons, spring onions, celery

Season the fish, cut into 8 even pieces and put to one side while you cook the pasta. Heat the oil in a large saucepan or sauté pan and in it gently fry the pasta until pale golden brown, taking care not to burn it, which is easily done. Have the stock simmering in another pan and add a ladle or so to the pasta. When it has almost been absorbed, add more, and so on until the pasta is tender. As with risotto, it is difficult to say exactly how much liquid you will need, as this depends on the thickness of the pasta, how dry it is, how humid the atmosphere is, and so on. But generally, you should allow one and a half times liquid to solid, and perhaps up to twice the amount. The finished dish should be very definitely moist, but not swimming in liquid; the liquid is inside the pasta, as it were.

While this is cooking, get griddle or grill very hot, and cook the salmon just before you are ready to serve. Put the pasta in a bowl, the salmon on a platter with the crudités, and the garlic mayonnaise in another bowl.

Arctic char with mint sauce

Serves 6

6 x 175g (6oz) arctic char fillets

freshly ground black pepper

fine sea salt

1 fresh lime

sauce

½ teaspoon coarse sea salt, crushed with about 15g (½oz) fresh mint leaves, plus extra for garnish

3–4 tablespoons crème fraiche

75mls (⅛ pint) each white wine and fish, chicken or vegetable stock

Season the fish on both sides with the salt and pepper. Grate the lime zest on to the fish flesh, and squeeze on just a little lime juice, keeping the rest for a salad dressing. Leave for 20 minutes, and then heat a large well-seasoned or non-stick pan, and cook the fish, skin side down, for about 5 minutes, when the skin will be quite crisp. Turn the fish over with a spatula, and cook the underside for a minute or two. Transfer the fish to warm plates, and pour the stock and wine into the pan to reduce them.

Stir in the crushed mint leaves and crème fraiche. Season with a dash of lime juice and a little pepper, if liked, and pour around the fish fillets. The crisp skin is very good to eat.

The perfect fish cake

YOU NEED, for each fish cake, equal proportions of flaked fish and dry mashed potatoes, quantities according to your appetite. There is no mystery to it. And there is no virtue in making it with anything other than cod or haddock. Salmon fish cakes are positively boring. And there is nothing to be gained by using more fish than potato. You also need salt and pepper for seasoning, flour or breadcrumbs for coating and olive oil for frying.

METHOD Mix fish and potato together in a bowl, and, if you wish, add some very finely chopped fresh parsley with the seasoning. Shape first into a ball, and then flatten to a cake. Dip in breadcrumbs, if you like, or flour. Heat a tablespoon or so of olive oil in a small frying pan, and gently lower in the fish cake. Fry until golden, and then turn it over carefully, and fry the other side until crusty and golden.

TO SERVE Tomato sauce, pesto, parsley or egg sauce, tartare sauce, mango chutney, or what you will.

Chilled herring roe mousse

Herring roes are inexpensive, widely available, quick to cook and highly nutritious. Whenever I cook them, I always think I should do so more often. They have long been a part of our gastronomic heritage, often used in savouries and breakfast dishes such as devilled herring roes, a simple dish in which the roe is fried in butter and spiced with cayenne or chilli and a little lemon juice, and served piled on toast.

On a recent visit to southern Spain, I came across a marvellous dish of scrambled eggs and herring roe, *revuelta de hueva de leche*, a speciality at Bar Bigote, on the waterfront in Sanlucar. It, too, is simple to make. Gently fry the roe in olive oil or butter for a few minutes, then pour on beaten eggs and cook until creamy, breaking up the roe with a wooden spoon as you stir. Season lightly and serve with toast, or Sanluquena style, with triangles of bread fried in olive oil.

Try this next dish using cold poached herring roe.

Serves 4

500g (1lb) cooked herring roe
½ teaspoon grated horseradish
2 tablespoons finely shredded watercress
salt
pepper
150mls (¼ pint) double cream, whipped
1 free-range egg white, whisked to peaks

Make a purée of the herring roe and horseradish, and then stir in the watercress. Season lightly, and fold in the whipped cream and whisked egg white. Chill until firmed up, and then serve in scoops with hot toast or crusty bread.

Smoked haddock and leek salad with pumpkin seed and sherry vinaigrette

Smoked haddock is one of my favourite foods. It is a versatile ingredient, good for breakfast or supper, in soups, salads and pastry dishes.

Serves 4

12–16 baby leeks, or 4 large ones
400g (14oz) undyed smoked haddock fillet
1 tablespoon aged sherry vinegar
1 teaspoon molasses, dark muscovado sugar
    or black treacle
1–2 teaspoons Japanese soy sauce
4–5 tablespoons pumpkin seed oil
freshly ground black pepper
2–3 tablespoons lightly toasted pumpkin seeds

Trim the leeks and rinse thoroughly. Split the baby ones down the middle. Cut the large ones into shreds. Steam or boil until tender, drain and rinse under cold water. Divide amongst 4 serving plates. Poach or steam the fish and place on top of the leeks.

Whisk together the rest of the ingredients, for the dressing. Pour this around the fish, and scatter the seeds on top before serving.

Potatoes

The British have always been, I had thought, amongst the world's connoisseurs of potatoes. Then I went to Colombia and Ecuador. In a supermarket in the fashionable part of Bogotá one Friday evening, I saw the locals, the *santaferenos*, choosing from a huge range of potatoes, and buying several different kinds – for soups, for stews, for frying, for baking and for mashing.

Potatoes now play a more prominent part in our own cooking, and not just a supporting role. You are meant to notice the architectural pile of square-cut chips, the truffled potato purée, the bright saffron mash and the crushed potato tart. And fortunately, we now have a wider variety to choose from, no longer just whites, reds and new potatoes.

Autumn is the best time of year for home-grown main-crop potatoes, which come on to the market in September. These are generally the potatoes more suited to boiling, baking and mashing. For salads and for crushed potatoes I find Charlotte, Pink Fir Apple and the Scottish variety, Shelagh, good.

With its restrained, subtle flavour and texture, the potato is a perfect foil for other foods, flavours and textures. Use it in the homeliest preparations, as well as the most luxurious. Bubble and squeak, stelk (the Scottish version of champ – potatoes mashed with onion, leeks or spring onions, sometimes other greens, served in a bowl with a puddle of melted butter in the middle) and colcannon are amongst our most economical traditional dishes. Rustic and simple, they are good on their own, or perhaps with a piece of ham or some grilled sausages. Cheese and butter, or herbs and olive oil, make a jacket potato an inexpensive yet highly appetizing treat. At the other end of the spectrum, potato combines with caviar, foie gras, smoked salmon, salmon roe, and indeed, with oysters. Hollow out and parboil small potatoes, brush with butter, slip in an oyster, and bake in a hot oven. Delicious.

Smoked haddock with leek mash

Serves 2

2 potatoes, peeled and diced
2 leeks, trimmed and thinly sliced
butter
salt and pepper
freshly grated nutmeg
milk
350g (12oz) undyed smoked haddock fillet, skinned

Put the potatoes and leeks in water, and boil until soft. Drain, keeping the water, if you like, as a soup or risotto base.

Mash the vegetables with butter, salt, pepper, grated nutmeg and a little milk. Divide the fillet in two, and place on top of the mash. Cover with a lid, and set over the lowest possible heat to prevent the mash from burning, but enough to let the fish cook in the steam.

Serve in heated shallow bowls, with or without a poached egg.

Smoked haddock with mashed potatoes, Savoy cabbage and Lancashire cheese sauce

Serves 2

1 large potato, peeled and cut into chunks
butter, milk or olive oil, to taste
6–8 Savoy cabbage leaves, central rib removed
2 x 175g (6oz) pieces undyed smoked haddock, skinned
freshly ground black pepper
pinch of ground mace
25g (1oz) butter
1 tablespoon plain flour
200mls (7oz) fish stock or milk
150g (5oz) crumbled farmhouse Lancashire

Boil and mash the potatoes, using butter, milk or olive oil, if you wish, to get the desired texture. Keep the potatoes warm.

Slice the cabbage leaves across into narrow strips, and

blanch in boiling water for 3 to 4 minutes. Drain, rinse, and put to one side.

Season the fish with the pepper and mace, while you make a béchamel sauce (p. 26) with the butter, flour and stock, or milk. When cooked, stir in the cheese.

Put the fish in a lidded non-stick pan with a slick of butter, and let the fish sweat, covered, until just cooked, about 4 to 5 minutes should be enough. If necessary, to heat it, drop the cabbage back into boiling water, or pour a kettle of boiling water over it. Divide the cabbage between two plates, top each with a mound of mashed potato, and place a piece of fish on top. Spoon over the sauce, and flash under a hot grill before serving.

Skate, smoked salmon and courgette terrine

Serves 8

4 sheets or teaspoons gelatine
600mls (1 pint) each good dry white wine and
    water
1 celery stalk, chopped
slice of fresh ginger – optional
piece of orange zest
2 bay leaves
1 sprig each of tarragon and thyme
handful of parsley stalks
1 teaspoon peppercorns
2 teaspoons salt
1kg (2lb) skate, carefully sliced from the bone
    (retain the bones)
250g (½lb) smoked salmon trimmings
200g (7oz) 'light' cream cheese or crème fraiche
4 courgettes, sliced lengthways and blanched

Soak the gelatine by just covering it with cold water, taken from the measured amount. Simmer the aromatics and skate bones in the remaining liquid in a saucepan for 30 minutes. Strain into a wide, shallow pan, such as a sauteuse, or frying pan.

Carefully lower the fish into the simmering court bouillon and poach for about 5 minutes. Remove the fish carefully, and drain it on a clean towel or kitchen paper.

Strain the cooking liquid and measure out just over 450mls (16oz) into a jug. Stir in the softened gelatine until it has dissolved. Season the liquid to taste, bearing in mind that as it cools, the flavour will weaken. (Remaining stock can be used for soup.)

Put to one side any large strips of smoked salmon, as

these can form a layer in the terrine. Blend the rest with the cream cheese and 150mls (¼ pint) of the gelatine liquid.

Layer the fish, smoked salmon cream and slices of courgette in a terrine lined with clingfilm. Pour on as much of the remaining gelatine liquid as the terrine will hold. Cover carefully and refrigerate until set. To serve, turn out, slice and accompany with a few salad leaves and a well-flavoured vinaigrette, dill mayonnaise or spicy tomato and loose horseradish sauce.

Baked Gulf red snapper

Serves 2

1 red pepper
1 onion, peeled and thinly sliced

Fish

1 fennel bulb, trimmed and sliced in thin wedges

2–3 tablespoons extra-virgin olive oil

2–3 tablespoons fino

thick piece of Gulf red snapper fillet, 400–500g
    (about 1lb)

2 tablespoons black olives

fresh mint or coriander

salt

pepper

½ lemon or orange

a few thin slices of chorizo or cured ham,
    shredded or not – optional

Peel the pepper, quarter, discard the seeds, and cut into strips. Put in a shallow ovenproof dish with the onion and fennel, add half the oil and wine, cover with foil, and cook in the oven or on top of the stove until the vegetables are soft, about 20 minutes or so.

Season the fish with salt, pepper and the grated citrus zest and juice. Place it on top of the vegetables, first cutting it into serving pieces, if you wish.

Add the rest of the olive oil and fino, the olives, and a tablespoon or two of chopped fresh herbs.

Cover with foil, and cook in the oven at 180°C/350°F/ gas mark 4, for about 30 minutes. About halfway through cooking, add the chorizo or ham if using it.

Some Scandinavian and other northern flavours

Niewe haring needs no recipe. In Amsterdam's Albert Kuyp market, where I first tasted the new season's herring one Saturday in June, you simply tilt your head back, open your mouth, and gobble the herring like a sea-lion. The faint-hearted might slip it between a split roll to eat as a sandwich.

Although new herring is no longer the seasonal treat it once was, since it is now frozen and sold all year round, the new season, which opens on 25 May, is still celebrated. Rollmops, pickled herrings, *matjes* herrings and cured herrings, plain and in sauces, are available loose and in jars from supermarkets and delicatessens, to make a well-stocked buffet, accompanied by cucumber salad, beetroot in sour cream, potato salad and hard-boiled eggs.

'New' herrings are worth buying in Schipol airport's departure lounge, together with packs of smoked eel fillets. I once returned from Amsterdam full of renewed enthusiasm for smoked eel, having visited my friend Jean Beddington, who has had her own restaurant there for many years. Her smoked eel terrine is justly famous, and I thought her eel and potato soup, of which my recipe is a version, a fine dish for a cool summer's night. And chilled, it would be most welcome on a warm evening.

Alternatively, serve the rich eel fillets with crisp vegetables and a sharp dressing in a salad, or quite simply with brown bread, rye bread or *vollkornbrot* and a wedge of lemon. It makes for a luxurious instant starter to any meal.

Smoked eel and potato soup

Serves 6

2 onions, peeled and sliced

500g (1lb) potatoes, peeled and diced

25g (1oz) butter

1 bay leaf

600mls (1 pint) milk

600mls (1 pint) fish stock

pepper

5 or 6 thin smoked eel fillets, each about 125g
    (generous 4oz), cut into pieces

Sweat the onion and potato in the butter until translucent, then add the bay leaf, milk and stock. Simmer until the veget-ables are tender. Sieve, and bring back to the boil, season with the pepper, stir in the eel, off the boil, and serve immediately.

Smoked eel and parsley pâté

Makes 750g (1¹/₂lbs)

500g (1lb) smoked conger eel

freshly ground black or white pepper

½ teaspoon ground nutmeg or mace
2 shallots, peeled and finely chopped – optional
2 tablespoons finely chopped parsley
250g (½lb) unsalted butter, softened, or, if you
     prefer, sunflower margarine

Remove any skin and bone from the eel, put in the food processor with the rest of the ingredients, and blend to a smooth paste. Pack into individual ramekins or a large pot, which you keep in the refrigerator, and from which you scoop quenelles of the pâté as you need it. It keeps for 7 to 10 days. Half quantities can, of course, be made.

On balance, I prefer to serve it with a wedge of lemon rather than add lemon juice 'to taste' in the blending. You could add a little finely grated lemon zest to the pâté, however.

Using olive oil instead of butter, you can make a softer paste, and add garlic to it so that it takes on Mediterranean flavours.

Smoked eel and potato salad with soy and lime dressing

Serves 6 to 8

500g (1lb) broccoli, freshly steamed and broken
     into florets
distinctive salad greens, such as lamb's lettuce,
     purslane, rocket, burnett, watercress, sorrel,
     spinach shoots or whatever you have
     available
225g (8oz) smoked eel fillets, diagonally sliced
500g (1lb) new potatoes, freshly boiled and
     sliced
8 tablespoons sunflower or groundnut oil
1 tablespoon toasted sesame oil
1 tablespoon lime juice
1 tablespoon soy sauce

Heap the salad leaves on individual plates, and arrange the broccoli, potatoes and eel as you wish. Whisk together the rest of the ingredients, for the dressing, and spoon over the salad.

Scallop and dill pudding

Many years ago, long before I had ever been to Norway, I made with scallops a dish similar to fish pudding in miniature, which I used to serve with a sauce made of scallop roe. I have now brought the dish up-to-date and simplified it. I process roe and scallops together, which gives a delicate coral mousse, light in texture and subtle in flavour. A butter sauce heightened with lime juice and zest is the best accompaniment; in Norway a prawn sauce would be served with the white fish pudding.

Serves 6 to 8

8 large scallops with large corals, cleaned and
     trimmed
500g (1lb) whiting or cod fillet, skinned
350g (12oz) crème fraiche
5 free-range eggs, separated
salt
pepper
1 tablespoon lemon juice
grating of nutmeg
2 tablespoons chervil, chopped

Put all the fish in a food processor, and process until smooth. Add the cream, egg yolks, seasoning and herbs, and mix until smooth. Whisk the egg whites, and carefully incorporate into the fish mixture. Pour into a buttered ring mould, place in a roasting tin with a little water, and cook in the middle of a preheated oven at 150°C/300°F/gas mark 2 for about 35 to 40 minutes. Remove from the oven, allow to cool slightly and turn it out on a platter, pouring a generous helping of sauce in the middle. Alternatively, allow to cool, then refrigerate overnight. Turn out, garnish with fresh herbs and salad leaves, and allow to come towards room temperature before serving.

Buried mackerel

This is a favourite recipe for curing mackerel in the style of gravad lax.

Serves 4 to 6

2 medium-sized mackerel, carefully filleted and
     with all the bones removed
2 tablespoons coarse sea salt
1 tablespoon light muscovado sugar
2–3 teaspoons freshly ground black pepper
2–3 teaspoons crushed coriander seeds
1 tablespoon finely chopped coriander leaves
4–6 tablespoons apple juice
red and green apple slices

spring onions

sprig coriander leaves

dressing

6 tablespoons apple juice

2 tablespoons groundnut oil

1 teaspoon toasted sesame oil

2 teaspoons toasted sesame seeds

Place 2 of the mackerel fillets in a shallow dish, skin side down. Mix the salt, sugar, pepper, coriander seeds and leaves. Spread this over the fillets; sprinkle on some of the apple juice, and place the other 2 fillets on top, skin side up. Spoon the rest of the apple juice over the fish. Cover with clingfilm, place a weighted board on top, and leave in the refrigerator for 12 to 24 hours.

Scrape off the salt mixture then, to serve, cut the fish diagonally into thin slices, and place on individual plates with a small salad of thin red and green apple slices, spring onions and a sprig of coriander leaves. Mix the apple juice and oils together, spoon over the apples, and sprinkle the toasted sesame seeds over the top.

Pickling

We have the Scandinavians to thank for the pickled herring. The Vikings, to be exact. They taught the English East Coast and Scottish fishermen how to fish for the prolific herring with drift nets. Such large catches could not be disposed of as fresh fish, and the fish were salted to preserve them throughout the months when there was no herring fishing.

Pickling was introduced as a way of counteracting the saltiness of the fish, to make it more palatable. Now we are more likely to buy fresh herring than salt herring, so if you want to pickle it, the fish needs to undergo a short brining first to give it the authentic flavour.

In Scandinavia cured and pickled herrings are eaten at breakfast and lunchtime, when they are a main feature of the extensive 'open table', sometimes with a mustard and dill sauce, with beetroot and sour cream, or with curry sauce.

In Britain we are more likely to see them served as a first course. Pickled herrings are easy to prepare and they keep well in the refrigerator. If a dozen pickled herrings is rather more than you want, the following recipe can be adapted to prepare 4 to 6 herrings.

I have used a very aromatic pickle. If you do not like cloves and cardamom or want a hotter pickle, add dried chillies and mustard seed instead. It is the kind of recipe open to infinite permutations, and I should mention that salmon, sea trout and brown trout can be prepared in the same way to very good effect, not to mention char, mackerel and sardines.

As with all pickle recipes, pickled herrings are much improved by using a mature spiced vinegar, one in which the spices have first steeped for about three months.

Pickled herrings

Makes about a dozen

12 herrings of even size

1.25 litres (1 quart) water

175g (6oz) sea salt

1.25 litres (1 quart) white wine vinegar, spirit
    vinegar, distilled malt vinegar, or rice vinegar

2 tablespoons Demerara sugar

2.5cm (1 inch) piece fresh ginger

1 tablespoon whole allspice

1 tablespoon peppercorns, black, white, or
    mixed

12 cloves

12 cardamom pods, cracked and split open

cinnamon stick

2 teaspoons coriander seeds

4 bay leaves

3 mild onions, peeled and thinly sliced

Begin the preparation at least two days before required.

The herrings should be scaled, gutted, cleaned and filleted. For rollmops, the fish are left whole after scaling, gutting and cleaning but the head and backbone are removed.

Place the fillets in a deep container, and pour over them the brine made from the water and sea salt. Let them soak for 2 hours. During this time, prepare the spiced vinegar by putting the vinegar and the sugar and spices, together with a small handful of the raw onion, in a saucepan, and bring it all to the boil.

Simmer for 4 to 5 minutes, and then remove from the heat, and allow to steep for 30 minutes. At the end of this time, pour the spiced vinegar through a fine strainer into a jug. Alternatively, the pickling ingredients can be loosely tied in a square of muslin or wrapped in a paper coffee filter, which you then fold over and staple.

Remove the herrings from the brine, pat them dry, and with a pair of tweezers, remove any remaining larger bones. Layer the fillets in an earthenware or glass dish with the rest of the onions layered between them. Pour the vinegar over them, cover, and leave for at least 48 hours before eating, for the pickle to mature.

Pickled herrings are excellent on their own, served with bread and butter or sour cream; but they are also a useful salad ingredient, mixed with apple and celery, for example, or best of all, with warm diced potatoes, chives and sour cream, or olive oil.

Fish with spices

Summer fish dishes suggest scallop or prawn salads, cold poached salmon with cucumber, mayonnaise and new potatoes, or perhaps an ailoli – a platter of cooked salt cod, eggs, potatoes, vegetables and a thick garlicky sauce. Good as they are, why not ring the changes by cooking fish with chillies and spices? Chilli-hot food does indeed cool you down. I can remember feeling pleasantly refreshed after eating bowls of tom yam kung, a hot and sour soup of prawns, on steamy Bangkok nights, and plates of fish-head curry in the permanently clammy heat of a Kuala Lumpur summer.

Whilst the 'noble' fish such as sole, wild salmon and salmon trout, turbot, John Dory and red mullet are best accompanied by classic sauces and cooked according to classical techniques, we have a much wider range of fish to choose from.

I have always found halibut a rather difficult fish, dense in texture and very easy to overcook so that it is often dry and dull. For this reason, it is a good fish to serve raw in marinades, as a tartare, or as a component of *ceviche*, a dish found all over South America. Lime juice and chilli are its main ingredients. The fish can be varied, as can the extra ingredients such as peppers, tomatoes, onion and coriander.

And halibut is marvellous in spicy stews. Laurent Farrugia at Chez Laurent in north London cooks as good a couscous as you will find this side of the Mediterranean. Until recently, he would serve fish couscous if ordered in advance, but it is so popular it now stays on the menu. My recipe is inspired by his but, if you get the chance, you should try his original version.

This makes a lovely main course for a large supper party, needing little else to make it into a feast. Warm pitta bread, olives, toasted almonds, chick-pea salad, cucumber salad, stuffed vine leaves or spicy meat balls to start with, and sticky honey pastries or a salad of oranges and apricots, scented with rose-water or orange-flower water, to finish. Lager, dry cider or full-bodied rosé wine, will quench thirsts and match the robust flavours of the stew.

For a smaller gathering, I would serve the peppered cod, one of the best of all our fish, firm-fleshed and full of flavour. Like all fish dishes, this cooks quickly, and can form the main course of a speedy dinner party. To start with, I would serve thin slices of Charentais melon, inter-leaved with slices of cured ham, such as Bayonne, Parma, San Daniele or Denhay. A soft fruit fool would be just the right note on which to finish, or, if the weather is cooler, a mixed berry and apple crumble with almonds and oat flakes in the crumble.

The fish cakes made from leftovers will make a good lunch or supper dish, but they can also be made as miniature appetizers for a drinks party.

The first recipe is the one I always serve before my Colombian chicken and potato stew, *ajiaco* (p. 51), but it will start off most meals quite readily, unless you plan to serve your best white burgundy.

Fish and shellfish *ceviche*

Serves 8

250g (8oz) lemon sole fillets, skinned
250g (8oz) cod fillet, skinned
250g (8oz) monkfish fillet or halibut steak, skinned
8 scallops, cleaned
1 pasilla chilli, soaked
3 shallots, peeled and chopped

Chillies

Whilst no one could argue that chillies are an essential ingredient, our cooking would be the poorer without it. At the same time that chocolate was being tentatively explored in the kitchens of Spanish palaces and monasteries, the conquistadors were bringing back chillies. Cultivation quickly spread, as the Spaniards travelled south and east. Thus, chillies are now an integral part of the cooking of many countries, especially in the tropics. These small, bright, hot red, green, orange and yellow chilli peppers have always been available from shops and markets which serve Asian and Caribbean communities.

Now both dried and fresh are widely available, from the exceedingly hot bird peppers, orange Thai peppers, cayenne, and the crumpled Scotch bonnet peppers to the milder Hungarian wax, Serrano and Anaheim. Dried chillies reconstitute well in hot water, and can then be added and used as fresh chillies in your recipe.

Chilli-based sauces and seasonings are excellent with bland foods, and they are an essential in fresh lively salsas made with raw fruits and vegetables. On the subject of chilli 'heat', I suggest that if you come across one that you have never used before, it is safest to assume that it is hot until proved otherwise, and proceed accordingly.

Appearance can be some guide: dark green chillies tend to be hotter than pale green ones, and hotter than red, because on ripening to red, they sweeten, although 'sweet' is a relative term. When following authentic regional recipes calling for chilli, it is best to assume that you probably do not have the same tolerance for chilli as the writer of the recipe.

2 tablespoons fresh coriander leaves, chopped
sea salt
freshly ground black pepper
juice and grated zest of 2 limes

Cut the sole fillet's in half down the middle, and then into thin strips. Dice the cod and monkfish or halibut. Remove the muscle from the scallops, and separate the coral from the flesh. Leave each coral whole, and slice the round part in half. Put all the fish in a china or glass bowl. Slice the softened chilli, having first removed the seeds, and stir with the rest of the ingredients into the fish. This is best prepared just before serving, but if you need to prepare it in advance, stir in the lime juice no more than 10 minutes before serving, or the acid will make the fish as tough as if you had overcooked it. If you cannot get dried chillies, use whatever fresh ones you can find, proceeding with caution.

Peppered cod with thyme and garlic-flavoured mashed potatoes

We might think of green mashed potatoes as a modern recipe. Alice B. Toklas, in *Aromas and Flavours*, published in 1959, gave a recipe for just such a dish, the potatoes made green with basil, watercress and parsley.

Serves 4, plus leftovers for fish cakes

1kg (2lbs) cod fillet
4 tablespoons black peppercorns
2 tablespoons breadcrumbs, lightly toasted
1 tablespoon ground almonds
1½ teaspoons sea salt
extra-virgin olive oil
2 tablespoons thyme
1kg (2lbs) potatoes, peeled
cloves of one or two heads of garlic, peeled

Divide the cod into six even pieces. Grind the peppercorns in a mortar, and mix with the breadcrumbs, almonds and half the salt. Brush the fillets with olive oil, and coat the flesh side with the pepper mixture. Place the fish on a baking sheet or grill pan, pepper side up. Pound the thyme with the remaining salt in the mortar. Boil the potatoes and garlic. Mash them, and stir in the thyme and a little olive oil. Bake or grill the fish for 10 to 12 minutes, depending on thickness and how well done you like it. Serve with the mashed potato. Balsamic vinegar is a good condiment to serve with this dish.

Pepper fish cakes with chilli tomato sauce

Serves 2 to 4

2 left-over peppered cod fillets
left-over mashed potato
flour
sunflower or olive oil, for frying
1 small onion or two shallots
4 ripe tomatoes
1 or 2 red or green chillies
1 teaspoon molasses sugar
sea salt

Flake the fish, and mix with the mashed potato. I like to use equal quantities of each; you may need to boil and mash more potatoes. Shape the mixture into round flat cakes, lightly coat in the flour, and fry in hot oil until golden brown all over and hot all the way through. Peel the onion, halve and seed the tomatoes, and seed the chillies. Put in the food processor with the sugar and salt, process briefly, and serve with the fish cakes. The contrast between hot and cold is very appealing, but the tomato sauce can be heated if you prefer. Do not cook it, however, as it is intended as an uncooked sauce.

Roasted aromatic salmon

Serves 8

8 x 175–200g (6–7oz) pieces wild salmon or
    sea trout fillet
melted butter or olive oil
salt
pepper
grated zest of a lemon and its juice
1 tablespoon spice mix or mild curry paste
    – see recipe

Brush the fish all over with the butter or oil. Season it lightly. Put the lemon juice and zest in a bowl and then the spice mixture of your choice. It might be the Moroccan *ras el hanout*, a Lebanese fish spice mixture, Chinese five-spice powder, garam masala or a Thai spice mix. You might want something less intrusive and mix a little cinnamon, cardamom, ginger and ground saffron with the lemon.

Rub this mixture into the fish and place skin side up on a buttered baking sheet. Leave for 10 minutes, and then place in a preheated oven at 220°C/425°F/gas mark 7 for 5 to 10 minutes, or until done to your liking. If the fillets are of uneven thickness, you may wish to remove the thinner ones first.

Pockets of salmon stuffed with spiced spinach on a bed of couscous

Almonds, ginger, sultanas and sweet spices are mixed with spinach, and this is stuffed into a split salmon fillet, which is then steamed and served on a bed of couscous.

Serves 6

6 x 175g (6oz) salmon fillets
salt
freshly ground black pepper
grated zest of 1 orange
3 tablespoons orange juice
75g (3oz) unsalted butter
750g (1½lbs) young spinach, trimmed,
    well-washed and drained
1 teaspoon freshly grated ginger
½ teaspoon each ground cumin, cardamom and
    coriander
2 tablespoons each light muscovado sugar,
    sultanas and toasted pine nuts or flaked
    almonds
350g (12oz) couscous

Trim the pieces of fillet to a neat shape, and remove any bones. Cut a pocket in each fillet, and season lightly, also using half the orange zest and juice. Use a little of the butter to grease a heatproof dish.

Put the rest of the butter, orange zest and juice in a frying pan, and in it cook the spinach with the ginger, spices and sugar. Drain off any excess liquid and stir in the fruit and nuts. Fill the fillets with the spinach, put in the buttered dish and steam for about 6 to 8 minutes. Transfer the fish to individual plates and serve with couscous cooked according to the directions on the packet, and mixed with chopped fresh coriander, a few more sultanas, nuts and orange zest.

Curried tuna tartare

Serves 4

1 large cucumber
18 radishes

500g (1lb) well-trimmed tuna fillet

2 shallots, peeled and finely chopped

curry

2 tablespoons sunflower or groundnut oil

1 tablespoon garam masala, 1 tablespoon
medium curry paste or 1 tablespoon
curry powder

fresh lime juice

sea salt

Thinly slice the cucumber and radishes, and put to one side. Dice, and then finely chop the tuna fish. Chopping produces a better texture than processing. Mix the fish with the shallots. Fry the curry in the oil for 5 to 10 minutes, and then allow to cool before mixing with the fish. Add lime juice to taste and a little salt.

Quickly shape the fish into equal flat cakes, and put on plates. Arrange the cucumber and radishes as you please, and if you wish, garland the tuna with some fresh coriander. Serve with toast or fresh chapattis cut into wedges.

This is an excellent topping for canapés.

Popadum with warmed smoked salmon, cucumber, chilli and mint sambal with mango chutney

Makes 6

6 popadums

750g (1½lbs) smoked salmon, in a piece

1 jar mango chutney

sambal

2 cucumbers

1 tablespoon salt

several sprigs of fresh mint and coriander

1 teaspoon sugar

freshly ground black pepper

1 or 2 small green chillies to taste, seeded and
chopped

1–2 tablespoons desiccated coconut, toasted

lime juice

Cut the ends off the cucumbers, and peel them lightly with a swivel-blade peeler, leaving on enough green for colour. Split them down the middle, and discard the seeds. Thinly slice the cucumber's (I use the slicing blade of the food processor). Put in a colander set over a bowl, and sprinkle with the salt. Leave for an hour or two, and then rinse thoroughly, and squeeze dry in a clean tea towel. Strip the leaves from

the herbs, and put in a food processor or mortar. Grind to a paste with the sugar, pepper and chillies. Mix the paste, cucumber and coconut together, and add the lime juice and further sugar or salt to taste.

Slice the salmon vertically from top to skin into 18 slices.

Fry or grill the popadums according to the directions on the package. Place one on each plate. On a hot greased griddle, or large frying pan, warm through the salmon pieces, or keep them cold if you wish, and place 3 on each popadum. Spoon on a heap of mango chutney and one of cucumber sambal. Serve immediately.

Fish for Lent

I support my local fishmonger in an effort, thereby, to support our dwindling band of fishmongers, our unhappy fishing fleet, and all those who encourage them to stay in business. If this part of our national life and ancient heritage goes the way of coal-mining and ship-building, we will be well on the way to becoming a nation of supermarkets, service industries and theme parks.

But my other reasons for shopping at our local fishmonger, two or three times a week, are far from altruistic. I do it because we like to eat fish, and I enjoy cooking it. Occasionally, I even get a bonus. Once, as I was buying undyed smoked haddock and a thick piece of cod fillet, the man next to me, an American, was saying not to worry about the roe with the scallops that he was buying, as he threw that part of the scallop away. This is a strange American habit, one I have never been able to understand. In the end they were given to me.

I blended them with a little crème fraiche and egg yolk, spooned the mixture into greased dariole moulds and steamed the little custards. I then turned them out and served them with the cod fillets, which I sweated in a covered frying pan. A simple sauce of cooking juices, white wine and chervil accompanied them.

Squid and potato salad

Serves 4 to 6

750g (1½lbs) waxy salad potatoes, such as
    La Ratte, Charlotte or Belle de Fontenay
500g (1lb) small fresh squid
4 tablespoons extra-virgin olive oil
2 shallots or one small onion, peeled and
    chopped
coarse sea salt
freshly ground black pepper
lemon juice
fresh chervil, parsley, coriander or basil

Scrub and boil the potatoes. Clean the squid, and slice the body into rings. Leave the tentacles whole. Fry the squid in half the olive oil, just for a few minutes until opaque and firm, but not enough to overcook it.

Peel the potatoes, or not, and slice them. Mix together while still hot the squid and potatoes. Add the shallots and the rest of the olive oil. Season, and sprinkle with lemon juice to taste, before stirring in plenty of chopped or shredded herbs.

Serve while still warm or at room temperature, not straight from the refrigerator. This makes a lovely starter, served piled into Little Gem lettuce or radicchio leaves. As an alternative to using more olive oil, you can dress the salad in a lemony or garlicky mayonnaise.

Mackerel with mustard and coriander

Serves 4

4 mackerel, about 300g (10oz) each
4 dessertspoons mustard, grain, Dijon, tarragon,
    as you prefer
4 tablespoons finely chopped coriander, parsley
    or watercress
2 crushed cloves garlic – optional
seasoning
4 tablespoons wholemeal breadcrumbs

Ask your fishmonger to gut the mackerel and clean them, leaving the heads on or off, according to your preference.

Slash each side of the fish diagonally in three places. Mix the mustard, coriander, garlic and seasoning, and spoon it into the slashes. Press the breadcrumbs into the surface.

Use two roasting bags, and place two fish in each, tightly closing the bag's but cutting a slice in each to let the steam escape. Bake in a medium oven at 180°C/350°F/gas mark 4 for 25 minutes.

Tuna burgers on mashed potatoes with *gremolata*

Tuna lends itself to many recipes and techniques more usually applied to beef. The burger is no exception, and is truly a modern classic.

Serves 4

500–750g (1–1½lb) tuna fillet
salt
pepper
4 spring onions
2 teaspoons capers

The perfect sole à la meunière

This might sound like a fancy French recipe, but it is an extremely simple dish to cook, and relies more on good ingredients than intricate techniques. Who knows if the dish was indeed first cooked by a miller's wife whose hands were still floury when her husband brought home some fresh sole?

YOU NEED, for 2 people, 2 Dover soles, skinned, cleaned and trimmed, salt, some milk in a soup plate, plain flour in another, freshly ground pepper, unsalted or clarified butter for frying, some parsley or chervil and wedges of lemon.

METHOD Season the fish with salt, dip in the milk, then in the flour, coating them well. Season lightly with pepper. Have the butter melted and hot, but not burning, in a frying pan, and fry the fish on both sides until done to your liking.

SERVE the sole on heated plates with the butter poured over it, some chopped herbs and the lemon.

NOTE This is not an easy dish to cook for more than two people unless you have several frying pans, an otherwise unoccupied stove top, and some help in the kitchen for dishing up.

zest of 1 lemon – one strip, and the rest grated
4 large potatoes
parsley, finely chopped
4 cloves garlic, peeled and crushed

Cut the fish into several large pieces, season lightly, and put to one side.

Put the trimmed and chopped onions, the capers, and the strip of lemon zest into a food processor, and process until finely chopped. Add the tuna, and 'pulse' only until chopped, still reasonably chunky, not to a paste. Form this mixture into patties and chill, while you peel, boil and mash the potatoes, adding milk, olive oil, or potato water, as you prefer.

Stir in the *gremolata* – the parsley, lemon zest and garlic mixture.

Heat a griddle or frying pan, oiled as necessary, and cook the tuna burgers until done to your liking. I prefer them seared on the outside and rare inside. Serve on top of a heap of mash.

Fried hake with green sauce

Northern Spain has rich fishing grounds, and hake is a classic of the Basque kitchen. Green sauce, not unlike our parsley sauce, is one of the four classic Basque sauces, together with the black squid ink sauce, the white almond sauce or *picada*, and the red Basque sauce using pimentos, tomatoes and onions.

Serves 4

4 x 175g (6oz) hake steaks
salt
pepper
flour
beaten egg
lightly toasted breadcrumbs
oil or butter for frying

sauce
60g (2oz) unsalted butter or olive oil
2 or 3 shallots, peeled and finely chopped
2 teaspoons plain flour
100mls (3oz) good dry white wine
100mls (3oz) fish stock
100mls (3oz) single, or whipping cream
3–4 tablespoons finely chopped parsley
1 tablespoon chopped capers – optional

salt
pepper

Lightly season the fish, and put to one side while you make the sauce. Heat the fat in a saucepan, and gently sweat the shallots until soft. Stir in the flour, and gradually add the wine and stock. Bring to the boil, stirring continuously to ensure a smooth sauce. Cook for 10 minutes, and then add the cream and herbs. Cook for a few minutes more, and season to taste.

Dip the fish steaks first in the flour and then in the beaten egg and breadcrumbs. Heat the oil or butter, or a mixture of both, in a frying pan, and fry the fish, carefully turning it over once. Hake is a delicate fish, needing gentle handling and cooking. Serve fish and sauce together.

Monkfish with rhubarb

In this next, rather seasonal, dish the tartness of the rhubarb fulfils the same sort of need for the taste buds as lemon in other fish dishes. Buy from the 'shoulder' end of the monkfish to give you a thick and even chunk.

Serves 4

750g (1½lbs) monkfish
25g (1oz) unsalted butter
2 or 3 sticks rhubarb
150mls (¼ pint) fish stock
seasoning
2 tablespoons chopped flat-leaf parsley or
    watercress, plus some whole leaves for
    decoration

Skin the monkfish very thoroughly, removing all gristle and gelatinous skin. Cut from the central bone, leaving two thick fillets. Cut each into 4 equal slices.

Gently heat the butter in a frying pan. Peel the rhubarb, and cut into slender batons about 5cm (2 inches) long, and cook gently in the butter for 2 or 3 minutes. Remove, and keep the rhubarb warm. Place the slices of monkfish in the pan in a single layer, and cook gently for 6 to 8 minutes, turning once. Remove with a slotted spoon while you quickly make the sauce.

Add the fish stock to the frying pan, which will also contain some cooking juices from the monkfish. Reduce by half over a high heat. Season to taste. Strain on to heated dinner plates, and arrange the monkfish and rhubarb on top. Garnish liberally with the greenery, which is also important for the overall flavour of the dish.

ELEGANT DINNER FOR SIX

English crab cakes

Spelt and chestnut-flour open ravioli with game ragout

Individual apple and marzipan tarts with blackberry sauce

This menu is for a dinner that is elegant rather than casual. The crab cakes are so named because they are entirely different from the Thai crab cakes we are now familiar with; these use traditional English seasonings, rather than chilli and lime leaf. The main course is easy to make, with full instructions for making the pasta, and the game ragout can be made in advance. Apples and blackberries make simply the best, most classic autumn dessert imaginable, and this is a particularly pleasing version.

A Barbera from Piedmont, a Côtes du Rhône or a red burgundy would go very well with the main course; a Vouvray or Montlouis *moelleux* with the tart; and a crisp Chablis *Premier Cru*, with at least three years' bottle age, with the crab cakes.

English crab cakes

Makes 6 or 12

75g (3oz) fresh breadcrumbs
2 tablespoons walnut or olive oil
2–3 tablespoons full-cream milk
1 teaspoon English mustard flour
good pinch each of ground nutmeg and mace
½ teaspoon Worcester sauce
½ teaspoon Tabasco
dash of Angostura Bitters
juice of ½ lemon or lime and its grated zest
1 teaspoon freshly ground black pepper
1 tablespoon freshly grated horseradish

500g (1lb) fresh white crabmeat
2 free-range eggs, separated
butter or olive oil for frying
lime, lemon and deep-fried parsley – for garnish

Soak the bread in the oil and milk. Mix the rest of the seasoning ingredients, including the horseradish, and then stir in the crabmeat, the soaked breadcrumbs and the beaten egg yolks. Mix thoroughly. Whisk the egg whites to firm peaks, and fold into the crab mixture.

Form into 6 or 12 cakes, and fry in the oil or butter until golden brown. Serve with wedges of lime or lemon, and garnish with deep-fried parsley. A homemade tomato sauce makes a nice accompaniment, as does a horseradish cream, together with watercress, rocket or mizuna, or a mixture of all three.

Spelt and chestnut-flour open ravioli with game ragout

Serves 6

Ragout

500g (1lb) hare, venison and pigeon, off the
    bone
1 onion, peeled and chopped or sliced
1 tablespoon extra-virgin olive oil
1 pinch each of mace, cinnamon, ginger and
    cumin
grating of nutmeg
level teaspoon freshly ground black pepper
5g (⅓oz) square of bitter chocolate
200mls (7oz) good dry red wine
150mls (5oz) game or other meat stock
1 bay leaf
sprig of thyme

Make sure the meat is of roughly even-sized small pieces. Dry them thoroughly. Brown the onion in the olive oil, and transfer it to a casserole. Brown the meat in batches, and transfer also to the casserole.

Add the spices, chocolate and half the wine to the pan. Bring to the boil, scrape up any residues stuck to the pan, and then add the remaining wine and the stock.

Bring to a full boil, pour it over the meat, tuck in the herbs, cover, and cook in a preheated oven at 150°C/ 300°F/ gas mark 2 for about 2 hours, or until the meat is tender. Or cook on a low burner, whichever is more convenient.

Allow the dough to rest for a while, and then roll it out as thin as you can get it, without breaking it up. Cut into squares, about 10cm (4 inches), or whatever will best suit the plate you plan to serve this on. I tend to serve one large ravioli per person, but you may prefer to make smaller ones and serve 2 or 3 each.

By now, you should have the ragout ready to serve, for all that remains is to boil the pasta for a minute or two until soft, drain it, and assemble each dish.

Place a sheet of pasta on the plate, pour on a ladle of ragout, top with another sheet of pasta, spoon on a little more ragout, top with a sage leaf, and serve.

If you do not want to go to the bother of making your own pasta, buy some lasagne sheets, boil, drain, cut to size, and use in the same way.

Individual apple and marzipan tarts with blackberry sauce

Serves 6

300g (10oz) short (p. 29) or puff pastry
200g (7oz) marzipan
6 apples
500g (1lb) blackberries
sugar to taste
icing sugar

Roll the pastry out into 6 rounds. Roll out the marzipan very thinly. Cut into 6 slightly smaller rounds. Place on top of the pastry, and raise the edges of the pastry to make a roughly fluted border.

Peel, core and thinly slice the apples, and arrange in the tarts. Dust lightly with icing sugar.

Bake for 25 to 30 minutes in a preheated oven at 180°C/ 350°F/gas mark 4.

Meanwhile, cook the blackberries gently, having first rinsed them, and, when soft, rub them through a sieve. Sweeten to taste, and serve with the apple tarts.

As an alternative to the blackberry sauce, use fresh or soaked dried apricots, cook, then sieve them, and add a dash of almond or orange liqueur, if you wish. And instead of a fruit sauce, you could serve a butterscotch, caramel or honey sauce; all will go very well with the apple and marzipan tart. The game ragout can be replaced with a creamy preparation of chicken and tarragon or chives, or a shellfish ragout with prawns, mussels, what you will, in a cream or tomato sauce with dill, basil or chervil.

Ravioli

100g (4oz) spelt flour
150g (5oz) pasta flour or plain flour
50g (2oz) chestnut flour or unsweetened
    chestnut purée
3 medium free-range eggs, lightly beaten
sage leaves

If you are using chestnut purée, you will not need to use all the eggs. Put the ingredients in a food processor, and mix until you have a soft, but homogeneous, dough. Or mix by hand on a worktop, making a well in the flour, with the eggs in the middle, and gradually drawing in the flour.

Berries and
soft fruits

In summer, peaches, plums, melons and glowing soft red berry fruit, strawberries, raspberries and figs are piled high in the shops, for us to eat our fill of before it's time for the crunch of autumn top fruit. It goes without saying that the best way to eat summer fruit is au naturel, but occasionally one might want to do something a little more elaborate, and in this chapter I have included many of the recipes I try out during the summer months.

Blueberries are an increasingly available summer treat, both grown here and imported from America. In America they are cheap enough for me to cook with in quantity. I make blueberry jam, blueberry cobblers and crumbles, and I love them combined with sliced peaches and orange juice in a colourful fruit salad.

Like cherries, they freeze well, and you can also adapt my cherry recipes and suggestions to blueberries. Not as 'wet' as many other fruits, blueberries are also excellent in baking, as in the easy-cake recipe, made like a traditional pound cake, with equal quantities of flour, sugar, butter and eggs. The mixing can be done all at once in the food processor, as long as the butter is soft to start with.

A bowl of crème fraiche or thick plain yoghurt, and one of light muscovado sugar are the perfect accompaniment for freshly picked, unhulled strawberries; this makes a delightfully easy ending to a summer lunch or dinner.

But if your strawberries need a little more assistance, I would not cook them, but slice them instead, and pour on boiled, then cooled red wine, sweetened with sugar and spiced with orange zest and cinnamon. This is especially good with vanilla ice cream and meringues. A grinding of black pepper and a sprinkling of sherry vinegar are the Spanish treatment for strawberries, while in Italy, balsamic vinegar is used to anoint the fruit. Anna del Conte, doyenne of Italian cookery writers in Britain, goes one better, having used this flavour combination to develop a covetable recipe for strawberry and balsamic ice cream.

I use strawberries and balsamic vinegar to make an unusual vinaigrette, which is an excellent partner for summer cold cuts, but try it too with cold poached salmon or smoked haddock. A salad of sliced smoked chicken, quail or cooked ham, interleaved with slices of ripe avocado, is especially good with this dressing.

Strawberry and balsamic vinaigrette

Serves 8

500g (1lb) ripe strawberries
2–3 tablespoons water
2 tablespoons balsamic vinegar
2 tablespoons extra-virgin olive oil
sea salt
pepper
fresh basil – optional

Hull the strawberries and rinse.

Put in a blender goblet with the water, blend and sieve. Whisk in the vinegar and oil, and then season to taste.

I find basil exceptionally good with strawberries, and I would shred some into the vinaigrette before using it.

Strawberry and mint terrine with strawberry sauce, flavoured with balsamic and pepper

If you feel the strawberries that we buy here need some added flavour or more elaborate treatment, try my terrine with the balsamic flavouring, very elegant but not too grand, for a Mediterranean-style buffet.

Serves 6 to 8

7 gelatine sheets, or 7 teaspoons gelatine
   granules
1 bunch mint
1kg (2lbs) fresh strawberries, hulled and wiped
750 mls (1¼ pints) clear apple, grape or pear
   juice
black peppercorns
1–2 teaspoons *aceto balsamico tradizionale di
   Modena*

Soak the gelatine in a little water.

Wash and dry the mint in paper towels, and take off the leaves. Wet a jelly mould or terrine, and 'stick' on the mint leaves, right side to the 'wall'.

Bring 200mls (7oz) of the juice to the boil, and stir in the softened gelatine. Stir until it has dissolved, and then add 400mls (14oz) more juice.

Take 200–250g (about ½lb) of the softest strawberries, and make a purée with them and the remaining 150mls (5oz) juice in a blender, adding a little freshly ground black pepper. Sieve into a jug, cover and chill.

When the jelly is cool, start the terrine by placing a layer of strawberries in the mould, covering with jelly and chilling until set. Add another layer of strawberries and jelly, and when this has set, continue in the same way until fruit and jelly have been used up.

Chill until firm, turn out, slice, and arrange on plates.

Spoon the strawberry sauce around the terrine, coarsely grind over each plate a little black pepper, and on to the sauce drop a few tears of *aceto balsamico tradizionale di Modena*.

Raspberry ice cream

This is based on a recipe developed by the eminent Victorian cook, teacher and ice-cream specialist, Agnes Marshall.

Note: this recipe contains raw eggs.

Serves 6

300–400g (10–14oz) raspberries, rinsed
thinly pared zest of half a lemon and half an
    orange
200g (7oz) caster sugar
300mls (½ pint) milk
300mls (½ pint) single or double cream
almond paste
8 free-range egg yolks
15g (½oz) glucose – optional, for extra
    smoothness

Gently cook the raspberries with the citrus zest and half the sugar until they collapse, about 3 to 4 minutes only, in fact hardly enough to cook them, just to heat them through. Remove the seasoning and sieve to a purée. Heat the milk and cream and almond paste. In a bowl, beat together the eggs, the rest of the sugar and the glucose, if using it. When warm, add a quarter of the cream mixture to the egg mixture, and thoroughly incorporate. When the rest of the cream mixture boils, pour it over the egg mixture, beating continuously.

Sieve the mixture into a clean saucepan, and cook gently until it will coat the back of a spoon. Cool, stir in the raspberry purée, then freeze in an ice-cream maker or in a box in the freezer. An ice-cream maker will turn the mixture and make it smooth. You will need to stir the mixture by hand or in a food processor during the freezing process for a really smooth ice cream if you freeze the mixture in a container.

Cook apricots with crushed cardamom seeds, cherries with cinnamon, gooseberries with orange zest and make them into fruit ice creams using this same recipe. Or try Mrs Marshall's banana ice cream – blend 6 ripe bananas with a glass of Curaçao and the juice of two lemons, sieve, stir into the basic custard, the recipe for which I give on p. 27, and freeze.

Serve the ice cream in cornets, and arrange bouquet-fashion in a container, or serve scoops on shortbread biscuits, with extra fruit purée.

Fig and raspberry tart

Serves 6 to 8

250g (½lb) plain flour
125g (4oz) unsalted butter, chilled and cubed
2 tablespoons caster sugar
pinch of salt
1 free-range egg, separated, the yolk lightly
    beaten
iced water
small punnet of redcurrants
sugar
kirsch or *eau de vie de framboise*
8 fresh ripe figs, quartered
about 400g (14oz) raspberries

Sift the flour into a heap. Rub in the butter, and then stir in the sugar and salt. Add the egg yolk and enough iced water to bind. Gather the dough into a ball, cover and rest it for 20 to 30 minutes. Roll out, and line a 25cm (10 inch) diameter tart tin or quiche dish, and place it on a baking sheet. Prick the base of the pastry all over with a fork. Cover with foil and dried beans or macaroni kept for the purpose of blind baking. Put in the top half of a preheated oven at 180°C/350°F/gas mark 4, and bake for 20 minutes. Remove the foil and 'weights'. Brush the pastry with lightly whisked egg white, and return it to the oven for 5 minutes more until set. Remove from the oven and cool.

Make the glaze by cooking the redcurrants until soft with 2–3 tablespoons of water, and then sieving them back into a saucepan. Add sugar to taste, and cook until just syrupy. Stir in the *eau de vie* and mix well.

Arrange the fruit in the tart. Brush with half the glaze,

and bake in the oven, preheated to 180°C/350°F/gas mark 4, for 10 minutes. Remove from the oven. When cool brush with the remaining glaze and serve. Make sure that you crowd the fruit into the tart, as it will shrink on cooking and leave gaps for the pastry to show through.

Blueberry and hazelnut cake, with cinnamon crunch topping

Makes 1 loaf

100g (4oz) butter, softened
100g (4oz) light muscovado sugar, plus
   2 tablespoons for the topping
100g (4oz) self-raising flour mixed with
   1 teaspoon baking powder
2 large free-range eggs
100g (4oz) hazelnuts
100g (4oz) fresh blueberries
1 teaspoon ground cinnamon

Blend the first four ingredients to a smooth batter. Grind the hazelnuts, but not too fine, and keep back about 1½ tablespoons. Stir the hazelnuts and blueberries into the cake mix and spoon into a loaf tin, 1kg (2lbs) in capacity, lined with baking parchment. Make a depression down the centre with the back of the spoon. Mix together the reserved hazelnuts, sugar and cinnamon and sprinkle on the surface of the cake. Bake for about 45 minutes in a preheated oven at 180°C/ 350°F/gas mark 4, or until a skewer inserted in the middle comes out clean.

Remove from the oven, cool in the tin for 5 minutes, then lift out by holding the baking parchment, and allow to cool completely on a wire rack.

Blue cheese mousse with figs

This next recipe makes a good cheese course and dessert combined, or serve it as a starter.

Note: this recipe contains raw eggs.

Serves 4

250g (8oz) blue cheese, such as Yorkshire Blue,
   Lanark Blue, Harborne Blue, Cashel Blue or
   Devon Blue
200g (7oz) ricotta
150mls (¼ pint) thick Greek yoghurt
freshly ground pepper
freshly grated nutmeg

2 free-range egg whites
fresh figs as available
rocket and watercress leaves – for salad

Put the cheeses and yoghurt in a food processor, and blend until smooth. Season with the pepper and nutmeg; the mixture will probably be salty enough.

Whisk the egg whites to firm peaks, and fold into the cheese. Line a pierced mould with wet muslin or cheescloth, and spoon in the cheese.

Place on a plate, and refrigerate for a few hours until firmed up. Turn out onto a plate, and surround with quartered fresh figs and a salad of rocket and watercress or other peppery leaves.

Strawberry and white chocolate tart in almond pastry

Serves 8

300g (10oz) plain flour
100g (4oz) ground almonds
175g (6oz) unsalted butter, chilled and diced
50g (2oz) icing sugar, sifted
1 teaspoon pure vanilla essence
1 free-range egg, lightly beaten
iced water, as necessary
200g (7oz) white chocolate
1kg (2lbs) strawberries
5 tablespoons redcurrant jelly
600mls (1 pint) whipping cream – optional

Sift the flour and ground almonds. Rub in the butter, stir in the sugar and add the vanilla essence, egg and enough water to bind to a smooth dough. Cover and chill for half an hour or so. Roll out the pastry and line a greased and floured 25cm (10 inch) loose-bottomed flan tin or ring set on a prepared baking sheet. The ground almonds make this quite a fragile pastry, and if you find it difficult to roll out, press it over the base and up the side of the prepared tin. Trim off the edges of pastry, and prick all over with a fork. Line with foil or greaseproof and cover the base with ceramic baking 'beans' or dried beans.

Bake 'blind' (empty) in a preheated oven at 180°C/ 350°F/gas mark 4, for 20 minutes. Remove the beans and lining paper and return the pastry to the oven for 5 to 8 minutes more to complete the cooking, pricking it again if it has puffed up. Remove from the ring and cool on a wire rack.

Melt the white chocolate gently in a bowl set over hot water and brush all over the inside of the cold pastry case. Once it has set, you can fill the tart. If you wish you can crush most of the strawberries, once hulled, with the whipped cream and pile into the tart, decorating the top with the best whole strawberries, in which case you will not need the redcurrant glaze. Alternatively, pack the strawberries in the pastry, pointing skywards. Melt the redcurrant jelly, allow to cool slightly but not set. Brush it over the strawberries. Serve the whipped cream separately, or, if you prefer, pouring cream, crème fraiche, vanilla ice cream or Greek yoghurt.

Canteloupe and strawberries with spiced claret syrup

Left-over red wine usually goes into sauces and casseroles, but from time to time, I use it for a syrup. Put equal volumes of red wine and sugar in a saucepan with a cinnamon stick, a few cloves, some nutmeg, and a spiral of orange zest. Bring to the boil, and simmer for 5 to 10 minutes. Allow to cool, and then strain into a clean juice bottle, and store in the refrigerator. Alternatively, bottle in glass while hot, and sterilize the bottles.

A few drops of this syrup are excellent with soft fruits. For a simple dessert, halve a ripe canteloupe melon, and scoop out the seeds. Quarter a few strawberries, and fill the centre of each melon half with them. Pour on a little syrup, and chill until required, not too long or everything in the refrigerator will smell of melon.

Red fruit jelly

This next recipe can be prepared a day in advance. Use whatever soft fruits are available. Blueberries, too, should be considered.

Serves 6 to 8

1 bottle Pinot Noir
caster sugar to taste
fresh lemon juice to taste
6 leaves or teaspoons of gelatine
1kg (2lbs) raspberries, strawberries, cherries
    and redcurrants

Bring the wine to the boil, and let it cook for a few minutes for the alcohol to evaporate. Sweeten the wine to taste, also adding lemon juice if you think it needs it, and in the hot liquid dissolve the gelatine, which you have first softened in a little cold water. Cool the liquid, and pour a little into a 1kg (2lb) loaf tin. When it has set, pack in a layer of prepared

fruit, wiped, topped and tailed, as necessary. Pour on a little more wine jelly, and let it set before adding the next layer of fruit. Continue until all the fruit has been used up and is covered with the last layer of wine set to a jelly. Any remaining liquid should also be poured into a tray and set, so that the jelly can be chopped and used to decorate the fruit jelly when it is turned out. A raspberry-flavoured chantilly will go well with this, and is made by whipping cream with *eau de vie de framboise* and a little icing sugar to sweeten.

Summer fruit in muscat wine

Serves 6

6 ripe apricots
3 white-fleshed nectarines

The perfect gooseberry crumble

This simple recipe makes one of the most appealing of all traditional English puddings. If you can add a couple of sprigs of elderflowers, well rinsed, the flavour will be ambrosial. Use the same method for apple, apricot, plum, pear, blueberry and other fruit crumbles in season.

YOU NEED about 1kg (2 lbs) gooseberries, topped and tailed, a vanilla pod, and golden granulated or light muscovado sugar to taste. For the crumble: 125g (5oz) plain flour, 75g (3oz) butter, 50g (2oz) ground almonds, 75g (3oz) light muscovado sugar and 25g (1oz) flaked almonds

METHOD Simmer the gooseberries in 2–3 tablespoons water for 10 to 15 minutes with the vanilla pod and the elderflowers, if using them. Remove the pod and flowers. Sweeten the fruit to taste and transfer to a buttered baking dish or individual ramekins. Rub the flour and butter together, stir in the ground almonds and sugar, keeping the mixture loose. Spoon the crumble over the fruit, and scatter on the flaked almonds. Bake at 200°C/400°F/gas mark 6 for 15 minutes.

TO SERVE Hot or warm, with cream, ice cream, a custard or crème anglaise sweetened with elderflower syrup.

a dozen or so large red dessert gooseberries

200g (7oz) cherries, stoned weight

500mls (18oz) muscat wine

Prepare this at least a day before required. Halve the apricots, slice the nectarines, top and tail the gooseberries and stone the cherries. Put the fruit in a large preserving jar, cover with the wine, seal the jar and refrigerate. Remember to take long forks or skewers to spear the fruit – fondue forks are ideal.

As an alternative try blueberries and blackberries as well as black cherries in red dessert wine such as sparkling Malvasia, Banyuls or Elysium made from the black muscat grape.

For a non-alcoholic version, use red or white grape juice to macerate the fruit.

Cherry time

High summer is the middle of the cherry season throughout Europe. By late June the trees are full of ripening fruit. In and around Fougerolles in the Franche-Comté sour cherries, *griottes*, are being harvested to make kirsch and maraschino, highly fragrant distilled white spirits, and to be preserved as *griottines*. French markets are piled with trays of cherries from the Tarn and Garonne valleys, and in the Basque country the curé of Itxassou will, with luck, not have to go over the border to buy cherries in Spain for the village's Fête des Cerises. A local chef once told me that this is what sometimes happens if the cherry season is late.

Cherries are not the only fruit that herald midsummer, but I find cherries the most tempting. Cherry jam is one of my favourites, yet stoning cherries can be a messy and lengthy process, and you really have to stone them if you are making jam or preserving them. There are gadgets such as olivestoners and also a French *truc* for stoning cherries in which the cherries are placed in a chute, a lever is pressed, the stones drop into a clear plastic container and the cherries slide into a bowl. Since the cherry season is so short in England too, perhaps we should not begrudge the time spent on them. Switch on the radio for some gentle music or the afternoon play and you will have stoned a kilo or two in no time. Then you can make jam, ice cream, sauce, Black Forest cake, pancake fillings, cherry pie

and various accompaniments to meat and poultry dishes.

There are two main types of cherries, sweet and sour. Over three hundred varieties of sweet cherries and six hundred varieties of sour cherries have been recorded, but as with most horticultural and agricultural produce, only a few varieties are available commercially. Some headway has been made in the reintroduction of traditional native apple varieties, and it would be very cheering to think that the same might happen for cherries. Brogdale Horticultural Trust in Kent, the home of the National Apple Collection, also maintains the hundreds of cherry varieties which used to be grown in Britain, such as the pre-1914 Newington Black, Rodmersham Seedling and the White Heart. You can visit, and decide which might be suitable for growing in your own garden or orchard.

Of the sweet cherries, we are most familiar with the gean or *guigne* and the heart or *bigarreau*; the first have soft, tender, juicy flesh and include Waterloo, Elton, Eagle, Early Purple and Black Tartarian. The hearts are firmer, sweet-fleshed with a slightly crisper texture, if something as tender as a cherry can be described as crisp. Windsor, Schmidt and Mezel in Britain, *burlat*, *reverchon*, *van* and *coeur de pigeon* in France, all belong to the heart or *bigarreau* group. One of the best-known is the Napoleon, pale-fleshed with a pinkish-yellow skin flushed with red. With its agreeable balance of sweetness and acidity, this one is excellent for preserves; it used to be known as the Kentish Nap. Of the modern hybrids, Stella is perhaps the most widely available, as is the Duke, a cross between a sweet and sour cherry.

Amongst the sour cherries, also known as morellos and amarelles, are the Montmorency and the Kentish cherry. These are excellent for preserves, but also for serving with meat dishes. Indeed, expect any dish described on a menu as 'Montmorency' to have cherries in it somewhere. They may no longer be, as they should, of the Montmorency variety, but it serves as a reminder of the small town of the same name just outside Paris, which used to supply Les Halles with cherries.

As well as English and French cherries, mention must also be made of one considered by some to be the very finest, the Moretta from Vignola near Modena in northern Italy. These are the best dessert fruit, crisp, juicy and full of flavour. In recent years, very fine cherries have also been imported from Valle del Jerte in Spain, from Washington State in America's Pacific Northwest, and, of course, from Turkey. I say of course, for there is evidence that in 69 or 74 BC – sources differ – Lucullus, the Roman general and epicure, brought the cherry tree to Rome from Pontus on the Black Sea, now Turkey, from a town called Cerasus, which has given its name to the cherry in many languages. Nevertheless, there is further evidence as early as the fourth century BC, in Theophrastus' writings, that the wild cherry, the gean or mazzard, *Prunus avium*, was known in Europe. It is thought that today's dark morellos and clear, red amarelles are descended from the Turkish cherry.

Cherries were first planted in Oregon in 1847, and are now an important crop. Some 25 years later, the Bing cherry was developed there by a Chinese orchardman named Bing. A hundred years ago, for Queen Victoria's Diamond Jubilee, the dish of flamed cherries and vanilla ice cream was devised in her honour by Escoffier.

In the thirteenth century cherry trees were planted in the royal garden at Westminster, and by 1629 thirty-five varieties of cherries were documented. Dried cherries we might think of as a trendy modern ingredient from California, but not a bit of it. Reference is made to them, as causing constipation, in the earliest French cookery book, written in Latin in the sixth century AD by Anthimus, a Greek doctor exiled in Ravenna at the court of Theodoric the Ostrogoth. Eaten as appetizers, to 'open the stomach', cherries were one of the few fruits to be eaten raw in medieval England. However, when there were gluts of fruit, they were dried or otherwise preserved.

There are, through the ages and in different cultures, far fewer recipes using cherries than apples, for example, the general view being that they are so much better raw. The earliest cherry recipe I have found is a medieval one, in which the cherries are picked at the Feast of St John, 24 June, when they will be beautifully ripe; they are then crushed to provide juice, and this is mixed with wine, breadcrumbs, sugar and a little butter, cooked gently for 10 to 15 minutes and allowed to cool and set. It is almost identical to a recipe cooked in Turkey today, *visneli ekmet tatlisi*. Morello cherries are used and when the pottage has set, it is spread with *kaymak*, Turkish clotted cream. Mrs Beeton has a very good

recipe for cherry tart, Miss Acton one for pickled cherries and Hannah Glasse a recipe for preserved cherries. My recipe for cherry jam is based on the one made almost certainly for Henrietta Maria, Charles I's queen. It is recorded in 1682, in *The True Preserve* by George Hartman, who was steward to Sir Kenelm Digby, the Queen's Chancellor, and publisher of many of his recipes, during and after his lifetime.

My first real encounter with cherries was not until I was a student in Freiburg in the Black Forest. Tom and I used to travel between there and Switzerland by scooter the length of the Basler Landstrasse. It was lined with cherry trees, for the local kirsch and jam industries. We would stop and pick some fruit every few kilometres, eat it, scatter the stones and stop for more. Sticky red mouths and fingers were one result, but I always hope that our scattering of stones on the verges produced more cherry trees in the ensuing years.

A note on buying cherries

Stemless cherries are now being sold in the shops, supposedly a little cheaper than the stemmed fruit. They are of a variety which can be harvested mechanically, by being gently shaken from the tree, when they detach themselves from their stems. However, I have always used the stems as a guide to the condition of the fruit. Bright green fresh-looking stems mean freshly picked cherries. Withered brown stems indicate fruit picked some time ago, and it will often be soft to the bite, rather than almost crisp. Without stems, how can one judge the freshness of the fruit? Sound, unsplit fruit will keep for up to six days in the refrigerator if covered.

Cooking with cherries

It goes without saying that the best way to eat cherries is freshly picked and au naturel, but occasionally one might want to do something a little more elaborate, and I have included some of my favourite cherry recipes and ideas.

Stir some stoned cherries into thick plain yoghurt, and you will never buy fruit yoghurt again. For an even more delicious cherry and yoghurt combination, one day I blended a handful of highly scented red damask rose petals with a couple of teaspoons of granulated sugar, stirred the result into thick plain yoghurt, and served it with cherries on the stem. Blend some ripe stoned cherries with skimmed milk, and float a scoop of frozen plain yoghurt, or vanilla ice cream, on top for a very superior milk-shake. Fill a plain sponge with whipped cream, into which you have folded ripe stoned cherries, and dust with icing sugar for a tea-time treat. Cherries are delicious in crêpes, and with pancakes for breakfast, stirred into maple syrup. Try cherries, too, in lovely dark red sorbets. And try a cherry and almond crumble, just the thing to serve after a summer dinner of mainly cold dishes.

Cherry jam

Makes about 2kg (4lbs)

1kg (2lbs) granulated sugar (depending on the
    sweetness of the fruit)
150mls (¼ pint) each raspberry and redcurrant
    juice, squeezed and strained from the fresh
    fruit
1.5kg (3lbs) stoned cherries
juice of one lemon, strained

Put the sugar and 150mls (¼ pint) of the juice in a saucepan, and heat gently until the sugar has dissolved. Add the rest of the juice and pour over the cherries in a bowl or enamel pan. Next day, bring everything to the boil, including the lemon juice, and boil rapidly until setting point is reached. Spoon into clean, hot jars, seal and label. Strawberry jam can be made in exactly the same way.

Kissel

I learned how to make kissel many years ago from a landlady whose family had lived in Russia. We also made it from redcurrants and other soft fruit. It is a lovely, jewel-coloured soft pudding, similar to the Scandinavian *rødegroed.*

Serves 4 to 6

500g (1lb) stoned cherries
1.15 litres (2 pints) water
150g (5oz) sugar
50g (2oz) potato flour

Simmer the cherries and water for 10 minutes. Crush, in the pan, with a large wooden spoon, electric hand blender or potato masher, and cook for a further 2 minutes. Strain into a clean saucepan, add the sugar, and heat the juice. Mix the flour with 2 tablespoons of cold water, and stir into the juice as soon as it comes to the boil. Stirring all the time, let the mixture boil for 1 minute. Remove from the heat, and then pour into a bowl. The mixture will set to a soft, smooth jelly-like texture as it cools. The mixture should not be allowed to boil for more than 1 to 2 minutes for its final cooking, or the starches will break down and the mixture remain liquid.

Visino (Cherry preserve)

Here is a recipe I learned from my Greek friend, Meni.

Makes about 1kg (2lbs)

1kg (2lbs) cherries, stoned
400–500g (about 1lb) unrefined granulated
    sugar
½ lemon

Leave the sugar and cherries to macerate in a bowl overnight. Use the lesser quantity of sugar if the cherries are very sweet.

Boil for 20 to 25 minutes, and add the juice of half a lemon towards the end of cooking. When setting point is reached, pot in hot jars, seal and label.

To make *visinada* use twice the amount of sugar, strain after cooking, and produce a syrup.

Cherries in red wine jelly

Serves 6

3 leaves or 3 teaspoons gelatine
450mls (¾ pint) good dry red wine
250g (½lb) stoned sweet cherries
sugar to taste

Soften the gelatine in 150mls (¼ pint) of the red wine. Put the cherries and remaining wine in a saucepan, and bring gently just to simmering point. Remove from the heat and strain the hot juices over the gelatine. Stir until the gelatine has dissolved. Sweeten the liquid to taste. Wet a 500g (1lb) loaf tin or jelly mould and put in the cherries. Pour on the liquid, and when cold, refrigerate until set. Turn out of the mould and serve.

Cherry meringue pudding

Serves 6 to 8

1kg (2 lbs) prepared cherries
150mls (¼ pint) full-bodied red wine, such
    as a Rhône
175g (6oz) caster sugar
600mls (1 pint) thick custard (see p. 27)
3 free-range egg whites

Put the fruit, wine and half the sugar in a saucepan, and cook gently until the fruit is just tender.

Spoon into an ovenproof glass bowl or dish, adding some of the juice but not enough to cover the fruit, which should provide a firm base for the custard. Spoon this smoothly over the fruit. Whisk the egg whites with half the remaining sugar, and then gradually add the rest until the meringue is firm and glossy. Spread over the custard, and cook in the bottom half of a very low oven at 150°C/300°F/gas mark 2 for about 45 minutes. The meringue should not be allowed to colour too much. Serve warm.

Swiss cherry crumble

I devised the next recipe a few years ago when staying in a friend's chalet in the Swiss alps. We would go down to the valley to shop, and, as it was early July, we feasted on cherries.

Serves 6

Crumble

6 heaped tablespoons plain flour
125g (4oz) unsalted butter, chilled and diced
2 tablespoons unsweetened muesli
2–3 tablespoons demerara sugar

Rub the flour and butter together until it resembles coarse breadcrumbs. Stir in the muesli and the sugar.

Fruit

25g (1oz) unsalted butter
500g (1lb) fresh or bottled morello cherries, stoned
1 teaspoon cornflour
1 teaspoon caster sugar
2 tablespoons kirschwasser

Butter an ovenproof dish, and put in the fruit. Mix the cornflour and sugar, and sprinkle over the fruit. Spoon the

crumble over the top, except for a small hole in the middle, which you keep open with a rolled paper tube. Bake the crumble for 30 minutes or so in a preheated oven at 200°C/400°F/gas mark 6, turning it down a notch or two after 15 minutes. Remove from the oven, take out the paper roll, and carefully pour in the kirschwasser. Serve warm. Incidentally, never buy Kirsch Fantaisie, not even for cooking; cherries have been nowhere near it.

Peaches

Late one summer, driving through the blue-grass country of northern Kentucky on two-lane black tops instead of the interstate motorways, we stopped late one afternoon at a farm-stand next to a peach orchard. We bought half a bushel of peaches, still warm from the sun, picked about an hour before, with fresh, firm leaves still attached. And truly, the first one was the most exquisite peach I have ever tasted. The skin offered a slight velvety resistance, and then yielded to a burst of sweet, yellow flesh, which dripped with juice. That is how fruit should be eaten, fully ripe, freshly picked, and eaten straight away, rather than being brought out of a cold store and stacked on shelves.

With store-bought fruit, try this lovely crumble recipe.

Peach, oatmeal and almond crumble with wine custard

Serves 4 to 6

Fruit

25g (1oz) unsalted butter
6 ripe, firm peaches, halved and stoned
1 orange
1 lemon
1–2 tablespoons light muscovado sugar

Butter an ovenproof dish, and in it place the peaches, hollow side up. Grate on the citrus zest, and squeeze on all the orange juice and half the lemon juice. Sprinkle with sugar all over.

Crumble

- 75g (3oz) unsalted butter, diced
- 25g (1oz) rolled oats
- 75g (3oz) plain flour
- 25g (1oz) ground almonds
- 50g (2oz) flaked almonds
- 75g (3oz) light muscovado sugar

Rub the butter into the oats and flour, to a breadcrumb texture. Stir in the ground almonds, half the flaked almonds, and the sugar. Spoon over the peaches, and top with the remaining almonds. Bake at 180°C/350°F/gas mark 4 in a preheated oven for 30 to 40 minutes. Serve warm with wine custard.

Wine custard

- 300mls (½ pint) sweet white wine
- 3 free-range egg yolks
- 2 tablespoons double cream

Boil the wine and reduce it by half. Place the egg yolks in a bowl, beat in the cream, and pour the boiling syrup slowly into the egg mixture, whisking continuously. Strain the mixture back into the saucepan. Cook over a very low heat, stirring all the time with a wooden spoon until just thick enough to coat the back of the spoon. Serve hot, warm or cold.

Mediterranean fruit

Loquat curd

For their brief season in late May, loquats are high on my shopping list. They are not widely available, and are easily damaged in transit. When ripe, the skin changes from unblemished, smooth, bloomy and apricot in colour, and develops brown patches. This puts off many buyers, and the fruit, particularly on street barrows and market stalls, is often sold very cheaply. Lovely in a simple compote or fool, loquats also make good sorbets, ice cream and jam. They can be substituted for apricots in many recipes, and make exotic chutneys and pickles, and a particularly rich and unusual curd.

Makes 6 to 8 servings, plus leftovers

- 500g (1lb) loquats
- 250g (8oz) caster sugar
- 3 free-range eggs
- 125g (generous 4oz) unsalted butter, diced
- lemon juice and grated zest, to taste

Rinse the loquats, removing any damaged parts, and halve them to remove seeds. Cook gently until soft, using as little water as possible – steaming is best. Rub through a sieve into a large bowl set over simmering water. Stir in the caster sugar, and then the eggs and butter. Stir frequently until the mixture thickens. It always takes much longer than I expect it to, and just starts to happen the instant before I decide to give up. Even then, I always wonder if it will thicken when cool. Of course, it will. Consider the amount of butter, which will cause it to set. This is a marvellous tea-time treat with fresh scones and clotted cream.

For a very simple dessert, cut rounds of brioche or challah, fry them in butter or simply toast. Spoon on the curd, and top with a little cream or crème fraiche. Keep the rest refrigerated, and use within 3 to 4 weeks.

Date and honey bread-and-butter pudding

Here is a Mediterranean fruit pudding recipe suitable for a cool night. I included it in the cookery course I taught in Andalusia, Spain, having been inspired by the Huerto del Curo, the date-palm groves in Elche near Alicante, and the small shops nearby selling the locally grown dates.

Dried stoned dates and honey together cook down to a rich, dark syrupy layer, between the baked bread and butter, soaked in a mixture of beaten egg, milk and dessert wine. You could use Malaga, muscatel or cream sherry. Unrefined sugar can be used in place of honey, if you prefer.

To make this pudding with Medjool-type dates would be generous indeed, and it would make a splendid pudding. (A more everyday type of dried fruit, such as you might use for baking, will also be very good.) And if these dates are a little hard, pour a small amount of boiling water over them, but not enough to wash away the flavour, only enough to soften them.

Serve the pudding warm, not steaming hot, and accompanied by chilled vanilla custard, ice cream, or thick yoghurt.

Serves 6

What you need is good white bread, sliced, and enough to loosely fill your chosen ovenproof dish. Generously butter the bread, one side only, with unsalted butter, and grease the dish with it.

Allow a handful of dates per person – 5 or 6 smaller ones, or 3 Medjool dates. Stone and chop them.

For six people, beat 3 free-range eggs into 500mls (18oz) milk and 100mls (4oz) sweet wine, together with a tablespoon of sugar.

Layer half the bread in the dish, and then cover with the chopped dates, the juice of half a lemon, and 2–3 tablespoons unrefined sugar, or honey. Top with the remaining bread.

Gradually pour the batter over the pudding, and allow it to stand for 45 minutes or so.

Bake in a preheated oven at 180°C/350°F/gas mark 4 for about 45 to 60 minutes, covering the top if it shows signs of burning or cooking too crisp.

If you have a Pyrex dish with a lid, put the lid on, the pudding will puff up to fill it, and the top will brown nicely but not be too crisp. As it cools, of course, the pudding will subside.

Apricot *clafoutis*

Ripe apricots need no cooking, but if they are not quite ripe, try them in this simple pudding. *Clafoutis* is the name of the traditional harvest dish from central France, a baked batter pudding stuffed full of ripe cherries. The name is now used in France and elsewhere to describe dishes cooked in a similar fashion, and sometimes not so similar. I have come across *clafoutis* baked in pastry crusts, but I do not believe it was ever intended to be such a complicated dish. Here it is in its simplest version. Like many custard/quiche-like dishes, this is best served warm with whatever accompaniment you like, clotted cream, ice cream, yoghurt, cream, or crème fraiche.

Serves 4

about 12 apricots
50g (2oz) unsalted butter
100g (4oz) self-raising flour, sifted with
   1 teaspoon baking powder
150mls (¼ pint) milk

2 free-range eggs
50g (2oz) light muscovado, or golden caster
   sugar

Halve the apricots, and discard the stones.

Use half the butter to grease a pie dish, and arrange the apricot halves on the bottom. Dot with the rest of the butter.

Make a thick batter with the rest of the ingredients, and pour over the fruit. Allow to stand for 15 minutes, and then bake for about 50 minutes in the middle of a preheated oven at 180°C/350°F/gas mark 4.

Dust with icing sugar, and serve hot, warm or cold with cream, yoghurt, custard or vanilla ice cream.

La compota

Here is the perfect recipe for combining dried fruit with fresh fruit.

Serves 6 to 8, with plenty of leftovers

200g (7oz) each of dried apricots, peaches,
   prunes and figs, plus the following, although
   optional: cherries, cranberries, muscatels
   and raisins
3 fresh hard pears, peeled, cored and quartered
3 fresh apples, peeled, cored and quartered
6 plums, halved and stoned
1 bottle good dry red wine
2 cinnamon sticks
about 200g (7oz) sugar

Soak the dried fruit overnight in 600mls (1 pint) water. The next day, drain the fruit, and put into a saucepan with the fresh fruit. Put the soaking liquid into another saucepan, together with the wine, cinnamon and sugar. Bring to the boil, and reduce by half. Pour over the fruit, bring slowly to the boil, and simmer for 10 to 15 minutes. Remove from the heat, and allow to cool.

Seville oranges and other citrus fruits

Oranges from the Alcalde

Every January, just as the Seville oranges begin to arrive, I alternate between writing a 'not the marmalade' column and one about nothing else. On the whole, I like to use these lovely sharp fruit in as many ways as possible, as well as for marmalade.

One January we were in Andalusia and the orange trees in Jerez were laden with fruit. It was so mild that the blossom was already coming out. Lack of rain meant that the oranges were very small, and few were being picked. The oranges belong, I discovered, to the town hall, to the *alcalde* or mayor. I was told that a contractor had been called in to pick them and sell them to Britain's marmalade-makers.

All this conjures up a romantic image of shady orange groves. In fact, the fruit trees line the narrow car-choked streets of the towns and cities of Andalucia, and who knows what poisonous fumes they absorb. The fruit was too tempting, however. To me, their small size indicated that, although not very juicy, they would be very concentrated in flavour. And so they proved to be. We picked some from trees furthest from the road in Jerez, and within less than twenty-four hours after returning to London, I had made a small batch of bright, tangy marmalade. The rest of the scrumped oranges, I used in my kitchen.

First I took one orange and peeled off long, thin strips of zest, put them in a decanter, and filled it up with a cream sherry. I rubbed a sugar lump over the orange to take up the rest of the fragrant essential oils, added it to the decanter, together with a splash of Iberian brandy. The idea is to leave this *vino aromatizado con naranja* for several weeks, and then serve it in small glasses as a digestif. It was a wine much enjoyed by the Jerezanos in the past. I also find it very good indeed for cooking – just a dash used in a duck casserole makes all the difference. And if you are a gin and tonic fan, forgo the lemon just once for a slice of Seville orange and you will look forward to it henceforth as a seasonal treat – an excellent tip passed on to me by the head of the Sherry Institute in London, somewhat heretically, I thought. Campari and soda benefits in the same way.

The juice of Seville oranges is very useful in the kitchen. I use it in fish cookery such as roasted skate with Seville oranges, scallops and red mullet with orange sauce, and it is particularly good with mackerel and other oily fish. My friend José Antonio Valdespino, at the restaurant La Mesa Redonda in Jerez, serves thin slices of tuna marinated in a little sherry vinegar and Seville orange juice with extra-virgin olive oil. Try this variation from my own kitchen.

Orange-marinated tuna fish

Serves 4 to 6

500g (1lb) trimmed fillet of tuna fish
extra-virgin olive oil
sea salt
freshly ground black pepper
1 or 2 Seville oranges, juice only – use the zest
    in another dish
fresh dill, chives or flat-leaf parsley

Slice the tuna fish as thinly as possible. Firming it up in the freezer helps. Brush each slice with the oil, and season lightly with salt and pepper. Leave for up to 3 hours, covered, in the refrigerator. Just before serving, brush with the orange juice. Decorate with the herbs and serve. You can serve this as finger food by placing the tuna fish on endive or Little Gem lettuce leaves.

Skate with olive oil and orange

Serves 4

1kg (generous 2lb) skate wings, in 4 pieces
4 tablespoons extra-virgin olive oil, plus extra for
    frying
sea salt
freshly ground black pepper
4 tablespoons plain flour
1 or 2 Seville oranges

Wipe the fish with kitchen paper. Brush with olive oil, grate on a little zest and brush with orange juice. Mix the seasoning and flour and coat the fish in it lightly. Fry the fish in olive oil, then arrange on heated dinner plates. Garnish with herbs, vegetables or salad leaves, and serve with boiled, steamed or mashed potatoes.

Heat the remaining fresh olive oil, mix with orange juice to taste, season and pour it over the fish at the table.

Charred squid salad with wilted greens and a mint and Seville orange dressing

Serves 4

750g (1½lbs) small squid, or 500g (1lb)
    ready-prepared squid rings
extra-virgin olive oil
sea salt
freshly ground black pepper
approximately 200g (7oz) prepared greens,
    such as shredded spring greens, watercress,
    spinach, rocket or chard
2 or 3 garlic cloves, peeled and crushed
handful of mint leaves
1 Seville orange
1 teaspoon honey or maple syrup

Clean the squid and cut into rings. Toss them in the oil and seasoning and cook them on a griddle or in an iron frying pan until cooked, with a little light charring here and there, but not burnt. Put to one side.

Cook the greens by stir-frying or steaming and season well. Heap the greens on four plates and top with the squid. Put any cooking juices in a bowl. Grind the garlic and mint leaves in a mortar, add the Seville orange zest, the honey, cooking juices and more olive oil and mix, with seasoning, finally adding the orange juice. Pour over the greens and serve. Instead of cooked greens you can use salad leaves. This dressing is also very good on the fat white spears of canned asparagus from Spain.

Fish steaks with orange and anchovy sauce, on a bed of spinach

Serves 2

2 cod or haddock steaks
salt
pepper
1 Seville orange

1 teaspoon extra-virgin olive oil
1 can of anchovy fillets, drained
1 bag of baby spinach, thoroughly rinsed and
    dried

Season the fish with the salt and pepper. Grate the orange for zest, rub some on the fish and squeeze a little of the juice on it.

Heat the oil in a non-stick or well-seasoned pan and fry the fish until done to your liking. Transfer to warm dinner plates.

Meanwhile crush or finely chop half the anchovies, keeping the rest for another dish, and add to the pan together with the rest of the orange juice and zest. Add a little more olive oil if you wish. Bring to the boil and stir in the spinach until just wilted. Serve with the fish.

Pot-roast pheasant with Seville orange

Pheasants, particularly hen pheasants, are large and plump by January, the end of the season. Even though they have, by this time, accumulated more fat than early in the season and can thus be roasted without barding, I still prefer to pot-roast them, preferably on a bed of onions, garlic and root vegetables, which caramelize nicely. The bitter-sweet juice of the Seville orange replaces the more usual lemon. Chicken and guinea fowl also respond well to this treatment. Before roasting a duck, prick it all over, and rub with the juice of a Seville orange, tucking some of the zest inside the body cavity.

Serves 4

1 large pheasant
1 Seville orange
salt
pepper
4 bay leaves
parsley stalks
2 parsnips
4 carrots
1 small celeriac or a celery heart
4 small turnips
2 tablespoons butter or extra-virgin olive oil
2 tablespoons Spanish brandy
4 tablespoons dry Amontillado or Oloroso
    sherry

Trim off any feathers and excess fat from the bird. Peel the zest from the orange and put it in the cavity. Halve the orange, discard the seeds, and squeeze out the juice. Rub the bird all over with the cut orange, season it, and put the bay leaves and parsley stalks inside the cavity. Peel the vegetables and cut into even-sized pieces, about the size of a cork. Heat the butter or oil, and fry the vegetables all over. Transfer them to a casserole, brown the bird all over, and place it on top of the vegetables. Pour the brandy over the bird, and, standing well back, light it. Deglaze the frying pan with sherry and the orange juice, and pour the juices over the bird. Cover and cook in a preheated oven at 180°C/350°F/gas mark 4 for about an hour.

Joint the pheasant, and serve it with the vegetables. Strain the juice into a jug, and serve separately. It can be enriched with cream if you like. A bunch of watercress or flat-leaf parsley will brighten up the dish, as will a few wedges of orange. When I picked the oranges in Jerez, I also came across a tree with pretty palmate leaves, the *Schinus terebinthifolius*, whose fruit is the pink peppercorn. Not a member of the pepper family, the pink seeds, nevertheless, add a pleasing piquancy to meat and fish dishes, as well as a note of colour. I used a few in the pot-roast bird recipe.

Seville orange marmalade

I make no claims for this being the best, easiest or most economical recipe for marmalade, but it works for me and makes just the right quantity, a few jars ranging in size from yoghurt jars to jam jars, some for me, some for friends. I am not interested in making as much marmalade from as few oranges as possible.

You need a large pan, a large measuring jug and a large weighing bowl on your scales, a long-handled spoon, and plenty of patience.

Marmalade-making is not rocket science. Quantities can never be exact. For example, you might simmer the oranges longer than I do; they might need it if they are less than fresh. Thus more water will evaporate in cooking them; you might push more pulp through your sieve than I do; that affects overall weight. Your oranges might contain more juice or pectin than mine. If, as I sometimes do, you use too small a pan, you will have to let it off the boil occasionally to stop it bubbling over. All this affects cooking time and quantities of sugar and water.

All that said, marmalade is not difficult to make, using this very basic recipe, and will leave you with the glowing satisfaction of having filled jars and jars for your store cupboard, as well as for presents.

Makes about 4–4.5kg (9–10lbs)

1.5kg (3lbs) Seville oranges
about 2.5 litres (4 pints) water
about 3kg (6lbs) granulated sugar
lemon juice, if necessary

Rinse the oranges, put in a large saucepan with the water and simmer for an hour or so until soft. Remove from the heat, and allow to cool.

Halve the oranges, scoop out the pulp and seeds into a sieve set over a bowl, and scrape through.

Finely slice the orange halves, or process for a few seconds in the food processor. Add to the sieved mixture and weigh.

For every 500g (1lb) of peel and sieved pulp, stir in 600mls (1 pint) cooking water, making up the quantity if necessary with water or lemon juice, or a little of both. Weigh it again.

For every 500g (1lb) of this mixture, add 625g (1½lbs) sugar and put everything in a large pan.

Heat gently, and when the sugar has dissolved, bring to the boil and continue cooking until setting point is reached; about half an hour at full boil will do it.

Allow to stand for 15 minutes to distribute the peel evenly. Fill hot, clean jars right to the top. Cover with waxed discs and cellophane covers, label, and store when cool.

Another version of Seville orange marmalade

Makes about 2.5kg (5lbs)

12 fresh Seville oranges
1.2 litres (2 pints) water
about 1.75kg (3½lbs) granulated sugar

Scrub the oranges well, rinse, and put in a lidded saucepan with the water. Cook covered, gently, for 2 to 3 hours until soft. Remove from the heat and allow to cool, overnight if this is convenient. Halve the oranges, scoop out the pulp and seeds into a sieve set over a wide pan. Rub through, and add the cooking liquid and the sugar. Heat gently, and when the sugar has dissolved, boil for a few minutes.

Meanwhile, finely slice the orange peel, or process for a few seconds in the food processor. Stir the orange peel into the boiling sugar syrup. Continue cooking just until the marmalade reaches setting point. Allow to stand for 15 minutes to distribute the peel evenly. Fill small hot, clean jars right to the top. Cover with waxed discs and cellophane covers, label, and store when cool.

There is invariably a little marmalade left over. Serve it hot over vanilla ice cream, use it to flavour a homemade ice cream, or stir it into a freshly made rice pudding.

Seville orange curd

Extremely rich and rather time-consuming to make, orange curd, like lemon curd, is something of a luxury. It is tempting to make it in large batches, on the principle that, since it takes so long to make, it is worth making plenty of it. It is a temptation to be resisted unless you plan to give lots away or use some of it immediately in Seville orange ice cream. The reason for this is that the curd does not keep long, no more than four weeks and preferably less. Since it contains raw eggs, it should be kept in the refrigerator. Do not let all this put you off making it. Seville oranges are such a rare treat that they deserve being made the most of. I pot my curd in 100g (4oz) jars. The following recipe will, I'm afraid, fill no more than 4. Lemons and limes can be prepared in the same way.

Note: this recipe contains raw eggs.

Makes about 500g (1lb)

3 Seville oranges
175g (6oz) caster sugar
2 or 3 sugar lumps
125g (4oz) unsalted butter, cut into pieces
4 free-range eggs, well beaten and sieved

Grate the zest from the oranges, and put to one side. Rub the sugar lumps over the oranges to extract the rest of the oil and flavour, and put in a bowl set over hot water, together with the rest of the sugar. Halve the oranges, and squeeze the juice into the sugar. Add the pieces of butter, and stir until the sugar has almost dissolved and you have a uniform mixture. Gradually beat in the eggs, and continue to cook over hot water until the mixture thickens.

This will take anything up to 40 minutes. The process should not be hurried, as you risk the mixture curdling. After about 25 minutes, stir in the orange zest. I do not like to add it earlier since it takes on a somewhat mar-

malady quality from long cooking, and I like to preserve the sharp, unique, fresh flavour of the bitter orange. The mixture should lightly coat the back of a spoon before you remove it from the heat. Do not worry if it looks pourable rather than spreadable. The mixture thickens as it cools. Pour into small, clean jars, allow to cool slightly, and then seal, label and refrigerate.

You can use the curd to make a number of easy yet luxurious chilled or iced puddings, such as soufflés, parfaits and ice creams.

Seville orange soufflé

Note: this recipe contains raw eggs.

Serves 6 to 8

3 tablespoons orange juice
3 teaspoons gelatine
450mls (¾ pint) double or whipping cream
approx. 125g (4oz) Seville orange curd
3 free-range egg whites
2 tablespoons caster sugar

Put the orange juice in a bowl, and sprinkle the gelatine on top. When it has softened, heat gently over a pan of hot water, and stir until the gelatine has dissolved. Cool. Whip the cream until firm, and fold in the curd and gelatine mixture. Whisk the egg whites with the caster sugar until firm, and fold into the mixture. Prepare a soufflé dish with a greased paper collar, and pour in the mixture, which will more than fill the dish but be held in place by the collar. Chill the soufflé until set. Carefully remove the collar and serve. Twists of orange zest, crystallized orange, mint leaves, toasted flaked almonds, etc. can be used to garnish.

Seville orange parfait

Note: this recipe contains raw eggs.

Serves 4

250mls (8oz) double cream
4–6 tablespoons Seville orange curd

Whip the cream, fold in the curd, spoon into wine glasses, and chill or freeze. If freezing, remember to allow the

Fruit

parfaits to soften in the refrigerator for a while before serving.

Seville orange ice cream

Note: this recipe contains raw eggs.

Serves 6 to 8

600mls (1 pint) single or whipping cream
about 125g (4oz) Seville orange curd

Mix together, and freeze. Before serving, 'ripen' the ice cream in the refrigerator, that is, allow the ice cream to come to a spooning consistency. It should not be served rock-hard.

Orange syllabub

Serves 4

1 Seville orange
1 teaspoon clear honey
2 tablespoons cognac
3–4 tablespoons rich Oloroso sherry
freshly grated nutmeg
150mls (¼ pint) chilled double cream
300mls (½ pint) chilled whipping cream

Grate the orange zest into a small bowl, and squeeze in 1 tablespoon of juice. Add the honey, cognac, sherry and a little nutmeg. Cover and refrigerate overnight.

The next day, stir in the creams, and whisk until foamy. Spoon into wine glasses, and chill until required. Serve with sponge fingers, brandy snaps, almond biscuits, or crisp cigarette-shaped wafers.

If you leave the syllabub for several hours, it will separate into a thick cream on top and clear liquorous whey at the bottom. It is very good like this but equally very good freshly whipped.

Almond and bitter orange pastries

Makes about 18

250g (½lb) sweetened shortcrust pastry (p. 29)
   or puff pastry
100g (3½oz) ground almonds
50g (2oz) caster sugar
1 tablespoon Seville orange marmalade, finely
   chopped
1 teaspoon orange-flower water
grated zest and 2 teaspoons juice from 1 Seville
   orange
lightly whisked white of a free-range egg

Roll out the pastry and cut into 18 circles. Mix the rest of the ingredients and divide amongst the circles.

Fold over the pastries into a pasty shape, having first dampened the edges, and seal them well. Bake in a preheated oven at 200°C/400°F/gas mark 6 for 10 minutes, and then turn down a notch, and bake for a further 5 to 10 minutes. Serve warm or cold, dusted with icing sugar. These are very good indeed with small cups of espresso.

More than Seville Oranges

January could be such a dreary month in a northern kitchen without our imports of oranges and other citrus fruit from southern Europe and elsewhere. I know we get excellent summer citrus fruit from the southern hemisphere, but it tends to get lost in the wealth of soft fruit – peaches, melons and apricots – that crowd our greengrocers' shelves, and, quite honestly, I never think of eating oranges in the summer. But in January and February, tumbling heaps of Valencias, navels, blood oranges, clementines and grapefruits of many colours join the seasonal Seville oranges.

In Andalucia I came across the bergamot, something like a squashed lemon with mild, almost bland, flesh and the most fragrant zest. Combined with a few lemons, the bergamots produce the most exquisite marmalade that I have ever made or tasted. Sadly, I have never come across the fruit elsewhere. When I find an ingredient like bergamot, with a haunting, unusual flavour, I try to capture its nuances in as many ways as possible, and as well as marmalade, I make *ratafia de limas*, infusing the lime zest in vodka for a few months and then adding sugar, and, indeed, I have also made a sugar flavoured with bergamot peel.

Our passion in this country for oranges goes back long before Nell Gwynne sold them at Drury Lane. One of the more poignant little footnotes to history is a loading bill showing that in 1289 a Spanish ship landed at Portsmouth with a cargo that included fifteen lemons and seven oranges for Queen Eleanor. The next year this former princess of Castile died. Not even the thirty-nine lemons, which were bought for her for 20 shillings, an enormous sum of money in those days, could save her.

The first Englishmen to taste oranges, however, were probably the Crusaders who, according to historian C. Anne Wilson, wintered in the citrus groves around Jaffa in 1191–92. In the sixteenth century both bitter and sweet oranges were imported, and by the middle of the next century they were being made into preserves. Citrus fruit, especially oranges, was also used to flavour meat and fish dishes. A look at the cookery books of the period is very revealing. Robert May, second-generation chef to the grand houses of England and France and author of *The Accomplisht Cook*, uses sliced oranges to garnish beef olives; stuffed leg of veal comes with lemon peel, sauce for carp includes orange juice, salmon is handsomely sauced with ginger, orange, herbs and plenty of spices; snails are cooked in a pie with pieces of chicken, marrow and bacon, seasoned with herbs and moistened with white wine, butter and orange juice. Clearly citrus fruit was extremely fashionable in the kitchen, much as lemon grass and Kaffir lime leaves are today. Of course, food fashions were much slower to change, taking perhaps a hundred years for fundamental changes to occur.

The following recipes reflect the variety of fish, meat and dessert dishes in which citrus fruit can play such a lively part. First a recipe for squid salad, full of flavour and contrasting textures and colours. For extra brightness you could add some diced tomato or halved yellow cherry tomatoes if your greengrocer or supermarket stocks them.

Roast chicken with lemon, garlic and Manzanilla

My winter cooking is often influenced by what I have cooked and eaten in Andalusia, and this next recipe is no exception; it makes a marvellous Sunday lunch. Fino or other good dry white wine can replace Manzanilla if you prefer.

Serves 4 to 6

1.25–1.75kg (3–3½lb) free-range chicken
1 lemon
1 onion
4 cloves garlic, or more, if you like
salt
pepper
about 150mls (¼ pint) Manzanilla sherry

Rinse and wipe the chicken all over. Remove the wing pinions and any excess fat from the cavity. Prick the lemon all over with a skewer and put it inside the chicken. Peel and slice the onion; peel the garlic, and put both in the bottom of a roasting pan, or the bottom half of a soaked clay chicken brick.

Lightly season the chicken, set it on top of the onions and the garlic, pour the Manzanilla over it, and place in the centre of the oven, preheated to 180°C/350°F/gas mark 4. Roast for 1¼ to 1½ hours, or until the juices run clear when a skewer is inserted into the thigh meat.

Remove the chicken, and put it in a warm place while you make the sauce. The juices from the pan can simply be boiled down slightly to reduce them, with the onion and garlic kept in, although they will have practically disintegrated. Or the sauce can be reduced and sieved, and even finished off with cream or butter, although I think this spoils the clean flavour of the lemon, which will have permeated the whole bird.

Carve, or joint the chicken, and serve the sauce separately.

In late autumn I love to go shopping in Gozo, especially to the vegetable vans in the car park in Victoria, or to the small shops around the main square. The island's prickly pears are really past their best, and anyway are difficult to deal with, but the first of the oranges are in the market, dull-skinned because they are unsprayed, mildly sweet and refreshing. Lemons, picked too early and green, are a ridiculous price, £1M, about £2 sterling a kilo; later in the season they cost a few pennies. The growers have to make their money now, for day by day on balconies and in sunny corners of walled gardens all over the island lemon trees catch the sun as it rises and their fruit is swiftly ripening. Soon no one will need to buy lemons – so they will be in abundant supply for homemade lemon curds and cordials.

Lemon cordial

Makes 1 litre (32 oz)

600mls (1 pint) water
thinly peeled zest and juice of 6–8 lemons,
    about 400mls (14oz)
50g (2oz) piece of fresh ginger, sliced
500g (1lb) granulated sugar

Put all the ingredients in a saucepan over low heat. Let the sugar dissolve, then bring to the boil, remove from the heat and steep overnight. Strain, bottle, label and keep in the refrigerator. Dilute a tablespoon or so in a glass of chilled sparkling water for a most refreshing drink. A little poured over ginger or vanilla ice cream is very good too.

Lemon sorbet

Serves 4

300mls (½ pint) freshly squeezed lemon juice
200mls (7oz) sugar syrup, made by boiling 200g
    (7oz) sugar with 200mls (7oz) water
1 tablespoon orange-flower water

Stir the liquids together and freeze, either in an ice-cream maker or sorbetière, according to the directions of the manufacturer, or in a freezer-proof container in the freezer compartment of the refrigerator.

If using the latter method, the mixture will require stirring from time to time, to break up the ice crystals.

It is a good idea to do the last stirring, when the mixture is quite well frozen, in a food processor.

Lemon and honey batter pudding

Serves 6

2 large lemons, with good skins
3 tablespoons clear honey
50g (2oz) unsalted butter
200g (7oz) plain flour
3 free-range eggs
450mls (¾ pint) milk

Pare a thin layer of zest from one of the lemons, taking care not to remove any pith. Cut the zest into long strips, and cook these in a little water for 5 minutes. Drain off the water, and add the honey to the pan. Cook the zest in the honey

The perfect lemon macaroon

Here is another useful addition to the citrus dessert theme, and a very useful recipe for a quick teatime treat. The macaroons are also excellent accompaniments to good ice cream and/or sorbet served for dessert.

YOU NEED, to make about 2 dozen, 150g (5oz) desiccated coconut, 1 tablespoon cornflour, 100g (4oz) caster sugar, 1 tablespoon lemon juice, 1 teaspoon lemon oil (optional), finely grated zest of a lemon, 1 free-range egg white and crystallized lemon peel for decoration.

METHOD Mix the coconut, cornflour and sugar, add the lemon juice, oil, zest and enough egg white to bind together in a firm paste. Shape into pyramids or quenelles, place on baking trays lined with rice paper or non-stick baking sheets, and bake in a preheated oven at 150°C/300°F/gas mark 2 for about 15 to 20 minutes, until just pale golden. Remove from the oven, top each with a piece of crystallized lemon peel, and cool on a wire rack.

until it begins to turn transparent, as if you were making marmalade.

Make a batter with the flour, eggs and milk, and stir the flavoured honey and lemon zest into it. Grate the zest of the second lemon into the batter and add the squeezed juice of one lemon. Stir thoroughly. Pour the batter into a hot and well-buttered dish, dot with the remaining butter and bake in the middle of a preheated oven, 200°C/400°F/gas mark 6 for 40 to 50 minutes or so, until well risen and golden brown.

Remove from the oven, cut into wedges and serve warm, rather than hot or cold. Any of the wide range of creams and plain yoghurts go well with this. As its name suggests, this is not a light sponge in texture, but a heavier-based pudding.

I once made some grapefruit curd, but did not cook it long enough and it was runny. I mixed in some whipping cream, and froze it into a pale, primrose-yellow parfait with a deep long-lasting flavour. With the juice of a couple of pink grapefruits, I made a lemon and gin syrup, and then I crystallized the peel.

This trio of grapefruit flavours made a very eleg-ant dessert, which I garnished with long, curved triangular tuiles, for which I cut out a cardboard template. None of the elements which make up this dish is difficult, but it is somewhat time-consuming. I give you the various stages because the curd recipe is useful, and the crystallized peel can be made without the other elements. Try dipping some in dark, and some in white, chocolate, either for presents, or for after-dinner sweetmeats.

Grapefruit curd

Note: this recipe contains raw eggs.

Makes about 600g

1 large or 2 medium grapefruits with good skins
8 free-range egg yolks or 4 whole eggs
150g (5oz) unsalted butter, cut into small cubes
350g (12oz) caster sugar

Grate the zest and squeeze the juice from the grapefruits, and put juice and zest in a double saucepan. Add the lightly beaten eggs, butter and sugar. Stir until the sugar has dissolved. Continue cooking and stirring until the mixture thickens, about 30 minutes.

Either use as described above in the introduction to this recipe or, for presents, pot in small, clean, dry jars, which you have warmed in the oven. Cover immediately. Label, refrigerate and use within 3 to 4 weeks.

For an easier dessert, you can use the curd with a good-quality cardamom or vanilla ice cream or lemon sorbet. Fill a clean squeezy bottle with the curd, scoop the ice cream or sorbet onto plates, and squeeze the curd around it in a jazzy design. Fabulous on black plates showered here and there with icing sugar.

Crystallized grapefruit peel

2 grapefruits, squeezed
water – see recipe
about 300g (10oz) caster sugar

Discard the pith, and cut the skin into neat strips. Cover with water, bring to the boil and cook until the peel is tender and translucent. Drain, rinse and return to the saucepan with 200mls (7oz) water and 200g (7oz) of the sugar. Cook gently until the sugar has dissolved, and continue to simmer the peel in the syrup, adding the remaining sugar after about 10 minutes.

When the syrup has almost been absorbed and the pieces of peel become sticky to the touch, but before they reach the brittle, cracking stage, transfer to wire racks. Leave them to dry out, overnight if you can, then roll them in caster sugar and store in an airtight box. Pink-fleshed grapefruit produces a pretty pale orange peel when crystallized, the yellow-fleshed grapefruit remains yellow. On the whole, for the curd I prefer the sharper yellow-fleshed, and for the syrup the pink-fleshed.

Grapefruit and gin syrup

Makes 250mls (8oz)

250mls (8oz) pink grapefruit juice
300g (10oz) caster sugar
4 crushed juniper berries
6 coriander seeds, crushed
piece of angelica stalk – optional
strip of orange zest
2–3 tablespoons gin – Plymouth Gin Export
    Strength is a good choice

Simmer the juice, sugar and aromatics until the sugar has dissolved, then boil for about 5 to 7 minutes. The aromatics are ingredients in the making of gin, and serve here to heighten its flavour. Strain, allow to cool slightly and stir in the gin.

Grapefruit ice cream

Note: this recipe contains raw eggs.

Serves 4 to 6

Take 400g (14oz) cold or chilled grapefruit curd (see above), fold in 200mls (7oz) whipping cream, whipped, and freeze in a container in the freezer, or use an ice-cream maker or sorbetière.

Autumn fruit

September is a happy month for English fruit, with plums, apples and pears ready for picking. And with luck, this lovely seasonal food will not have to spend too long in store before it reaches the shops.

The top fruit and stone fruit can also be supplemented by wild food – by cobnuts, hips, haws, rowanberries, crab-apples, elderberries and blackberries. Much of this does not make for good eating purely as fruit, but is fine in jellies, preserves and sauces for game or other meat. In our street in north London the rowanberries ripen so early that I sometimes miss them. Otherwise, I make a few small pots of this smoky-flavoured, garnet jelly for use with winter pork and venison dishes.

I love jams made from greengages and damsons, relatively expensive to produce and fiddly to make because of the stones. The end result is worth it, though, and like anything homemade, makes a lovely present – and even more special if you can find the small, golden mirabelle plums. Alternatively, you can preserve these in a mixture of sugar syrup and vodka, to serve as after-dinner treats in the winter. If you do this, add an extra dimension of flavour by stirring in a few crushed mirabelle kernels. These small, colourful fruits, like damsons and greengages, also make lovely sauces to serve with ices and mousses, and go especially well with the cream cheese heart recipe on p. 133.

While sweet melons remain plentiful, I do not ignore imported fruit entirely. I particularly like the freshness of the following salad, served before a substantial main course. It is, however, also very good as an accompaniment to a slice or two of ham or other cured or smoked meat, and, indeed, fish, as a light luncheon or supper dish.

Melon, cucumber, mint and mozzarella salad

Serves 4

1 ripe honeydew or other sweet melon
1 cucumber
1 or 2 mozzarellas
4 sprigs of mint
sea salt
white pepper
extra-virgin olive oil
cider vinegar
lettuce leaves
mint – for garnish

Discard the seeds from the melon, and dice or scoop it into balls. Lightly peel the cucumber, halve it, discard the seeds, and dice it.

Dice the mozzarella. Keep the tops of the mint sprigs for garnish, and then tear up the leaves and crush them with the sea salt to a paste. Add the pepper, olive oil and a little cider vinegar.

Mix all the ingredients together, and serve chilled in lettuce leaves, garnished with mint.

Crisp orchard pickle

We do not use pickles and chutneys a great deal at home, so they tend to mature nicely in the jar, and I'm always glad to have a jar or two on hand for presents as well. Serve this one with some farmhouse Cheddar and a thick slice of good bread; instant lunch, instant bliss.

By the way, a reader once sent me a most useful tip for dealing with very hard pears: poach them in lemonade rather than water, and they quickly become tender.

Makes about 2kg (4lbs)

1 lemon
500g (1lb) firm pears, such as Conference
750g (1½lbs) apples, Bramleys for preference, or a crisp green apple
1kg (2lbs) firm Victoria or Marjorie Seedling plums
salt
600mls (1 pint) distilled pickling malt vinegar
1 cinnamon stick
8 crushed cardamom pods
175g (6oz) unrefined granulated or light muscovado sugar

Squeeze the lemon into a large glass, china or ceramic bowl. Peel, core and dice the pears and apples, and turn them in the lemon juice. Halve the plums, and remove the stones and cut up the fruit. Put in the bowl. Sprinkle liberally with the salt, about 110–140g (4–5oz), cover and refrigerate or keep in a cool place for 24 to 36 hours.

Meanwhile, prepare the vinegar. Since it is already spiced, it does not need long cooking. Put in a saucepan with the spice and sugar. Heat gently until the sugar has dissolved, and then boil for two minutes. Cool. Rinse the fruit thoroughly. Drain and dry it, and pack it into jars. Pour the cold strained vinegar over the fruit, seal, label, and store it for a couple of weeks before using.

Crisp plum and walnut roll

As this next recipe is not made with homemade strudel dough, but bought filo, it does not deserve to be called a strudel, but it is made in the same way, and the plums make a nice variation on the more usual apple filling.

Serves 6

2 tablespoons fresh white breadcrumbs, fried in
    butter
150g (5oz) walnut pieces, crushed
½ teaspoon cinnamon
4 tablespoons Demerara sugar
500g (1lb) plums, halved, stoned, and very
    thinly sliced
2 sheets filo, about 25 x 30cm (10 x 12 inches)
4 tablespoons unsalted butter, melted

Mix the breadcrumbs, walnuts, cinnamon and sugar, and mix half of this with the sliced plums. Brush both sheets of filo with melted butter, and scatter the dry plumless mixture between the two sheets.

Heap the plum mixture along the length of the filo, about a third in from the lower long edge. Fold in the two short ends, and the lower edge, and then carefully roll up the parcel.

Place on a parchment-lined baking sheet, and bake in a preheated oven at 180°C/350°F/gas mark 4, for 35 to 40 minutes until golden brown. Serve hot or warm, dusted with icing sugar and accompanied by cream or Greek yoghurt.

Plum and hazelnut crumble

While there are plenty of plums still about, I like to make the occasional plum crumble. Here is a version made with hazelnut oil instead of butter –

same calories but less saturated fat. As with the previous recipe, pears or apples can be used instead.

Serves 6

750g (1½lbs) plums
6–7 tablespoons hazelnut oil
75g (3oz) dark muscovado sugar
100g (¼lb) wholemeal flour
75g (3oz) ground hazelnuts
25g (1oz) flaked or chopped hazelnuts

Stone the plums, and poach until just tender with a couple of tablespoons of water. Spoon into an ovenproof dish brushed with hazelnut oil. Mix the sugar, flour and hazelnuts, and then gently work in the oil, rubbing and lifting until the mixture resembles breadcrumbs. Whilst the nuts, flour and sugar can be mixed in the food processor, it is best then to add the oil and work by hand, since using oil, in any kind of baking, in place of 'dry' fat produces a heavier texture.

Whole hazelnuts that you grind yourself to an uneven texture are also very good in a crumble. Walnuts and walnut oil can be used in the same way. If you are unable to get nut oils, one of the light flavoured olive oils would do very well. Spoon the crumble topping over the fruit and bake in a preheated oven at 180°C/350°F/gas mark 4 for 20 to 25 minutes, until the top is golden brown.

Rhubarb soup

As an alternative to the sublimely rich and dark chocolate desserts which seem to be a feature of every New York pastry chef's repertoire, I have looked for sweet inspiration to the fruit desserts. Pâtissier François Payard does 'pomme, pomme, pomme', fresh Macintosh apple, in a light apple syrup with apple sorbet and crisp chips of dried apple. At Chanterelle, a blood-orange soup turned out to be rather similar – syrup, sorbet and segments of the fruit. In due season I make similar desserts with gooseberries, peaches, raspberries and pink grapefruit. Forced rhubarb will perform the variation admirably. Try this refreshing rhubarb soup.

Serves 4 to 6

1kg (2lbs) rhubarb
4 crushed green cardamom pods

1.15 litres (2 pints) water

juice and finely peeled zest of an orange

200g (7oz) sugar, or more to taste

1 teaspoon cornflour – optional

Top and tail the rhubarb. Keep one stalk apart, and chop the rest to put in a saucepan with all the ingredients, except the sugar and cornflour. Cook until the rhubarb is soft. Discard the orange zest and cardamom. Put a sieve over a bowl, and pour in the contents of the pan.

Sweeten the resulting rhubarb juice to taste, and thicken it slightly by rubbing a tablespoon or two of the rhubarb through the sieve. Alternatively, use cornflour to thicken it, if you prefer.

While the rhubarb is still hot, mix it with the remaining sugar, to taste, and stir. When the sugar has dissolved, allow the rhubarb to cool, add about 150mls (¼ pint) of the rhubarb juice, and then freeze to a sorbet texture. Cut the remaining stick of rhubarb into neat batons about 4cm (1½ inches) long and 1cm (½ inch) thick. Poach in a little syrup for a couple of minutes, no more, as they should retain some firmness.

To serve, ladle some rhubarb 'soup' into chilled bowls, place a scoop of rhubarb sorbet in the middle, and float the rhubarb batons around it. A curl of orange zest or a sprig of mint can be used for garnish, if you wish.

Cream cheese hearts with damson sauce

The next recipe makes a very simple, rich and stylish dessert. It goes particularly well with damson, but I make this at all times of the year and use for the sauce whatever fruit is in season. If there is nothing much available, I fall back on that indispensable store-cupboard standby, a packet of dried apricots.

Serves 4

100g (4oz) each thick Greek-style plain yoghurt, curd cheese, sieved cottage cheese and crème fraiche

75g (3oz) unrefined caster sugar, plus extra for the sauce

2 free-range egg whites

500g (1lb) damsons, poached in a little water

Blend the yoghurt, cheeses and cream until smooth, and stir in the sugar. Whisk the egg whites to form peaks, and fold into the mixture.

Spoon the mixture into pierced moulds, lined with wet cheesecloth, place on a plate, and refrigerate for about 12 hours to drain and firm up. Sieve the damsons and sweeten the purée to taste.

When ready to serve, turn the hearts out onto individual plates, carefully peel off the cheesecloth and pour the sauce around.

English apples

Why is it that English apples are quite so seductive? They are not velvety and luscious like peaches, nor bursting with juice like muscat grapes. The tropical languor conjured up by fragrant mangoes is quite absent, as is the frank sensuousness of biting into a ripe, warm fig. In comparison, the apple is a rather brisk, tart, uncompromising, sensible fruit, rather like a Scottish grandmother. And yet, did it not cause the downfall of Eve? I'm sure it wasn't the only fruit in the Garden of Eden, but I do know how she felt.

Scrumping apples was a time-honoured October activity in the village where I grew up in Yorkshire. We would go out just after dusk had fallen, the air smoky with bonfires. The smallest child would squeeze through the gap in the railings of the orchard attached to one of the large houses, and hand the booty over to the big ones. And inevitably, as with Eve, the magisterial voice of authority was not far away. In my case, it was the village bobby addressing the school next day, all seventeen of us, on the sanctity of private property.

Still, every year, I look forward to each of the apple varieties as they are harvested. It was not like this when I lived in France; those dull Grannies and Goldens held little appeal. Not many years ago, it looked as if English apples were going the same way, towards vast monocultures, with traditional orchards fast disappearing. Now, supermarkets have recognized the benefits in being seen to be promoting home-grown, seasonal food. They work with growers to ensure that traditional varieties of orchard fruit are maintained and replanted. Much of the credit for this renewed interest in traditional English apple varieties must go to the charity Common Ground, who some years ago suggested an Apple Day, held in the third week of October. It has caught the public imagination and there are now apple-related activities all over the country during that period.

I always look out for the first russets, James Grieves and Coxes in my greengrocer's, but prefer my Coxes to be picked as late as possible for optimum flavour. It is quite ridiculous to pick them in early September. A ripe Cox, 'the Chateau d'Yquem of apples', is a late autumn treat. As Edward Bunyard, in his *Anatomy of Dessert*, says of November, a 'month which welcomes the ripening Cox, the mellowing Comice, is a time for rejoicing. With some game in the covers and some Burgundy in the cellar, let the population be reduced by all possible means. Let them go to lands of everlasting veal and unripened oranges, let them quaff their Chianti and other acidulous beverages, we grudge them not their fare.'

My apples and pears will be for eating raw, and also for cooking. Pears are particularly good in puddings. Apples I find work well not just with sweet ingredients, but with savoury ingredients too.

On the question of whether to use cooking apples or dessert apples in cooked dishes, I do believe that is a matter of personal taste. It is also a subject to rouse strong feelings amongst readers, I have discovered over the years. When I first learned to cook, I used Bramleys and other cooking apples in my pies, flans and puddings, because that is what my mother taught me. Then I went to live in France, where they do not have Bramleys, and so I learned to use Golden Delicious and Reinettes. Now, I sometimes use one, sometimes the other.

Queer gear

In greengrocers' language, 'queer gear' denotes exotic fruit and vegetables, the kind we get from the tropics and the Mediterranean, usually in the autumn and winter. From then until early in the New Year, when the first of the citrus fruit reaches us from Seville and Sicily, we have a wealth of exotica from which to choose: pomegranates, quinces, persimmons, prickly pears, custard apples, as well as an array of unusual vegetables.

Pomegranates

When we visit Gozo in the autumn, I buy as many exotic fruit as I can, especially the pomegranates. As always, skin colour is an unreliable indicator of ripeness. The leathery skin of much of the fruit is pale and unripe-looking, but when broken open, reveals deep, ruby, juicy flesh enclosing the seeds. I use some of the seeds to make a salad with cucumber, to serve with marinated *lampuki*, dolphin fish which is caught locally, but I bring most of the fruit home to London with me.

Pomegranates in the kitchen

To get at the seeds, cut a slice off one end of the fruit, and then score the skin through into five or six segments. Peel off the skin and then gently break up the tightly packed mass of seeds. Discard all traces of the thin yellow membrane and pith, which is extremely bitter because of the high tannin content. Put the red fruit in a plastic sieve, and crush with a wooden or plastic spoon. This way the seeds themselves, suspended in the juicy red droplets, will not be crushed to release their bitterness into the juice. Alternatively, but not quite so satisfactory because some of the tannin escapes, halve the fruit and squeeze it, not too hard, on a lemon-squeezer. It is a quicker method nevertheless.

The juice, combined with a little oil and seasoning, makes a very good marinade, particularly for poultry and game, with which season the fruit coincides perfectly. With its gentle acidity, pomegranate juice also makes a most satisfactory dressing for salads and vegetables that is very kind to any wine that you might be drinking with it. The juice marries particularly well with hazelnut oil and walnut oil. The seeds, too, look very good mixed in with salad leaves and just as good in a fruit salad made with green and purple fruit.

Fruit

The reddest, most richly flavoured juice makes a stunning cocktail when mixed with champagne. And to finish a meal with a flourish, freeze it into a granita. Or try this idea from Elizabeth David's *Summer Cooking:* having discarded the skin and pith from 6 pomegranates, crush the fruit with a fork, mix with a little icing sugar, rosewater and lemon juice, and serve well chilled, if not iced. I can think of few better ways to end a rich autumn meal.

Pomegranate margarita

Serves 1

1 ripe pomegranate
1 measure tequila
1 teaspoon icing sugar
1 teaspoon lime juice

Moisten the rim of a glass with lime juice, and dip it in salt, if you like. Chill the glass. Halve the pomegranate, and use a lemon-squeezer to extract the juice. Stir in or shake the rest of the ingredients with the pomegranate juice, and serve in the chilled glass.

Pomegranate and cucumber salad

Serves 4 to 6

1 cucumber
2 medium pomegranates
2 or 3 shallots, or a small onion
1 lemon
sea salt
freshly ground black pepper

Halve the cucumber, and discard the seeds. Thinly slice it, grate coarsely, or put through the julienne disc of a food processor. Lightly salt the cucumber, and put in a sieve.

Break open the pomegranates, and pull out the fruit, avoiding the bitter yellow pith. Put in a bowl. Peel and finely chop the onion. Rinse and dry the cucumber, and mix both with the cucumber. Halve the lemon, and squeeze half the juice into the bowl. Cut the remaining half into 3 or 4 slices, remove the peel and pith, and cut into tiny segments. Add this and some seasoning to the salad, mix, and serve. You can add olive or walnut oil, if you wish, but I like this salad just crisp, sharp and lemony, without oil.

Custard apples

This is the name given to many members of the large Annonaceae family to describe what should more properly be labelled cherimoya and sugar apple. Guanabana and sweetsop are other names under which you may find these exotic fruits. I came across many varieties in the markets of Colombia, including the much larger soursop that is used there to make the most refreshing drink from the milky opaque flesh which has the creaminess of custard and the light acidity of pineapple.

You may be lucky enough to find two types of custard apple, or annona, at the supermarket or greengrocer's. Both are a dull dusty green, increasingly marked with brown as the fruit ripens. An irregular heart shape, the fruit is heavy when held in the hand, and when ripe is soft and yielding. If bought hard, it will ripen when kept in a brown paper bag in a warm place. One type of fruit, the sugar apple, has softly rounded protruding scales and the other, the cherimoya, is covered in shallow indentations like fingerprints.

Custard apples in the kitchen

There are a number of ways to make the most of the delicate flesh and subtle flavour. The pulp can be turned into mousses, fools, iced soufflés and ice creams as well as the cooling fruit drinks found in Colombia and the Caribbean. There would be no point at all in cooking this rare exotic treat. I think it is best eaten quite simply, perhaps as a solo treat.

Cut the ripe fruit in half, spoon out the soft custardy pulp, and eat it from the spoon, discarding the shiny black seeds. Eaten this way, custard apple is indeed a most descriptive name for it.

Persimmons

In the late autumn Italian markets glow with the rich translucent orange of the persimmons from Cesena, just down the Via Emilia towards the Adriatic. Some of this fragile fruit finds its way to our greengrocers here, carefully wrapped in blue tissue paper and cradled in wood shavings. Swollen and taut-skinned, it looks almost overripe, and you will sometimes find it being sold at knockdown prices because the greengrocers cannot get rid of the fruit.

Do not be tempted to bite into a firm persimmon. It will be unripe and so full of tannin that it will scour your mouth. It will also curdle cream without a doubt. The Israeli Sharon fruit is a hybrid of the persimmon, or kaki, but without the tannin, and can be eaten soft or firm. It is slightly smaller and squarer than the kaki and good in salads, both sweet and savoury. As with all members of the family, the fruit is high in vitamins C and A.

Persimmons in the kitchen

The very best way to use them when they are really ripe is to put them in the freezer at the beginning of the meal. Take a thin slice off the top, and eat the sweet, semi-frozen flesh with a spoon. A squeeze of lime or lemon enhances the flavour. The pulp can also be made into a purée, mixed with cream or syrup, frozen and then served in the skins which have been left in the freezer (see recipe below). Fold the pulp of ripe fruit, Sharon or kaki, into thick Greek yoghurt, fromage frais or whipped cream for an easy mousse, or mix it with homemade custard for a fool.

In America, where there is also a native persimmon, a much smaller fruit sometimes called a 'Virginia date', persimmon pudding is a traditional dish. Here the pulp is mixed with a traditional sponge mixture and steamed. The familiar Sharon or kaki can be used, and the chopped pulp can also be added to a muffin mixture and baked.

The colour and rich sweetness of the fruit pulp make it very tempting to marry it with savoury dishes; try mixing it with ginger and spices as a sauce to accompany roast ham, pork or duckling.

Chilled persimmon creams

Serves 6

6 fully ripe persimmons with sound, unblemished
   skins
finely grated zest of a lemon
1 scant tablespoon icing sugar
250mls (8oz) double cream or crème fraiche

Sharon or kaki fruit can also be used for this recipe.

Take a thick slice off the top of each persimmon to make the lid. With a pointed spoon, carefully scoop out the persimmon flesh, keeping the skins intact, and put the flesh into a blender, together with the lemon zest and icing sugar. Blend until smooth. Fold the persimmon purée into the cream, divide the mixture among the fruit skins which you have put for a while in the freezer, replace the lids, and chill until required.

Tropical fruit

Nothing transports the senses more easily than tropical fruit. One whiff of papaya, and I am back in a garden in the Philippines. A slice of star fruit, and I remember an extraordinarily refreshing, pale, silky-green juice served to me one hot day in Kuala Lumpur. A slurp of mango with its juices running down my arm might recall Thailand. Anything with coconut transports me to Colombia's Caribbean coast.

Autumn and winter are the time to look for them at better greengrocers' and supermarkets, alongside the ubiquitous, but nevertheless agreeable and useful, kiwi fruit, the fragrant kumquat and the tiny lantern-like physalis, or Cape gooseberry. I use the hard unripe kiwi fruit in salsa recipes as a substitute for tomatillos, paper-husked tree tomatoes.

When I am able to get more than enough quinces than I need for jelly and quince cheese, I experiment with this most fragrant fruit. I use it with poultry pot-roasts, in pies with apple and in Moroccan tagines. Quince has an affinity with tomato, I have discovered, and I now have another recipe to add to my vegetable and fruit soup repertoire.

Melon and mango salsa

Makes 6 to 8 servings

250g (½lb) melon, diced small
1 mango, peeled and diced small
juice of 1 lime
juice of ½ orange

Quince

With its yellow, waxy skin and faint grey down, the large, knobbly, slightly pear-shaped quince is one of our most delightful and rewarding fruits. It is worth having just for its scent alone. One or two in a fruit bowl will perfume the room with a sweet autumnal fragrance. No wonder our grandmothers used quince to scent the linen cupboard.

I do not have access to quince trees so I buy them from my local greengrocer, who gets them from Cyprus or Turkey. They are expensive, and to make a little go a long way, I slice a few into an apple pie for extra depth of flavour. I keep some to cut up and put inside a chicken or guinea fowl while it is roasting.

The rest I use to make a quince and onion compote, which I flavour with cardamom and serve with game or poultry dishes. To make it, I peel, core and chop the quinces, and cook with a little water until soft. Meanwhile, I peel, chop and fry some onions until wilted, and then add the quince together with crushed cardamom seeds, some brown sugar and wine vinegar, and cook to a jammy consistency. It can be served hot or cold, and will keep like chutney if enough sugar and vinegar are used to preserve it.

Quince is one of the few fruits that are not eaten raw. Even when fully ripe, the fruit is extremely hard and dry and fairly astringent. Most often the quince is used to make richly coloured sweetmeats. Because of its high pectin content, it is also combined with low-pectin fruit to make jellies. In Portuguese the word for quince is *marmelo*, and the fruit is made into *marmelada*, (whence our marmalade), a thick fruit paste which is marvellous at breakfast with rolls or lightly toasted bread. In Spain a similar preparation is *membrillo*, which slices like cheese and which, indeed, is very good served with cheese, especially farmhouse Lancashire. *Pâté de coing* is a French sweetmeat in which the quince paste is cooked until stiff, then sliced or cubed, rolled in sugar and allowed to dry. In the Languedoc quinces make a sweet pie filling, flavoured with rum, to be served at harvest time. They are also very good simply baked in the oven like apples or jacket potatoes; the flesh is scooped out, mixed with, preferably, one of the unrefined sugars for extra flavour, plus cream, and eaten hot.

Fruit

---

3 or 4 spring onions or baby leeks, trimmed and
    finely sliced
1 clove of garlic, peeled and crushed
1 tablespoon light muscovado sugar
salt
pepper

Mix all the ingredients together, cover, and allow to stand for at least 30 minutes to let the flavours develop.

Pickled physalis salsa

Makes 6 to 8 servings

175g (6oz) physalis, or Cape gooseberries,
    husks removed
100g (3–4oz) seedless raisins
1 green pepper, seeded and diced

6 spring onions, trimmed and finely sliced
6 tablespoons light muscovado sugar
4 tablespoons white wine vinegar
1 clove of garlic, peeled and crushed
1 teaspoon freshly grated ginger
salt
pepper

Mix all the ingredients together. Cover and refrigerate for up to a week. Mango, papaya or pineapple salsa can be made in the same way.

Quesadillas with kiwi salsa

Serves 2 as a starter

2 flour tortillas
125–150g (4–5oz) Gouda or Edam cheese,
    thinly sliced

salsa

1 onion, peeled and finely chopped

1 tablespoon sunflower oil

1 green chilli, seeded and thinly sliced

4 unripe kiwi fruit, chopped

1 tablespoon light muscovado sugar

2 tablespoons pumpkin seeds

salt

pepper

lime juice to taste

1 tablespoon fresh coriander, chopped

Make the salsa first.

The easiest way to prepare this is to sandwich the two tortillas with the cheese, and put the round on a baking sheet in a low oven until the cheese is melted. Then cut into wedges, and serve with the salsa. Alternatively, heat the *quesadilla* in a non-stick frying pan, set over a low heat and with a lid set slightly askew. If you cannot get tortillas, you can make a similar dish with two large crêpes or pancakes.

To make the salsa, gently fry the onion in the oil until wilted, and then stir in the chilli, fruit and sugar, and cook for 5 minutes or so. Pound the pumpkin seeds to a paste with a little salt, pepper and lime juice, and stir it into the salsa to thicken and season it. Stir in the chopped coriander.

Tropical fruit sundae

Serves 1

1 scoop ice cream or sorbet: vanilla, coconut,
    mango, passion-fruit or rum and raisin

2 tablespoons prepared fruit, mango, pineapple,
    guava, physalis, custard apple or persimmon

A generous helping of rum syrup, almond liqueur or rum butterscotch sauce, and a scattering of toasted flaked almonds, coconut, pine nuts, hazelnuts or brazil nuts finishes off the sundaes nicely, without further adornment.

To make 2 servings of rum butterscotch sauce, melt 2 tablespoons each of unsalted butter and unrefined soft brown sugar in a saucepan. When melted and bubbling, stir in 2 tablespoons each of rum and cream. Allow to boil for a couple of minutes, and then remove from the heat.

Mango and coconut crumble

Not-too-ripe mangoes are diced and baked in individual pots with a crunchy topping of coconut and molasses sugar, which also flavours the simple coconut cream sauce served with the pudding.

Serves 6

175g (6oz) unsalted butter

2 large mangoes

juice of 1 lemon

175g (6oz) molasses sugar

175g (6oz) plain flour

75g (3oz) desiccated coconut

Use a little of the butter to grease 6 individual dishes. Peel and dice the mangoes, discarding the stones. Toss the fruit in the lemon juice, and sprinkle with 2–3 tablespoons molasses sugar so that a good syrup is produced.

Put the fruit in the dishes. Dot with another 25g (1oz) of the butter. Rub the remaining butter into the flour until it resembles fine breadcrumbs. Stir in the remaining sugar and the coconut, and spoon the crumble mixture on top of the fruit, pressing it down a little.

Bake in a preheated oven at 180°C/350°F/gas mark 4 for 30 minutes or so, until the crumble topping is golden.

Coconut cream sauce

1 can unsweetened coconut cream

2 tablespoons molasses sugar

Gently heat the coconut cream, sweeten to taste with the molasses sugar and serve with the crumbles.

Mango fool

For a simpler dessert without pastry, try this very easy mango fool.

Serves 2 or 3

1 large ripe mango

1 tablespoon rum – optional

light muscovado sugar to taste

200mls (7oz) double cream or thick custard (p. 27)

1 tablespoon toasted flaked almonds

Peel the mango and pare off a couple of slivers for garnish. Roughly chop the fruit and blend or process until smooth, with rum if you like, and sugar if necessary. You might find a dash of freshly squeezed lime or lemon intensifies the mango flavour. Fold the whipped cream or custard into the mango purée and spoon into wine glasses. Chill until required, and serve topped with the slivers of mango and toasted flaked almonds.

Mango tarte Tatin

Serves 6

250g (½lb) short pastry (p. 29) or puff pastry
2 or 3 firm, rather than overripe, mangoes
100g (4oz) golden caster sugar
100g (4oz) unsalted butter
1 or 2 tablespoons rum – optional

Peel and slice the mangoes. Put the sugar and butter in a shallow but sturdy cake tin, or tarte Tatin pan, or a small frying pan that will go in the oven and heat gently until the sugar has melted. Raise the heat, and allow the mixture just to reach caramelization.

Remove from the heat, and arrange the mango slices in the pan. Roll the pastry into a circle, just a little larger than the pan.

Cover the fruit, and tuck the pastry down the inside of the pan. Put in a preheated oven at 180°C/350°F/gas mark 4, and bake for 20 to 25 minutes. Then run a spatula around the edge, invert a plate over the top, and turn out the tart, fruit side up. Any juices remaining in the pan, stuck to the bottom, can be loosened with a little water, caramelized, and poured over the fruit. Sprinkle the fruit with rum before serving.

A rum or passion-fruit custard is delicious with this tart, or you can make a chantilly by whipping some cream and folding in a little icing sugar and rum, or passion-fruit juice.

Fruit

If you enjoy eating game, you have to keep an eye on the calendar, as different game birds and animals are available at different times through the autumn and winter.

An organization to promote game in Britain, the Game Marketing Executive, has been set up under the aegis of the Ministry of Agriculture, Fisheries and Food and the Countryside Business Group, and, as a result, we see more game in the shops in due season. But I was disappointed to see, in some of its promotional literature, that guinea fowl and quail were listed with other game.

In this country, with our cool climate, quail has never been a game bird, unlike, for example, in the southern states of America, where quail shoots are held regularly. Here, quail are kept in pens in barns and reared like chickens. And, like chickens, they will enjoy good, bad or indifferent conditions, depending on the producer and the regime that is followed.

Most rabbit too is farmed rather than wild, so the best thing is to ask your butcher for a wild, clean-shot rabbit. This makes for very good eating when carefully cooked, unlike the softer, white, rather delicate, not to say bland, meat of farmed rabbit. Hare, on the other hand, is never farmed, and, like grouse and some wild ducks, remains truly wild game.

The saying that we are what we eat is equally true of animals and birds. I will always prefer to eat wild game. A partridge that has fed on corn left behind from the harvest, a young grouse that has eaten nothing but heather shoots, and a boar that has rooted around eating acorns, roots, chestnuts and crab-apples will taste very different from the creatures that have been reared on a carefully formulated and processed feed. In addition the game bird or animal is well exercised, both in searching for its food and in escaping from its predators, and this affects the flavour and texture of the meat.

Having checked first with your guests, game is a good choice for entertaining, and an excuse to open wonderful bottles of wine and serve even greater delicacies. One autumn, I was brought a white truffle from Italy, and grated it over a risotto made only with grouse stock, no meat at all. It was heavenly and more than matched the extraordinary burgundy my husband Tom opened for our friends, a 1983 La Tâche Domaine de la Romané Conti. A few weeks before that a grouse and porcini risotto

went well with a 1985 Gevrey-Chambertin *premier cru* Lavaur. We have a slight preference for burgundy with game in our house, but others will prefer Côtes du Rhône. With paler game, such as pheasant and partridge, Alsace wines are extremely good. The last time I cooked hare, we served a 1984 Valbuena Vega Sicilia with it. With roasted partridge breasts on a celeriac and potato galette, served with quartered and glazed baby beetroot and stir-fried cabbage, we drank a glorious 1985 Château Rayas Châteauneuf-du-Pape.

As accompaniments to game, plain, homely root vegetables are clear winners, with wild mushrooms a close second, and chestnuts, cabbage and some fruits in the running, as in the first recipe, a variation on the classic duck with orange. With dark game such as this I like to serve wild rice.

Braised wild duck with kumquats

Serves 2

1 oven-ready wild duck
salt
pepper
2.5cm (1 inch) chunk of fresh ginger, peeled, sliced and slivered
12 pickling onions, peeled
2 teaspoons olive oil or butter
12 kumquats
a few fresh coriander sprigs
150mls (¼ pint) fino sherry, or good dry white wine

Remove any fat from the duck's cavity, chop off the wing pinions and wipe the bird all over with paper towels.

Preheat the oven to 180°C/350°F/gas mark 4. Lightly season the bird all over, insert the slivers of ginger under the skin, and put a few in the cavity.

Fry the small onions all over in the oil or butter until golden brown. Put them in a small casserole, put the bird on top, having browned it all over, and put the kumquats around it, together with some coriander stalks.

Pour most of the fat from the frying pan, and deglaze it with the sherry. Pour the boiling pan juices over the bird. Cover, and cook for 35 to 40 minutes in the oven.

Let the bird rest before carving it; surround it with the kumquats and onion, garnish with fresh coriander leaves.

Boil up the cooking juices, add more seasoning if necessary, and hand separately. Serve with wild rice.

Pastilla de faisán

The pheasant *pastilla* recipe is based on a wonderful pigeon *pastilla* we ate in Paris, at Darkoum, one of the city's best Moroccan tables. Incidentally, I call the dish *pastilla*, not *bstila*, *bisteeya* or any of the other transliterations. This is what Madame and Monsieur Lamrini call it on their menu, and I consider them the experts. In its original version, young pigeon and over a hundred layers of tissue-like *ouarka* dough are used.

Serves 6 to 8

6 free-range eggs
200 mls (7 oz) strong pheasant stock
150 g (5 oz) butter, melted
12 sheets of filo pastry – about 225 g (½lb)
3 tablespoons caster sugar
125 g (4 oz) flaked almonds, fried gently in butter
1 teaspoon powdered cinnamon
750 g (1½lbs) cooked pheasant, off the bone
150 g (5 oz) chopped dried fruit (apricots, prunes, peaches or pears, or a mixture)
1–2 tablespoons pickled lemon, chopped – optional
2 teaspoons each cardamom, cumin and coriander seeds, crushed
icing sugar, toasted almonds, black olives, fresh mint leaves – to garnish

Beat the eggs with the stock, and cook gently in a non-stick frying pan, as if you were making scrambled eggs. When the mixture has thickened slightly, remove the pan from the heat, and let it cool. Preheat the oven to 180°C/350°F/gas mark 4.

Brush a round cake tin with butter and brush the first two sheets of pastry with butter, and line the tin with them, buttered side up so that the edges hang over the rim. Cut the next four sheets to the diameter of the tin, brush them with melted butter, and lay them in the bottom of the dish. Sprinkle half the caster sugar, almonds and cinnamon on to the pastry, and spoon on three-quarters of the egg mixture.

Shred or mince the pheasant, and mix it with the dried fruit, pickled lemon, spices and the rest of the sugar, almonds and cinnamon. Spread this mixture in the dish, and spoon over the remaining egg mixture.

Cut four more sheets of dough to fit the tin, brush them with melted butter, and arrange them on top of the filling. Fold over the overlapping pastry as neatly as possible. Then cut two final sheets to fit, brush them with butter, and place them on top.

Bake for 40 minutes, raise the temperature to 200°C/400°F/gas mark 6, and cook for a further 10 to 15 minutes until golden brown.

Serve hot or warm, thickly dusted with icing sugar. Heat a couple of skewers and use them to make grill marks in the sugar. Olives, almonds and mint leaves can also be used to garnish. This sweet and savoury pie is also very good cold.

Pheasant breasts with pomegranates

Pheasant breasts make an elegant dish, easy to prepare and very attractive. If you cannot get pomegranates (see p. 134) use apple juice or cider to marinate the meat, and garnish with peeled, sliced apple cooked in butter. If, by chance, you have quinces, the pheasant is even better with this lovely fragrant fruit, thinly sliced, cooked to a pink translucence, and finished off with butter.

Pheasant is always a good buy in December. More plentiful than earlier in the season, the birds, whilst still young, have put on a bit more flesh.

Serves 4

4 trimmed pheasant breasts
1 or 2 pomegranates
1 carrot
1 stick of celery
1 onion, peeled and thinly sliced
black peppercorns
pink peppercorns – optional
garlic, to taste
4 tablespoons rich game stock

Place the breasts in a single layer in a shallow dish. Cut the pomegranates in half. Pick the seeds out of one half, and keep these intact for decoration, about 1 dessertspoonful per plate.

Squeeze the rest on a lemon-squeezer, and strain the juice over the pheasant. Add the carrot, celery, onion, crushed peppercorns and garlic to the marinade. Stand for a few hours, or overnight.

Remove the pheasant from the marinade, which you strain into a small saucepan.

Heat the grill, and cook the pheasant under quite fierce heat, turning it over once, so that it is brown, but not burnt, on the outside and moist and juicy inside.

Keep the meat warm while you finish off the sauce by adding the game stock to the marinade, and reducing it to a good gravy-like consistency.

Divide the sauce among four heated serving plates, place the pheasant breasts on top, scatter some pomegranate seeds over each serving, and serve with a few steamed broccoli florets and a purée of celeriac, carrot, garlic and cardamom, or wild rice and a cauliflower and potato mash.

Partridge and cabbage pies

Serves 4

500g (1lb) short or puff pastry
500g (1lb) partridge fillets, from the breast and
    legs of 3 or 4 birds
50g (2oz) butter
1 onion, peeled and sliced
225g (½lb) cabbage, finely shredded and
    blanched
1 teaspoon each sea salt, juniper berries,
    allspice and black peppercorns, crushed
2 tablespoons chopped flat-leaf parsley, or
    chervil
2 hard-boiled free-range eggs, shelled and
    chopped
4 tablespoons cooked wild or basmati rice
milk-and-egg wash to glaze and seal the
    pastry
100mls (4oz) game or partridge stock

Fry the meat in butter for a couple of minutes or so, remove, and put to one side. Fry the onion until soft, and then stir in the cabbage and spices, and cook 2 to 3 minutes more. Remove from the heat, and stir in the herbs.

Roll out the pastry, and cut out 8 circles, four large ones and four smaller ones. Put the smaller ones on a baking sheet lined with baking parchment. Heap the cabbage, partridge, rice and chopped egg on each pastry circle, leaving a 1cm (½ inch) border. Brush this with the egg wash. Lay the larger pastry circle on top, and pinch down to seal it, pressing it all the way round with the tines of a fork.

Make a small hole in the centre of each pie, and keep it open with a roll of greaseproof paper. Brush the pies all over with the glaze, and bake in a preheated oven at 200°C/400°F/gas mark 6 for 20 minutes. Turn the heat down a couple of notches and carefully pour in the stock, removing the paper, and bake for a further 10 to 15 minutes.

Pot-roast partridges

Partridges are usually very tasty in November/ December, and this next recipe makes a good dinner-party main course. So, too, does the previous, more rustic recipe.

Serves 4

4 oven-ready partridges
4 bay leaves
4 sprigs of thyme
4 curls of orange zest, taken from 1 orange
50g (2oz) butter
4 tablespoons cognac or brandy
salt
pepper
75mls (⅛ pint) good dry white wine or vermouth

If necessary, untruss the birds and remove the barding fat. Put a bay leaf, a sprig of thyme and a piece of orange zest in the cavity of each bird. Rub them all over with orange juice, and rub the butter over the breasts.

In a heavy casserole, brown the birds all over, and then flame with the cognac or brandy. Season lightly, and then pour in the wine. Bring to the boil, cover the casserole, and then bake in the oven for 45 minutes in a preheated oven at 180°C/350°F/gas mark 4.

Transfer the birds to a serving platter, and boil up the pan juices to make a gravy. Garnish with bunches of watercress, curls of orange zest or orange wedges, and serve with the gravy.

Venison steaks with blackcurrant sauce

Serves 2

2 venison medallions, about 175g (6oz) each
2 tablespoons crème de cassis liqueur
2 tablespoons fruit vinegar, sherry vinegar or
    balsamic vinegar
3 cloves
3 juniper berries
6 peppercorns
2 tablespoons walnut oil
25g (1oz) butter
1 teaspoon sunflower oil
4 tablespoons game stock
salt
freshly ground black pepper

Put the meat in a dish. Mix the liquids, crush the spices and mix all together with the walnut oil. Pour this over the meat, cover, refrigerate and leave for an hour or so, turning it once.

When ready to cook, bring the meat to room temperature, and reserve the marinade. Dry the meat well, and heat a frying pan with half the butter and all the sunflower oil, or use a non-stick frying pan. When hot, sear the meat on both sides, lower the heat and cook until done to your liking.

Remove the meat from the pan and keep it in a warm place, loosely covered, on a plate. Sieve the marinade into the frying pan, and raise the heat. Allow to reduce slightly, and then stir in the stock, and once that is bubbling, quickly add the remaining butter, and season to taste. Pour in any cooking juices that have drained out of the meat. Serve the sauce with the meat. Mashed potatoes and glazed kohlrabi slices make very good accompaniments.

Venison cobbler with a pumpkin topping

A cobbler, with its golden scone-dough topping, makes a handsome centrepiece for a casual supper for friends and family. Here I add pumpkin to the topping, and suggest this as an alternative to turkey for a Thanksgiving dinner, a holiday we usually celebrate, even though Tom has lived here for over thirty years.

Serves 8

Cobbler

    1.5kg (3lbs) diced venison – use boned leg or
        shoulder
    1 tablespoon plain flour
    ½ teaspoon each salt and freshly ground pepper
    3 tablespoons olive oil
    3 tablespoons brandy
    75mls (⅛ pint) port
    1 tablespoon red wine or balsamic vinegar
    600mls (1 pint) good dry red wine
    sprig of rosemary

Toss the venison, a few pieces at a time, in a bag with the flour and seasoning. Brown the meat in the olive oil, flame with the brandy, then add the port, vinegar and red wine. Bring to the boil, tuck in the sprig of rosemary, cover,

and cook it at 150°C/300°F/gas mark 2 for about three hours.

Topping

    300g (10oz) self-raising flour
    75g (3oz) butter or lard, diced
    75g (3oz) Parmesan, grated
    100g (4oz) raw pumpkin, grated
    ½ teaspoon each freshly ground pepper and
        nutmeg
    2 tablespoons plain yoghurt, mixed with 75mls
        (⅛ pint) cold water
    50g (2oz) flaked almonds

Rub the flour and fat together in a bowl, and then stir in the cheese, the pumpkin and seasoning. Stir in enough liquid to make a soft, pliable dough. Transfer to a floured board, and knead it lightly.

Roll out to fit the top of whatever ovenproof dish you are serving the stew from, cut into wedges and lay them on top of the stew, or cut into rounds and arrange on top. Sprinkle with the flaked almonds. Bake at 200°C/400°F/gas mark 6 in a preheated oven for 15 to 20 minutes.

Pappardelle with wild venison sausage sauce

Pappardelle are broad, flat noodles, which, when cooked, wind and fold themselves around a chunky meat sauce, as in this dish. If you cannot get or make pappardelle, tagliatelle or fettuccine can be used instead.

Serves 4, as a main course

    500g (1lb) wild venison sausages
    1 onion, peeled and chopped
    1 celery stalk, trimmed and finely chopped
    2–3 garlic cloves, peeled and finely chopped
    1 tablespoon extra-virgin olive oil
    150mls (¼ pint) game, beef or chicken stock
    1–2 sprigs marjoram or oregano
    1 tablespoon balsamic vinegar
    500g (1lb) fresh pappardelle

Remove the meat from the sausage skins. Fry the vegetables and garlic in the olive oil until wilted. Raise the heat, add the meat, and brown it briefly. Add the stock and the herbs. Simmer for about 40 minutes, uncovered, until the meat is tender and the sauce reduced. Finally, add the balsamic vinegar. Stir the sauce into the freshly cooked and drained pasta. In Tuscany a red wine vinegar would be used, although over the Apennines in Emilia Romagna, they would use balsamic vinegar.

Venison burgers

Another casual meal uses finely diced or coarsely minced venison. Season the meat with freshly ground pepper, a little ground mace or nutmeg, some cumin and allspice. Add a dash of Jalapeño Tabasco, Angostura Bitters and Worcester sauce. Shape into patties and cook on a hot griddle.

You will also need half a ciabatta per person, alfalfa sprouts, and then whatever else you like on burgers. While the patties are grilling, split and toast or bake the bread, on which a slick of olive oil and a scraping of garlic will do no harm. Heap on the alfalfa sprouts, any other salad or toppings, then the grilled venison burger and finally the top layer of bread. It couldn't be simpler.

Hare and celery casserole

Hare is always exceedingly good value, divided into joints for jugged or casseroled hare for four, a roast saddle for two, and leftovers to serve in soup or with pasta.

Do not be daunted by the length of the hare recipe. It is no more than the standard casserole recipe, which you can adapt to other meats, first frying the onions, then browning the meat, next adding the prepared vegetables, and finally deglazing the pan and adding the seasonings. After that, once in the oven, the casserole looks after itself.

Serves 6

1 hare – see recipe
1 bottle red wine
1 onion, peeled and sliced
2 or 3 garlic cloves, peeled and sliced
2 tablespoons olive oil
1 head of celery
2 tablespoons plain flour
2 bay leaves
6 juniper berries, crushed
seeds of 3 cardamom pods
freshly grated nutmeg
salt and pepper

Have the hare jointed by your butcher, with the saddle cut into three pieces. Wipe all over inside and out with damp paper towels, and snip off the transparent skin on the back and legs. The boniest bits, from the rib cage, can be removed altogether and used for making stock.

Put the wine in a saucepan and reduce it by half. If the wine was quite thin and sharp to begin with, it will now be even more so. Add three or four small sugar lumps. There's nothing like chaptalization to round out an iffy wine.

Gently fry the onion and garlic in the oil until golden brown, and transfer it to a casserole.

Separate the celery stalks, remove the stringy parts and any brown ends. Rinse thoroughly and cut into thumb-size batons. Put these too in the bottom of the casserole.

Brown the pieces of hare in the same pan in which you fried the onions, and transfer them to the casserole. Sprinkle the flour in the frying pan, and stir and scrape up the residues, gradually adding the wine, stirring to make a smooth sauce. If it becomes lumpy despite your best efforts, simply strain the mixture through a sieve over the meat. Add the seasonings to the casserole, stir in well, put on the lid and cook in a low oven, 150°C/300°F/gas mark 2 for about 3 hours, or at 180°C/350°F/gas mark 4 for 1½ to 2 hours.

This casserole is delicious served with garlic mashed potatoes – you boil the peeled garlic with the potatoes and mash both together. If you like the flavour, you can add a little creamed horseradish to the mash, or serve it separately.

Roast saddle of hare with chestnuts, mushrooms and shallots

Sometimes I cook this next recipe with quartered, peeled firm pears or apples instead of the mushrooms. The slight sweetness accompanies the hare very well.

Serves 2

saddle of hare
1 tablespoon extra-virgin olive oil
freshly ground black pepper
pinch each of ground cloves, nutmeg and salt
2 or 3 crushed juniper berries
1 teaspoon fresh thyme leaves

Prepare the meat a few hours in advance, the night before or in the morning, whichever is more convenient. Make sure it is well trimmed.

Brush it all over with the oil, and rub in the spices and herbs. Cover, and leave in a cool place, or refrigerator.

The hare will take only about 15 minutes to roast and 15 minutes to rest, so prepare your vegetables in advance.

Peel some shallots, wipe some cap mushrooms, and prepare some chestnuts. Vacuum-packed and peeled chestnuts from France are now available in 200g (7oz) packs from well-stocked delicatessens and other food shops. They can be boiled in the bag, or gently fried in butter, saving a good deal of work, and the end results are not too different from preparing them from scratch.

Blanch the shallots for a few minutes, drain and put them in a frying pan with a little butter. Cook for 15 minutes or so, and then add the chestnuts, and after a further 10 minutes add the mushrooms and fry on a lower heat for 5 to 8 minutes.

The hare can go in the oven, preheated to 230°C/450°F/gas mark 8, when you start cooking the chestnuts. Roast it for 15 minutes, and then remove, and keep it warm for 5 to 10 minutes before carving in long slices.

Add a little wine to the juices in the roasting pan, and boil up to make gravy.

Hare ragout with red-wine risotto

For the following recipe, make the ragout first. The *soffrito* of vegetables is a base for many Italian sauces. I find it worth making double or triple the quantities given here, and storing it for later use. And indeed, I usually make at least double quantities of the meat sauce to use on another occasion. It is particularly good with pasta, and makes an excellent lasagne. Minced or chopped venison, beef, veal or pork can be made into rich meat sauces following the same method.

Note: I have always reckoned on a pinch being the amount you pick up between forefinger and thumb, and a good pinch being what you pick up with thumb, forefinger and middle finger.

Serves 4 to 6

Ragout

1 onion
1 celery stalk
1 carrot
1 leek – optional
2–3 tablespoons extra-virgin olive oil

hindquarters of a hare
5 tablespoons good dry red wine, i.e. a good
    splash of it, and the same of milk
a good pinch of nutmeg
1 bay leaf
3 or 4 peeled plum tomatoes, i.e. half a 400g
    (14oz) can
salt
pepper

Peel, trim and chop the vegetables finely, keeping the onion separate. Fry this gently in the olive oil, and when translucent, add the remaining vegetables. Cook until soft. Meanwhile, remove the meat from the bones, and dice it. Keep the bones to cook with the sauce for extra flavour.

Fry the meat with the vegetables until it loses its raw exterior. Raise the heat, and add the wine. When it has evaporated, add the milk and nutmeg. When the milk has been absorbed, add the bay leaf, rub the tomatoes through a sieve into the sauce, and simmer, partially covered, on the lowest possible heat for up to 2 hours.

The sauce can then be cooled and refrigerated for later use, or towards the end of cooking time you can start the risotto, which will take 40 to 45 minutes.

Risotto

1 onion or 2 shallots, peeled and finely chopped
1 celery stalk, trimmed and finely sliced
2 tablespoons extra-virgin olive oil
about 500g (1lb) risotto rice
300mls (½ pint) full-bodied red wine
about 1 litre (2 pints) vegetable, chicken or
    game stock
seasoning
1–2 tablespoons unsalted butter – optional
chunk of fresh Parmesan

Sweat the vegetables in the oil until translucent, and then stir in the rice until well coated in oil. Have both wine and stock simmering, and add half of the wine to the rice. Stir it well, and when the wine has been absorbed, add the rest of it. When this, too, has been absorbed, start adding the stock, only pouring in more once the previous batch has been absorbed. Keep stirring. You might find the rice done to your liking before you have added all the liquid, but I like a creamy risotto, and I tend to use a good deal of stock or boiling water at the end, if I have used up all the stock.

Just before serving, season to taste, and stir in the butter, if using it, to give an extra gloss. Spoon the risotto into heated soup plates, and spoon some of the hare ragout on top. Let each person grate their own cheese onto the risotto.

Roasted onions are very good with game, as is a purée of celeriac and garlic. When roasting onions, it is best to leave them exactly as they are, with all the outer skins, as these help to prevent the onions from burning. Place them in a clean, greased ovenproof dish, with a couple of tablespoons of water. Cook for 1 to 2 hours, depending on size, at 180–200°C/350–400°F/gas mark 4–6. If cooking them at the higher temperature, cook towards the bottom of the oven.

They look good served as they are; pop them out of their skins at the table. Do not waste the skins. Pour some water into the cooking dish, where the onion juices will have caramelized to a nice brown. Pour into a saucepan with the onion skins and, when you have done with them, any game bones or carcasses. Simmer together to make a well-flavoured, clear, dark brown broth. Use it for the previous recipe or the two on p. 148.

Wild rabbit glazed with mint, honey and cider

Lentils or mashed potatoes are good with this rabbit dish, as is a purée of onions or leeks, or a heap of sauerkraut. If hot vegetables do not appeal, serve instead either a green salad or a chunky salad of fennel, apple, walnuts and white radish.

Serves 4 to 6

hindquarters and back joints of two wild rabbits
5 or 6 sprigs of fresh mint
½ teaspoon each sea salt and freshly ground
    black pepper
1 teaspoon each ground cumin and coriander
3 tablespoons cider
1 tablespoon cider vinegar
1 tablespoon clear honey
1 teaspoon mustard, or more to taste

Chop the hindquarters in two, and the back into two joints.

Strip the leaves from the mint, and roughly tear them. Put in a mortar with the salt, pepper and spices, and grind with a pestle to a paste. Gradually add the liquid, the honey and mustard.

Mint

This would have to be my desert-island herb, which surprises me, because I did not use it for years. It took me a long time to get past my loathing of mint sauce. Tarragon used to be my favourite, when I loved cooking *poulet à l'estragon* and adding the pungently anise-scented herb to creamy fish sauces. Also in the seventies, living in north London and shopping at Cypriot grocers', I would use coriander with everything. Then basil became a passion, and I would bring large bunches back from every trip to Italy, some for pesto, some for salads. I still love these herbs, and to them would add chervil, savory and lovage.

But nothing is quite as versatile as mint. Important in many kitchens, from Thailand and Vietnam to Morocco and Italy, mint is as good with fish as it is with meat. Shredded into bulgar wheat salads and in spring rolls, it is excellent too with vegetables. Try it in a chilled melon and cucumber soup or in a tomato salad. Add it to fruit compotes. Crystallize the leaves to garnish desserts, and even use it in ice creams, sorbets and syrups.

But if using mint in desserts, do not leave for more than an hour or two before eating. Mint's fragrant oils are very volatile, and the flavour rapidly deteriorates, as I learned to my cost once, making a mint sorbet the day before I needed it. And do not forget that fresh mint makes a wonderful infusion, excellent for the digestion.

Brush this paste on the meat, and leave for 20 to 30 minutes for the flavours to penetrate.

Put the joints of rabbit in a single layer in an oiled roasting tin and bake in a preheated oven at 180°C/350°F/gas mark 4 until tender. This is wild meat; it may take 40 minutes, it may take very much longer, depending on the age of the animal. Baste the meat from time to time, and cover with foil if it shows signs of drying out.

Game broth with parsnip dumplings

Serves 4 to 6

1.25 litres (2 pints) game broth
4 heaped tablespoons parsnip purée
4 tablespoons self-raising flour
1 small free-range egg yolk

For the dumplings, mix the last three ingredients together until smooth. Take small pieces, about the size of your little finger's first joint, and roll them down the tines of a fork. This will produce gnocchi-like shapes. Slide them into the simmering stock, and when they float to the top, the soup is ready. To preserve the limpid clarity of the broth, you may prefer to poach the dumplings in water, transfer them to heated soup plates, and then pour on the boiling game broth. As you bring this to the boil, a drop of Madeira, rum or sherry will enhance the flavour.

Wild rice and game soup

Serves 4

1 small onion or 2 shallots, peeled and finely
    chopped
2 teaspoons olive oil
1 medium carrot, peeled and diced
1 small turnip, peeled and diced
1 celery stalk, trimmed and sliced
900mls (1½ pints) game stock
100g (4oz) cooked game, off the bone
75g (3oz) cooked wild rice
2 tablespoons dry Amontillado sherry or Madeira
salt
freshly ground black pepper
coriander or flat-leaved parsley – for garnish

In a heavy-based pan or a casserole, fry the onion in the oil until golden brown. Add the vegetables, and fry for 2 or 3 minutes.

Pour on the stock, bring to the boil, and simmer until the vegetables are tender. Add the meat, rice and sherry, and cook for a further 5 minutes.

Season to taste, garnish with coriander, or flat-leaved parsley, and serve immediately.

Peppered country casserole

This last recipe is an immensely versatile dish, using a mixture of diced venison, rabbit and pigeon, although other combinations of meat and game can be used. I like to add plenty of spices and pepper to the casserole, but no single one dominates – they simply add to the layers of flavour.

Serve the casserole with jacket potatoes put in the oven at the same time, or dauphinois potatoes. Root vegetables or green vegetables will accompany it very well too.

The casserole can be made and served immediately, or it can be cooked 2 to 3 days before required and refrigerated. It reheats well. Sometimes I serve the casserole with a crumble, sometimes with a herb cobbler topping, and sometimes with a crust of flaky pastry. Leftovers, chopped up and mixed with plenty of gravy, make a fine sauce for chunky pasta. Without the gravy, it makes good potted game, mixed with softened butter, spices and a little port or Madeira.

Serves 6, plus leftovers

1.5kg (3lbs) meat, off the bone, as described
    above, using 500g each venison, rabbit and
    pigeon breasts
2 onions, peeled and chopped or sliced
2 tablespoons olive oil
1 pinch each of mace, cinnamon, ginger and cumin
grating of nutmeg
level teaspoon freshly ground black pepper
5g (⅙oz) square of bitter chocolate
600mls (1 pint) good dry red wine
300mls (½ pint) game or other meat stock
2 bay leaves
sprig of thyme
watercress – for garnish

Make sure the meat is of roughly even-size pieces. Dry them thoroughly. Brown the onion in the olive oil, and transfer it to a casserole. Brown the meat in batches, and transfer also to the casserole. Add to the pan the spices, chocolate, and half the wine. Bring to the boil, scrape up any residues stuck to the pan, and then add the remaining wine and the stock. Bring to a full boil, pour it over the meat, tuck in the herbs, cover, and cook in a preheated oven at 150°C/300°F/gas mark 2 for about 2 hours, or until the meat is tender. Serve from an earthenware dish, garnished with a sprig or two of watercress.

Steak and game pie

I would suggest serving the next dish with a purée of celeriac and a crisp, green vegetable, such as broccoli or Savoy cabbage. The pie is also rather good cold.

Serves 6 to 8

500g (1lb) lean cut of beef, such as blade, chuck, rump or topside
750g (1½lbs) game off the bone, e.g. pheasant breasts or leg, hare, rabbit, partridge
2 tablespoons plain flour
½ teaspoon freshly ground black pepper
¼ teaspoon salt
pinch of ground mace
2 tablespoons sunflower or groundnut oil
1 onion, peeled and sliced
300mls (½ pint) beef or game stock
300mls (½ pint) brown ale, or dry cider
1 bay leaf
250g (½lb) puff pastry
for glaze, beaten free-range egg and milk

Cut the meat into bite-size cubes. Put the flour and seasonings in a paper bag, and shake a few pieces of meat in it at time to give them a light dusting of flour.

In a heavy pan or flameproof casserole heat the oil, and fry the onion until golden. Push to one side, and brown the meat, a few pieces at a time. Pour on a little of the stock, and scrape up any residues stuck to the pan. Add the rest of the stock, the ale or cider, and the bay leaf. Bring to the boil, reduce the heat to a simmer, cover, and cook for about an hour until the beef is tender. Cool the meat quickly, and either cover and refrigerate until required or transfer it to a pie dish.

Preheat the oven to 200°C/400°F/gas mark 6. Roll out the pastry, and cover the meat in the pie dish with it, pressing down well to seal at the edges. Lop off any excess pastry, and use it for trimming the pie. Slash the top to let the steam escape. Brush with the egg-and-milk glaze. Bake for 30 to 35 minutes.

Game

Grains

Wild rice

Wild rice has always seemed such an exotic food, from so far away, even though it is now widely available in our food halls, supermarkets and delicatessens. Although today it is grown on a commercial scale and mechanically harvested and processed in Canada, California and elsewhere, it originated in the lakes of Minnesota, where it is still harvested by native Americans in canoes and dried in the traditional way. Recently, travelling through Minnesota, we stopped at Cass Lake, where the Leech Lake band of Chippewa (Ojibwe) Indians harvest, process and sell this rice, as well as other Ojibwe foods, such as canned smoked white fish from the lakes.

It is here that the Mississippi River and its headwaters provide the clean, unpolluted water acreage in which the wild rice thrives, as a natural, organic product. This wild rice is relatively pale, with long, large grains, compared to the very dark paddy-grown rice.

Although it was the wrong time of year to see the harvest, we ate the rice in a small restaurant on the reservation. It was especially good as wild rice pancakes for breakfast. But in fact, our first taste of Minnesota came with the meal we were served on North West Airlines, flying into Minneapolis. A wild rice and pecan salad served with sliced smoked duck breasts was very good indeed, and led me to plan some recipes of my own on my return.

Smoky flavours go very well with wild rice, as we discovered at another stop, the Bistro in Bismarck, North Dakota, where chef Jason Wagner had a delicious smoked chicken, corn and wild rice chowder on the menu. My salad of scallops, bacon and wild rice is inspired by those dishes, and I have developed a version of the soup, which makes a very satisfying bowlful.

Wild rice, botanically an aquatic grass not a rice, is a nutritious food, with a protein content of 14 per cent. It contains nine essential amino acids, and is particularly rich in lysine. A good source of fibre, it is also gluten-free. Still rather expensive, wild rice is nevertheless economical. Since it expands to about 4 times its original volume in cooking, 2 to 3 level tablespoons of uncooked wild rice provides an individual serving.

I like to serve it with game and grills, as well as in salads. And I always cook enough to supply leftovers for using in soups or stuffed vegetables, and now pancakes.

Of course, all rice is as versatile as this, and it is a good idea to have several varieties in stock. I usually have a large bag of basmati rice to serve with curries; Jasmine rice for oriental dishes; Carnaroli, Vialone or Arborio for risotto; Calasparra rice for paella and Portuguese baked rice dishes; short-grain rice for puddings, and Chinese congee and Camargue rice for fun. This 'red' rice, which grows solely in the paddies of Provence, is processed very little, and thus cooks to an agreeable chewiness. It, too, is good in salads.

Rice salads are best freshly cooked and served. If you have to prepare them in advance, it is important to cool them quickly, then cover and refrigerate until required. Try to bring back to room temperature in time for eating.

You can use other grains in recipes that normally use rice. Barley 'risotto' was once rather fashionable. I like it cooked with wild mushrooms and a well-flavoured stock. It will not cook to the creamy texture of white rice, neither does spelt, which is now set to take over from barley in the fashion stakes. In Paris, Alain Solivérès at Les Elysées makes a spelt 'risotto' with black truffles. In Auch, André

Spelt

This is a northern European grain, which was cultivated first by the Romans. An antique wheat variety, spelt produces an excellent flour for bread, which can also be used in pasta. The whole grains can be used like wheat, barley – or even rice, as a look-alike 'risotto'; it would be a pity to ignore our native grains for exotic imports, particularly now that spelt and spelt flour are available in healthfood stores and some supermarkets.

Daguin used to combine one of his famous duck dishes with spelt (*épeautre*) and pearl onions. You can find this wholesome grain, an ancient variety of hard wheat which used to be widely grown in Britain, in health food stores, and, I expect, before too long, in supermarkets. Spelt flour is produced under the Doves Farm label, is already available in supermarkets and I find it excellent for bread-making, either on its own or combined with strong white flour.

To cook wild rice

For every two level tablespoons of wild rice you put in the saucepan, add three times its volume, 6 tablespoons, of water. Or, more simply, using a measuring jug, for 125mls (4oz) rice (4 servings), add 375mls (12oz) water or stock. Bring to the boil, stir, cover, and then cook on the lowest possible heat until the water has been absorbed and the rice grains have broken open and cooked to the texture you like, chewy or soft. This can take from 25 to 50 minutes.

Wild rice, scallop and bacon salad

Serves 2

50g (2oz) wild rice
150mls (6oz) water
1 shallot, peeled and finely diced
4 rashers smoked streaky bacon, rind removed
50g (2oz) pecans or walnuts, roughly chopped
2–3 tablespoons walnut oil
sprigs of chervil, chopped, with some left whole
        for garnish
salt
lemon juice, sherry vinegar or cider vinegar
freshly ground black pepper
6 scallops

Cook the wild rice as explained above, and when it is cooked, stir in the shallot. Meanwhile grill or fry the bacon till crisp. Crumble it and stir, with the nuts, walnut oil and some chervil, into the rice. Add to taste salt, pepper, lemon juice or vinegar.

Grill the scallops or sear in a hot pan, just a minute or so on each side, and serve on top of the rice, with the rest of the chervil for garnish.

Wild rice, corn and smoked chicken soup

Serves 6 to 8

2 tablespoons olive oil
1 large onion, peeled and finely chopped
1 celery stalk, trimmed and thinly sliced
1 leek, trimmed, thinly sliced and rinsed
2 tablespoons plain flour
½ teaspoon dill seeds or fresh dill
1.5 litres (2½ pints) chicken stock
150mls (¼ pint) good white wine
kernels cut from 3 fresh corn cobs
150g (5oz) cooked wild rice
200g (7oz) smoked chicken, diced or shredded
cream and fresh dill or parsley – optional

Heat the oil in a large saucepan, and stir in the first three vegetables. Cook until golden. Add the dill, stir in the flour and gradually blend in half the stock. Cook for 5 minutes, then stir in the remaining stock and the wine, bring to the boil, and simmer gently until the vegetables are tender. Add the corn, rice and chicken. Bring to the boil and simmer for 5 minutes before serving. To serve, swirl in the cream and scatter on the herbs, if using them.

Wild rice hotcakes

Makes 10 to 12

1 free-range egg
300mls (½ pint) semi-skimmed or skimmed milk
1 heaped tablespoon plain yoghurt
200g (7oz) plain flour
1 teaspoon baking powder
100–150g (4–5oz) cooked wild rice
oil or butter for frying, or use a non-stick pan

Beat the egg, milk, yoghurt, flour and baking powder to make a thick, smooth, lump-free batter. Stir in the wild rice, and wait until the batter begins to froth and bubble slightly on the surface. This indicates that the mixture is aerating because of the baking powder's action and will produce a light batter.

Make sure the pan, and fat, if using it, are hot. Pour in the batter until it covers the area of a small saucer. Do not shake the pan or spread the mixture. When the surface is matt, dry and full of holes, turn it over, and cook the under-side for 2 to 3 minutes. Stack the hotcakes on a plate set over a pan of hot water, until you have cooked all the batter.

These are marvellous for a leisurely breakfast served with maple syrup or crisply cooked bacon.

Rice

We often think of rice as an oriental ingredient, whether as a partner to curry or as a foundation for sushi, but it is also widely used throughout the Mediterranean. Indeed, it is grown extensively in southern Europe, as well as further north in the broad sweep of the Po Valley in Italy.

Black risotto with coral aioli

The last time I made this risotto, I served it as a first course before a main course of sole fillets. I used the sole bones to make the stock, and the edge trimmings from the fillets I chopped and stirred into the risotto. You could also use prawns and a shellfish stock, or small chunks of monkfish.

Serves 6

1 onion, peeled and finely chopped
2 tablespoons olive oil, or butter
250–275g (about 10oz) Carnaroli, Arborio,
    Vialone, or other risotto rice
1–1.25 litres (about 2 pints) fish stock
2 sachets squid ink
4–6 large diver scallops
cloves of fresh garlic, to taste
olive oil
lemon juice
salt
pepper

In a large pan gently fry the onion until soft. Stir in the rice until well coated, and then pour on a ladle of boiling stock and stir. Once it has been absorbed, add more stock, gradually using up all the stock until the rice is cooked through. You may add boiling water if you like your risotto creamy and the rice has absorbed all the stock. Or, if you prefer your risotto drier and firmer, do not use all the stock.

About halfway through cooking, add the contents of the ink sachets.

Meanwhile, separate the corals from the scallops, and poach the corals gently for a minute or so. Cut the scallops into strips, and cook them briefly in a little oil in a hot frying pan.

Put the corals and the peeled, chopped garlic in the blender, and process until smooth. Then gradually add about 80mls (3oz) oil, as if making mayonnaise, together with a dash of lemon juice and seasoning.

Spoon the risotto into heated soup plates, put a spoonful of the coral aioli on top, and some strips of scallop on top of the sauce. Serve immediately.

Red risotto

From the Camargue, that strange, low-lying country of black bulls and white horses in the south of France, comes an unusual strain of red rice, now being sold in Britain. Not as refined as white rice, it takes longer to cook and retains more bite. But it can be used to good effect in traditional rice recipes, and I have devised a red risotto to make the most of its colour.

Serves 2

1 pink shallot, peeled and chopped
2 tablespoons olive oil
125g (4oz) red Camargue rice
1 beetroot, cooked and grated
2 or 3 dried porcini, broken into pieces, and
    soaked
100mls (3oz) good dry red wine, hot
up to 250mls (about 8oz) vegetable or chicken
    stock, hot
seasoning
Parmesan cheese
chopped chives – optional

Fry the shallot in the oil, and then stir in the rice until coated with oil. Add a handful of the beetroot, the porcini and their soaking water, and the red wine. Simmer, stirring until the liquid is absorbed. Add a ladle of stock, and let the rice absorb it, before adding more liquid, and so on. Add the seasoning.

Once you have added half the stock, stir in the remaining beetroot. If the rice is not cooked to your liking once you have used all the stock, add boiling water.

Serve the risotto in heated bowls, and sprinkle with chopped chives, if you like. You can stir some grated Parmesan cheese into the risotto before serving it, or pass it round separately.

Rice is a major ingredient in the cooking of the Iberian peninsula, and I was told, when visiting Murcia, not to miss Alicante, described as the queen of rice-cooking. Our lunch at Darsena, right in the centre of the city overlooking the port, was well worth the journey, with its menu of 50 rice dishes. These will have been made from rice grown around Valencia, or possibly Seville. But in that part of Spain is an even more interesting rice-growing region, Calasparra.

To get there, take the N301 from Murcia north towards Albacete. After about 50 kilometres, take the Calasparra turning – it is the next one after the Jumilla turning – then drive about 28 kilometres to the town. The cooperative is on the Andalusia road, but, of course, the *tierras arroceras* are tucked away in small high valleys between the mountains, down twisting narrow lanes. These *tierras*, or rice paddies, have been in the same two hundred or so families for ever. They are small and are still worked by the families.

When we visited El Peralejo in spring, they were repairing the ditches and canals, which had been filled in and damaged by earth washed down from the mountains during recent storms. The previous summer had been very hot, with forest fires destroying much of the tree cover on the hillsides so that there was nothing to hold the soil back. By 1 May, they would have flooded the *tierras* by drawing water from the Rio Segura, and then sown the seeds. This is done in the old-fashioned way, broadcasting by hand.

Unlike Valencia and Seville, with their broad flat *tierras* at sea level, here the rice lands are about 500 metres above sea level, and much cooler; therefore, with a growing season six weeks longer than in other parts of Spain, harvesting begins in mid-October. This longer growing season gives a harder grain, which, of course, the locals say is the best rice in the world.

The land is organically cultivated with a lower yield than other rice-growing areas, and because it is labour-intensive, the rice is more expensive. Only half of the *tierras* are cultivated each year – the rest are left fallow. The area's Denominacion de Origen is heavily protected and rigorously controlled, and has finally just been recognized by the EU.

Until now, throughout the rice-growing world, there has been long-grain, round-grain and medium-grain rice. Calasparra has always been seen as a medium-grain rice. But the EU has decided that now there is only long-grain and round-grain rice, Indica and Japonica, and Calasparra is deemed to be round-grain rice.

The most prized variety of Calasparra rice is Bomba. Joaquín Salinas, director of the cooperative, told me that the locals recommend four parts water to one part rice with a cooking time of 24 to 25 minutes, on average, but it depends on how wet or dry you like your rice. When asked, he said his favourite rice dish was a local one cooked with white beans and dried whole red peppers, and it is indeed a very good one.

Four to five tonnes of Calasparra rice comes to Britain, ten times as much to France, and ninety to a hundred tonnes to Germany; in all some 20 to 30 per cent is exported. But much stays in Calasparra and nearby areas, as the people love it, eating it three times a week at least.

Arroz y alubiones empedrao
(Rice and beans with red peppers)

Serves 4 to 6

200g (7oz) dried white beans, large broad
    or butter beans, or the smaller cannellini,
    or haricot beans
3 tablespoons olive oil
3 cloves garlic, peeled and chopped
6 spring onions, trimmed and chopped
2 dried red pimentos
2 tomatoes, peeled, seeded and chopped
300g (10oz) Calasparra rice
½ teaspoon salt
good pinch of saffron
2 tablespoons chopped parsley
water

Soak the beans the night before, and the next day simmer until tender.

About 45 minutes before you want to serve the rice, heat the oil in a paella pan, and in it gently fry the onions, garlic and crushed pimentos for a few minutes. Remove, and put to one side.

Fry the tomatoes, and then add the rice, the rest of the ingredients, and 3 times as much water as rice, including the bean cooking liquid. Bring to the boil, add the beans, and cook for about 20 minutes. Serve immediately.

Stuffed vine leaves

Makes 36

36 vine leaves, packed in brine or freshly picked
350g (12oz) cooked meat, finely chopped or
    minced
350g (12oz) cooked rice, wild, basmati or
    Camargue
4 ripe tomatoes, seeded and chopped
1 onion, peeled and finely chopped
2 tablespoons pine nuts
2 tablespoons finely chopped mint, sage or
    coriander
crushed garlic – optional
sea salt
freshly ground black pepper

Bring a large pan of water to the boil, and drop in the well-washed vine leaves. Bring back to the boil, drain, rinse, and pat the leaves dry. If you use vine leaves packed in brine, drape these over a colander and rinse with a kettle of boiling water and dry them.

Mix the meat with the rest of the ingredients. Spoon a little on to a leaf and roll up into a cork shape. Place in an oiled ovenproof dish, and fill the rest of the leaves in the same way. Sprinkle with olive oil, and bake for 20 minutes at 180°C/350°F/gas mark 4 in the top half of the oven.

A cucumber and yoghurt salad is good with hot stuffed vine leaves. They are also very good cold.

Couscous

Although not a grain, but in fact a pasta-type preparation made with semolina, couscous is served as and acts like a grain, which is why I include this recipe here.

Couscous with vegetables

Serves 6 to 8

Couscous

The easiest way to prepare this, since most couscous that we buy is pre-cooked, is to measure out 70–85g (2½–3oz) per person, and for every portion, sprinkle on a tablespoon or two of hot water. Stir, cover with a tight-fitting lid, and set over a very low heat, using a heat-diffusing mat, if possible, to avoid burning. Check after 10 minutes, and break up the couscous with two forks to separate the grains. It will still be very firm, so add the same quantity of water once again and cover for 5 to 10 minutes. You might need to do this a third time before it is cooked to your liking. The grains should be dry, tender and fluffy, not at all soggy. An alternative cooking method is to steam the couscous in a sieve over the vegetable stew.

Grilled vegetables

2 aubergines
8 courgettes
4 peppers – red, yellow or both

Slice the aubergines lengthways, somewhat less than 1cm (½ inch thick). Slice the courgettes into thick, oblique slices with a broad cut surface, and quarter and seed the peppers. Place on a well-oiled grill pan or griddle, and cook at a moderately high heat, turning once until the vegetables are tender and a good colour. When cool enough to handle, peel the peppers.

Spiced green vegetable and chick-pea stew

2 onions, peeled and chopped
2 leeks, trimmed, sliced and washed
2 celery stalks, trimmed and sliced
2 tablespoons olive oil
½ teaspoon ground cardamom
½ teaspoon ground cumin
½ teaspoon ground coriander
½ teaspoon mixed spices
175g (6oz) green beans, topped, tailed and
    sliced, if necessary
175g (6oz) Savoy cabbage, shredded
1.15 litres (2 pints) vegetable stock or water
400g (14oz) drained canned chick-peas, or
    soaked and cooked chick-peas

Gently fry the first three vegetables in the olive oil in a saucepan or casserole. Sprinkle on the spices, and stir these in. Add the green vegetables and stock, and simmer for 20 minutes. Add the chick-peas, and cook for a further 10 minutes. Chop the coriander, and stir in before serving. Broccoli, kohlrabi and cauliflower can also be used in the stew.

Couscous

We have a local restaurant that is the very barometer of culinary fashion. Chinese when we first came to live in the area twenty years ago, it has been Thai, Mexican, Mediterranean, a tapas bar, and it is now Al Kasbah, with drawings of tagines and couscoussieres everywhere, for couscous is the staple of the moment. The French have been enjoying it for years.

Going to the local North African restaurant for *couscous royale* has been a part of French restaurant culture for as long as going out for a curry has been a part of ours. It is a most versatile staple, good hot or cold. Grain-like but, in fact, a type of pasta, couscous accompanies grills and stews, spicy or not, of meat, fish and vegetables, or in any combination. Easy to prepare by following the directions on the packet, most of

the couscous we buy is pre-cooked, requiring only moisturizing to allow it to swell, and gentle reheating. I usually pour on about a quarter of its volume of boiling water, stir with a fork put the lid on the pan and set it over the lowest burner, on a heat-diffuser, until ready, adding more water if necessary, and forking the 'grains' through to separate them.

To left-over couscous can be added sugar, cinnamon, and a dash of rose or orange-flower water. Steam it in a buttered basin, turn it out, and serve with cream for dessert or with hot milk instead of porridge for breakfast. You can also put in almonds and dried fruit before steaming it.

Meanwhile, of course, as we begin to explore the possibilities of couscous, the French have taken to basmati rice, and it is to be found by name on all the best menus in France.

To serve

fresh coriander, olives, toasted almonds and
raisins – for garnish

Heap the couscous on to a platter or a shallow bowl, arrange the grilled vegetables around it, and garnish with olives, coriander leaves, almonds and raisins.

The stew is served separately and eaten with the couscous and grilled vegetables. Harissa, the hot chilli sauce, is the usual accompaniment – a little on the side, to be added to each mouthful. It is usually sold in colourful blue and yellow tubes under the name Cap Bon. If you buy it in small cans, transfer the contents, once opened, to a small plastic or glass container. I keep it in the refrigerator where it seems to last almost indefinitely.

Fish couscous

To make the spice mixture used in this recipe, which is enough for several dishes, combine 1 tablespoon each ground allspice, black pepper, cardamom, chilli, cinnamon, cloves, coriander, cumin, ginger, paprika, and 1 teaspoon of powdered mace or nutmeg. If you grind the spices yourself, the mix-

ture will be that much fresher and more fragrant. Mix all together and store in a jar.

Serves 4

500g (generous 1lb) halibut steak in one piece
2–3 tablespoons groundnut or sunflower oil
1 onion, peeled and sliced
2 red peppers, seeded and sliced
4 courgettes, trimmed and sliced
1 aubergine, diced
about 250g (8oz) cabbage, shredded
spice mixture (see above)
600mls (1 pint) water
250g (8oz) cooked or canned chick-peas
fresh coriander leaves
salt
more coriander leaves and toasted flaked
almonds – for garnish

Heat the oil in a large frying pan, and fry the onion until golden brown. Stir in the rest of the vegetables, and fry for a few minutes, until coated with oil. Sprinkle on 2–3 tablespoons spice mixture, and stir well to coat the vegetables. Add the water, bring to the boil, partially cover, and simmer for 30–40 minutes. Add the drained chick-peas, and stir in some chopped fresh coriander. Check the seasoning, and add salt if necessary.

Divide the halibut into four equal pieces by removing the centre bone, or cook on the bone, as you wish. Rub 2–3 tablespoons of the spice mixture over the fish. Put the fish in the pan with the vegetables, cover, and let the fish steam for 8 to 10 minutes. Remove from the heat, and transfer the vegetables and fish to a shallow bowl.

For four people, you will need about 400g (14oz) couscous, to be cooked according to the directions on the packet. This can be done while the vegetables are cooking. Serve the pile of steaming couscous on a serving platter, decorated with coriander leaves and toasted flaked almonds.

For a hint of fruity sharp sweetness to the fish couscous, you can add some chopped pickled lemon or mango chutney.

Trahana

Like couscous, *trahana* is not a grain. I include the next recipe because *trahana* is an ingredient that readers write to me about occasionally; they pick it up on holiday in Greece, or friends send it to them. It is available here from shops selling Greek products and is imported by Odyssea. It is wonderfully tasty stuff, and almost identical to the Hungarian *tarhonya*, Turkish *tarhana* and the *kishk* of the Arabian peninsula.

Trahana is a portable instant food: wheat flour is mixed with yoghurt, sheep's milk or soft cheese, moistened, rolled into balls, and left to dry, not unlike couscous. Then, in former times, it could be packed into saddlebags, loaded onto camels or horses, and used as 'fast food' by being reconstituted in hot water at a desert encampment or on the Magyar plain.

Turkey and *trahana* soup

Turkey stock can be replaced with chicken, duck or game stock to good effect.

Serves 4

1 onion, peeled and finely chopped
2 celery stalks, trimmed and finely sliced
1 leek, trimmed, sliced and thoroughly rinsed

1–2 teaspoons turkey fat
1.25 litres (2 pints) turkey stock
150–200g (5–7oz) *trahana*
3 tablespoons chopped fresh coriander
100g (4oz) feta cheese, crumbled

Fry the vegetables in a saucepan in the turkey fat until golden brown. Add the stock, and cook for 20 minutes. Then add the *trahana* and half the coriander.

Cook until the *trahana* is soft, and then stir in the remaining coriander and the feta cheese, and serve in heated soup plates, with warm pitta bread.

Trahana can be replaced with couscous or with bulgar wheat, but the flavour and texture of the soup will not be quite the same.

Quinoa

Quinoa is the very small seeds of a grass originally grown in Latin America but now more widely cultivated. The small grains make a tasty and unusual alternative to other cereals.

Warm quinoa and lentil salad with mint and sherry vinaigrette

Combining both grains and pulses, this is an extremely nutritious dish, and full of flavour.

Serves 6 to 8

230g (½lb) Puy or other small 'blue' lentils
125g (4oz) quinoa
extra-virgin olive oil
sherry vinegar
fresh mint leaves, shredded or chopped
fresh basil leaves, shredded or chopped
6–8 spring onions, trimmed and chopped, or 3
    shallots, peeled and chopped – both optional
seasoning

Cook the pulses and grains separately, in water; the lentils in at least twice their volume, the quinoa in 2 to 3 times its volume. Drain and mix them, and stir in, to taste, the olive oil and vinegar, and then add the herbs, as much or as little as you like, the onions, if using them, and some seasoning. Serve warm.

Pulses

Mussel, bean and celery soup

Serves 2

2 celery stalks, trimmed and diced
300mls (1½ pint) light chicken or fish stock
1 can cannellini or haricot beans
1 litre (1¾ pints) mussels
2 tablespoons finely chopped parsley
freshly ground pepper

Cook the celery in the stock until soft, and meanwhile prepare the mussels by scrubbing, cleaning, rinsing and steaming until they open. Strain the juices into the stock, and when cooked enough to handle, remove the mussels from the shells. Sieve some of the beans to a purée and thus thicken the soup.

Add the rest of the beans and the parsley. Bring to the boil, season with the pepper, and drop in the mussels. Allow them to heat through, and serve the soup.

The addition of herbs such as savory or basil will nicely complement the flavour of the mussels.

Try this variation. Dice some smoked bacon, and fry the celery and some chopped onion with it; then add a couple of peeled, diced potatoes with the stock, and you have a warming chowder, substantial enough for a main course.

Golden lentil soup

Serves 2

1 onion, peeled and diced
a little olive oil
400mls (14oz) chicken, ham or vegetable stock
100g (4oz) orange lentils
salt
pepper
mace or nutmeg

Fry the onion until golden brown in the olive oil, and then add stock and lentils and a touch of seasoning. Cook until the lentils are soft, and then sieve or liquidize, and add more seasoning to taste as you reheat the soup before serving.

To add some crunch to the soup, scatter on some croûtons, crisp bacon bits or duck skin, as you like.

White bean, sage and ham soup

Serves 4 to 6

250g (½lb) cannellini or haricot beans (dry weight), soaked overnight
1 meaty ham bone, smoked or unsmoked, to taste
2.25 litres (4 pints) water
1 celery stalk, trimmed and sliced
1 onion, peeled and sliced
1 leek, trimmed and sliced
2 or 3 sprigs of fresh sage
3 sprigs flat-leaf parsley
pinch of coarse sea salt
pinch of white pepper
100g (4oz) soured cream or crème fraiche

Put the soaked beans, ham bone, water and vegetables in a large saucepan, together with the sage and parsley stems. Bring to the boil, skim any foam from the surface, partially cover, and simmer for 3 to 4 hours.

Remove the ham bone and the herb stems. Blend the soup until smooth, sieve, if you wish, and return it to the saucepan. Thin the soup, if you like, with ham or vegetable stock or water.

Tear up the herbs, and grind them to a paste in a mortar with the sea salt and pepper. Heat the cream in a separate pan and stir in the herbs until well blended.

Bring the soup to the boil, ladle into soup bowls, and swirl the sage cream on top. Serve immediately.

Black bean terrine

Serves 4 to 6

approx. 600mls (1 pint) volume of cooked black beans
2 leaves or 2 teaspoons gelatine, softened in as little water as possible
300mls (½ pint) vegetable or chicken stock
1 small chilli, seeded and chopped, or dried chilli flakes, to taste
50–75g (2–3oz) chorizo sausage – optional
2 spring onions, peeled, trimmed and chopped
1 tablespoon fresh coriander leaves

Put the gelatine in the stock, and heat just until it dissolves. Put all the ingredients in the food processor, having first skinned the chorizo and chopped it in chunks. The mixture should not be blended too smooth; in fact, the whole thing can be made by hand, mashing the beans, finely chopping the other ingredients, and mixing in the stock and gelatine.

Line a 1kg (2lbs) loaf tin with clingfilm. Pour in the mixture, tap it down to eliminate any air pockets. Loosely cover with clingfilm, and leave until set. Turn out the terrine and serve it sliced. Sour cream or yoghurt, mixed with chopped chillies, spring onion or coriander, or all three ingredients, is good with this, as is a fruity salsa, some warm bread and a tomato salad.

Spiced salmon kebabs on a bed of golden lentils

Serves 4

Lentils

250g (½lb) red lentils
1 piece of cinnamon stick
2 cloves
6 cardamom pods, split open
1 small onion, peeled and finely chopped
2 tablespoons olive oil or groundnut oil

Rinse and drain the lentils. Fry the spices and onion in the oil for a few minutes. Add the lentils, and pour in about 450mls (¾ pint) water. Bring to the boil, cover and reduce the heat to the merest simmer. Cook until the lentils are tender, topping up with more water if necessary. Meanwhile, prepare the fish.

Kebabs

750g (1½lbs) salmon fillet
50g (2oz) melted butter, olive oil or groundnut oil
1 tablespoon ground coriander
2 teaspoons ground cumin
1 teaspoon ground allspice
½ teaspoon ground cardamom
½ teaspoon ground turmeric
½ teaspoon ground black pepper
¼ teaspoon dried chilli flakes
16 bay leaves

Skin the salmon, and remove as many bones as possible. Heat the fat in a small pan, and fry the spices in it for 4 to 5 minutes. Remove from the heat and allow to cool slightly. Brush this paste all over the fish, and cut into even-size pieces to thread on 4 skewers, interspersed with bay leaves. Have the grill moderately hot, and grill the salmon skewers for a couple of minutes on each surface.

Serve on the lentils, perhaps with a yoghurt, mint and cucumber sauce. Make this by shredding and pounding fresh mint and a little salt in a mortar. Mix it with plain yoghurt and grate in some cucumber.

Dinner party for six

'Scotch' eggs with an oriental dip

Pheasant breasts with wild berries and celeriac

Lemon syllabub in an almond pastry tart

A very elegant version of Scotch eggs, stuffed pheasant breasts served with celeriac and a berry sauce, and lemon syllabub in an almond pastry tart, make for a delightful autumn dinner, suitably festive for entertaining. And parts of the meal can be prepared in advance, which is always a help.

Quail eggs are fiddly things to shell, and I would not usually recommend them for a meal for six, cooked single-handed. But these can be boiled in advance, and their 'jackets' and dipping sauce prepared ahead of time, leaving you only to deep-fry and then serve them. They are delicious morsels, and this is a useful recipe to keep for the holiday season, when you want a change from cheese straws and sausages on sticks to serve with drinks.

You do not, of course, need to make all three mixtures for coating the quail eggs; choose whichever you prefer and adjust the quantities accordingly. As an alternative to the oriental dip, tartare sauce is worth considering, and a spicy tomato ketchup would go well with the crisp, deep-fried coated eggs.

The pheasant season opens on 1 October and lasts until January. They are at their very best in late November and December. As the meat veers more towards blandness than gameyness, I have chosen to accompany it with the robust flavours of black pudding, cabbage, celeriac and berries. Together these produce a richly appetizing dish, pleasing to the eye as well as to the palate.

Rather than roast a couple of pheasants to serve six people, I prefer to buy three birds, use the breasts in this recipe, and the legs for a casserole, game crumble or a pheasant sauce for pasta. The sinewy meat on the legs responds better to slow,

moist cooking, whereas the tender breasts can be cooked quickly, with dry heat, or cooked in the oven. This recipe, as with most recipes for pheasant, will do equally well with chicken. You might, for example, use chicken liver instead of black pudding for the stuffing, and make the sauce with cranberries and a little chopped kumquat for a more piquant sauce.

Root vegetables are marvellous with game, absorbing its deep, savoury gravy and offering as a foil a nice earthy sweetness; swedes, parsnips, carrots, turnips and celeriac can be used singly, or in combination. And they can be cooked in various ways. Thinly cut and deep-fried, they make a good alternative to game chips; cut into rough chunks and roasted in the oven, they become tender inside, with dark, chewy caramelized edges. Or you can boil and mash them to a purée, adding herbs, spices and other aromatics. Carrots and parsnips with cardamom is a favourite in my house, as is celeriac and potatoes with mustard seeds. Or you can peel and slice the vegetables, and then cook them in water with a little butter, adding, as they begin to glaze, a dash of lemon, lime or orange juice and a grating of zest. In the following recipe I use sliced celeriac, as one might use a savoury toast under roast grouse or woodcock. Whenever I use celeriac, I always prepare more than I need, dropping the rest into acidulated water to keep it white. Then I cut it into julienne strips, and make celeriac remoulade with a creamy mustard dressing. This is particularly good topped with some freshly cooked juicy mussels.

Dairy-based desserts have always been a mainstay of traditional British cooking. This is to be expected since our cream is the envy of pastry cooks around the world. Junkets, trifles, syllabubs, custards and creams are suave, silky and satisfying desserts. I prefer to keep the flavours simple rather than complex, and thus I prefer vanilla or lemon to chocolate and coffee cream desserts.

The dessert recipe combines a crisp, rich, almond pastry shell, which you can make in advance, with a foamy cloud of whipped cream syllabub, flavoured with white wine and lemon. It is a most delectable dessert, and very pretty to look at. This recipe too is open to many permutations. Substitute 25g (1oz) flour in the pastry for an equal amount of cocoa, to make chocolate almond pastry. Fill it with chocolate cream and top with poached pears, or fill the pre-baked plain almond pastry tart with pastry

cream and on top place dried apricots, which you have first poached to soften them.

'Scotch' eggs with an oriental dip

Makes 24

24 quail eggs
100g (4oz) cooked salmon
100g (4oz) prawns, shelled
100g (4oz) crabmeat
salt
pepper
1 tablespoon chives, finely chopped
1 tablespoon coriander, finely chopped
1 tablespoon basil, finely chopped
2 free-range egg whites
breadcrumbs
oil for frying

dip

1 fresh red chilli, seeded and chopped
1 teaspoon freshly grated ginger
1 clove garlic, peeled and crushed
1 teaspoon Dijon mustard, or ½ teaspoon
    wasabi paste
1 tablespoon rice or sherry vinegar
1–2 tablespoons light muscovado sugar
1 tablespoon toasted sesame oil
2–3 tablespoons soy sauce
100mls (4oz) groundnut oil

Boil the quail eggs for 3 minutes. Cool and shell.

Separately process the fish with a little seasoning and herbs – salmon with the chives, prawns with the coriander and crab with the basil.

Whisk the egg whites lightly, and divide among the three mixtures, using them as a binder. Use each mixture to wrap 8 quail eggs. Roll them in the breadcrumbs, and chill for an hour or so to firm them up.

Heat a pan of groundnut or sunflower oil to 170°C/ 325°F, and fry the eggs until golden brown. Drain. Mix the ingredients together for the spicy oriental dip and serve with the eggs.

Pheasant breasts with wild berries and celeriac

Serves 6

3 whole pheasant breasts; use the carcasses for
    the stock
2–3 tablespoons butter
1 large mild onion, peeled and thinly sliced
200g (7oz) blueberries, or bilberries
2 tablespoons elderberries
several sprigs of flat-leaf parsley, finely chopped,
    plus extra for garnish
2 garlic cloves, peeled and crushed
200g (7oz) black pudding
6 large cabbage leaves, blanched
flour
salt and pepper
100mls (4oz) fino or dry Amontillado sherry
1 bay leaf
1 celeriac

Remove the pheasant breasts from the bone, chop the carcasses, and put in a saucepan of water. Bring to the boil. Skim the foam from the surface, and simmer. Reduce until you have about 500mls (18oz) stock. You can prepare this the day before.

When ready to prepare the dish, which should not now take much more than 40 to 50 minutes, melt the butter, and in it gently cook the onion until soft and golden. Add half the blueberries and all of the elderberries, parsley and garlic, and once the onion is soft, add the crumbled black pudding, and mix well.

Make a pocket in the pheasant breasts, and fill with the mixture. Wrap them in the cabbage leaves, and tie with thread. Dust with the flour, and fry on all sides. Season and place in a shallow earthenware casserole dish.

Pour in the sherry and the stock, and add the bay leaf. Cook in the oven at 180°C/350°F/gas mark 4 for about 20 to 25 minutes.

Meanwhile, trim the celeriac and cut into 6 rounds. Blanch them for 10 minutes, then brush with oil or butter and cook in the top of the oven until golden brown.

To serve, put some celeriac on each plate, cut each pheasant breast in half, and place the two pieces at an angle on the celeriac, with the meat juices from the pan around it and extra berries and parsley for garnish.

You can replace the black pudding with coarse Lincolnshire or other sausage meat, crumbling and lightly frying before you add it to the stuffing. Dried cranberries, blueberries or cherries, soaked in a little brandy, can be used to replace the fresh berries, if you prefer. For a more homely version of this dish, pot-roast two whole pheasants, stuffed with the berries, herbs and sausage meat, and serve with braised cabbage and roasted celeriac chunks.

Lemon syllabub in an almond pastry tart

Note: This recipe contains raw eggs.

Serves 6

200g (7oz) plain flour
100g (3½oz) unsalted butter, chilled and diced
50g (2oz) ground almonds
1 free-range egg yolk
icing sugar
chilled water

syllabub
300mls (½ pint) double cream
300mls (½ pint) whipping cream
1 free-range egg white

grated zest of a lemon, infused overnight in
   3–4 tablespoons muscat wine, sweet Loire
   wine or cream sherry, with a little freshly
   grated nutmeg
icing sugar for dusting
freshly grated nutmeg

Rub the flour and butter together, and then with a knife stir in the ground almonds and then the egg yolk, a tablespoon or so of sifted icing sugar, and enough chilled water to bind it to a dough.

Chill it, wrapped, for half an hour. Roll out the pastry, and line a tart tin about 20–25cms (8–10 inches) and bake blind for 20 to 25 minutes in a preheated oven at 180°C/350°F/gas mark 4. Remove from the oven and cool.

Whisk the creams to firm peaks, add the wine and lemon zest, and then separately whisk the egg white and fold into the cream.

Dust the pastry case with icing sugar, and spoon in the syllabub. Grate nutmeg on top before serving.

As with all my ingredients, I try to buy organic meat when I can, or meat that comes from traceable sources with high standards of animal husbandry. This might mean shopping at the local butcher, buying meat mail-order or visiting farm shops on my travels. Supermarkets too are paying attention to the consumer, and most of them stock a range of organic meat.

There are so many other good things to eat that it would be a pity to eat meat every day. With a richly varied diet, one can afford to eat good meat a couple of times a week.

My meat recipes come from all over, many of them collected on my travels, some developed in my own kitchen. They include quickly cooked dishes, ideal for when time is short, and some delicious slow-cooked dishes which are perfect for entertaining.

As a general rule of thumb in meat cookery, the less money you spend on the meat, the more time is needed to prepare it. Tender cuts of meat are the most expensive ones, and these take the least time to cook.

Stock

During the ban on beef on the bone, one had to think about alternatives, not only to beef on the bone, but to stock made from beef bones.

First of all, it is worth considering whether you really need stock. The secret of a good meat sauce for spaghetti is not stock, but slow cooking.

Instead of trying to cook in 10 to 20 minutes, slow down. Plan your time in the kitchen so that when you have time available, you use it to make several dishes that benefit from extra preparation and cooking time, for use later in the week. Make a batch of ragout, or meat sauce, and freeze some.

A quick sauce for a steak does not need stock, either. Sear the meat in a greased heavy stainless-steel frying pan, and once the steak is cooked, deglaze the pan with wine, let it boil for a few minutes, season, and serve with the steak.

If you must have stock at all costs, use about 100g (4oz) of the cheaper cuts of beef to a litre (1¾ pints) of water, with some celery leaves, a bay leaf and a slice of ginger. Simmer for an hour or two.

A cheaper way of acquiring stock for a casserole is to buy your meat in a whole piece, trim it, dice it and use the trimmings to make a little stock while you fry the meat, onions and vegetables.

However, if you are really in a hurry, there are a number of ingredients which can add flavour to your cooking. Wine, vermouth, soy sauce, miso (fermented soy bean paste, sometimes with rice and other cereals added) and dried mushrooms, especially ceps and shiitake, are invaluable for their flavouring and savoury qualities.

To add colour as well as flavour, halve an onion and let it caramelize slowly, cut side down, in a small heavy frying pan, and then add water, bring to the boil, simmer for 5 minutes and strain, to produce a rich brown juice. This is, to my mind, rather more effective than adding a piece of onion skin to the stockpot.

Another type of flavouring, which at first might seem bizarre when added to meat, is that of cured or dried fish. This technique is much used in oriental cooking with, for example, dashi, Japanese stock ingredients of dried tuna flakes and seaweed, and Chinese and Vietnamese fish sauce, or nuoc mam; and in Sri Lankan cooking, where Maldive fish, pounded dried tuna or other oily fish are used. But a dash of anchovy essence will do just as well, adding a surprising, yet subtle, depth of flavour.

Beef

Of all the cuts of beef, steak is one of the most popular. Steak cuts for grilling or frying come in a wide range. The fillet yields the lean, very tender and most expensive tournedos, mignon and the thicker chateaubriand; in my view these pieces, although tender, can lack the flavour of other steaks. The entrecôte is the lean, tender piece cut from the boneless sirloin, by which name the steak is also known. Porterhouse steak is cut from the wing end of the sirloin, and the T-bone steak is cut right across the sirloin, to include the bone and the fillet. Rump steak is the large, long cut taken from the top of the rump, a full-flavoured and tender piece of meat. The very tasty, tender and inexpensive feather steak comes from the forequarter, normally used for stewing or braising beef. Also inexpensive is the skirt steak from the belly of the animal, and the flank steak from the forequarter, juicy and delicious when cooked rare, dry and tough when overcooked.

Do not salt the meat before cooking, as this will draw the juices to the surface, and the meat will steam rather than sear. This is not a spelling error. You cannot 'seal' meat. It has been proved conclusively that meat juices are not sealed in on contact with high heat.

The frying pan or grill should be lightly greased so that the meat does not stick on contact and then tear on removal. Have the pan or grill very hot before putting in the steak. Cooking time depends entirely on the thickness of the meat and your judgement as to what constitutes 'done'. A meat thermometer takes away some of the guesswork, and eventually you will be able to judge by looking at and touching the meat. Rare beef is 51°C (123°F), 60°C (140°F) is medium and 70°C (158°F) is overdone.

Grilled skirt steak

Meat that has undergone tenderizing by a commercial product is disagreeable, as you may well know if you have had it in restaurants. However, a quick dip in pineapple juice, which contains the powerful tenderizing enzyme papain, can do wonders for a piece of beef. I once had some lightly smoked beef fillet which had been marinated in pineapple juice, but this was rather a pointless exercise given that the cut is naturally tender. But I adapted the idea and sometimes use it for skirt steak.

This is a very flavoursome piece of meat, but it can sometimes be chewy and even tough. The secret is to cook it quickly and serve it rare, since the longer it cooks the tougher it becomes. I think it is best to buy one large thick piece of skirt, and slice it for serving. A ridged cast-iron grill that rests on two rings on the hob is excellent for fast grilling, imitating the appearance, if not the flavour, of the charcoal grill.

Serves 3 or 4

500g (1lb) beef, either thick skirt or goose skirt, in a piece
2 mild onions, peeled and thinly sliced
150mls (¼ pint) unsweetened pineapple juice
6 juniper berries, crushed
freshly ground black pepper

Remove any thick membranes from the meat.

Put a layer of onion in a bowl, the meat on top, and another layer of onion on top. Pour over the juice, and scatter on the juniper berries and pepper. Leave for 40 minutes or so, turning the meat once.

Heat the grill, and when it is very hot remove the meat from the marinade, dry it thoroughly, and grill it for 6 to 8 minutes on each side, turning it carefully once. Remove from the grill, and allow to rest in a warm place before carving.

A little sauce can be made by frying the onion in butter until soft, adding the spices, pineapple juice and a little beef stock, and cooking for 20 minutes or so. This is best done before you put the beef under the grill.

Rub the mixture through a sieve for a thick oniony sauce, or simply allow the liquid to strain through for a liquid one.

Steak and chips go wonderfully well together (see p. 197 for how to make the perfect chip).

Steak tartare for two

For the next recipe I usually buy a tail-end piece of fillet steak, less expensive than the thick end of the fillet. Finely chop or mince it rather than using the food processor, as this produces a better texture.

300–400g (10–14oz) well-trimmed steak, finely chopped
2 free-range egg yolks
additional flavours, to taste – finely chopped shallots, parsley, capers, gherkins, salt, freshly ground black pepper, Worcester sauce

Mix the steak with one egg yolk per person, and then, if you are following tradition, the shallots, parsley, capers and gherkins. The mixture is then seasoned and shaped into two patties or mounds. I prefer to leave out the gherkins, and I use a very light hand with the Worcester sauce.

Fresh toast is the traditional accompaniment, although in Brussels and Paris it is usually served with a heap of *frites*.

Meat

Tripe

Pinkly grilled calf's liver and sautéed chicken livers, roasted veal kidneys and devilled lamb's kidneys, brains in brown butter sauce, sweetbreads sliced and fried to a golden brown, black pudding, pig's ears and feet, oxtail: I like to cook offal of all kinds, but I think tripe may be my favourite. I came to like it as a child when my father would occasionally cook it for supper.

As well as being a great favourite in the north of England, tripe is part of the robust rural cooking of many countries, including Portugal, Mexico, Spain, Italy, Brazil, China, Turkey and France. In Taiwan it is cooked with black beans and ginger. In Istanbul tripe soup is a great restorative after a night out.

In France Madame Saint-Ange had several tripe recipes in her book, as did Escoffier, and both listed tripe à l'anglaise, dipped in breadcrumbs and fried. You will not find tripe recipes in all English cookery books, however. Mrs Marshall, Mrs Peel and Mrs Acton offer nothing between trifle and trout. Mrs Beeton, on the other hand, not only gives recipes for tripe, but describes the laborious process of dressing it, which requires much stripping, scraping and cleansing before hours of boiling in several changes of water. Dressing tripe has been likened to cleaning out the Augean stables.

In Britain it is usually sold dressed. And with it, you can make several delicious dishes. One, a Hannah Glasse recipe, takes a large square of tripe – honeycomb is best – which is rolled around a forcemeat of breadcrumbs well seasoned with salt, pepper, herbs, nutmeg and lemon peel and bound with an egg. The roll is then basted with butter and roasted. Another favourite dish of tripe is based on a classical recipe of ancient Rome, tripe with honey and ginger sauce, which one could well imagine found its way to Britain too.

Beef Stroganoff for two

For this quick recipe, as for the previous one, I use rump steak, feather steak or the tail-end of fillet, which your butcher should let you have cheaper than the premium cut.

    400g (14oz) steak
    1 shallot, finely chopped
    150g (5oz) button mushrooms
    25g (1oz) butter
    2 tablespoons soured cream or crème fraiche

Slice the steak, flatten the slices, and cut into finger-size pieces. Fry the shallot, then the mushrooms, in the butter, and when soft, add the meat. Cook for a minute or two on a high heat, and then add the crème fraiche or soured cream. Season to taste and serve.

This is excellent served over a bed of rice, especially a mix of basmati, wild rice and Camargue red rice.

The recipe can be adapted to other tender cuts of meat, such as chicken breasts, pork fillet, veal and turkey, all equally good served with rice. These should all be well cooked, and indeed there is no merit in undercooking the beef, as its juices would then stain the cream sauce.

Steak with balsamic vinegar

The traditional balsamic vinegar of Modena – *aceto balsamico tradizionale di Modena* – is so mellow that one can use it to deglaze the pan for a quick sauce, as one might use wine.

Serves 2

    2 fillet steaks
    1 tablespoon extra-virgin olive oil
    salt
    freshly ground black pepper
    2 tablespoons traditional balsamic vinegar of
        Modena

Trim any fat from the meat. Heat the olive oil in a heavy frying pan, and fry the meat on both sides until it is done to your liking.

Season, and place on serving plates. Put the vinegar in the pan, boil, and scrape up any residues, and spoon on to the steaks. Serve immediately.

Quick Caribbean beef steak

Basing it on the traditional sweet beef pot roast of Cartagena in Colombia, I have used the essential ingredients of rum and molasses sugar to make this quickly cooked dish, choosing an inexpensive yet flavoursome cut of beef.

The meat is marinated overnight in spices and onions, and then quickly fried and the pan deglazed with wine, rum and molasses sugar to produce a richly flavoured sauce to accompany the meat, which is served with coconut rice or mashed potatoes.

Serves 6 to 8

1kg (2lbs) skirt steak in a piece, or 6 x 175g
    (6oz) feather steaks
2 onions, peeled and grated
½ teaspoon crushed allspice
1 teaspoon salt
2 teaspoons freshly ground black pepper
2 tablespoons wine vinegar
4 whole cloves
1 bay leaf
4 tablespoons molasses sugar
4 tablespoons each water, rum and dry red wine

Rub the meat all over with the onions, allspice, salt, pepper and vinegar. Stick the cloves and bay leaf into the meat. Cover, and marinate for several hours or overnight.

Heat a well-seasoned or non-stick frying pan and cook the steak on each side for 4 to 5 minutes. Remove and keep it warm. Add the sugar and liquids to the pan and cook for 3 to 4 minutes until you have a well-flavoured sauce. Serve the meat, sliced if using skirt steak, on top of the rice or mashed potatoes and pour the sauce over it.

Roast rib of beef

Roast beef is the perfect Sunday lunch for family and friends, especially when you serve it with all the trimmings, crisp light Yorkshire puddings, proper gravy and golden roast potatoes.

Serves 6

a wing rib joint of 2 ribs, weighing about 2 kg
    (4–5lbs)
freshly ground black pepper
flour

Have the chine bone cut through and separated from the rib, but not removed.

Season the meat with the pepper, and dust the fat side with flour. Roast in a hot oven, at least 200°C/400°F/gas mark 6, for 22 minutes per kg (10 minutes per lb), for rare to medium-rare beef, and then remove from the oven. Cover the meat loosely with foil, and keep it warm for 15 to 20 minutes before you carve it into nice, evenly pink slices.

When cooked, the wing rib is one of the easiest joints to carve, even though it is on the bone. To carve, all you do, with a sharp knife, is simply remove the loosened chine bone and detach the meat from the rib bone or bones. Cut into short, vertical slices. The same applies even with a larger joint with 3 or 4 ribs. The rib bone is worth keeping for a little beef stock, as it will have browned in the oven to give any stock a good colour.

Gravy

Make this while the beef is resting. Pour off any excess fat and sift a tablespoon of flour into the roasting tin. Scrape up any juices stuck to the bottom and work in the flour. Add a little boiling water, stock or red wine and stir until the mixture forms a slightly thickened sauce, adding more liquid as necessary. A splash of port or Madeira is a good addition, as is a hint of mustard. Strain into a small saucepan and let the gravy simmer for 5 minutes or so, before pouring into a warm jug. I should say 'gravy boat', but I have never had a gravy boat; I suppose that is because I have never had a dinner service.

Yorkshire pudding

One Sunday I thought I'd be rather smart and cook and serve a large Yorkshire pudding in my new enamelled cast-iron rectangular roaster. Disaster. The pudding remained as flat as a pancake. The secret to a good Yorkshire pudding is the thinnest possible tin, to keep the temperature high.

2 free-range eggs
250mls (8oz) each milk and water, mixed
250g (8oz) plain flour
½ teaspoon salt
2 tablespoons dripping from the roasting pan

Beat the eggs with the liquid. Gradually beat in the flour and the salt until you have smooth batter, and then let it stand for 30 to 40 minutes. Place the dripping in a roasting tin or

Yorkshire pudding tin, and place it in the top of a preheated oven at 200°C/400°F/gas mark 6 to heat up almost to smoking point.

Pour the batter into the hot roasting tin, and bake for about 25 minutes, until the pudding is well risen and golden. Cut it into squares, and serve either before the meat course, with gravy, or alongside the meat. You can, of course, make the Yorkshire pudding in individual tins, in which case bake for 12 to 15 minutes.

Potted beef

Here is a good way of using up leftovers from a joint of beef, good on toast or in sandwiches.

Using the food processor, put diced cooked beef in the bowl, a pinch of mace, some freshly ground black pepper, softened butter in equal proportion to the meat, or less butter if you prefer, and a dash of port or Madeira, as well as 2–3 tablespoons of gravy if there is any left. Blend until smooth, spoon into a bowl, and pour clarified butter over the top, which will seal it until required. Refrigerate.

Classic daube of beef

Serves 6 to 8

1 onion, peeled and thinly sliced
3 celery stalks, trimmed and cut into batons
2 tablespoons extra-virgin olive oil
1kg (2lbs) beef, cubed
3 tablespoons seasoned plain flour
½ bottle full-bodied red wine
finely pared zest and juice of an orange
2 tablespoons black olives
8 pieces dried tomato, each snipped into 2 or 3
    pieces
freshly ground pepper
1 bay leaf
sprig of rosemary
½ teaspoon fennel seeds – optional
salt, if needed

In a frying pan fry the onion and celery in the oil until the onion is golden brown. Transfer to a casserole. Dust the meat in the seasoned flour and brown it in the frying pan. Add it to the casserole. Pour the wine into the frying pan and boil it up, scraping up any cooking residues. When reduced

by about a third, pour it over the beef. Cut the zest into fine shreds and stir it and the juice into the beef, adding also the olives, tomato, pepper and herbs. Put the lid on and cook the casserole in a preheated oven at about 180°C/350°F/gas mark 4 for 2 hours. Check the seasoning when you are ready to serve. Olives are quite salty and you are unlikely to need to add extra salt. Jacket or mashed potatoes are perfect with this, and instead of another vegetable accompaniment, I would serve a green salad afterwards, to mop up any remaining gravy.

Left-over daube is excellent reheated and served with fresh pasta or gnocchi, and it also makes a very good filling for homemade ravioli.

Steak and kidney pudding

In Victorian times, when fresh oysters were inexpensive, they were a traditional ingredient in steak and kidney pudding, placed on top of the filling, just under the suet crust. In this recipe I have used mushrooms, but this does not mean that you cannot also add the oysters.

These ingredients fill a 1.75 litre (3 pint) pudding basin.

Serves 6 to 8

1kg (2lbs) rump, chuck or blade steak
250g (½lb) ox or veal kidney
250g (½lb) button or cap mushrooms, brushed
    and sliced
1 large onion, peeled and chopped
about 200mls (7oz) water, stock or ale
salt
freshly ground black pepper

crust
250g (½lb) self-raising flour
pinch of salt
125g (¼lb) suet, grated
iced water

Trim the meat, and dice it into 4cm (1½ inch) cubes. Halve the kidney, snip out the core, remove any fat, and dice the kidney.

Make the pastry by sifting the flour and salt into a bowl, then add the suet and lightly rub into the flour until you have the texture of breadcrumbs. Gradually add a little iced water. This amount of fat and flour will take about 125mls (4oz). With your hands or a knife, work it together just until you have a soft, pliable, but not wet dough. Lightly and briefly, knead the dough on a floured work surface until just smooth, then roll it out with quick, light strokes. Flour the dough if necessary, but sparingly, to stop it sticking, and roll out to a diameter of 30–35cm (12–14 inches).

Grease the pudding basin, and fold the dough in four. Cut away a quarter and save this for the lid. With the broad edge outwards, fit the pastry into the basin. Press it to the sides. It will overhang the edges of the basin. Leave enough to build a pastry rim around the lip of the basin, to which you can anchor the pastry lid.

Pile the steak, kidney, onion and mushrooms into the lined pudding basin. Add the liquid, and season lightly.

Gather together all the remaining pastry trimmings, and roll out a round of pastry to generously fit the top of the basin. Pinch together where the lid joins the pastry walls, to seal it well. Cover with a round of greased greaseproof paper, pleated down the middle to allow the pudding to rise, and tie a pudding cloth over it. Place on a steamer rack in a saucepan, and pour in enough boiling water to come a quarter of the way up the basin. Cover with a lid, and steam for 2 to 2½ hours, adding more boiling water if there is a danger of the pan drying out.

Turn the pudding out onto a heated serving plate. Serve by cutting into wedges and transferring to hot dinner plates.

Carrots, celeriac and other traditional root vegetables are excellent accompaniments to the homely steak and kidney pudding.

Oxtail casserole with apple and horseradish mash and herb dumplings

Like steak and kidney pudding, oxtail soups and casseroles are perfect winter food. Slow cooking warms up the kitchen and fills the whole house with good smells.

Serves 4

2 oxtails cut into chunks
1 tablespoon olive oil
1 large onion
2 bay leaves
300mls (½ pint) brown ale
300mls (½ pint) water or beef stock
6 stoned prunes
1kg (2lbs) potatoes
1 Bramley apple

about 2 tablespoons grated horseradish, or to taste
butter and milk for mashing
salt and pepper

Brown the oxtail in the olive oil, and transfer the pieces to a casserole. Peel and slice the onion, and lightly brown it too, before adding it to the casserole. Tuck in the bay leaves.

Pour the ale into the frying pan, and bring to the boil, scraping up any caramelized cooking juices stuck to the bottom of the pan. Pour over the oxtail.

Add enough stock or water to come about three-quarters of the way to covering the meat. Simmer on the stove or cook in a very low oven, about 150°C/300°F/ gas mark 2, for 2 to 3 hours until the meat is tender.

Strain the cooking juices into a bowl. Cool, and then refrigerate until next day, when you can lift off the layer of fat.

When the meat is cool enough to handle, remove all the bones, put the meat in a container, cover, and refrigerate until next day. You can make this dish on the same day you serve it, but I think it is even better the following day.

Peel and boil the potatoes, and when they are almost done, add the peeled, cored and sliced Bramley, and continue boiling until both are soft. Drain and mash with the milk and butter, adding the horseradish and seasoning to taste.

Meanwhile, chop the prunes, and mix them with the meat and a few spoonfuls of the by now jellied cooking juices. Reheat thoroughly, and reduce the remaining cooking juices, if they need it, and add to the meat. Serve in large shallow soup plates, with a helping each of mash and herb dumplings.

Herb dumplings

Serves 4

100g (4oz) soft white breadcrumbs
100g (4oz) plain flour
1½ teaspoons baking powder
50g (2oz) finely chopped or grated suet
grated rind of a lemon
grated rind of an orange
1 spring onion, finely chopped
2 tablespoons herbs, finely chopped
seasoning
2 free-range eggs, lightly beaten

Mix together all the dry ingredients, including the suet, and then bind to a soft dough with the eggs. With floured hands, form into small balls, or shape into quenelles with two wet teaspoons. Lower into boiling water, and poach for 15 minutes or so, then drain and serve with the stew.

Veal

When I can, I like to buy free-range English veal. Unlike veal from loose-housed calves – or worse, from calves housed in the infamous crates – this meat comes from young animals reared with their mothers, and suckled either at pasture, or if the weather is unsuitable, in airy barns. Their diet is grass or hay, as well as their mothers' milk, which produces a light pink meat rather than the iron-deficient flesh of crated calves.

Much of the veal sold in Britain comes from Holland, which imports many of the young live calves from Britain to be reared in the crated system now banned here. No straw, no room to turn around or exercise in any way and a diet of milk powder produce the white, tender flesh for which people are prepared to pay high prices. I prefer to pay an even higher price for free-range veal, choose one of the less expensive cuts and make it go further with other ingredients.

Because veal is good cold and slices well, it is worth buying and cooking a larger joint than you need. In any case, larger joints cook better than small ones, shrinking less and staying juicier.

Roast rolled veal with kidney

Serves 8 to 10, plus leftovers

2kg (4lbs) boneless breast or, a much more
    expensive cut, loin of free-range veal
1 or 2 veal kidneys, fat removed
salt
pepper

chopped-up veal bones
75g (3oz) unsalted butter
1 tablespoon flour
150mls (½ pint) good red or white wine,
    depending on what you are serving with
    the veal, i.e. use red if you are serving a
    red wine
300mls (¼ pint) water or stock

Open out the breast or split the loin almost in two. Halve the kidneys lengthways, lightly season, and place down the middle of the breast or split loin. Roll up tightly, and tie with string at intervals. Lightly season the roll and place it, seam side down, on the chopped bones in a roasting tin, and put in a preheated oven at 180°C/350°F/gas mark 4 for 40 minutes, adding a few tablespoons of the water to the roasting pan as the meat browns. Turn the meat over, and roast for a further 40 to 45 minutes, adding a little more water as it browns but not enough to cause the meat to steam.

Remove the meat from the roasting tin and let it rest, covered, in a warm place for 15 minutes or so before carving. Remove the bones and sprinkle the flour in the roasting tin, add the wine and bring to the boil, scraping up all the residues stuck to the pan. Add the rest of the water, mix well, and cook for 5 minutes or so. Season the gravy to taste, and strain before handing round with the meat.

Roasted fennel and potatoes are good companions for roast veal, as are crisp green vegetables such as broccoli and green beans.

Cold roast veal with salmon sauce

Roast veal is delicious when cold, and quite worth cooking specially to serve as part of a cold buffet if the weather forecast is good. Any that is left over can be thinly sliced and served as *vitello tonnato* with a tuna fish mayonnaise sauce. You can also substitute cold cooked salmon for the tuna fish to make *vitello salmonato*.

Serves 4 to 6

500g (1lb) cooked free-range veal in a piece
125g (4oz) cooked salmon
1 small tin of anchovies
4 tablespoons olive oil
2 free-range egg yolks
juice of ½ lemon
freshly ground black pepper
1 tablespoon capers

Slice the veal thinly, and lay on a long platter in overlapping slices. Combine the rest of the ingredients except the capers, and blend or process until smooth and shiny like mayonnaise. Roughly chop the capers, and stir these into the sauce. Pour over the veal, and leave in a cool place for a couple of hours for the flavours to blend.

Veal casserole with saffron and root vegetables

Serves 4 to 6

good pinch of saffron
500–750g (1–1½lbs) diced English free-range
    or farmhouse veal, plus any bones
1 tablespoon plain flour
2 tablespoons olive oil
12 pickling onions, peeled
2 parsnips
2 carrots
1 celeriac root

grated zest of an orange and its juice
300mls (½ pint) good dry white wine
seasoning
2 cloves
1 bay leaf
1 sprig of thyme

Soak the saffron in a little hot water. Dust the meat with the flour, and brown it lightly in the olive oil, together with any bones. Transfer to a casserole.

Fry the onions, and add to the casserole. Peel the root vegetables, cut into even batons, and add to the casserole, together with the orange zest and juice.

Deglaze the frying pan with the white wine, stir in the saffron and its liquid, bring to the boil and pour over the meat. Season lightly, tuck in the cloves, bay leaf and thyme, cover, and cook gently for an hour or so in a preheated oven at 180°C/350°F/gas mark 4.

Serve with rice or gnocchi. Alternatively, this is very good made the day before required and finished off with a cobbler topping I like to add herbs, cheese, saffron or other flavourings to the cobbler. Perhaps not saffron in this case,

Saffron

This edible gold has been a precious spice in our store cupboards since the earliest times. The slender, dry red filaments, almost insignificant in themselves, add a rich colour, fragrance and inimitable flavour to food, qualities which were much prized in medieval times throughout Europe, and later in the New World. Most of the saffron we buy is grown on the Spanish plains, although excellent saffron also comes from Greece, as well as Egypt, Iran, Kashmir, India and Morocco. Unfortunately, it is easy to imitate the appearance of dried saffron, although not its flavour, with the dried petals of the safflower, a member of the thistle family from which safflower oil is derived. If you are offered very cheap saffron, it is almost certainly not saffron.

Legend has it that saffron was brought into Cornwall by the Phoenicians, who came to trade for Cornish tin. A nice legend, but unfortunately there is no evidence to suggest that

the Phoenicians ever reached the British Isles. Indeed, Portugal is the furthest north they are thought to have settled, since there was plenty of tin for the Phoenicians in the Iberian peninsula.

Saffron is more likely to have been introduced by the Romans and also brought back from the Middle East by the Crusaders, and later by pilgrims. Later still it might have come from the home-grown crop around Saffron Walden.

I use saffron a good deal in my cooking, in both savoury and sweet dishes. Although we are more accustomed today to use saffron in risottos, paellas and bouillabaisse, there are a number of traditional English recipes which use it. Saffron cakes, buns and biscuits are still made in Devon, Cornwall, Northumberland and Ireland, especially at Easter time. But I also like to use saffron in sauces with fish, in vinaigrettes and, of course, in the fashionable saffron mash.

but to complement the sweet root and orange flavours in the casserole I would use finely chopped spring onions and parsley. And to give a good rise to the dough, I use plain yoghurt.

Onion and parsley cobbler

tops a casserole for 6

280g (10oz) plain flour
4 teaspoons baking powder
½ teaspoon baking soda
½ teaspoon salt
125g (4oz) butter or lard
2 tablespoons parsley, finely chopped
3 tablespoons yoghurt
3 tablespoons water
6 spring onions, trimmed and finely chopped

Sift the dry ingredients together, and cut in the fat, and then rub in lightly to form a breadcrumb texture. Stir in the parsley. Beat the yoghurt and water together, and stir into the flour mixture to form a soft dough, adding more water if necessary. Roll out to about 2.5cm (1 inch) thick, and cut into rounds.

Bake on a sheet for 12 to 15 minutes at 200°C/400°F/ gas mark 6, and arrange around the top of the casserole. Alternatively, transfer the meat to an ovenproof serving dish, arrange the scones around the top, and then bake.

Roast best end of veal with herb and mustard crust

Have the meat prepared by your butcher. The chine bone should be removed and the thick, fatty piece of meat removed from the rib bones, which should be scraped clean. The joint will now be easy to carve in slices across the grain of the meat, parallel to the rib bones. Keep the bones and trimmings for stock.

Serves 4 to 6

1.5kg (3lb) boned and trimmed best end of
    free-range veal
150mls (¼ pint) rich veal stock
splash of wine – optional

crust
4 cloves of garlic
2 shallots

4 tablespoons finely chopped fresh parsley, with
    a little tarragon or chervil, if available
2 tablespoons Dijon mustard
4 tablespoons soft white breadcrumbs
3 tablespoons olive oil
juice of ½ lemon
salt and pepper

Peel and finely chop the garlic and shallots, and mix with the rest of the ingredients for the crust. Spread the mixture over all the meat. Cover closely with clingfilm, or foil, and refrigerate overnight so that the meat takes on some of the flavours of the crust.

Next day, bring the joint to room temperature. Preheat the oven to 150–175°C/300–325°F/gas mark 2. Place the joint in a roasting tin, and cook it in the middle of a slow oven for about 2 hours. Every 40 minutes, pour on a tablespoon of veal stock.

Remove the meat from the oven, and keep it warm while you make the gravy. Gently pour out any fat from the roasting tin, and then set it over a low heat. Scrape up any caramelized cooking juices with a metal spoon, add a little water and the rest of the stock. Boil and scrape until you have a good mixture. A spoonful or two of whatever wine you are serving with the veal would not come amiss, but it is not essential.

Carve the veal into thinnish slices, and arrange on a serving platter with the gravy handed separately, or arrange a couple of slices on each heated dinner plate, pour on a little gravy, and add whatever vegetables and/or starch you have chosen to accompany the veal.

Seared liver and bacon

Calf's liver is delicious, rather expensive, but quick to cook, and makes a good standby.

Serves 2

4 rashers streaky bacon, rind removed
250–350g (8–12oz) free-range calf's liver, cut
    into 3 or 4 slices
1 tablespoon plain flour
¼ teaspoon salt
¼ teaspoon pepper
1 tablespoon extra-virgin olive oil or butter
2 or 3 sage leaves

If the rashers of bacon are long, cut them in half. Fry them in a frying pan until done and just beginning to crisp.

Meanwhile, shake the liver in a bag with the flour, salt and pepper. Shake off any surplus flour. Remove the bacon from the pan, and keep it warm. Drain away the bacon fat.

Heat the butter or olive oil, and fry the liver on both sides until cooked to your liking. Put it on heated plates with the bacon. Add a tablespoon or so of water to the pan to deglaze. Bruise the sage, and stir it into the pan juices briefly before pouring them over the liver.

Some might say that creamy mashed potatoes are the only thing to serve with liver and bacon, but consider also polenta or aubergine purée.

Polenta-grilled calf's liver with crisp sage leaves

Serves 2

250–350g (8–12oz) sliced free-range calf's
    liver
3–4 tablespoons medium or coarse polenta
½ teaspoon freshly ground pepper
good pinch of salt
10 or 12 sage leaves
extra-virgin olive oil

Mix the dry ingredients, and dip the liver in it. Heat and oil the grill or griddle, and cook the liver on both sides until done to your liking.

Brush the sage leaves with the oil, and place under the grill, or on a griddle or in a frying pan. Use moderate heat, and cook until just crisp. Serve with the liver.

Calf's liver with balsamic on potato and garlic *fonduta*

Serves 4

750g (1½ lbs) Arran Victor or other good
    potatoes
1 head of garlic
100mls (4oz) boiling milk
150g (5oz) Fontina cheese
50–75g (2–3oz) Parmesan, grated
1 tablespoon each olive oil and unsalted butter
500g (1lb) free-range calf's liver, in 4 slices
2 tablespoons plain flour mixed with ½ teaspoon
    each salt and freshly ground black pepper
2–3 tablespoons *aceto balsamico tradizionale di
    Modena*

Aceto balsamico tradizionale di Modena

Traditional balsamic vinegar from Modena is exquisite, rare and expensive, about £40 for 100mls (4oz). The inexpensive industrial balsamic, an imitation, can be copied at home by adding caramel to cider vinegar.

Made from the local white Trebbiano grapes, after acetification the traditional balsamic vinegar is aged and decanted into a succession of barrels of different woods, each barrel smaller than the next, including chestnut, oak, cherry and ash. Juniper is no longer used, I'm told, because it is considered too aromatic, but a small piece of juniper wood might be put into one of the oak barrels. Ageing will last at least 12 years, and often more than 25, when it is entitled to be called *stravecchia* (mellow).

A set of new barrels will cost in the region of £500, and before they can be used they are steamed to sterilize them, and then seasoned for a month by filling them with strong vine-gar.

The vinegar was never originally intended as a commercial product. It was made in homes in the Modena and Reggio Emilia district, just as households in Britain will make marmalade. Unlike marmalade, it was so precious and costly to produce that it was often used as a dowry.

There are many uses for this fine vinegar with its intriguing sweet and sour flavour and rich fragrance. At the end of the meal, before pudding, finish off the last of the red wine with a few flakes of fruity Parmesan cheese 'baptized' with *aceto balsamico tradizionale di Modena*. Try a little sprinkled on strawberries, or on a salad of herbs and edible flowers.

Peel the potatoes and garlic cloves. Boil and mash to a smooth purée with the milk. Beat in the cheeses and keep the *fonduta* warm by standing the pan in a roasting tin of hot water on top of the stove on a very low gas.

Meanwhile heat the oil and butter in a heavy frying pan. Dip the liver in the seasoned flour and fry for a few minutes on each side until done to your liking.

Spoon the *fonduta* on to hot serving plates, place the liver on top, and spoon on the *balsamico* mixed with the pan juices. This is very good accompanied by a generous bunch of watercress.

Veal kidney meat loaf

Serves 6, plus leftovers

1 free-range veal kidney
salt
pepper
nutmeg
100mls (4oz) dry or fruity white wine
2–3 tablespoons flat-leaf parsley, finely chopped
500g (1lb) free-range boneless stewing veal
500g (1lb) free-range or organic belly pork
1 onion, peeled and finely chopped
1 free-range egg, lightly beaten
few leaves of tarragon, finely chopped

Remove the fat from the kidney, halve, and snip out the core. Season it lightly with the salt, pepper and nutmeg. Moisten well with white wine, and roll it in the chopped parsley.

Trim the meat, dice, and mince it. Mix in the rest of the ingredients, including the rest of the wine.

Press half the mixture into a 1kg (2lbs) loaf tin, put the kidney on top, and press the rest of the mixture around it. Or make the mixture into a loaf shape and transfer onto a shallow roasting tin.

Bake in a preheated oven at 180°C/350°F/gas mark 4 for about 50 to 60 minutes.

Lamb

Breaded lamb chops

This first lamb recipe makes a quick meal for two, and is delicious served with a cucumber salad, yoghurt and pitta bread.

Serves 2

6 or 8 best-end-lamb cutlets, chine bone removed
2–3 tablespoons flour
1 free-range egg, beaten
4 or 5 tablespoons fresh soft breadcrumbs
grapeseed or olive oil for frying
2 red peppers, quartered, seeded, grilled and peeled
1 lemon

Beat the meat to flatten it slightly. Flour the cutlets and then dip them in the egg and breadcrumbs. Put about 1cm (⅓ inch) oil in a frying pan and, when hot, fry the cutlets on both sides until done to your liking. Quickly fry the peppers in the oil and serve with the cutlets, together with lemon wedges.

Poached leg of lamb with onion sauce and samphire

Serves 6

2kg (generous 4lb) whole leg of lamb
2 bay leaves
2 onions, peeled and stuck with half a dozen cloves
parsley stalks
1 carrot, peeled and sliced
1 small turnip, peeled and sliced
1 leek, washed and sliced
1 celery stalk, trimmed and sliced
salt
pepper
500g (1lb) samphire, trimmed, picked over and thoroughly rinsed
2 slices bread, crusts removed
double cream – optional

Trim and tie the leg of lamb to hold its shape. Fill a large saucepan or fish kettle with enough water to cover the lamb. Gauge how much water first, by putting the leg in, pouring in enough water to cover it, then removing the leg. Put in the herbs, vegetables and lightly add salt and pepper, but not yet the lamb. Bring to the boil, put in the lamb, and when the water comes back to the boil, turn down the heat as low as possible and poach for 15 to 18 minutes per 500g (1lb). Remove the lamb from the pot, and put it to rest in a warm place for about 15 minutes before carving.

While the meat is resting, prepare the accompaniments. To make the sauce, dip the bread in the cooking liquid, then squeeze it out. Put in a blender or food processor with the now soft onions, having removed all but a couple of cloves. Blend until smooth, adding cooking juices or double cream until you have the consistency you prefer. Sieve, season to taste, reheat and keep it warm.

Strain the cooking liquid into a clean saucepan and bring it to the boil. Drop in the samphire, blanch for 30 seconds, then strain and serve with the lamb and onion sauce.

Spiced lime cutlets

Spicy food is excellent for picnics, and lamb cutlets make neat and easy-to-eat finger food.

Makes 18 to 20

3 racks of lamb, chined and very well trimmed,
    and cut into cutlets
juice of a large lime
1–2 tablespoons extra-virgin olive oil
1 teaspoon each freshly ground black pepper,
    ground coriander and cumin
½ teaspoon each ground cardamom, cloves,
    cinnamon and salt

The meat should be trimmed to give a clean rib bone with just the eye of the meat attached. Rub all over with the lime juice and olive oil. Mix the pepper, spices and salt together very thoroughly and dust each cutlet liberally with the mixture. Arrange on non-stick baking sheets, and roast the cutlets in a preheated oven at 200°C/400°F/gas mark 6 for 8 to 15 minutes, depending on the thickness of the meat and how well done you like it. Allow to cool before wrapping.

Chicken drumsticks, quail and duck breasts can all be cooked using the same basic recipe. You can also replace the dry spices with a flavoursome curry paste, either Indian or Thai.

Spiced roast lamb

Serves 4

½ leg of new season's lamb, about 1kg (2lbs)
1 tablespoon extra-virgin olive oil
½ teaspoon each ground cardamom, cloves,
    cinnamon, coriander, cumin and black
    pepper or cayenne

Remove any large chunks of fat, and rub the lamb all over with the olive oil. Massage in the spices, place the meat on a rack and roast for 45 to 60 minutes at 200°C/400°F/gas mark 6. Remove from the oven, and allow to rest before dividing up. I say 'dividing up' instead of 'carving' because, with a joint like this, I like to separate it along the muscles and give everyone a chunky, juicy piece. It's a matter of taste, though, and others will prefer to slice the lamb. Green beans are, as always, a good accompaniment, as are flageolets, soaked and then cooked until tender.

Shepherd's pie

Potato-topped pies are perfect food for informal entertaining as they are easy to eat, with a fork only. Shepherd's pie, and all its relations, are a treat, and not difficult to achieve. You can assemble the shepherd's pie in advance and put it in the oven just 30 to 40 minutes before you want to serve it.

Serves 4 to 6

1 medium onion, peeled and finely chopped
1 tablespoon olive oil
750g (1½lbs) cooked lamb, minced or finely
    chopped
200mls (7oz) lamb stock or gravy
2 tablespoons port
1 teaspoon Worcester sauce
pinch of grated nutmeg
pinch of ground allspice
pinch of chopped fresh rosemary
1 tablespoon finely chopped parsley
salt
pepper
1kg (2lbs) mashed potatoes

Lightly brown the onion in the olive oil. Mix with the rest of the ingredients, except for the potatoes, and spoon into an ovenproof dish. Spread the mashed potato over the top, and score with the tines of a fork.

Bake for about 45 minutes in the top of a preheated oven at 180°C/350°F/gas mark 4.

Moroccan lamb tagine

Dried fruit combines with meat and spices here in a fragrant tender stew, which is best accompanied by saffron-flavoured rice, or couscous, to soak up the juices. Boned shoulder, or fillet, is suitable for this dish.

Serves 6

750g (1½lb) lamb, off the bone
1 tablespoon olive oil
1 medium onion, peeled and chopped
2–3 cloves of garlic, peeled and crushed
½ teaspoon ground cinnamon
½ teaspoon ground cardamom
1 teaspoon cumin seeds
1 teaspoon coriander seeds, crushed
200mls (7oz) lamb or veal stock
4 carrots or small turnips, peeled and sliced, but
    not too small (about 1–2.5cm (½–1 inch)
    chunks)
150g (5oz) dried apricots, soaked in warm water
    for ½ hour
½ preserved lemon, or juice and pared zest of
    ½ lemon
salt
freshly ground black pepper
freshly grated nutmeg
chopped fresh coriander leaves

Trim any excess fat from the lamb, and cut the meat into 5cm (2 inch) cubes. Brown them in the olive oil, and put to one side. Lightly brown the onion, and then add the garlic and spices. Cook these dry for 2 to 3 minutes, and then gradually add the stock, scraping up the residues.

Put the meat in a casserole, pour the spiced stock and onion over it, and add the carrots, apricots and lemon to the pot. Season to taste.

Cover and cook at 180°C/350°F/gas mark 4 for 1 to 1½ hours. Simmer for about 15 to 20 minutes and, just before serving, grind on some nutmeg and scatter with the chopped coriander leaves.

Haggis Parmentier

No, this is not a recipe for making haggis from scratch with the sheep's pluck, but a very appetizing way of cooking it.

Serves 4

500g (1lb) haggis
1kg (2lbs) good mashing potatoes, peeled
1 small turnip, peeled and diced – optional
salt
pepper
freshly grated nutmeg
2 tablespoons fresh breadcrumbs
25–50g (1–2oz) butter

Cook the haggis according to the instructions on its wrapper, and while it is cooking, boil the potatoes, and the turnip, if using it. Drain, mash and season with the salt, pepper and nutmeg. Spread a layer of mash on the bottom and sides of an ovenproof dish. Halve the haggis, and scoop it over the mash. Top with the remaining mash, scatter with breadcrumbs, dot with butter, and bake in the top half of a preheated oven at 200°C/400°F/gas mark 6 for 25 to 30 minutes. Before covering the haggis with its layer of mash, you could, with advantage, sprinkle it with a little whisky or malt.

Pork

Despite the fact that pork has never reached the formal realms of haute cuisine, it is one of the most rewarding and versatile meats to cook with. And organic and truly free-range pork is as different from the industrialized variety as it is possible to imagine.

The Middle White pig is one of Britain's traditional breeds, and is now classified as a Rare Breed. I have never tasted better pork than that from the Middle White, with which I first became acquainted when filming at Heal Farm in North Devon, where

Ann Petch rears a small herd of all the rare breeds of British pigs. Richard Vaughan of Pedigree Meats of Herefordshire also sells meat from Middle Whites and is one of a growing band of farmers who have converted from conventional, large-scale, fast-turnover farming, in his case to specializing in rare breeds, which his wife originally reared for showing.

The Middle White is highly prized by the Japanese, who, I am told, pay the equivalent of about £60 a kilo (2lbs) for its meat, which makes it even sadder that we have allowed stocks in Britain to dwindle to no more than two hundred registered sows. In an effort to create a market for this excellent meat, and that from rare native breeds of sheep and beef cattle, the Rare Breeds Survival Trust has approved a number of butchers around the country to sell it. It is well worth hunting these out.

The depth of flavour of this type of pork is very fine. I have roasted it, cooked it in a pot with rice and oriental spices, and made goulash. The chops are delicious for a quick weekday meal.

The trotters I added to a *poule au pot* (see p. 50), which produced a lovely rich broth. The bonus came next day when I brought the trotters to room temperature, allowing me to prise them apart, brush them with melted butter, roll them in fresh breadcrumbs and bake them. They were excellent with mashed potatoes, pickles and mustard.

Whenever I make goulash, usually in the autumn or winter – but it's good for an English summer, too – I always make more than I need for one meal so that there will be enough for goulash soup later in the week. On one occasion, rather than soup, I made a filling for soft tacos. It was very simple. I shredded the pork and reheated it in its sauce, together with a generous splash of Tabasco and a heaped tablespoon of chopped fresh coriander. The flour tortillas I wrapped in foil and heated, and served them and the pork with cream cheese, shredded iceberg lettuce and homemade guacamole, for an easy and inexpensive supper.

For the goulash, use Hungarian paprika if you can for real authenticity, choosing one of the sweet (i.e. mild) ones rather than a fiercely hot one, since what is important here is the colour; the hot paprika can be used in place of the chilli or cayenne. Since I do not like caraway seeds, I prefer to substitute dill seeds.

Pork *paprikash*

Serves 4, plus leftovers

2 large onions, peeled and cut into wedges
1 tablespoon grapeseed oil
1.5 kg (generous 3 lbs) pork shoulder
2 tablespoons sweet paprika
1 tablespoon plain flour
small or large pinch of chilli powder, cayenne pepper or hot Hungarian paprika, to taste
1 teaspoon dill seeds
150 mls (¼ pint) pork or chicken stock
330 mls (1 small bottle) dry cider or decent red wine
salt
pepper

Fry the onions in the oil in a large flameproof casserole until golden brown. Remove and put to one side. While the onions are cooking, remove the skin and fat from the meat, then carefully separate the skin from the fat. Discard the fat or render and use as lard. Cut the meat into cubes, and brown them in the oil. Sprinkle on the paprika, flour, chilli and dill, and stir in well, continuing to cook. Pour on a little stock, and vigorously scrape up any bits stuck to the bottom. Add the rest of the stock, cider or wine and the pork skin.

Bring to the boil, cover, and simmer very gently for about 2 to 2½ hours, seasoning after an hour. Sometimes potatoes are peeled, cut up and added to the stew about half an hour or so before the end of the cooking, or you might serve the goulash with boiled or steamed potatoes, broad noodles or dumplings. I also serve mine with potatoes mashed with finely chopped fennel tops.

To make a goulash soup from the leftovers, cut the meat into smaller pieces, together with any potatoes. Put them and the gravy in a saucepan, together with stock – 600 mls (1 pint) will serve 2. Stir well, bring to the boil, and simmer for 15 minutes. Serve with soured cream and chopped fresh dill.

Pork and mango casserole, with black beans and rice

This next is a very good recipe for a party, as it will not spoil if left a little longer than the recommended cooking time. Simply turn down the oven temperature.

Serves 8 to 10

1 large onion, peeled and thinly sliced

2 tablespoons sunflower oil

1.5 kg (3 lbs) pork shoulder, off the bone,
    trimmed and diced

1 tablespoon ground cumin

½ teaspoon each ground black pepper, allspice
    and ginger

300 mls (½ pint) chicken or pork stock or cider

50g (2oz) dried mango, cut into pieces

6 celery stalks, trimmed and sliced

3 or 4 chorizo, or other paprika pork sausages

fresh coriander – optional

Using a heavy frying pan, brown the onion in the oil and transfer to a flameproof casserole. Fry the pork in batches until it, too, is browned all over. Stir in the spices until the meat is well coated. Transfer it to the casserole. Pour the liquid into the frying pan, scrape up any cooking residues and bring to the boil. Pour the liquid over the meat and stir in the mango pieces and celery. Put the casserole on the hob, bring to the boil, cover with a lid, then simmer on the lowest heat, preferably with a heat-diffusing mat, and cook for two hours. Alternatively cook in the oven for about 2½ hours at 150°C/300°F/gas mark 2.

You can cook the casserole to this point the day before required. When ready to serve, slice and add the chorizo, and reheat the casserole for 30 to 40 minutes. The chopped fresh coriander can be added just before serving. You can double or triple the quantities and make a huge casserole in advance, reheating it in batches as required. Accompany with a bowl of rice, and a bowl of black beans or black-eyed peas.

Cider- and honey-glazed loin of pork with gooseberry, apple and sage stuffing

Serves 4 to 6

1 loin of pork weighing about 2 kg (3½ lbs), bone
    out, but keep the skin

3 sprigs of sage

150 mls (5oz) stock, water or wine

4 tablespoons English cider

4 tablespoons English cider brandy

2 tablespoons English honey

stuffing

1 small onion, peeled and finely chopped

1 small Bramley, peeled, cored and diced

1 handful of gooseberries, if available

100g (4oz) soft brown breadcrumbs

5 or 6 sage leaves, chopped

75g (3oz) walnut pieces

2 cloves of garlic, peeled and crushed

salt

pepper

Discard any excess fat from the meat and skin. For the stuffing, finely chop any meat trimmings, together with the onion and fruit. Mix with the breadcrumbs, sage, walnuts, garlic and seasoning. Make a deep horizontal slit the full length of the loin, and open it out flat. Spread the stuffing over the meat. Roll it up, and tie at intervals, tucking back any stuffing which escapes.

Preheat the oven to 180°C/350°F/gas mark 4. In a heated non-stick frying pan, fry the pork all over until well browned. Place a sprig of sage on a rack, or on crumpled foil in a roasting pan of a size just large enough to hold the meat; place the meat on top, lay two more sprigs of sage on top of the meat, and cover it with the pork skin.

Place in the top half of the oven, and roast for about 1½ to 2 hours, basting under the skin from time to time with the cider, brandy and honey mixed together. The meat juices should run clear when a skewer is inserted into the centre of the joint. If the juices are pink, the meat is not yet cooked.

Remove the pork from the oven, and keep it warm. Skim excess fat from the roasting pan, and then add a little stock, water or wine to the pan juices. Boil and strain into a jug or gravy boat.

A gratin of potatoes and a dish of baked onions are very good with this traditional roast.

Caramelized pork hocks with pease pudding

The joint of meat you require is the fist-sized knuckle or hock, above the trotter. It does not hold a great deal of meat, but what there is is exceedingly tasty, and you have the bonus of the luscious skin, which in this recipe cooks to a burnished sticky savouriness.

Serves 4

4 pork hocks – see recipe

1 leek, trimmed, sliced and well rinsed

1 celery stalk, trimmed and sliced

1 carrot, peeled and sliced

200 mls (7oz) cider

1 tablespoon cider vinegar

1 tablespoon dark muscovado sugar

1–2 teaspoons Worcester sauce

½ teaspoon ground allspice

split peas – see recipe

Put the knuckles in a large casserole with a well-fitting lid. Add the leek, celery and carrot, and cover with water. Bring to the boil, skim impurities from the surface, cover with the lid and cook for about 4 hours at 150°C/300°F/gas mark 2.

Strain the liquid into a shallow pan and reduce it to about 200mls (7oz), keeping the hocks covered and in a warm place. Add the cider, vinegar, Worcester sauce, sugar and allspice to the pork gravy and boil down to sufficient to well moisten, but not drown, the meat and pease pudding.

Meanwhile put the split peas in a saucepan, cover with water and simmer until tender, adding more water as they absorb it. It is worth cooking more than you need for this dish in order to produce a soup later in the week. You can also serve some crisp steamed cabbage or curly kale with the pork and pease pudding.

Grilled breaded pig's trotters with tartare sauce

Serves 2

2 pig's trotters

300mls (½ pint) water

1 bay leaf

freshly ground black pepper

4 cloves

50g (2oz) butter, melted

75g (3oz) breadcrumbs

100g (4oz) mayonnaise

a few sprigs of tarragon, chopped

2 small gherkins, chopped

Remove basket and trivet from the pressure cooker, and put in the pig's trotters, water, spices and seasoning. Close the lid, bring to full pressure, and cook over a low heat for one hour and fifteen minutes. Release the steam slowly, uncover, and lift out the pig's trotters. The cooking liquid can be used to give body to soups, stews and terrines. When cold, it will set to a stiff jelly.

When the pig's trotters are cool enough to handle, brush them all over with the melted butter, and roll them in the breadcrumbs. Cook under a hot grill, turning occasionally.

To make the sauce, simply mix the mayonnaise with the chopped tarragon and gherkins. If you do not want to bother

with the sauce, mustard, chutney or a salsa make good alternatives, and a bowl of undressed watercress, to eat with your fingers, is a good accompaniment.

Tamales

Tamales are a good dish to do for a party. If possible, try to get a couple of helpers, as the tamales should be wrapped in banana leaves or cornhusks, which takes time. If you can't get cornhusks or banana leaves, foil or greaseproof paper will do.

Serves 8 to 10

500g (1lb) cornmeal (polenta)

4 tablespoons plain flour

1 teaspoon salt

2 tablespoons olive oil

2 tablespoons wine vinegar

½ teaspoon cumin seeds

chicken or beef stock, to mix

500g (1lb) raw chicken, off the bone

500g (1lb) pork spare rib chops

500g (1lb) lean pork, rind removed

250g (8oz) chipolata sausages

4 onions, peeled and finely chopped

8 tomatoes, peeled, seeded and chopped

up to 300mls (½ pint) stock, mixed with dry
    white wine or water

seasoning

12 olives, stoned and chopped, mixed with
    2 tablespoons capers and 3 tablespoons
    seedless raisins

Sift the polenta, flour and salt together. Mix in the olive oil, vinegar, cumin seeds, and enough stock to make a smooth paste that is firm enough to handle.

Dice the chicken, pork and sausages into small bite-size pieces. Cook in a heavy saucepan with a little of the onion and tomato for about 30 minutes. Season to taste. In a separate pan cook the remaining onion and tomato until soft.

Cut greaseproof paper into 8–10 squares. Spoon a tablespoon of the cornmeal paste into the centre of each, and flatten it to about 1cm (½ inch), hollowing the centre slightly. On top, pile a little meat, some of the tomato and onion mixture, and some of the olives, capers, raisins and beans. Top with some more paste, and smooth top and bottom together to seal the filling inside.

Carefully wrap the greaseproof paper around each

tamale so that it is watertight, tying them, if necessary. Steam for at least an hour.

The tamales can be served with hot sauce, if you like, eaten in the fingers when cooled a little, or with knife and fork.

Yorkshire pork pie

Makes ten 2cm (³/₄ inch) slices

filling

500g (1lb) fat belly of pork

125g (4oz) streaky bacon

500g (1lb) lean pork meat, off the bone, such as
     tenderloin

¼ teaspoon freshly grated nutmeg

1 teaspoon freshly ground black pepper

1 tablespoon finely chopped fresh parsley

½ tablespoon finely chopped fresh sage

1 Bramley apple, peeled, quartered, cored and
     diced

200g (7oz) Wensleydale cheese

pastry

up to 750g (1½lbs) plain flour

1 level tablespoon salt

250g (8oz) lard

200mls (7oz) water

jelly

300mls (½ pint) rich chicken or pork stock

2 sheets or 2 teaspoons gelatine, softened in
     water

Preheat the oven to 170°C/325°F/gas mark 3.

Discard the rind from the belly of pork and the bacon, and mince the two together. Fry quickly, in batches if necessary, just enough to remove the raw look. Put in a bowl. Dice the lean pork and fry it lightly all over, draining off any cooking liquid into the stock. Mix the meats together, and add the spices, seasoning, herbs and apple. Cover, and stand in a cool place.

Make the pastry, either in a bowl or on a marble slab, or in a food processor. Sift together the flour and salt, keeping back about 5 tablespoons of flour. Put the lard and water in a saucepan, and bring them to the boil. Stirring continuously, slowly add the flour. When dry and liquid ingredients are thoroughly blended together in a hot, smooth (rather than sticky) mass, turn it out onto a worktop, and knead, adding more flour as necessary, to form a workable pastry.

Cut off a quarter of the pastry to use as a lid, and press or roll out the rest to line a 1.25kg (3lb) loaf tin, pie mould, spring-form mould or cake tin, leaving about 1cm (½ inch) pastry hanging over the rim of the tin. Wet this. Fill with the pork mixture, moulding it to a mound in the centre. Shave the cheese into thin slices and cover the pork with it.

Roll out the remaining pastry, and use to cover the pie. Press the edges together, and roll them over inside the rim of the loaf tin (that way, it will be an easy matter to slide a palette knife all the way round the pie when cold to ease it out of the tin), and make a fluted edge by pinching together at intervals.

Roll out the pastry trimmings to make stick-on decorations, if you wish. Make a pencil-diameter hole in the top of the pastry, and keep it open with a small roll of greaseproof paper. Brush the pie with the milk or egg to glaze it, and lay two or three layers of greaseproof paper, or foil, on top so that the crust does not bake too brown. Bake in the centre of the oven for 1¼ hours. Remove the paper for the last 15 minutes. Let the pie cool for 2 to 3 hours.

When you have taken the pie out of the oven to cool, prepare the jelly. Boil the stock, remove from the heat and stir in the softened, drained gelatine. Once the pie is cool, slowly pour in, through the hole in the pastry, as much of the stock as you can. Allow the pie to cool completely. Then wrap in foil or greaseproof paper, to store. Do not keep the pie for more than two or three days in the refrigerator before eating.

Torta tal-majjal bil-qara ahmar
(Gozitan pork and pumpkin pie)

Serves 6

about 300–350g (10–12oz) long-grain rice

1 large onion, peeled and finely chopped

2 tablespoons extra-virgin olive oil

500g (1lb) minced pork

cloves of garlic, to taste, peeled and chopped

500g (1lb) pumpkin, peeled and diced small

1 tablespoon each chopped fresh mint, parsley
     and marjoram

2 tablespoons finely chopped celery

2 bay leaves

1 glass white or red wine

salt, pepper, lemon zest

1 teaspoon carob syrup – optional

500g (1lb) puff, flaky or shortcrust pastry (p. 29)

Cook the rice in just under twice its volume of water, lightly salted, until barely cooked. Tip into a sieve, and then spread it out on a tray or baking sheet to cool quickly.

Meanwhile, fry the onion in the oil until golden brown, add the pork, and brown it lightly. Stir in the garlic, pumpkin, celery, the herbs, wine, seasoning, and grated zest of a lemon. Add the carob syrup, if using it. A splash of Worcester sauce and a dash of Angostura Bitters, or a teaspoon of honey, might replace it – just some little secret ingredient from your store cupboard.

Partially cover, and simmer until the pork and onions are tender, about 45 minutes to an hour. Spoon this mixture on to a tray, leave to cool, then refrigerate it until required. (Spooning a warm filling into an uncooked pastry shell will melt the fat in it too soon, and make it soggy.)

Roll out just over half the pastry, and use it to line a rectangular ovenproof dish, lightly greased and floured first. Mix the rice and pork, and spoon into the pastry case. Remove the bay leaves. Roll out the remaining pastry, and cover the pie, sealing the edges well.

Bake in a preheated oven for 15 minutes at 200°C/450°F/gas mark 7, and then for a further 10 to 15 minutes at 180°C/350°F/gas mark 4. Serve hot with a green salad.

Rillettes

Rillettes are not very far removed from the English potted meat, which is essentially cooked meat, pounded to a paste, and mixed with a little fat to make it rich and spreadable.

With a food processor, you can make all manner of potted meat and fish. All you need to do is cut the cooked meat into pieces, and put it in the bowl of the food processor with about half the quantity of softened butter, perhaps a little wine, vermouth, Madeira or port, some seasoning and herbs, and process until smooth.

Try venison with port and nutmeg, salmon with vermouth and chives, chicken with sherry and mace, duck with orange liqueur and black pepper. It is a very good way of using cooked leftovers.

Serves 6

500g (1lb) belly pork, diced
salt and freshly ground pepper
1 bay leaf
dried sage

grated nutmeg
100mls (4oz) water

Preheat the oven to 150°C/300°F/gas mark 2. Put the belly pork in a casserole with all the seasoning and water. Cook at the bottom of the oven for about 3 hours, until all the fat has melted and the meat is cooked.

Discard the bones and any skin from the casserole. Then place a sieve over a basin and pour a ladleful of the remaining meat and fat into the sieve. Take a fork in each hand and literally pull all the meat apart. It should all finish up in shreds.

Pack loosely into a jar, pot or pâté dish, and add a little of the melted fat. Continue until all the meat has been shredded and potted and all the fat poured around it. Make sure that the top has a good layer of fat, which will form the seal once refrigerated.

Brawn

Pork cheese, head cheese, jellied veal, jellied ham, galantine of chicken are all later variations of the Anglo-Saxon *bawr-en*. This was originally the head meat of the wild boar, which was served set in a jelly, in an intricate and often lifelike shape, highly garnished, as the centrepiece of the high table in medieval times.

Recent recipe books give traditional methods of preparing brawn, but I am not certain that many of us have the time and, let's face it, the nerve to deal with a whole pig's head, ears, snout and all. However, jellied meats can make extremely good summertime dishes and are not difficult to cook. The principle is the same whatever meat you use. Gelatine-rich meat is cooked on the bone, in stock or water and wine, with herbs and other flavourings until the meat is tender. The meat is removed, chopped and placed loosely in a mould, the juices reduced, degreased and strained over the meat. The whole is allowed to set, and then is turned out and sliced for serving with, for example, a small green salad of bitter or pungent leaves such as endive, rocket or watercress, or with bread and pickles for a simple lunch.

Rabbit or chicken can also be cooked in this way, as long as you cook with it a chopped pig's trotter, which is rich in gelatine. Calf's foot or cow's heel are other sources of gelatine, but the pig's trotter is usually easier to come by.

These are not dishes for long keeping, especially in summer. Warm aspic or gelatine preparations are the perfect culture for bacteria, so chill the dish quickly and refrigerate as soon as possible. One of the least expensive jellied meats to prepare is the knuckle of bacon. When cooked with a little white wine and mixed with parsley, it makes a delicious dish for which a lentil salad will be the perfect companion.

Jellied bacon and parsley

Serves 4 to 6

1 knuckle of bacon, about 1kg (2lbs)
300mls (½ pint) dry white wine
1 onion
3 cloves
1 bay leaf
6 parsley stalks
6 peppercorns
2 tablespoons finely chopped parsley
salt
pepper

Soak the bacon for at least four hours in cold water to get rid of excess saltiness, changing the water a few times. If the bacon was not too salty to begin with, you can always add salt later if necessary, but a too salty brawn will not be good to eat.

Put it in a saucepan with the wine, the onion peeled and stuck with the cloves, the bay leaf, parsley stalks and peppercorns. Add the water, bring to the boil, skim the surface and simmer, partly covered, for 1½ to 2 hours, until the meat is tender. Remove the knuckle from the pan, keeping the stock simmering. Quickly remove the meat from the bone, and put the bone and skin (not the fat) back in the pan to extract more gelatine. Remove any sinews from the meat, and dice it neatly. Season it to taste.

Wet a mould, terrine or pudding basin, and put the meat in it, loosely, not packing it down, as the liquid is meant to fill the spaces between the meat. Cool, cover and refrigerate. Strain the liquid into a chilled bowl. This is to bring the temperature down as quickly as possible so that you can chill the stock in the refrigerator in order to remove the fat from the surface. Once this has been done, liquefy the stock again. Add seasoning if necessary. Stir in the parsley, and pour the stock over the meat.

Refrigerate, covered, until it sets again. Eat within two days.

The pleasures of pasta

A convenience food that is elegant? Fashionable food that is comforting? Nutritionally impeccable food that is also deeply satisfying? Pasta is all these things, and more. And it is hardly surprising that it has moved far beyond its national boundaries to become everyone's favourite food.

Pasta is never boring. Each season brings its own delights in the form of accompanying sauces: wild mushroom or pumpkin in autumn, hearty, meaty ragouts in winter, the vivid green flecks of fresh garden peas and broad beans in summer, enlivened with a few shreds of prosciutto.

In winter I can look to the store cupboard for some anchovies, chillies and dried tomatoes, to stir with fruity olive oil into some good dried pasta. Or if I want to make pasta for filling, I might cook a mixture of oyster mushrooms and plain mushrooms, to which I have added some soaked dried porcini. As an alternative, I like leeks or fennel, cooked until soft, mixed with crumbled Gorgonzola and finely chopped almonds or pine nuts. These mixtures go into ravioli, agnolotti, capelletti, mezzalune or tortelloni – rounds, half-moons, rect-angles or squares, large or small, as you wish. Or consider making different shapes, emulating the designer pasta now available, such as calzone and caramelle. The first are long filled rectangles, not unlike pillows; the second look like sweets in paper wrappers.

For a long time, I have felt that much of the commercial fresh-filled pasta available is inferior to anything one could make, and I rarely buy it. This is not of course to be confused with some excellent fresh pastas made on the premises in Italian deli-catessens and other good food shops. And on the subject of supermarket pasta, what about the rows and rows of pasta sauces? They are pale copies of the real thing, requiring gums and stabilizers of all kinds, as well as using often inferior ingredients. Spaghetti carbonara is traditionally made by stir-ring a series of ingredients in to a pan of freshly cooked pasta, not by making a sauce and pouring it over.

Whenever I want pasta with an unusual filling or am aiming for a particularly fine-textured pasta, I make my own, dragging out my pasta-roller which I bought in 1982 after travelling over the New Year around Marseille, Nice and San Remo. Here I had my first encounter with pesto, and saw in the market the fragile winter bunches of basil with their roots still attached and wrapped in soft blue paper. It was not long before I was making pasta of every colour and flavour, including chocolate ravioli filled with ricotta, raisins and pine nuts, which I used to serve with wood pigeon and other dark game dishes.

A couple of years later, I was introduced prop-erly to the world of dried pasta, *pasta secca*. I revis-ited Liguria, and spent some time in the Agnesi factory. I watched the whole process, from wheat arriving from America in the grain ship, through the milling and sifting stages, the mixing, the extruding and cutting in giant pasta machines with *trafile*, or dies, in many different shapes, after which the pasta was hung up to dry before being packaged.

Years later, I saw the first part of the process when one summer my husband Tom and I drove through Minnesota, right across North Dakota and into Montana, where we stayed on a farm belonging to distant cousins in Plentywood, right near the Canadian border in what used to be bandit country. Not only did we see the young durum wheat growing, but we went to the Lutheran church with the family on a rainy Sunday morning, to hear the pastor acknowledge all the farmers' smiling faces. While we were at the farm, every millimetre of rain was measured and monitored.

We went to the grain elevator run by the farmers' cooperative, and watched as the young manager, JR, weighed in a grain truck full of durum wheat. He took out a sample, measured the volume, then weighed it before and after dockage, having run it over a sieve to sift out and weigh the foreign matter, or dockage. Then he took a smaller sample of grain, ground it and tested it in an infra-red monitor for protein content. On the basis of those calculations, the price for the load was established. From there it was to be sent by rail, on the local Soo Line, to one of the larger centres for shipping, to perhaps finish its journey in Liguria, who knows.

Dried pasta is not better than fresh pasta, and vice versa. They are different – in texture, taste and use. And we are lucky that we now have such a wide variety of excellent pastas to choose from. There are the familiar commercial ranges of dried pasta, but even these do a premium range. I like Menucci's pappardelle, for example. But there are also the more artisan ranges, such as Castiglione, La Molisa, La Casa del Grano. Often these brands will specialize in regional pasta, such as *orecchietti* from Puglia and *malloreddu* from Sardinia.

Homemade pasta

If you want to make your own pasta, some of the larger supermarkets sell pasta flour, imported from Italy, *farina di grano duro*. Or you can use a mixture of bread flour, i.e. strong flour and plain flour, or simply bread flour. In every case, the proportion is *un etto*, or 100g (4oz) for every egg. Allow a good 100g (4oz) flour for each medium-size free-range egg. This is enough for one generous portion as a main course.

If you are making pasta in a food processor, simply put in the eggs and flour, and process until loosely bound together. Knead by hand on a floured work surface until smooth, let it rest, covered, for 15 minutes, then roll out to the thickness of a 20p coin. The resting period is important, to let the dough relax and become elastic again.

To make the dough by hand, pile the flour on to a work surface, make a well in the centre, and slide in the whole eggs. Draw the flour from the edges to the centre, covering the eggs, and, working with your fingertips, gradually mix in the flour and eggs until thoroughly amalgamated. Knead the dough for 10 to 15 minutes, until it is smooth and satiny.

Use the pasta to make the following recipe.

Mushroom caramelle

Serves 4 as a starter

approx. 350g (12oz) mixed mushrooms, wiped
    clean and finely chopped
6 dried porcini slices, soaked and chopped
    – optional
2 tablespoons olive oil
salt

pepper
pasta dough made from 200g (7oz) flour

To make the filling, gently cook the mushrooms, including the porcini if using them, in the oil, and then cook on a high heat until most of their liquid has evaporated. Season lightly, and allow to cool before using.

Roll out the dough thinly, and with a fluted cutter, cut into rectangles.

Spoon a little filling in the centre of each rectangle, moisten one short edge of the pasta, and roll up the small parcel, pressing the wet edge along its length to seal.

Twist and pinch the two ends so that you have something which resembles a boiled sweet. If you cook these as soon as they are made they will take 3 to 4 minutes only, but nearer to 10 minutes if you allow the pasta to dry out. Toss in oil or butter before serving.

The best way to cook pumpkin is first to bake it in large chunks in the oven until tender. This dries it out a little and concentrates the flavour. I use the same method for the parsnips with which I make the parsnip and walnut pasta below. This was inspired by a visit to Emilia Romagna, where our friends the Lancellottis make a marvellous *tortelloni alla zucca* (pumpkin). I discussed the parsnip version with Angelo Lancellotti, and he thought it would work. It does.

One of the reasons that I welcome the first cold snap of the autumn is that pasta-making is much easier in a cooler, drier atmosphere. With luck and perseverance, I can roll out the dough to number 6 on my pasta machine, which is very thin and perfect for stuffed pasta. The lower notch makes for a rather stodgy ravioli with very thick edges. Hand-rolling, of course, produces even better pasta.

Parsnip and walnut pasta

Serves 4 to 6

2 parsnips, roasted
100g (3½oz) walnuts, ground
75g (3oz) ricotta
½ a nutmeg, grated
100g (4oz) freshly grated Parmesan
50g (2oz) Gorgonzola
2 teaspoons orange marmalade, with the peel
    finely chopped

good pinch freshly ground black pepper

1 tablespoon breadcrumbs

pasta dough made with 300g (10oz) flour

Halve the parsnips, scoop out the flesh, and mix to a stiff, smooth paste with the rest of the filling ingredients.

Roll out the pasta dough, and cut into rounds or squares; fill and shape into half-circles or triangles, sealing the edges after moistening with water. Or spoon the filling at intervals on a sheet of pasta dough, moisten the spaces between, and cover with another sheet of dough. Press down all around the fillings, and cut into squares. As you cut them, place on a cloth-covered tray until you are ready to cook them.

Drop into a large pan of boiling water, and simmer for 2 to 3 minutes. Drain, toss gently in butter or olive oil, which can, if you like, be infused with lovage or sage. Any left-over filling can be used to make dumplings to serve in a game broth.

Gorgonzola and pear ravioli

This is a cross between stuffed gnocchi and pasta, and I dreamt up the recipe, literally, writing it down when I woke up, and then testing it in my kitchen.

Serves 4 as a starter

50g (2oz) salted butter

2 tablespoons milk

seasoning

250g (8oz) freshly mashed potatoes

75g (3oz) pasta flour

2 ripe pears

125g (4oz) Gorgonzola

mace or nutmeg

olive oil or butter, and sage – for garnish,
    see recipe

Make the dough by first beating the butter, milk and seasoning into the mashed potatoes. Then add the flour. You may need more or less than the recipe states, depending on how moist your potatoes are.

Let the dough rest, covered, for 20 minutes. Break off egg-sized pieces and roll out, either by hand or in a pasta machine, to no more than the thickness of a 10p coin. Peel, core and chop or grate the fruit. Crumble the cheese and mix with the pear. Season with a little mace or nutmeg. Cut the dough into circles or other shapes. Put a teaspoon of cheese and fruit in the centre. Wet the edges of the dough, fold over, and seal. Set aside on a board covered with a tea towel, and

continue until you have used up all the dough and filling. Any left-over dough can be rolled out, cut into narrow strips, and allowed to dry for use in soup another day.

Bring a large pan of water to the boil, and slide in the ravioli. After 3 to 4 minutes, remove with a slotted spoon and serve immediately, sprinkled with a little olive oil or butter in which you have infused a leaf or two of sage. Freshly grated Parmesan can be handed round, but I do not really think it is essential.

Baked fish and pasta

For this recipe choose a short chunky pasta, such as penne, fusilli or macaroni. The fish can be cod, haddock, monkfish or one of the grander fish such as sole, brill or turbot. Mussels, scallops or cold-water prawns add a different texture, flavour and colour. It is a versatile dish.

Serves 6 to 8

500g (1lb) pasta

olive oil or butter, for tossing

500g (1lb) firm white fish, filleted and skinned

250g (½lb) prepared shellfish

25g (1oz) butter

25g (1oz) plain flour

600mls (1 pint) milk, skimmed, semi-skimmed or
    whole

150mls (¼ pint) dry white wine or fish stock,
    according to taste

1 tablespoon fresh dill, chopped, or 2 teaspoons
    dried dill

pinch of nutmeg

salt

pepper

2 tablespoons breadcrumbs

1–3 tablespoons freshly grated Parmesan

Cook the pasta for three-quarters of the time stated on the packet. Drain, rinse and toss in a little olive oil, or butter to stop it sticking. Cut the fish into 2.5cm (1 inch) pieces. The shellfish should be removed from their shells and armour plating. Make a béchamel sauce (p. 26) with the butter, flour and liquid. Cook for 10 minutes, and then add the herbs and seasoning. Combine the fish, sauce and pasta and spoon into a greased ovenproof dish. Mix the breadcrumbs and Parm-esan, and sprinkle over the dish before putting it in a preheated oven, at 180°C/350°F/gas mark 4. Bake for 20 to 25 minutes.

Fresh tagliatelle with caviar

Serves 2, substantially

pasta made from 200g (7oz) flour – see above
25g (1oz) unsalted butter
2 or 3 tablespoons crème fraiche
shot of vodka – optional
pepper
2 or 3 ripe tomatoes, peeled, seeded and diced
30g (1oz) caviar, or more

Divide the pasta into pieces, and roll each through a pasta-roller several times, finally on the thinnest setting. Allow to dry on a clothes rack or tea towels for 20 to 30 minutes before cutting into tagliatelle. Spread them out to dry a little, and then curl them into loose 'nests', a few strands at a time.

Cook in boiling, lightly salted water when you are ready. When cooked, drain, and stir in the butter and the sauce, which is no more than this simple mixture – a good spoon-ful or two of crème fraiche, some vodka, a little pepper and two or three ripe tomatoes, peeled, seeded and diced.

Serve the tagliatelle in heated soup plates, and top each serving with a spoonful of caviar.

Herb-printed pasta

Herb-printed pasta reminds me of pressing flowers as a child. I have come across this method of dec-orating pasta in several restaurants over the last few years. It is not difficult to do, and if you do not want to make your own pasta you can use wonton wrap-pers (a small round roll of dough), which can be bought in Chinese supermarkets. Use small sage leaves, flat-leaf parsley, basil, coriander, rosemary flowers, sage flowers, tarragon and chervil.

Serve the pasta hot with olive oil, Parmesan and fresh raw tomatoes, peeled and diced, or chopped black olives, or lightly fried mushrooms. You can also serve two sheets of the pasta as an open ravioli, and put a spoonful of luxurious filling between the sheets: crab meat, chopped and cooked wild and cultivated mushrooms, shredded goose or duck mixed with ginger, soy and spring onions.

Makes 24 sheets

48 squares of thinly rolled homemade pasta, or
   wonton wrappers

3 tablespoons water
1 tablespoon cornflour
herbs
oil

Keep the pasta covered with a damp cloth, and use two pieces at a time. Mix the water and cornflour, and brush one side of each wrapper with the 'paste'. On one of them, arrange the herbs. Press the other piece on top, and cut decorative fluted edges with a pasta-cutter. Place on a clean towel, and continue with the remaining wrappers. Cook in a large, shallow pan of boiling water, and then remove with a slotted spoon, drain, and fold in oil before serving hot or cold.

You can also fold the squares diagonally to make trian-gular pasta.

You can make herb-printed lasagne especially easily with a hand-cranked pasta-roller. Having rolled out two sheets of pasta to the third notch, arrange the herbs on one sheet and cover with the other, pressing down firmly. Put the roller back to the widest setting and roll the pasta through, then on each subsequent setting. You will see that the herbs stretch too, and you may not be able to roll it through the last setting without tearing the pasta.

Baked walnut lasagne with pesto

Serves 4

350g (12oz) shelled walnut halves
100g (4oz) pine nuts
6 tablespoons walnut oil
1 or 2 garlic cloves, peeled and crushed
   – optional
6 tablespoons finely chopped flat-leaf parsley
400g (14oz) lasagne sheets
50g (2oz) butter
freshly grated Parmesan or other suitable
   cheese
fresh pesto

Drop the walnut halves into boiling water for a few minutes to loosen the skin. Drain, and rub off the skin. This stage can be left out if you prefer.

Lightly toast the pine nuts in a dry pan, and then pound all the nuts together. Gently fry them for a few minutes in a little of the walnut oil, together with the garlic if using it, and the parsley. Remove from the heat, and add a little boiling water and the remaining oil so that the mixture has a looser spreading consistency.

Cook the sheets of lasagne according to the directions on the packet, drain, and line a buttered ovenproof dish with some of it. Spread a layer of walnut paste, and top with lasagne sheets. Alternative layers of paste and pasta, and continue until you have used up all the paste and pasta. Dot with flakes of butter and cheese, and bake for 15 to 20 minutes in a hot oven. Serve with the pesto.

Double vegetable lasagne

Serves 6 to 8

1.5kg (3lbs) leeks, trimmed, sliced, rinsed and
    drained
1 litre (1¾ pints) milk
75g (3oz) butter
75g (3oz) plain flour
200g (7oz) grated Parmesan
freshly grated nutmeg
1 large onion, peeled and chopped
2 tablespoons olive oil
1 large aubergine, diced
4 courgettes, diced
400g (14oz) canned tomatoes
1 tablespoon finely chopped basil
freshly ground black pepper
salt
400g (14oz) lasagne sheets
1 mozzarella cheese, diced
25g (1oz) shaved Parmesan

Simmer the leeks in the milk until tender. Drain them, put to one side, and save the milk.

In a large saucepan melt the butter, stir in the flour, cook for a few minutes, and gradually add the milk, stirring and cooking until you have a nice smooth sauce. Stir in the cheese, season with the nutmeg, and put to one side.

Make the second filling by frying the onion in the olive oil until wilted, and then fry the aubergine, letting it brown a little. Add the courgettes and tomatoes, and cook until you have a ratatouille, letting most of the liquid boil away. Stir in the basil, and season to taste.

Cook the lasagne according to the directions on the packet, or for 3 to 4 minutes, if fresh. Drain on damp tea towels.

To assemble the lasagne, spread a layer of sauce in the bottom of an earthenware ovenproof dish, and cover it with a single layer of lasagne. Mix the leeks with the mozzarella, a little seasoning and a few spoonfuls of sauce, and spread this over the lasagne.

Spoon on another layer of sauce, and cover with a layer of lasagne. Add the ratatouille layer, and spread some sauce over it.

Cover with a last layer of lasagne, and spread on the remaining sauce. Put the Parmesan shavings on top, and bake in a preheated oven at 180°C/350°F/gas mark 4 for 45 minutes or so.

To replace the fillings I have suggested, alternative layers might be: pumpkin with cheese and nutmeg; mixed mushrooms; fennel and blue cheese; spinach, ricotta, pine nuts, sultanas and mozzarella, and these same fillings can be used inside ravioli.

Another vegetable lasagne

Serves 4

40g (1½oz) butter
40g (1½oz) plain flour
300mls (½ pint) each skimmed milk and
    vegetable stock, hot
2 tablespoons thick Greek yoghurt or fromage
    frais
seasoning
1 large aubergine
2 large red peppers
oil
6 leeks
250g (½lb) firm potatoes, such as Francine,
    Charlotte or La Ratte
8–10 sheets lasagne
rosemary or thyme
Parmesan cheese

Melt the butter in a heavy saucepan, stir in the flour, and cook for a minute or two before gradually adding the milk and stock, stirring continuously to ensure a smooth sauce. Cook for 10 minutes, and remove from the heat. After 10 to 15 minutes, stir into the yoghurt or fromage frais and seasoning.

Slice the aubergine and quarter the peppers, remove the seeds, brush with oil, and grill or bake both vegetables until soft. Trim and slice the leeks, rinse thoroughly and blanch for 5 minutes in boiling water. Thinly slice the potatoes, and parboil them.

Oil or butter a rectangular dish, and spoon some of the sauce over the base. Wet the sheets of lasagne and arrange a layer on top of the sauce. Make the next layer with the aubergine and pepper, slicing the pepper if necessary.

Spoon on more sauce, and cover with a layer of damp

lasagne sheets. The second layer of vegetables is the leeks and potatoes. Top this with more sauce, and a final layer of wet lasagne sheets. Spread the rest of the sauce on the lasagne, and on top of that add a generous shaving of Parmesan. Add a little snipped rosemary or thyme to each layer.

Bake for about 30–40 minutes in a preheated oven at 180–200°C/350–400°F/gas mark 4–6.

Ricotta, herb and prawn lasagne

Serves 4

sauce – choose from the immediately preceding
    two recipes
500g (1lb) ricotta, cubed
2 tablespoons each finely chopped chervil,
    chives, parsley and basil
couple handfuls of baby spinach, blanched,
    dried and chopped
salt and pepper
8–10 sheets lasagne
500g (1lb) peeled prawns

Make 300mls (½ pint) sauce, and mix with the prawns. Keep back 100mls (4oz) sauce. Mix the ricotta with the herbs, spinach and seasoning. Oil a rectangular dish, and build up layers of sauce, lasagne and ricotta, finishing with lasagne and sauce.

Bake for 20 minutes at 180°C/350°F/gas mark 4 in a preheated oven. Then spoon on the remaining sauce and prawn mixture, and return it to the oven for about 5–8 minutes. Serve hot and bubbling.

Seafood and spinach lasagne

Serves 4

sauce – choose from Double vegetable lasagne
    or Vegetable lasagne (p. 189)
500g (1lb) monkfish, diced
300g (10oz) peeled prawns
250g (½lb) baby spinach, blanched and dried
2 tablespoons chives, finely chopped
2 tablespoons chervil, finely chopped
salt and pepper
8–10 sheets lasagne

Make 300mls (½ pint) sauce. You can use fish stock instead of vegetable stock in the sauce for this recipe. Mix the fish,

spinach, herbs and seasoning with half the sauce. Spoon more sauce into the bottom of an oiled rectangular dish, and build up layers of lasagne, fish mixture and sauce.

Bake for 35 minutes in a preheated oven at 180°C/350°F/gas mark 4, and serve hot and bubbling.

Macaroni pie

This pie is different from the Neapolitan *pasticcio* and the one described in Lampedusa's *The Leopard*, and much more like the pasta pies of Modena and Bologna, using cream and mushrooms rather than meatballs and tomato sauce. You can, in place of the turkey, use chicken, chicken livers or game.

Serves 6 to 8

300g (10oz) plain flour
150g (5oz) butter, chilled and diced
pinch of salt
iced water
2 shallots, peeled and finely chopped
1 celery stalk, trimmed and finely sliced
2 tablespoons each olive oil and butter
300g (10oz) mushrooms, thinly sliced
2 tablespoons plain flour
600mls (1 pint) milk, hot
1 bay leaf
2 sprigs tarragon
salt and pepper
nutmeg
3 *boudin blanc* or Italian sausages
500g (1lb) macaroni
2 mozzarella cheeses, drained and diced
500g (1lb) lightly cooked turkey meat, shredded
    or diced
200g (7oz) can petits pois, drained
75g (3oz) Parmesan, grated
milk and free-range egg, beaten, or saffron-
    infused water for glaze (see p. 191)

Rub the flour and butter together to a crumb-like consistency, and stir in the salt and enough water to bind the pastry. Cover with clingfilm, and refrigerate until required.

To make the sauce, fry the shallots and celery in the olive oil and butter until the shallots are translucent. Add the mushrooms and herbs, and cook uncovered until the vegetables are soft. Stir in the 2 tablespoons of flour and gradually blend in the milk until you have a smooth mushroom sauce. Season to taste. Put aside until required.

Heat a frying pan, slice the *boudin* or squeeze the sausages out of the skins into small balls, and fry them until well browned all over.

Cook the pasta for 2 to 3 minutes less than the time stated on the packet, drain it while still al dente, rinse under cold water, and drain again.

To assemble the pie, roll out two-thirds of the pastry, and line a spring-form cake tin, about 7.5cm (3 inches) deep and 22–25cm (9–10 inches) in diameter.

Mix the pasta with about 300mls (10oz) of the mushroom sauce, and stir in the peas, mozzarella, turkey and sausage. Spoon into the pastry case, sprinkling with the Parmesan. The pasta should be well moistened with the sauce, as it will absorb more liquid as it cooks. Spoon on the rest of the sauce, sprinkle on more Parmesan, and top with a lid rolled from the remaining pastry.

Cut out pastry decorations for the top. Make a small slit in the pie crust to allow steam to escape. Brush with egg and milk, or saffron-infused water.

Bake in a preheated oven at 200°C/400°F/gas mark 6 for 10 minutes, and then turn down to 180°C/350°F/gas mark 4 for about 30 minutes.

Remove from the oven, and transfer to a large serving platter. Add watercress, rocket, wedges of lime and mandarin and pomegranate for a festive appearance. Just before serving, you can pour a drop or two of white truffle oil through the hole in the pastry lid, and its scent will suffuse the whole pie.

Macaroni cheese

Serves 4 to 6

500g (1lb) macaroni or penne
2 tablespoons fresh breadcrumbs
50g (2oz) butter
300mls (½ pint) single cream or thin béchamel
125g (¼lb) ricotta, crumbled
1 mozzarella cheese, sliced and diced
75g (3oz) fresh Parmesan, grated
75g (3oz) Dolcelatte or Gorgonzola cheese
freshly ground black pepper
pinch of nutmeg

Cook the pasta for about 10 minutes in boiling water and drain. Rinse and drain again. While the pasta is cooking, fry the breadcrumbs in half the butter, and put to one side. Heat the cream or sauce in a saucepan, and stir in the cheeses until melted. Season with the pepper and nutmeg, and stir into the pasta together with the remaining butter. Pour into

a buttered ovenproof dish, scatter the breadcrumbs on top, and bake for 15 to 20 minutes in a preheated oven at 180°C/350°F/gas mark 4.

Alternatively, you can cook the pasta fully, drain it, and immediately mix it with the cream and melted cheese and remaining butter. Scatter the breadcrumbs on top, and finish under a hot grill for a few minutes.

Pasta pronto – dried pasta with easy sauces

Let me pass on the method of cooking dry pasta that I learned from Eva Agnesi, president of one of Italy's best pasta companies in Liguria.

Put the pasta, allowing 100–150g (3½–5oz) per person, into a large pan of boiling water. You can salt the water, or not. It is traditional to salt the water, but over the years I have become used to pasta cooked in unsalted water.

Bring the water back to the boil, and boil it fast for 2 minutes. Then move the pan off the heat to the back of the stove. Cover with a tight-fitting lid, and leave for the full 10 to 15 minutes, or whatever is specified on the packet.

Give the pasta a stir, and then strain it through a colander, over your serving bowl, using the hot water to heat the bowl. Do not over-drain the pasta.

Let it stand while you combine, in the pan, the pasta with your chosen sauce ingredients. Tip the water out of the bowl, and slide in the pasta and sauce from the saucepan. Serve immediately.

Pasta is the convenience food par excellence. While the water is boiling, you can assemble the rest of the ingredients; just some crushed garlic and anchovies, extra-virgin olive oil and a handful of rocket or watercress stirred into the freshly cooked and drained pasta makes a wonderful dish. Or some tomatoes from which you have first removed the seeds, then chopped, and stirred into the pasta with mascarpone or some diced mozzarella. When tomatoes are just going to be heated through, as in the sauce just mentioned, I do not bother peeling them. But if they are an ingredient in a slow-cooked sauce, it is preferable to remove the skin – otherwise it rolls into tough little spindles, which do nothing to enhance the dish.

Here are some more easy recipes for sauces to accompany *pasta secca*.

Anchovy and caper sauce

Serves 4 to 6

400g (14oz) can chopped tomatoes in juice, drained
2 or 3 cloves of garlic, peeled and sliced
1 can anchovies in oil, drained and chopped
2 tablespoons capers, well rinsed
8 black olives, stoned and chopped

Put the tomatoes in a sauté or small frying pan, preferably non-stick, and cook until they have lost much of their liquid. Add the rest of the ingredients, and cook together for a few minutes.

Freshly ground pepper and some torn-up basil can be stirred into the sauce when you mix it with the pasta.

Peas, ham and rosemary sauce

Serves 4 to 6

150mls (5oz) double or whipping cream, or crème fraiche
good sprig of fresh rosemary, plus 4 or 5 leaves crushed with salt
200g (7oz) can petits pois
50g (2oz) prosciutto – the cheaper ends and off-cuts can be used

Scald the cream and rosemary sprig. Remove the sprig, and stir in the crushed herb and the peas. Shred the prosciutto, and combine it with the sauce and pasta.

Herb pesto

One day, having more than a sprig of fresh basil in the fridge, I collected together all the fresh herbs I could put my hands on, mainly leftovers from those thin plastic supermarket envelopes.

To the basil I added the leaves of a sprig of oregano, 6 or 8 stalks of coriander, 3 or 4 sprigs of tarragon, some flat-leaf parsley, 3 or 4 mint leaves, and some spring onions. I put all that in the food processor with about 75g (3oz) each of good Parmesan and pine nuts, processed it until grainy, and then added pepper and extra-virgin olive oil until I had a fairly stiff paste.

Not basil pesto, but a great improvement on much of what you buy in jars, the big difference being that I do not add lemon juice, which is added to commercial pesto to preserve it.

When you drain the pasta, leave a little water, 1 to 2 tablespoons, in the bottom of the pan, mix in the pesto, and then return the pasta to the hot pan to mix it before transferring it to a hot serving bowl.

Prawns and oyster mushrooms with fennel

Simply dice a fennel bulb and fry in olive oil, add torn-up oyster mushrooms and, when cooked, some unpeeled prawns. Mix with cooked pasta and, instead of grated Parmesan, fresh breadcrumbs fried in olive oil.

And quicker still: if you have some good gravy or sauce left over from a Sunday roast, stir it into freshly cooked pasta which you also mix with fresh rocket leaves.

Potatoes for pleasure

If you have entered 'the zone', the transatlantic diet which bans starches, read no further for I write in celebration of the potato. On the other hand, if you regard it as a treat, or just as an essential adjunct to the main course, there will be something here for you.

Sometimes, I like to treat potatoes as the main element of a dish; other times, they will accompany a piece of fish or meat. Either way, it is worth buying the right ones for the job, and storing and preparing them properly.

I remember being astonished the first time I went to produce markets in South America. There was such a wide range of potato varieties, all sizes, shapes, colours and textures, which, even though I knew the importance of potatoes in Andean cooking, left me very curious. Comparisons with potato supplies at home did not show ours in a favourable light. Of course, matters have improved in recent years, but it still surprises me sometimes to be offered only 'reds', 'whites' and 'baby new potatoes'. Thus, it is an empty counsel of perfection to advise that X is best for baking, Y is good for chips, and Z is best for salads. Too often, we have to take what we can get.

And individual taste comes into play too. Whilst certain varieties are recommended for chips because they take on a floury centre when cooked, there are those who may prefer a chip made from a waxy potato.

I have included a recipe and method for making chips. My excuse for cooking them once in a while is to keep my hand in, but the truth is that, just occasionally, there is nothing more appealing than a plate of steak and chips, or fish and chips. They do take a little time and trouble to prepare, but are infinitely worth it as a treat. I would not cook them for more than two people, however. If I wanted a larger quantity, then homemade oven-baked chips are probably the answer. Proceed as for the perfect chip, and, when you have dried the chips, spray with a little olive oil, put on baking trays, and cook at 180°C/350°F/gas mark 4 for 30 to 35 minutes.

We might think of fish and chips as a British 'invention', but I was only a little surprised to learn that it was a Belgian who had first persuaded us to eat chips with our fish. Certainly, cooked food was available from city cookshops throughout Britain from the Middle Ages, but it was the age of the railway which brought fish to inland cities at lower prices, and fried fish soon became a favourite fast food of the factory workers of the Industrial Revolution.

The first chips in Britain were sold by the Belgian Edouard de Gurnier, who opened a stall in the old Green Market in Dundee in 1874, and they rapidly caught on as an ideal partner to the crisp, battered, deep-fried fish.

Belgian gastronomic magazines seem to devote a good deal of space to the origin of the chip. Chef Pierre Wynants believes it should not be called the French fry but rather the Belgian fry. Some claim that the first instructions for frying the chip in two stages came from the Belgian kitchen, although others claim that the chip was popularized in Belgium by French refugees after 1851, following Louis Napoleon's coup d'état. I tend to accept the story, which goes back about two hundred years, that the poorer inhabitants of Namur and the surrounding region used to catch small fish in the Meuse, which they would deep-fry. When the river froze and cut off their supply of free food, they would cut up potatoes in the shape of the small fish and fry them instead.

Roland Barthès, the philosopher, however, felt that the chip was a gastronomic symbol of Frenchness; '*la frite est le signe alimentaire de francité*'.

A walk through my nearest supermarket the other day produced ten potato varieties, two of them 'vintage' varieties, the all-purpose Up-to-date, and the floury British Queen, suitable for mashing and roasting. Alongside were all-purpose Desiree and red-skinned Romano, the ubiquitous King Edward, the Maris Piper for baking and chipping, large Caras for baking, the Kerrs Pink for chipping, baking and roasting, the waxy white Estima, and the 'new' Nicola for salads. And my local greengrocer, Brian Lay, in Hampstead had small red Rosevals from Provence, a real treat, and delectable with the first of the wild salmon.

Some of the recipes that follow are based on

ones that I learned to cook after I had been to Colombia. When I was there, I gathered recipe leaflets from the local supermarkets in Bogotá. The original croquettes had chopped Brazil nuts in them, but I like to use a mixture of sesame, pumpkin and sunflower seeds, which I mix and lightly roast or toast myself. These make a good vegetable first course, or, if made small, can be handed round with drinks.

Potato and toasted seed croquettes

Serves 6

500g (1lb) all-purpose or floury potatoes
25g (1oz) butter
salt and pepper
nutmeg
2 free-range eggs, lightly beaten
50g (2oz) plain flour
125g (generous 4oz) mixed seeds (see above),
    lightly toasted
oil for frying

Boil the potatoes, peel when cool enough to handle, and then mash with the butter; add the salt, freshly ground black pepper and nutmeg to taste.

Beat in the eggs and flour, and then stir in the seeds.

Form the mixture into small balls or cork shapes. Roll them in flour, and then fry them in plenty of very hot oil until golden brown. It is best to fry a few at a time, to maintain the oil's high temperature.

Let the croquettes drain on kitchen paper before you serve them.

Simple potato and bacon soup

Serves 6

50g (2oz) butter or olive oil
6 large waxy potatoes, peeled and diced
2 white or brown onions, peeled and sliced
1 litre (1¾ pints) milk
250mls (8oz) chicken or vegetable stock
2 or 3 cloves garlic, peeled and sliced
6 large sprigs of parsley
1 sprig of thyme
2 bay leaves
salt and pepper

6 slices streaky bacon, smoked or green, as
    preferred, rind removed, then grilled, or fried
    and crumbled
6 tablespoons cream

Heat the butter or oil in a large saucepan, and add the potatoes and onions. Cover and sweat them over a low heat for 10 to 15 minutes without letting them brown, add half the milk and stock, the garlic, herbs and seasoning, and cook, partially covered, until the vegetables are soft. Rub through a sieve or blend the mixture, having removed the herbs first.

Return the soup to the saucepan, add the rest of the liquid, bring to the boil, add more seasoning if necessary, and serve in hot soup bowls with the cream and crumbled bacon for garnish. For a vegetarian version, use the appropriate stock, and garnish with grilled or fried smoked tofu or toasted seeds.

Curried potato and cashew roulade with mango and cardamom sauce

Serves 4 to 6

75g (3oz) clarified butter, sunflower margarine or
    groundnut oil
3 tablespoons cashews
1 large onion, peeled and thinly sliced
1 generous tablespoon medium curry paste
350g (12oz) waxy potatoes, peeled, coarsely
    grated, and dried
3 tablespoons plain flour
300mls (½ pint) semi-skimmed milk, hot
4 large free-range eggs, separated
200g (7oz) thick Greek yoghurt
1 tablespoon each finely chopped mint and
    coriander

sauce
6 tablespoons pineapple or apple juice
1 tablespoon mango chutney, strained
seeds of 6 cardamom pods
1 small ripe mango, peeled and finely diced

Heat half the fat, and in it first gently fry the cashew nuts until golden brown, and then put them to one side.

Fry the onion in the fat until wilted and golden brown, then add most of the curry paste and the potatoes, and cook for a few minutes more. Put to one side.

In a saucepan melt or heat the remaining fat, stir in the flour, and then gradually add the milk and cook until you have a smooth thick white sauce. Remove from the heat, and stir in the egg yolks and curried potato and onion.

Whisk the egg whites until firm, and fold them into the yolk mixture. Spoon into a lined, greased Swiss roll tray, and bake in a preheated oven at 200°C/400°F/gas mark 6 for 12 to 15 minutes, until the mixture is golden brown and just firm to the touch. Turn it out onto a clean tea towel, and carefully roll it up from one of the thin ends.

To make the filling, lightly crush the cashew nuts, and stir into the yoghurt with the herbs. Unroll the roulade, spread on the filling, and re-roll it.

Make the sauce by cooking the remaining curry paste with the juice, chutney and crushed cardamom seeds. Stir in the mango, and serve with the sliced roulade.

Potato and oxtail tart

Serves 4

1 oxtail cut into chunks
1 tablespoon olive oil
1 large onion
2 bay leaves
½ bottle good red wine
300mls (½ pint) water or beef stock
1.35kg (3lbs) large potatoes
6 stoned prunes
75–100g (3–4oz) butter, salted or unsalted, as you prefer
seasoning
butter

Brown the oxtail in the olive oil in a frying pan, and transfer the pieces to a flameproof casserole. Peel and slice the onion, and lightly brown it too, before transferring to the casserole. Tuck in the bay leaves. Pour the red wine into the frying pan, and bring to the boil, scraping up any caramelized cooking juices stuck to the bottom of the pan. Pour over the oxtail.

Add enough stock or water to come about three-quarters of the way to covering the meat. Simmer on the hob or cook in a very low oven for 2 to 3 hours until the meat is tender.

Strain the cooking juices into a bowl. Cool, and then refrigerate until next day, when you can lift off the layer of fat.

When the meat is cool enough to handle, remove all the bones, put the meat in a container, cover, and refrigerate until next day.

When ready to make the tart, peel and thinly slice the potatoes. Blanch them for 30 seconds or so in boiling water, and then drain and rinse under the cold tap. Lay the slices on a clean tea towel to dry.

Chop the prunes, and mix them with the meat and a few spoonfuls of the by now jellied cooking juices.

Line with greaseproof paper and thickly butter a cake tin about 20–25cm (8–9 inches) in diameter and about 4cm (1½ inches) deep. Neatly arrange slices of poatato over the bottom of the tin, overlapping them to cover it completely; two layers will not be too much. Season lightly. Take the longer slices of potato, and arrange these around the side of the tin, overhanging the top slightly.

Put the meat mixture in the potato-lined tin, make it level, and fold over the potatoes at the edge. Cover with another neatly overlapping layer of potatoes. Season the top. Butter the surface, and cover loosely with a sheet of foil or greaseproof. Bake in a preheated oven at about 190°C/375°F/gas mark 5 for 45 to 50 minutes, until the potatoes are cooked through and nicely browned.

Before turning out onto a plate, weight the tart down for 15 minutes or so to firm it up and make cutting a little easier. With a sharp knife, cut into wedges, and serve. I like to serve this with a purée of swede and garlic, lightly flavoured with clove or cardamom, or creamed cabbage flavoured with nutmeg.

Potato salad

Serves 6 to 8

1.5kg (3lbs) new potatoes
scant teaspoon coarse sea salt
2 teaspoons cumin seeds
1 teaspoon black peppercorns
2 or 3 shallots, peeled and chopped
butter
extra-virgin olive oil
sherry vinegar

Scrub and boil the potatoes until tender. While they are cooking, grind the salt, cumin and pepper. When cool enough to handle, peel, then dice or slice the potatoes, and in a bowl mix them with the shallots. Add the seasoning and enough oil to dress them. Sprinkle the vinegar with a light hand. A sour-cream dressing works well, if you prefer it to oil and vinegar with potatoes.

The perfect chip

YOU NEED one large potato per person. To achieve a light, fluffy chip, crisp and golden on the outside, choose a firm but floury-textured potato such as Desiree, Maris Piper, King Edward, Romano, Roseval, Pentland Dell and Bintje. For the fat you have a wide choice. Duck and goose fat, chicken fat and beef dripping all have their aficionados, and they are efficient for frying as they have a high smoke point. Others will prefer not to use animal fats, and will look to olive oil or sunflower, groundnut or canola (rapeseed) oil. Products labelled simply 'vegetable oil' are perhaps the least appealing, since they may include palm and coconut oils, both high in saturated fats.

Do not use any fat more than two or three times, as high heat breaks down the molecules in the oil and causes it to deteriorate. If you can, use fresh each time.

METHOD Peel the potatoes and slice about 1cm (1/3 inch) thick, and into strips of similar width. It will give good results: a thicker chip like this will absorb less fat than thin-cut chips. Place in a bowl of lightly salted water for half an hour. Drain the chips and then dry them thoroughly in a clean tea towel to avoid the fat spitting as moisture hits it.

Cooking the chips in two stages gives more control over the end result. Stage one cooks the potato gently, until barely done. Stage two, at a higher temperature, gives the chips their characteristic golden crispness. Unless you are cooking no more than a couple of handfuls of chips, do them in batches, to prevent the temperature of the oil falling too much.

Heat the oil in a deep-fryer or heavy saucepan, to a temperature of 190°C/375°F. If you do not have a cooking thermometer, a cube of bread dropped into the oil will immediately sizzle and turn brown by the time you have counted to ten, when the oil is hot enough.

Lower the chips into the oil, and fry for about 5 minutes, moving them around with a heat-proof spatula or slotted spoon to ensure even cooking. Remove and drain on crumpled kitchen paper. Finish the stage-one cooking of the rest of the chips.

For stage two, heat the oil to 200°C/400°F and put the chips back in the oil in batches, then fry for 2 to 3 minutes until they are golden brown. Remove from the fat, drain on kitchen paper and then serve them, or keep them warm in the oven while you finish cooking the rest of the chips.

TO SERVE Chips cooked like this are good enough to eat on their own, dipped Belgian-fashion into really good mayonnaise; or, of course, served with a perfectly grilled steak or a piece of cod, with or without batter, as you prefer. I also like to give them a sprinkling of coarse sea salt before serving them.

Rösti (Swiss-style fried potatoes)

Serves 6

1kg (2lbs) waxy, not floury, potatoes, boiled in their skins the day before
75–100g (3–4oz) butter, lard or olive oil
salt
water

Peel, thinly slice the potatoes, and cut into thin strips. Heat half the fat in a large frying pan, and put in the potatoes. Sprinkle lightly with salt, and fry them until they have soaked up the fat. Add the remaining fat, and then gather the potatoes into a cake in the centre of the pan, squashing well down to bind it together.

Sprinkle with a little water, no more than a tablespoon or so, lower the heat, and cover with a lid or foil. Shake the pan occasionally to stop the potatoes catching, and cook for about 15 minutes until golden brown on the bottom; turn out the rösti, and slide it back into the pan to cook the underside for a few minutes. Slide onto a serving plate, and serve cut into wedges. There is, of course, no such thing as the one and only rösti recipe. Others will advocate using raw grated potatoes and giving them an extra 10 to 15 minutes' cooking time.

Edith's potato cake

My mother-in-law remembers her mother, who went to America from St Petersburg, making what her children used to call a potato pizza. During a visit to Pennsylvania to stay with my mother-in-law, she and I tried to recreate the recipe as it sounded so good. It was. Now, whenever I bake bread, I save some dough for the potato cake.

Serves 6

1 teaspoon dried yeast
150mls (¼ pint) warm water
pinch of sugar
250g (½lb) strong plain flour
½ teaspoon salt
500g (1lb) potatoes
175g (6oz) hard or semi-hard cheese, such as
    red Leicester, Cheddar, Parmesan, Gruyère
salt and pepper

With the first five ingredients make a smooth, elastic dough, cover and let it rise in a warm place. While the dough is having its final rising, peel and boil the potatoes and grate the cheese. When the potatoes are soft, drain them very thoroughly. Mash and season them. Stir in most of the cheese, which will melt in the hot potato. Roll the dough out on a floured worktop, and lay it on a large oiled baking sheet or on an oiled griddle. Spread the potato mixture on top, and sprinkle with the remaining cheese. Bake in a preheated oven at 200°C/400°F/gas mark 6 for 15 to 20 minutes until both top and pastry are golden brown and crisp.

Experimenting with this recipe, I found I had more dough and more filling than I needed. I pinched off pieces of dough, each about 50g (2oz), flattened each piece, spooned a little filling into the centre, and closed the dough over it, pinching it together. When baked, these filled bread rolls were perfect to serve with soup. On another occasion, when I had cheese and potato mixture left over, I worked in a fair amount of flour and used the dough to make potato gnocchi.

Roots

Why do even the best restaurants persist in serving those awful flabby mangetouts? I was in a country-house hotel in Scotland one winter looking forward to a gala dinner in which surely the local potatoes and swedes as well as salmon and beef would feature. I was disappointed. Filo pastry swathed everything and physalis garnished every empty space on the plate. 'Seasonal vegetables' turned out to be the ubiquitous limp khaki pod from Guatemala and a pallid spike of baby corn from Thailand. 'New' potatoes were simply small imports. Where were the bashed neeps? The parsnips? The home-grown potatoes? This last was a particularly sad omission, since we were not many miles from the late Donald Maclean's potato collection in Perth, where he grew hundreds of varieties.

Root vegetables are at their sweet, crunchy best in winter, and the perfect partner for other winter food such as game, casseroles and roasts. I like to peel and slice them very thinly, and use them raw in salads. Thinly sliced, they make a nice alternative to the usual sticks of vegetables served as crudités with a dip. Roots prepared in this way and then dried can be deep-fried into excellent crisps. Carrots, beetroot, parsnips and celeriac make particularly good crisps.

More versatile than might at first be apparent, root vegetables can be roasted, grilled, stewed or mashed. Some can form the basis for sweet dishes, others are good in soups.

My favourite 'mash' is to cook a root vegetable with an equal amount of potatoes and the peeled cloves from a head or two of garlic. I might add a couple of bay leaves, cloves or crushed cardamom pods. Olive oil, butter, milk or soured cream – any of these – are good mashed into the drained, seasoned vegetables.

Thinly sliced roots can also be used in place of more conventional pastas or pastry, as clever chefs have shown us: celeriac in place of lasagne sheets, turnip slices to make ravioli, potato and celeriac to make meat versions of tarte Tatin.

If you want something more exotic, there are many imported roots now in our markets and supermarkets: yams, taro, eddo, large green oriental radishes, mooli or white radishes. Some of them are best cooked and mashed, but others are delicious raw. The one I like best is the jicama, or yam bean. It resembles a spinning-top, pointed at top and bottom of a sphere, and is the sweetest of all the roots. Native to Central America, it is eaten in Mexico raw as an appetizer, thinly sliced, dipped in lime juice, and then dusted with salt and powdered chilli. Mix it on a platter with slices of apple and kohlrhabi for a light, crisp salad.

Completely different are the comforting, creamy soups you can make from root vegetables. One of the very best versions I have tasted was served as part of the Christmas Day menu on British Airways flights. Unusual for a winter soup, it was served chilled, and it was unusually good.

Parsnip soup

Serves 8

40g (1½oz) butter or olive oil
1 medium onion, peeled and chopped
1kg (2lbs) parsnips, peeled and chopped
1.75 litres (3 pints) vegetable or chicken stock
seasoning
150mls (¼ pint) single cream
fresh coriander – for garnish

Melt the butter or heat the oil in a large saucepan, and sweat the onion until soft. Add the parsnips and stock, and cook until the parsnips are soft. Allow to cool slightly before liquidizing the soup. Return it to the pan, season to taste, bring to the boil, and serve with the cream poured on top. Garnish with the coriander. If you plan to serve the soup chilled, use oil not butter, and check the seasoning just before you serve it. Cold soups need a little more seasoning than hot soups.

Carrot, chilli and coriander griddle cakes

I have often written about root vegetables and juicing. Here is a recipe for using up the pulp after making carrot juice.

Makes 12 to 18

2 free-range eggs
100g (4oz) plain flour
300mls (½ pint) milk
about 175g (6oz) raw carrot pulp or finely grated
   carrot
1 green chilli, seeded and finely chopped
2 spring onions, trimmed and finely chopped
a few coriander leaves, shredded
salt
pepper

Make a smooth batter with the eggs, flour and milk, and then stir in the rest of the ingredients. Heat a griddle or heavy frying pan, greasing it as necessary, and drop soupspoons of the batter onto the hot surface. When the batter is dry on top, turn the griddle cake and cook the other side. Pile up the cakes on a plate set over a pan of simmering water to keep them warm. Serve them with some soured cream and smoked fish.

Sweet potato pie

If you cannot get sweet potatoes, you can make this pie with carrots or parsnips, or, of course, pumpkin, which this pie closely resembles. Such pies are very popular in the southern states of America, and I have included the recipe for a biscuit-crumb shell as an alternative to short pastry.

Serves 6

250g (½lb) ginger nuts or digestive biscuits
2 free-range egg whites, kept separate
350g (12oz) cooked, drained and mashed sweet
   potato
75–100g (3–4oz) light muscovado or Demerara
   sugar
½ teaspoon freshly grated nutmeg
½ teaspoon ground cloves
½ teaspoon ground cinnamon
good pinch of mace
pinch of salt
2 free-range eggs

Reduce the biscuits to crumbs, and mix with one egg white. Lightly grease a pie dish, and line it with this mixture, pressing it to the sides and bottom. Bake for 8 to 10 minutes in a preheated oven at 200°C/400°F/gas mark 6. Allow to cool. This crust can be made the day before required, if convenient. Shortcrust pastry can, of course, be used instead. Mix the remaining ingredients thoroughly, and pour into the baked pie shell. Bake for 40 to 50 minutes in a preheated oven at 200°C/400°F/gas mark 6.

In praise of salsify

It is all very well for me and other cookery writers to extol the virtues of buying locally grown vegetables in season, their low cost, their freshness, their 'appropriateness' with other seasonal food. Low cost? Not long ago I went into a supermarket in Plymouth to buy, amongst other things, parsnips. I didn't need many, but the bag came to £3.64. Ah well, supermarkets, I hear you say. Why didn't I go to a local greengrocer? In fact, Stokes of Bodmin did have parsnips, but I also wanted Jerusalem artichokes, radicchio, Chinese leaves, fennel, kohlrabi, uncooked beetroot, butternut squash and salsify.

In the end the boss in Bristol, Julian Barcyk, was immensely kind and helpful and went to great lengths to buy the vegetables I needed early in the morning at the wholesale market in Bristol, and to send them down to Bodmin by road later in the day. He kept his fingers crossed that he would be able to sell anything I didn't need.

Later in the month, when I wanted salsify over Christmas, Brian Lay, in north London, was willing to get it for me, but he said I would have to take the whole box, as he would never be able to sell the rest. 'No demand,' he said. We like salsify, but even so, a 5kg box took some dealing with. This is one of the most delicately flavoured of our root vegetables, with a fine texture, yet we can't, apparently, be bothered with it.

I wouldn't go as far as saying that it tastes anything like its familiar name, 'vegetable oyster', but it is a most welcome addition to the winter table. Of course, those who grow it will already know this. What a pity it is not grown in Britain on a commercial scale. Most of the vegetables we eat in winter seem to be grown in Holland. Perhaps if more of us start asking our greengrocers for it, we will see more of it about.

Of course, I know one of the reasons why we ignore salsify in favour of baby corn, mangetouts, green beans, and tasteless baby carrots in their plastic packs. Salsify and scorzonera, its close relation, are a devil to prepare.

There are two schools of thought as to the best method of preparing them: one is that the vegetables should be scrubbed hard, topped and tailed, boiled or parboiled, and then peeled, cut up, and finished off. The second is that the roots should be scrubbed hard, peeled, rinsed, cut to fit the pan, and then boiled or parboiled.

The first method is said to prevent 'bleeding'. It does not, since the roots, as well as being topped and tailed, have to be cut to fit the pan. A sticky substance is exuded, whichever method you use. But I do find the roots much easier to peel when they are raw and firm, rather than partly cooked and limp. It really is worth persevering; the end results are lovely, especially when you finish off the salsify in a silky béchamel, with or without a little cheese, and scattered with breadcrumbs and butter for a crunchy golden finish. The leftovers make a remarkably good soup. The vegetable is also very good steamed and dressed with olive oil, lemon juice and seasoning. Or try it with an oriental dressing.

Gratin of salsify

Serves 4, plus leftovers

1.5kg (3lbs) salsify
1 teaspoon lemon juice
25g (1oz) unsalted butter
25g (1oz) plain flour
150mls (5oz) cooking liquid plus 150mls (5oz) milk, or use 300mls (½ pint) cooking liquid mixed with dried milk
salt
pepper
nutmeg
50–75g (2–3oz) grated cheese – optional
25g (1oz) breadcrumbs

As you scrub, peel and cut up each root, drop it into a saucepan of water, to which you have added the lemon juice.

Cut into 3cm (1½ inch) lengths, or into 7.5–10cm (3–4 inch) lengths, and then quarter lengthways, if you want slender rather than chunky pieces. Rinse and cover with fresh water. Bring to the boil, and simmer until just tender to the knife point.

Drain. You can use some of the cooking liquid for the sauce.

Melt half the butter, stir in the flour, and gradually add the liquid, stirring until you have a smooth paste. Simmer for 10 minutes, and then season and stir in half the cheese, if using it.

Combine the cooked salsify and sauce, and spoon into an ovenproof dish. Scatter the rest of the cheese on top, dot with the remaining butter, and sprinkle on the breadcrumbs. Bake at 180–200°C/350–400°F/gas mark 4–6 for 15 to 30 minutes.

Salsify, walnut and Cheddar soup

Serves 2

200g (7oz) left-over salsify gratin
50g (2oz) walnuts
400mls (14oz) chicken or vegetable stock
seasoning
75g (3oz) grated Cheddar

Put the left-over gratin, most of the walnuts and the stock in the blender, and process until smooth. Reheat, season to taste, and pour into heated soup bowls with the cheese sprinkled on top, together with the remaining walnuts, roughly crushed.

Beetroot is another 'bleeder'. I have not yet become as fond of it as I am of salsify, but I am beginning to recognize its merits, as early memories of vinegary beetroot at last begin to fade. Beetroot too responds well to oriental dressings; or, as a vegetable accompaniment, serve young beets in a cream sauce, or béchamel, well flavoured with cardamom rather than nutmeg, for a change.

I like to use beetroot juice in a vinaigrette with walnut oil, as well as in the classic borscht. It marries particularly well with tomatoes, however, in the rich velvety soup recipe I give below, the acidity in the one being offset by the earthy sweetness of the other.

Beetroot and tomato soup

Serves 4

1 tablespoon olive oil
1 onion, peeled and finely chopped
1 celery stalk, trimmed and finely chopped
1 small carrot, peeled and finely chopped
3 garlic cloves, peeled and crushed
1 tablespoon dill seed, or chopped fresh dill

400g (14oz) can plum tomatoes
2 or 3 cooked but not pickled beetroot, peeled
    and diced
1 litre (32oz) vegetable stock
2–3 tablespoons soured cream
fresh dill

Heat the olive oil in a heavy saucepan, and sweat the onion, celery and carrot for 20 to 30 minutes without browning. Add the garlic and dill, and cook for 2 to 3 minutes more. Add the tomatoes, and cook on a high heat until much of their juice has evaporated.

Put in the beetroot and the stock, bring to the boil, and simmer for 10 to 20 minutes. Blend or rub through a sieve and return the soup to the saucepan, bring to the boil, then serve immediately.

Spoon a little cream into each soup bowl, if liked, and garnish with fronds of fresh dill, if available.

Baby beet, avocado and potato salad with dill, ginger and mustard mayonnaise

Serves 2 or 3

8 baby beets
12 small potatoes, peeled
2 tablespoons good mayonnaise
1 teaspoon mustard
½ teaspoon honey
½ teaspoon fresh grated ginger
fresh dill
salt
pepper
lemon or lime juice to taste
1 small ripe avocado

Separately boil the vegetables until tender. Pop the beets out of their skin, and then put in a bowl with the potatoes.

Mix the mayonnaise, mustard, honey, ginger, dill and seasoning, including a dash of citrus to sharpen the flavour, and then mix into the vegetables. Peel and dice the avocado, and mix this in too.

If you like raw onions, a red onion peeled and thinly sliced is a good addition to this salad.

Beetroot, potato and herring salad with dill cream

Serves 4 to 6

4 sheets or 4 teaspoons gelatine
600mls (1 pint) beetroot cooking liquor
2 tablespoons sherry vinegar
4 beetroot, cooked, peeled and diced
about 750g (1¼lbs) small waxy potatoes
small bunch of dill
sea salt
freshly ground black pepper
150mls (¼ pint) whipping cream, whipped
6 rollmops

Soak the gelatine in a little of the beetroot liquid, and when soft, stir it into the rest of the liquid and the sherry vinegar. Heat gently, stirring until the gelatine has dissolved. Cool as quickly as possible – outside the back door, on a balcony or over a bowl of ice. Wet a ring mould, and scatter the beetroot in it. Pour over the cold liquid, and refrigerate until set. The jelly can be prepared the day before required.

Scrub and boil the potatoes, and while they are cooking, make the dill cream. Strip the feathery leaves from the stems, which can be put in with the potatoes. Put the leaves in a mortar with a pinch of sea salt and some pepper. Grind with a pestle until you have a paste. Fold this into the whipped cream.

To assemble the salad, turn the jelly out onto a platter. Fill the centre with the potatoes, cooled, mixed with some of the dill cream. Arrange the rollmops on top, and garnish with more dill. Alternatively, chop the rollmops and some shallots, and fold the mixture, together with the cream, into the potatoes.

There are other ways of serving this combination. The simplest is to dress the chopped beetroot with sherry vinegar and walnut oil, and put it in the bowl. Serve the remaining ingredients, rollmops, potatoes and dill cream, in separate bowls too, and forget about the jelly.

The jelly can also be set in individual glass bowls or china dishes, and the salad, herrings and cream piled up on top.

This is a dish for beer and akvavit rather than wine.

White root salad

A cool, crisp, pale assemblage, this salad is a perfect recipe to follow a spicy main dish, such as a vegetable curry.

Serves 8

250g (8oz) each mooli (white radish), celeriac,
    young parsnips and fennel
lemon juice
2 tablespoons Dijon mustard
6 tablespoons cream or plain yoghurt
1 garlic clove, peeled and crushed
1 teaspoon ground cumin
½ teaspoon ground coriander
coarse sea salt

Peel the vegetables, then slice and shred them. As you deal with each piece, drop into a bowl of salted water with lemon juice added to prevent browning.

To make the dressing, mix the rest of the ingredients except the salt. Drain the vegetables thoroughly, and mix with the dressing. Sprinkle the salt on top, and serve immediately.

It is best to make this salad just before required so that the vegetables will not be in the water too long, thus losing much of their flavour, texture and nutrients.

Stir-fried kohlrabi and Chinese leaves with toasted sesame seeds

Serves 4 to 6

2 kohlrabi
1 head Chinese cabbage
2 tablespoons sesame seeds
2 tablespoons groundnut oil
2 tablespoons water
2 tablespoons rice or cider vinegar
1 tablespoon soy sauce
2 teaspoons light muscovado sugar
2–3 teaspoons toasted sesame oil
freshly ground black pepper or Szechuan
    pepper

Peel and quarter, then cut the kohlrabi into slim wedges. Trim and shred the Chinese cabbage.

In a wok, sauté pan or stir-fry pan, dry-toast the sesame seeds, and put to one side. Heat the groundnut oil and in it stir the vegetables until wilted. Add the water and vinegar, put the lid on, and shake the vegetables.

Let steam for a few minutes, and then add the rest of the ingredients. Stir in to mix well, cook for a few minutes more, and then serve, scattered with the sesame seeds. This is very good as part of an oriental meal, but it is excellent too with flattened and grilled organic chicken breasts.

Salad of leeks, ham and Jerusalem artichokes with a mustard dressing

Serves 4 to 6

500g (1lb) Jerusalem artichokes
250g (½lb) slender leeks
salad leaves
250g (½lb) cooked ham, shredded
1 tablespoon cider vinegar
1 tablespoon grain mustard
2–3 cloves garlic, peeled and crushed – optional
salt
pepper
extra-virgin olive oil

Scrub and boil the artichokes for 4 to 5 minutes. Peel them when cool enough to handle.

Trim, then steam or boil the leeks.

Put the salad leaves on plates, and arrange the leeks, when cold, on top. Slice the artichokes, when cold, very thinly, and mix with the ham. Heap on top of the leeks.

Make a dressing with the remaining ingredients, and pour over the salad.

Baked onions

Serves 6

Take 6 medium onions, about 75–100g (3–4oz), and cut the stalk ends level. Place on a baking sheet and bake until soft, for about an hour at 200°C/400°F/gas mark 6. Cut a lid off each onion, scoop out most of the centre, leaving one or two layers as a wall. Blend the onion centres until smooth, mix with a little cream or grated cheese, or if you have it, potato and cheese purée, put the mixture into the onion skins and return the onions to the oven for 5 to 10 minutes for the flavours to mingle. Serve as a separate course or as an accompaniment.

Celeriac

The celeriac is one of my favourite winter vegetables. It might look like a simple country bumpkin next to the cool and elegant fennel, the cosmopolitan green beans and mangetouts and the dandyish radicchios, but it is worth getting below that rough, tough, knobbly exterior to the dense, crisp white flesh beneath, with the pronounced flavour of celery, to which it is related.

Celeriac in the kitchen

This large root vegetable needs peeling before cooking. Because the white flesh oxidizes rapidly on contact with air, it is best to quarter the root and rub the cut surfaces with lemon. Then peel each quarter and drop it into a saucepan of water, to which you have added a little more lemon juice or vinegar.

Celeriac is a marvellous partner to dark game such as hare and grouse. I dice it small and add it to game soups and consommés. Larger chunks are cooked in game pies and casseroles. One of the best ways of using celeriac is to boil it with potatoes and plenty of peeled garlic cloves, then drain and mash with olive oil. It is excellent when served with a dish that has plenty of gravy.

Celeriac can be used like potatoes in other ways: chips and crisps are particularly good, the crisps making a perfect canapé for a sliver of marinated salmon or scallop. A gratin of celeriac, sliced or mashed, is delicious with roast beef.

Fresh shellfish combines very well with the celeriac's earthy sweetness. I like to blanch slices of celeriac, then cut it into thin julienne strips before combining with freshly cooked mussels and a creamy mustardy dressing. Celeriac on its own in such a dressing is the *céleri-rave* of the traditional French hors d'oeuvres trolley.

Ideally suited to our climate, celeriac has featured very little in traditional English cooking. But it seems to fare better in the modern kitchen. The Troisgros restaurant in Roanne cooks small 'olives' of celeriac with duck liver, and Peter Kromberg at the Intercontinental in London uses celeriac for a 'lasagne', taking very thin broad slices of celeriac, blanching them, and then layering them with filling. It is an idea I used most successfully when I made a lasagne for a friend who cannot eat wheat products. Try it with a filling of mixed shellfish.

Celeriac and potato cake, based on the Swiss rösti

Serves 4

1 potato, weighing about 250g (½lb)
1 chunk of celeriac, of equal size
salt and freshly ground pepper
25g (1oz) unsalted butter

Peel and parboil the vegetables. When they are cool enough to handle, shred them on a grater or in the food processor. Mix together, and season with the salt and pepper.

Melt half the butter in a small frying pan, and press the vegetable mixture into it. When cooked and brown on one side, slide it on to a plate. Melt the rest of the butter, and cook the celeriac cake on the other side until golden brown. Cut a wedge for each serving.

An exotic root: the Jerusalem artichoke

In America Jerusalem artichokes are called 'sunchokes', which gives a hint as to the plant's main characteristic. Like its relation, the sunflower or girasol, of which the vegetable's name is said to be a corruption, the Jerusalem artichoke is heliotropic, growing towards the sun.

Although their irregular shape means that there is a good deal of waste, the unique, slightly sweet, nutty flavour of Jerusalem artichokes makes them well worth the small effort needed to deal with them.

Jerusalem artichokes in the kitchen

The simplest way to prepare them is to scrub them thoroughly to rid the interstices of any soil, cut off any bruised parts, and steam or boil them until tender. The vegetables can also be parboiled and sliced and baked au gratin. Peeled, boiled and mashed, Jerusalem artichokes make an excellent

base for a soufflé. Try it seasoned with a little ginger or nutmeg, and mix in some grated Parmesan. Because they too oxidize when peeled, drop the vegetables into water and lemon juice to stop them discolouring as you peel them.

Because of the sweetness, not unlike that of the heart of the globe artichoke, it is as well to choose carefully what you will partner the vegetable with. I like it best with strong game dishes, with roast lamb, beef or pork and with grilled lamb chops, all simple, direct flavours.

Jane Grigson in her *Vegetable Book* described how well Jerusalem artichokes go with prawns in salad. Mix with a creamy dressing, and add some toasted flaked almonds and something oniony or garlicky such as Chinese chives.

A creamy vegetable soup is one of the nicest things to make with Jerusalem artichokes. Both Jane Grigson and Escoffier had recipes for a 'Palestine' soup, a creamy purée using stock, flavoured with herbs and spices. The French chef's version included toasted hazelnuts. I like to use them with left-over chicken and a stock made from the carcass.

These are good recipes to keep on hand because you can replace the artichokes with celeriac, sweet potatoes or a mixture of onions and potatoes, and make similar switches in the gratin and rösti recipes.

Chicken and artichoke soup

Serves 4 to 6

1 onion, peeled and sliced
2 tablespoons unsalted butter
1 level tablespoon plain flour
6 large Jerusalem artichokes, well scrubbed and sliced
freshly ground nutmeg
pinch each ground cloves, cardamom, cinnamon and white pepper
150mls (¼ pint) milk, semi-skimmed or skimmed
850mls (1⅔ pints) chicken stock
salt to taste
shreds of cooked chicken
cream or herbs

In a large, heavy saucepan, sweat the onion in the butter until soft. Stir in the flour, parsnips and spices, and gradually add the milk. Bring to the boil, and simmer until the vegetables are soft. Blend with the chicken stock until smooth. Bring back to the boil, adjust the seasoning, and stir in the chicken. Serve in heated bowls with a swirl of cream or a sprinkling of herbs. If you prefer, potatoes or celery can replace the parsnips.

Gratin of Jerusalem artichokes

Serves 4

500g (1lb) Jerusalem artichokes
salt and freshly ground white pepper
200mls (7oz) thin béchamel sauce or single
    cream

15g (½oz) unsalted butter
1 tablespoon freshly grated Parmesan or
    Gruyère – optional

Preheat the oven to 180°C/350°F/gas mark 4. Scrub the vegetables well, and cut off any bruised or knobbly bits. Slice them, and drop into a large pan of boiling water. Simmer for 2 to 3 minutes and then drain.

Butter an ovenproof dish, and put in a layer of artichokes. Season lightly, and then pour on a little of the sauce or cream. Dot with a little butter, and sprinkle on half the cheese. Add the rest of the artichoke slices, more seasoning, sauce or cream, butter and grated cheese. Bake in the oven; you can place them at the bottom of a hotter oven, depending on what else you are cooking.

VEGETARIAN DINNER FOR SIX

Baked parsnip chips with spiced bean relish

Vegetable tart with English goat's cheese

Spelt frumenty or 'risotto' with cider and mushrooms

Chocolate creams

At least twice a week, I like to cook without fish or meat, and I return home laden with bags from the greengrocer. I realize how lucky I am to be able to shop there, within walking distance; long may he and others like him flourish. I buy half a dozen vegetables, whatever is in season, and then decide what to do with them when I'm back in my kitchen. Combining them with grain in some form, rice, pasta, bread or pastry, and some pulses – beans, lentils, or chick-peas – contributes all the essential nutrients, and besides produces a colourful and satisfying meal.

The following menu is an unusual mixture of roots, pulses and grains. The parsnips are not roasted or mashed, but thinly sliced to make oven-baked chips. This makes the ideal utensil for scooping up the savoury and spicy bean dip. This can be made in advance, and any leftovers can be mixed with vegetable stock for the perfect autumn soup. In fact this whole meal would be suitable for a seasonal celebration, perhaps a Hallowe'en dinner, in which case you could serve the bean relish or the spelt risotto in a baked hollowed-out pumpkin. The pumpkin flesh can be saved for a pie or soup.

I am in two minds whether to call the spelt dish 'risotto' or 'frumenty'. The latter is probably more appropriate, because spelt is not rice, and risotto is made from rice. But frumenty, a very old English dish, is an utterly archaic word, used to describe medieval pottages of boiled wheat, dried fruit and other ingredients, the precursor of our Christmas pudding. Perhaps 'risotto' is the best way to describe the dish, after all. But do note that spelt does not behave in the same way as rice. If you are a true risotto aficionado, you may not like the 'risotto'. My husband Tom says that life is too short to acquire a taste for spelt. But I like it. It retains a slight chew, even when cooked and stirred at length. Like rice, it does give off some of its starch and becomes nicely creamy when cooked. This ancient grain is enjoying something of a comeback, particularly in France, and is available from healthfood shops here.

The vegetable tart can, of course, be adapted to suit your own preference for vegetables and cheeses. Hard sheep's milk cheese would also be very good melted over leeks, and blue cheese over fennel.

The chocolate creams are very intense and best served in small containers, such as espresso cups. It is such a simple recipe, requiring only two ingredients, that I feel almost guilty in giving space to it. Nevertheless, it is so good and so useful that it deserves an outing. Vegans can eat it, as well as those on low-sugar and low-fat diets. The secret is to use a top-quality chocolate with the highest content of cocoa solids. The cream is best made the day before required and will keep, covered and refrigerated, for several days. The soya cream substitute is a UHT product, and you can therefore make the dessert with store-cupboard goods. Add some raw food in the form of juicy pears to follow or precede the chocolate, and a salad of chicory, fennel and celery, or sticks of the same as crudités to serve with the parsnips and bean relish.

Slice the parsnips lengthways, about the thickness of a one-pound coin. Brush with the oil, or use an olive-oil spray. Place on a baking sheet, and bake at 180–200°C/350–400°F/gas mark 4–6 until crisp and golden. You may need to turn the trays, and the slices, from time to time, to stop them burning.

Meanwhile, to make the dip, put the rest of the ingredients except the seasoning and lemon in a blender or food processor, and blend until smooth.

Season to taste, and pile into a bowl. Serve with the lemon wedges and the parsnip chips. If you prefer, you can use black beans or chick-peas for the dip.

Vegetable tart with English goat's cheese

You can use mushrooms and leeks in this tart, as well as courgettes. The fennel should be quartered and blanched first until reasonably tender; otherwise, it will not cook in the same time as the other ingredients. Courgettes I blanch whole and then slice, unless they are no more than little-finger length, in which case I halve them lengthways.

Serves 6 to 8

300g (10oz) strong plain flour
1 teaspoon fast-action easy-blend yeast
1 teaspoon salt
about 150–200mls (5–7oz) hand-hot water
2 tablespoons extra-virgin olive oil
3 or 4 courgettes, topped and tailed
2 round fennel bulbs, trimmed and blanched
250g (8oz) English goat's cheese
coarse sea salt

Sift the dry ingredients together, and then stir in the water. You may not require it all, or you may need a little more, to produce a soft, but not sticky, dough.

Knead for 10 minutes on a floured worktop until you have a smooth, classic dough. Cover and put to one side while you prepare the vegetables.

For a tart some 30cm (12 inches) across, parboil the courgettes and blanch the fennel as described.

Oil your tart tin, and roll out the dough to fit. If you haven't got a paella pan, use a roasting tin, a Swiss roll tray or any other broad flat container that will go into the oven. A pizza tray or stone is, of course, ideal.

Brush the dough with olive oil, and arrange the vegetables on it. Dribble on a little more olive oil, and sprinkle with the salt.

Baked parsnip chips with spiced bean relish

Serves 4 to 6

6 or 8 parsnips, scrubbed, or peeled if
   necessary
extra-virgin olive oil
500g (1lb) cooked, drained haricot or cannellini
   beans, or drained canned beans
2 or 3 garlic cloves, peeled and crushed
1–2 teaspoons fresh thyme or oregano
2 red chillies, seeded and chopped
1–2 tablespoons fresh coriander, finely
   chopped
salt
pepper
1 lemon, cut into wedges

Bake in the centre of a preheated oven at 200°C/400°F/ gas mark 6 for about 30 minutes. Add the sliced goat's cheese and bake for another 15 to 20 minutes. Serve warm or hot.

Spelt frumenty or 'risotto' with cider and mushrooms

Serves 4 to 6

250g (8oz) spelt grains
sprig of rosemary
2 tablespoons extra-virgin olive oil or butter
500mls (18oz) dry or medium cider, boiling
at least 500mls (18oz) vegetable stock, boiling
250g (8oz) mixed fresh mushrooms, sliced
a few pieces dried ceps, soaked in hot water

Fry the spelt grains in oil until well coated, and then add the rosemary and a quarter of the cider, and cook over a brisk heat until it has been absorbed. Ladle in more cider, stir, and cook until the mixture is drying, and then continue adding liquid in the same way, using the stock once the cider is finished.

Fry the mushrooms in a little butter or oil, and add them and the soaked ceps to the frumenty, and continue cooking until the grain is tender.

Serve in heated soup bowls, handing round grated cheese separately, if you wish.

Chocolate creams

Serves 6 to 8

200g (7oz) Soya Dream or other cream
    substitute made from soya beans
200g (7oz) chocolate, broken into pieces

Heat the soya 'cream', and when hot but not near boiling, pour it over the chocolate pieces in a bowl. Vigorously beat the mixture until cold, then spoon into small ramekins or espresso coffee cups. Cover with clingfilm, refrigerate until set and then serve.

The texture is very smooth and creamy, and the good-quality chocolate quite masks any soya flavour.

This is a very easy recipe. I like it because I can serve it to friends who cannot eat milk products, and it is also low in sugar and fat. Those with a very sweet tooth might not like it.

You can use the cream, too, as a filling for a fatless sponge cake.

If I were seriously rich and had a large kitchen, I sometimes think I would like to employ a pâtissier. Their skill and art, which I know I could never emulate, always fill me with admiration. Over the years, I have had the good fortune to work with many gifted pastry chefs, both here and abroad. And each time I work with them on my recipes, my desserts invariably emerge much improved, and with more elegance and refinement.

Chocolate Jonathan was never as good as when made with Ah Kit at the Mandarin Oriental in Hong Kong. At the Intercontinental in London, when I first cooked there in 1987, Ernst Bachmann was the pâtissier, and sceptical though he was about my lavender sorbets and custards, he also showed me many techniques for improving my desserts – one was to thickly butter a cake tin and line it with flaked almonds before spooning in the sponge mixture; this was one that he rather frowned upon, I seem to remember, since it was a non-fat, low-sugar, wholemeal flour sponge, about as far removed as possible from the sumptuous, elegant confections which emerged from his kitchen.

One of his protégés was Claire Clarke, one of the best pâtissiers in Britain, with whom I shared the delightful task of making bread, desserts and sweetmeats for a British gala dinner in Paris a few years ago. Together we devised a baked apple with a crumble topping, to be served very plain – no coulis, no garnish – just a single oval scoop of mead ice cream. And she tells me that she continues to make my damson jellies for sweetmeats. But these homely dishes are nothing compared to the sublime confections that I have experienced in New York.

Towering architectural structures, frivolous, frothy confections, baroque and decadent combinations of flavours – transatlantic desserts have to be the most spectacular and original. Why do one thing with an apple when you can do three things, such as award-winning pâtissier François Payard's 'Pomme, pomme pomme' devised when he was at Restaurant Daniel? At Vong, you can eat white-pepper ice cream with bananas and passion-fruit, or liquorice ice cream with poached pears. The warm, runny-centred chocolate cake served all over Manhattan is a great delight, as are the tall desserts at the Gotham Bar and Grill and Aureole. Take your sweet tooth to New York for fruit soup, chocolate millefeuille with chicory, crisp fig Napoleon

with grape sorbet, and mango sundae with chilli-macadamia nut brittle.

Desserts and dessert wines make a very happy marriage at the end of a meal, and it is always worth hunting out the unusual bottle or half-bottle. *Vin de paille* from France and Schilfwein from Austria have the honeyed, concentrated flavour which comes from ripe grapes being laid on mats to further dry in the sun. Muscat de Beaumes de Venise and other sweet muscats, Mauzac Nature *à méthode Gaillacoise* from the Languedoc and Cerdon du Bugey, demi-sec and very grapey, are all good with pastry, cake and batter desserts. With the sharper fruit-based desserts, I recommend sweet Loire wines or late-harvest Rieslings or other German/Alsace varietals, from Australia, Austria, California, England and Canada; as well as, from Germany, Mosel Auslese or the even sweeter Trockenbeeren Auslese. These have enough acidity to balance that in the fruit.

To further perfect your baking and dessert-making, there are some items of equipment I highly recommend. And a browse through a good kitchenware shop or mail order catalogue from Lakeland or Divertimenti will provide further inspiration. A mandolin to make thin slices of fruit to turn into elegant, translucent fruit crisps is a good investment, as you can also use it for vegetable preparation. Professionals use Silpat baking sheets, available from catering suppliers such as Nisbet's in Bristol, but you can find similar non-stick products for domestic cooks. The cook's blow-torch is a delight to use, easy to operate and with a neat, precise flame, ideal for caramelizing crème brûlée. It is also, I have to report, perfect for lighting the cigar aficionado's puro, and you may never see it again. Wire racks for cooling cakes and pastries are essential, and you can now get multi-tiered racks, which are useful if you are baking in quantity. For grating, the ICTC Microplane does all that it claims, and I have got rid of my box grater. Precision-cut and thus easy to clean, it allows citrus fruit, ginger, nutmeg and garlic to glide over the tiny teeth with ease; no pressure required. And finally, to add a finishing touch to many desserts, I like the citrus oils available from Lakeland, which add a subtle boost of pure flavour.

I try to tell myself that there is little inclination and time to make a pudding every day, and at home fresh fruit generally finishes our meals. The reader might be forgiven for being sceptical about that, given the size of this chapter, and the fact that there is also a whole chapter devoted to fruit and one to chocolate, for even more dessert recipes.

this combination of ingredients is to fill unbroken meringue nests with the whipped cream and heap the poached fruit on top, or vice versa.

A miscellany of desserts

Caramel pears with rosemary

Serves 6

6 pears, peeled and cored
6 tablespoons Demerara or light muscovado sugar
1 sprig of rosemary, plus 6 for decoration
4 tablespoons crème fraiche

Put the pears in a heavy saucepan with a lid. Add the sugar, a tablespoon of water, and a sprig of rosemary. Cover, and cook gently until the pears are tender.

Transfer them to individual bowls or a serving bowl, and spike each with rosemary through the fatter part of the pear. Remove the rosemary sprig from the pan, and add the cream. Bring to the boil, and cook until the caramel thickens. Pour over, or around, the pears. Sage or lavender can be used in place of rosemary.

Meringues with poached fruit

Serves 2

150mls (½ pint) whipping cream
3 or 4 plums, quartered and poached with a little
water and sugar to make a thick syrup
2 individual meringue nests, broken into pieces

Whip the cream, and fold in the fruit, syrup and the meringue pieces. Spoon into wine glasses, or other serving dishes, and serve immediately. It is a good idea to have fruit and cream already chilled. An alternative method of serving

Fruit and nut casserole

Serves 6 to 8

675g (1½lbs) dried fruit such as apricots,
prunes, figs, peaches, pears and apples
1.75 litres (3 pints) hot Earl Grey or jasmine tea
1 lemon grass stalk
2.5cm (1 inch) piece of ginger, peeled and
shredded
2 bay leaves
12 allspice berries
50g (2oz) each pine nuts, hazelnuts, flaked
almonds, walnut pieces
3 tablespoons sweet muscat wine – optional

The perfect banana split

Appealing to the child in all of us, the banana split is one of the easiest ways to finish a meal. And good ingredients make it into a real treat.

YOU NEED, for each person, one ripe but not over-ripe banana, two scoops of the best and strongest vanilla ice cream (I recommend Hill Station's Strong Vanilla Bean), whipped cream (optional), hot chocolate sauce (which you can make yourself by melting 8oz Valrhona chocolate in 2 table-spoons cream), and toasted flaked almonds for decoration.

METHOD In a shallow glass dish arrange the banana, split down the middle, and add the ice cream. Top with the whipped cream and, if using, pour the hot chocolate sauce over the top. Scatter the almonds on top of that.

ALTERNATIVES Serve the chocolate sauce separately, and for those who do not like their chocolate ration this way, heat some luxury caramel spread (*dulce de leche*) and offer it instead.

Put the dried fruit in a lidded flameproof casserole, and pour on the hot tea. Add the lemon grass, ginger, bay leaves and allspice. Bring to the boil, cover, and cook in a preheated oven at 170°C/325°F/gas mark 3 for 1½ to 2 hours.

Remove from the oven, and allow to cool. Toast the nuts in a heavy frying pan until just crisp and golden.

When the fruit is just warm, stir in the nuts, and the wine, if using it. This is very good served with chilled thick Greek yoghurt.

English mead jelly with Cornish fairings

Serves 6

6 sheets or teaspoons gelatine
600mls (1 pint) English mead
200mls (7oz) English white wine
slice or two of nutmeg, cinnamon stick or blade
of mace
1–2 teaspoons lemon juice, to taste
sugar or English honey, to taste

Soak the gelatine in about 3 tablespoons cold water in a large jug or bowl until soft. Put the mead and wine in a saucepan, bring to the boil and add the spice. Steep for 15 minutes and strain over the gelatine. Sharpen with the lemon juice and sweeten with sugar if you think it needs it, then pour into your most elaborate jelly mould. When set, turn out and serve with Cornish fairings and clotted cream. Alternatively, set in a terrine and serve slices of the jelly on individual plates with two or three biscuits and a scoop of cream or vanilla ice cream.

Makes 2 dozen Cornish fairings

200g (7oz) self-raising flour
2 teaspoons ground ginger
1 teaspoon mixed spice
pinch of saffron, rubbed to a powder
pinch of salt
175g (6oz) golden caster or light muscovado
sugar
175g (6oz) unsalted butter, softened

Sift the dry ingredients together, and cream the sugar and butter. Stir the two together, mixing thoroughly. Form the mixture into twenty-four balls. Place on greased or lined baking trays, and press down with the base of a glass – a decorative one if you wish.

Bake for 8 to 10 minutes in a preheated oven at 180°C/350°F/gas mark 4 until golden brown. Transfer to a wire rack to cool.

These will stay crisp for a few days if put in an airtight container, once completely cold.

Tarts, pies and crumbles

Banana tart

This banana tart recipe can be made up as a large one, but I like the appearance of the individual tarts, which are really no more than a circle of pastry. Use plain or sweet shortcrust, flaky or puff (p. 29).

Vanilla, cinnamon- or cardamom-flavoured ice cream can be served with the warm tart, or chocolate if that combination appeals. If it does, you might even want to make your own chocolate short pastry. Substitute 25g (1oz) cocoa powder for 25g (1oz) of the measured flour.

Serves 4

250g (½lb) pastry
1 tablespoon couscous or coarse semolina
5 or 6 ripe but still firm bananas
juice of a small lemon
4–5 tablespoons icing sugar

Roll out the pastry and from it cut out four circles the size of small saucers. Use the remaining pastry to make decorations – knots, hearts, flowers and leaves, whatever you wish. Put the circles on a baking sheet, and sprinkle the couscous or semolina in the centres. This absorbs excess juice and prevents the pastry from going soggy. Slice the bananas and arrange on the pastry circles, leaving a 1cm (⅓ inch) border. Sprinkle the fruit with the lemon juice and dust with a little of the sugar. Place in the top half of a preheated oven at 200°C/400°F/gas mark 6, and bake for 10 minutes.

Remove from the oven, brush the pastry border with

water, and shake on more sugar. Brush the pastry trimmings, and dust these with sugar too. Place them on the baking sheet, and return to the oven for a further 10 to 15 minutes. After 5 minutes, turn down the heat to 180°C/350°F/gas mark 4. Remove from the oven, dust the tarts lightly with icing sugar, decorate with the pastry trimmings and serve warm.

Curd tart with fragrant tea-soaked sultanas

Serves 6 to 8

100g (4oz) sultanas
1 pot of Earl Grey or jasmine tea
250g (½lb) sweet shortcrust pastry – see p. 29
350g (12oz) curd cheese
150mls (¼ pint) single cream
100g (4oz) caster sugar
1 or 2 tablespoons rosewater
grated zest of a lemon
freshly grated nutmeg
4 free-range eggs
nutmeg

Cover the sultanas with the hot tea while you get on with the rest of the tart. Line a greased and floured tart tin or quiche dish with the pastry. Prick the bottom, and bake blind for 10 to 12 minutes at 200°C/400°F/gas mark 6. Let the pastry cool, and lower the oven temperature to 180°C/350°F/gas mark 4. Beat the curds with the rest of the ingredients until smooth. Drain the sultanas, dry them, and scatter in the bottom of the pastry case. Pour the curd mixture over them, and bake for about 40 minutes until set. The surface should not brown but remain pale.

Dust lightly with freshly grated nutmeg before serving.

Peach and almond tart with bourbon butterscotch sauce

Serves 6 to 8

250g (½lb) sweet shortcrust pastry – see p. 29
200g (7oz) almond paste
6–8 peaches
2 tablespoons Demerara sugar

Line a 25cm (10 inch) loose-bottomed tart ring with the pastry. Flatten the almond paste, or roll it out, and line the bottom of the pastry case with it.

Peel and slice the peaches, then arrange them over the almond paste. Sprinkle with the sugar, and bake for about 35 minutes in a preheated oven at 180°C/350°F/gas mark 4.

Serve warm, with the sauce.

Bourbon butterscotch sauce

6–8 peach kernels, crushed
250g (½lb) granulated sugar
100mls (4oz) water
300mls (½ pint) double cream
2–3 tablespoons Bourbon

Boil the kernels with the sugar and water for 2 to 3 minutes, and then strain into a clean saucepan. Cook the syrup until it caramelizes, and then stir in the cream and bourbon.

Cook for 2 to 3 minutes to amalgamate the flavours and evaporate the alcohol.

Serve with the peach and almond tart, or with vanilla ice cream.

Taffety tart

This next is a recipe dating back to at least Elizabethan times; variations on the theme occur in cookbooks over a period of a hundred years or so. The combination of lemon, rosewater and aniseed is exquisite, and the tart is very easy to make.

Serves 4

250g (½lb) puff or sweet shortcrust pastry
  – see p. 29
2 medium Bramley apples, or 4 dessert apples,
  if you prefer
2 tablespoons rosewater
4 tablespoons caster sugar
1 tablespoon fennel seed, or aniseed
grated zest of a lemon
25g (1oz) butter, softened

Roll out the pastry, and cut 4 circles from it. Transfer them to a buttered, floured baking sheet.

Peel, core and slice the apples and arrange on the pastry, flavouring them with half the rosewater and sugar, the fennel seed or aniseed, and the lemon zest. Brush with some of the butter.

Bake in a preheated oven at 180°C/350°F/gas mark 4 for 15 to 20 minutes. Remove from the oven, and raise the heat to 200°C/400°F/gas mark 4.

Brush the tarts with the remaining butter, scatter on the remaining sugar, and sprinkle on the rest of the rosewater. Return the tarts to the oven, and let them glaze and brown for 5 minutes.

Serve hot or warm, plain, or with clotted cream, apple sorbet or vanilla ice cream.

Treacle tart

Nineteenth-century developments in sugar–refining gave us golden syrup, which must have been a boon for bakers. It is the ideal ingredient for gingerbread and spice cake, but, above all, in treacle tart. Open tarts in the north of England are given elaborate pastry trimmings such as latticework, whorls and gables. A latticed treacle tart is very handsome, but tastes just as good without it.

Serves 4 to 6

250g (½lb) shortcrust pastry – see p. 29
50g (2oz) fresh breadcrumbs
freshly grated nutmeg
grated zest of a lemon
1 tablespoon lemon juice
250g (½lb) golden syrup

Grease a 20cm (8 inch) pie plate. Roll out the pastry and line the plate with it, to cover the rim. Mix the breadcrumbs with the nutmeg and lemon zest. Mix the lemon juice with the golden syrup, and spoon into the dish. Sprinkle the breadcrumbs over the top. Slash the pastry rim at 1cm (⅓ inch) intervals, and fold in alternate cut parts towards the centre. This gives a 'gable' tart, looking like the battlements of a castle. Bake for 25 to 30 minutes in a preheated oven at 190°C/375°F/gas mark 5.

To make a properly latticed treacle tart, you need 350g (¾lb) pastry. Use two-thirds of it to line the pie plate. Roll out the remaining pastry into 8 or 10 strips about 1cm (⅓ inch) wide and slightly longer than the top surface of the tart. Lay half the strips of pastry across the tart at equal distance apart. Press down, and seal the strips to the tart at one side only. Fold back alternate pastry strips, and lay on another strip at right angles, beginning the second layer of lattice. Return the folded-back strips as they were, and then fold back the alternate strips. Lay on a second strip of pastry at right angles to the first layer, making sure that it is an equal distance from the first strip. Return the folded-back strips to their original position, and fold back the alternate strips, i.e. the ones you started with. Lay on another strip at right angles, and continue until all the strips have been interwoven. Moisten the ends of the pastry strips, and then flatten, seal and trim off the ends. Bake. This sounds much more complicated than it is, as you will see once you get started.

Pecan and maple tart

This is an exceedingly rich tart, as it should be. You can substitute walnuts or even hazelnuts or almonds for the pecans, but no low-fat, low-sugar substitutes, please. If using almonds, I would leave out the maple syrup and replace it with extra corn syrup or golden syrup, keeping the flavour delicate to complement the almonds. Corn syrup can be found in shops which stock American food products such as Selfridges, the Rosslyn Delicatessen, Harvey Nichols and Jerry's Home Store, all in London.

Serves at least 6 to 8

200g (7oz) plain flour
100g (3½oz) unsalted butter, chilled and diced
pinch of salt
50g (2oz) caster sugar
1 small free-range egg, lightly beaten
iced water

filling

75g (3oz) light muscovado sugar
100g (3½oz) unsalted butter
150mls (5oz) pure maple syrup
150mls (5oz) corn syrup or golden syrup
4 free-range eggs, lightly beaten
1 teaspoon pure vanilla essence
¼ teaspoon salt
250g (½lb) shelled pecans

Rub the flour and butter together, and stir in the salt and sugar, and then the egg and enough iced water to bind.

Roll out the pastry, and line a 20 to 25cm (8 to 10 inch) greased tart tin. Prick the pastry all over, line with grease-proof paper, weight down with ceramic baking beans (dried beans will do, and can be stored and re-used for the same purpose), and bake blind for 8 to 10 minutes in a preheated oven at 200°C/400°F/gas mark 6. Add in the beaten eggs.

Remove from the oven, take out the beans and paper, and let the pastry case cool. Put the sugar, butter and syrups in a saucepan, bring to the boil and cook for about 5 minutes. Remove from the heat and stir in the vanilla essence, salt and pecans. Add in the beaten eggs.

Pour the mixture into the tart. Bake in the preheated oven at 180°C/350°F/gas mark 4 for about 30 minutes, until the filling has just set and the top is lightly browned.

For a short cut, put the contents of a jar of *dulce de leche*, luxury caramel spread, in a bowl. Beat in the eggs and softened butter, then stir in the salt, vanilla and pecans.

Prune and Armagnac tart

Serves 6

500g (1lb) *mi-cuit* prunes (semi-dried prunes
    from France sold under the Merchant
    Gourmet label)
150mls (¼ pint) Armagnac
pinch of ground cinnamon
4 free-range egg yolks and one whole egg
125g (5oz) caster sugar
40g (1½oz) plain flour, sifted
500mls (18oz) single cream or full-cream milk
1 cinnamon stick
250g (½lb) sweet shortcrust pastry – see p. 29

Stone the prunes and soak them in the Armagnac with the
cinnamon while you make the custard, or pastry cream, and
bake the tart shell. Put the eggs and sugar in a large bowl
and whisk until well blended. Whisk in the flour until
smooth. Scald the cream and cinnamon stick in a saucepan
and pour it in a thin stream onto the eggs, whisking all the
time. Return the mixture to the saucepan and cook it on a
very gentle heat until it thickens, stirring all the time. Do not
cook on high heat, as the egg will set as if scrambled. Strain
the custard into a bowl, cover with cling film, and when
cool, refrigerate until required.

Roll out the pastry and line a 25cm (10 inch) loose-
bottomed tin. Prick all over with a fork, cover with
greaseproof paper and weight down with baking beans.
Bake for 15 minutes in the centre of a preheated oven at
180°C/350°F/gas mark 4. Remove from the oven and carefully take out the baking beans and greaseproof. Return the
pastry to the oven for a further 10 minutes to complete
cooking. Cool the tart shell on a wire rack.

When ready to assemble the tart, strain the liquid from
the prunes and boil it to a glaze. Spoon the pastry cream
into the tart shell and arrange the prunes on top. Brush all
over with the glaze and allow to cool. Serve within 2 to 3
hours. If you prefer not to use alcohol, soak the prunes in
grape juice or Earl Grey tea.

Baked apricot and cardamom tart

Serves 4

250g (½lb) sweet shortcrust pastry – see p. 29
500g (1lb) apricots, stoned and halved
3 free-range eggs
200mls (7oz) single or whipping cream

100g (4oz) caster sugar
seeds of 6 cardamom pods

Line a 20–25cms (8–10 inch) flan ring with the pastry, and
cover with the fruit, cut side down. Beat the remaining
ingredients, and pour over the fruit. Bake in a preheated
oven at 200°C/400°F/gas mark 6, for 15 minutes, and then
turn down to 180°C/350°F/gas mark 4, for a further 30 minutes. Serve hot, warm or cold.

A variation on this is to separate the eggs, and use a
little more cream to beat with the egg yolks. Make a meringue
(p. 28) with the whites and extra caster sugar, and spread
over the pie. Bake at 180°C/350°F/gas mark 4 for 35 minutes,
and then at 150°C/300°F/gas mark 2 for 15 to 20 minutes.

A classic apple pie

In Yorkshire and Lancashire, a piece of cheese is
as common an accompaniment to apple pie as
cream or custard. Wensleydale and Lancashire are
particular favourites. Use Bramleys, Egremont
Russets, James Grieve or Howgate Wonder for the
filling.

The perfect Bakewell tart

Sometimes known as Bakewell Pudding, this is
traditionally baked in a deep oval dish with slop-
ing sides. A loose-bottomed tart tin can also be
used, in which case the shorter cooking time
should be used.

YOU NEED, for 6 people, 250g (½lb) puff pastry,
raspberry jam, 100g (4oz) caster sugar, 4 free-
range eggs, 100g (4oz) butter, melted, 100g (4oz)
ground almonds, 1 tablespoon lemon juice.

METHOD Line a 20cm (8 inch) tart tin with the
pastry, and spread it with a generous layer of
jam. Whisk the sugar and eggs until thick and
pale. Stir in the melted butter, then fold in the
ground almonds and add the lemon juice. Spread
the mixture evenly over the jam. Bake in a
preheated oven at 200°C/400°F/gas mark 6 until
nicely browned on top, for about 30 to 40 minutes.

Serves 6

25g (1oz) unsalted butter

400g (14oz) plain or sweet shortcrust pastry
 – see p. 29

50g (2oz) ground almonds

500g (generous 1lb) apples, peeled, quartered,
 cored and sliced

2 cloves

50g (2oz) golden granulated sugar

Butter a 25cm (10 inch) pie plate and reserve the rest of the butter. Divide the pastry in two, and roll out half of it to line the pie plate. Sprinkle the base of the pie with the ground almonds, to absorb the juices. Arrange the fruit on top, tuck in the cloves, dab on the remaining butter and sprinkle with sugar.

Moisten the rim of the pie base. Roll out the second piece of pastry and cover the pie with it. Seal and trim the edges. Decorate the top with pastry trimmings if you wish. Make a hole for the steam to escape, and bake in a pre-heated oven at 200°C/400°F/gas mark 6 for 12 minutes, then turn down to 180°C/350°F/gas mark 4 for another 30 minutes or so. Serve hot, warm or cold.

Pumpkin pie

Serves 6

250g (8oz) plain or sweet shortcrust pastry
 – see p. 29

350g (12oz) pumpkin, cooked and mashed

125g (4oz) golden syrup

50g (2oz) light muscovado sugar

¼ teaspoon freshly ground black pepper

½ teaspoon ground ginger

1 teaspoon each ground cinnamon and mixed
 spice

3 free-range eggs, lightly beaten

300mls (½ pint) full-cream milk, or half-and-half
 mixture of milk and single cream

Roll out the pastry, and use it to line a 9–10 inch (23–25.5cm) pie dish. Mix the pumpkin, syrup and sugar until thoroughly blended. Stir in the spices, and beat in the eggs. Pour in the milk, and blend thoroughly before pouring into the pastry case.

Bake in a preheated oven at 220°C/425°F/gas mark 7 for 15 minutes, and then turn down to 180°C/350°F/gas mark 4 for a further 35 minutes, or until set and a skewer inserted in the centre comes out clean.

Blueberry, sloe gin and almond crumble

Serves 4

about 350g (12oz) blueberries

100mls (4oz) sloe gin

100g (4oz) plain flour

75g (3oz) butter

50g (2oz) ground almonds

75g (3oz) light muscovado sugar

40g (1½oz) flaked or chopped almonds

Simmer the blueberries in the sloe gin for a few minutes. Sweeten if necessary, but the sloe gin should be sweet enough. Spoon the fruit into individual ramekins. Rub the butter and flour together, stir in the ground almonds and sugar, keeping the mixture loose.

Spoon the crumble over the fruit, and scatter the almonds on top. Bake at 200°C/400°F/gas mark 6 for 15 minutes. Serve hot or warm, with a custard or crème anglaise and a little more sloe gin. If you do not make your own, the Plymouth Gin company has started making a very good sloe gin, as well as a companion damson gin.

Puddings

Steamed mango and ginger pudding

Serves 4 to 6

2 small mangoes, one soft, one firm

150g (5oz) each butter and light muscovado
 sugar

200g (7oz) self-raising flour

2 large free-range eggs

2.5cm (1 inch) piece fresh ginger, grated

grated zest of lemon

Peel the mangoes. Dice the firm one to serve with the pudding, and make a purée of the other with a tablespoon each of butter and sugar.

Spoon all but one tablespoon of the purée into the bottom of a greased 1 litre (32oz) pudding basin. Cream the remaining butter and sugar until light, and beat in the eggs, flour, ginger, mango purée and lemon zest. Pour the batter into the prepared pudding basin. Cover with a piece of greased, pleated greaseproof paper, tie on, and steam for 1½ to 2 hours. Or cook it under pressure for 20 minutes.

Turn out, and serve hot or warm with the diced mango and some crème fraiche, yoghurt, custard, or what you will. The pudding will also have made its own sauce.

Sharrow Bay icky sticky toffee sponge pudding

Often imitated, never bettered.

Serves 4 to 6

50g (2oz) unsalted butter
175g (6oz) granulated sugar
175g (6oz) chopped stoned dates
275mls (9oz) water
1 teaspoon bicarbonate of soda
2 free-range eggs
175g (6oz) self-raising flour
½ teaspoon pure vanilla essence
600mls (1 pint) double cream
75g (3oz) Demerara sugar
2 tablespoons black treacle

Cream the butter and sugar. Boil the dates in the water until soft and add the bicarbonate of soda. Beat the eggs into the creamed mixture, then fold in the flour, dates and liquid and the vanilla essence. Pour into a deep greased cake tin or soufflé dish, or individual pudding basins, cover loosely with foil and bake for 40 to 45 minutes at 180°C/350°F/gas mark 4, less time for smaller individual puddings. While the pudding is baking, boil together the cream, sugar and treacle until you have a nice golden caramel sauce. When cooked, turn the pudding out and pour the sauce over the top.

Clafoutis

This is a simpler dessert than a fruit tart, and the only thing that takes time is the preparation of the fruit.

Cherries and apricots are suitable fruit for baking in a batter pudding. Watery acidic fruits such as rhubarb and gooseberries do not work as well, and I would not use soft fruit in this way, except for blueberries and bilberries. Sliced apples

The perfect summer pudding

Nothing captures the flavour of summer better than this uniquely English pudding. When there is a glut of fruit, it is worth making extras in lidded, plastic Christmas pudding containers and freezing them.

YOU NEED, for each pudding, a generously heaped basinful of prepared fruit, of which redcurrants and raspberries are essential, blackcurrants a good idea, gooseberries too, but strawberries and cherries less good; sugar to sweeten, and several slices of firm white bread with crusts removed.

METHOD Tip the fruit into a saucepan, gooseberries before the others, if using them. Sprinkle with sugar, add 2–3 tablespoons of water and simmer gently for a few minutes before adding the rest of the fruit and barely cooking, just until the juices run. Add more sugar as necessary. Cut each slice of bread into two wedges, dip in the juice and line the bottom and sides of the pudding basin. Spoon in the fruit, top with more bread and a little more juice, to fully soak the bread. Cover, weight the top and refrigerate for 24 hours. Turn out and serve with the rest of the juice and some cream.

or pears, halved plums, stoned greengages, when in season, will all make very good puddings, particularly if you add a little matching eau de vie or liqueur to the batter.

Alternatively, flavour a crème chantilly to serve with it. Yoghurt, fromage blanc, crème fraiche, single, double or clotted cream are all suitable accompaniments, or you can serve a thick sauce or thin syrup of the same fruit or complementary fruit.

The rest of the ingredients are inexpensive and readily available in most of our store cupboards and refrigerators – milk, butter, eggs, sugar and flour. Clafoutis is almost identical to the English 'hasty pudding', a thick batter poured over fruit and baked in the oven. Although clafoutis can be served straight from the oven, I like it best when just warm.

Serves 6

50g (2oz) unsalted butter

2 free-range eggs

2 free-range egg yolks

5 heaped tablespoons self-raising flour

300mls (½ pint) milk

1 tablespoon kirsch – optional

50g (2oz) sugar

350g (12oz) stoned cherries or apricots

Butter generously a 20–25cm (8–10 inch) pie dish or quiche dish, place on a baking sheet, and put in the oven. Heat the oven to 180°C/350°F/gas mark 4.

Meanwhile, beat the eggs, flour, milk, kirsch and sugar together until smooth. Remove the hot pie dish from the oven, pour on half the batter, then add the fruit and remaining butter and the rest of the batter. Return the dish on the baking tray to the oven as quickly as possible. Lower the heat to 170°C/325°F/gas mark 3, and bake for 45 to 60 minutes.

Frances Bissell's Christmas pud

My recipe for Christmas pudding is nothing if not versatile. As long as you keep roughly to the balance of ingredients, you can add and substitute to taste. It will not do any harm to have 1.25kg (3lbs) fruit instead of 1kg (2lbs) fruit and 250g (½lb) of nuts. If nuts are off the menu, make up the quantity with dried fruit, preferably one of the more exotic ones such as cherries or cranberries. If you prefer not to use alcohol, use concentrated apple juice, which will help to keep the pudding moist but will increase the sugar content.

The main feature of the pudding is that it contains less sugar, less fat and more fibre than most commercial varieties. I am able to do this because I do not have to conform to certain rules about shelf life that manufacturers have to adhere to. That said, though, many have commented that the pud does keep from one year to the next, although it was never designed to.

Suet is not essential in the pudding. I sometimes replace it with fruit and nut oils, although grapeseed oil would also be an excellent substitute, as is vegetarian suet. And for a lighter texture, I use brown breadcrumbs instead of flour. But if gluten allergy is a problem, use rolled oats instead of breadcrumbs. Indeed, a mixture of oats and breadcrumbs works well anyway.

If you do not have the fortified wine, use 150–200mls (5–7oz) spirits or liqueur.

For those who have never tackled a Christmas pudding before, do have a go. Don't be daunted by the long list of ingredients. These can all be bought in one trip. The recipe is very easy, just a matter of mixing, then steaming in a pudding basin, and the end results will impress your family and friends mightily.

To accompany the pudding, I have given a recipe based on the classic brandy butter recipe but using a mandarin orange liqueur. And, of course, you can vary the recipe to make other flavoured butters, using almond liqueur, rum, Calvados or English cider brandy, cherry brandy, *eau de vie de poire*, and my favourite, if you can find it, *eau de vie de coing*, quince eau de vie. It is worth looking for on a pre-Christmas French shopping trip. Crème fraiche or vanilla ice cream are suitable alternatives to these rich butters.

Serves 8 to 10

250g (½lb) fresh wholemeal breadcrumbs

250g (½lb) roughly chopped muscatel raisins

250g (½lb) roughly chopped sultanas

250g (½lb) roughly chopped dried apricots

250g (½lb) chopped stoned prunes

250g (½lb) chopped walnuts, almonds or extra
    dried fruit

1 large Bramley apple, peeled and grated, or
    2 peeled, grated carrots

1 teaspoon each ground cinnamon and mace

½ teaspoon each ground cardamom, cloves and
    allspice

2 tablespoons candied orange peel or coarse-
    cut marmalade

juice and grated zest of 1 orange

4 free-range medium eggs

75mls (3oz) brandy or orange liqueur

150mls (5oz) fortified muscat wine, port,
    marsala or Oloroso sherry

Put all the dry ingredients in a large bowl, and mix thoroughly, either with a large wooden spoon or your hands. Put the marmalade, orange juice and zest, eggs, brandy and wine in another large bowl or in a blender or food processor, and beat until well blended and frothy. Pour the liquid over the dry ingredients. Mix again until the mixture is moist. Cover and let it stand for a couple of hours at least, and, if possible, overnight to let the spice flavours develop.

Oil or butter the pudding basin or basins (the mixture approximately fills a 2 litre (4 pint) basin, and spoon in the mixture. As the pudding contains no raw flour, it will not expand very much during cooking, and you can fill the basin to within a centimetre or two of the rim. Take a large square of greaseproof paper, oil or butter it, and tie it over the top of the pudding basin with string.

Place the basin in a saucepan, standing it on a long triple strip of foil to help you lift the hot basin out of the saucepan once the pudding is cooked. Pour in boiling water to reach halfway up the pudding basin, cover the saucepan, and bring it back to the boil. Lower the heat, keep the water at a steady simmer, and steam the pudding for 5 hours. Make sure the water is kept topped up. When the pudding is cooked, remove it from the pan and allow it to cool completely before wrapping it, basin and all, in fresh greaseproof paper and foil.

When you want to serve it, steam for a further 2 hours. You can, of course, for both stages of the cooking, use a pressure cooker, which will greatly reduce cooking times, as will a microwave. Manufacturers' instructions should always be followed.

To make smaller puddings, pack into 250g (½lb) pudding basins, cover and prepare in the same way, but steam for about an hour only. To reheat, a small pudding of this size will take 20 to 30 minutes of conventional steaming, from room temperature. A homemade Christmas pudding makes a lovely present, especially when accompanied by a flavoured butter to serve with it.

Mandarin butter

250g (½lb) unsalted butter
175g (6oz) icing sugar, sifted
pinch of ground mace
4 tablespoons Mandarine Napoleon liqueur
2 tablespoons cognac

Have all the ingredients at room temperature. Blend until smooth, pack into pots or jars, seal, label, and refrigerate until required. If you start with the butter at room temperature and use a food processor, the butter can be made very quickly. You can use the same proportions to make larger quantities for giving as presents.

Cranberry, pear and walnut pudding

At Christmas, for a quick yet seasonal pudding and as an alternative to the usual rich pudding and brandy butter, try this version which uses cranberries, pears and walnuts.

Serves 6 to 8

250g (½lb) fresh cranberries
3 ripe Conference pears
125g (generous 4oz) walnut halves
100g (4oz) unrefined granulated sugar
3 large free-range eggs
125g (4oz) sifted self-raising flour
75g (3oz) melted unsalted butter

Wash and pick over the cranberries. Drain and pile on a clean tea towel to dry. Peel, core and slice the pears. Mix them with the cranberries, walnuts and 25g (1oz) of the sugar, and put them in a buttered baking dish, about 5cm (2 inches) deep and about 1.25 litres (2 pints) capacity. Beat together the eggs, the rest of the sugar, the flour and butter until smooth, and pour over the fruit. Bake for 45 to 50 minutes in a preheated oven at 170°C/325°F/gas mark 3 until risen and golden. When it is done, a knife point inserted into the centre will come out clean.

Creams, fools and custards

Coeurs à la crème

Serves 6

250g (½lb) thick Greek-style plain yoghurt
150g (5oz) curd cheese or sieved cottage cheese
2 teaspoons rosewater
clear honey or caster sugar, to taste
3 free-range egg whites

Blend the yoghurt and curd or cottage cheese, mix in the rosewater until smooth, and sweeten to taste. Whisk the egg whites to form peaks, and fold into the cheese.

Spoon the mixture into muslin-lined moulds, place on a plate, and refrigerate for about 12 hours to drain and firm up.

When ready to serve, turn out onto plates, and carefully peel the muslin from the moulded cheese mixture.

Baked vanilla cheesecake

This cheesecake recipe is an old-fashioned one, baked in a shortcrust rather than on a biscuit-crumb base. I learned it from Mary Ann, who was a Peace Corps Volunteer in Nigeria when I was a VSO there. It appeared on many party tables whenever we could find and afford the dairy products.

Serves 8 to 12

300g (10oz) sweet shortcrust pastry – see p. 29
250g (½lb) cream cheese or soft fresh cheese
150g (5oz) unrefined granulated or caster sugar
5 medium-size free-range eggs
2 tablespoons plain flour
1½ teaspoons pure vanilla essence
juice of half a lemon
300mls (½ pint) single cream
300mls (½ pint) milk

Roll out the pastry, and use it to line a cake tin, baking dish, flan ring or other suitable container capable of holding a volume of about a litre (32oz).

Place the container on a baking sheet, as this will conduct heat right through the pastry, which holds a rather dense mixture.

To make the filling, first cream the cheese and sugar, beat in the eggs and flour, and then the remaining ingredients. Pour into the pastry case, and bake in a preheated oven at 180°C/350°F/gas mark 4 for 45 minutes to 1 hour 15 minutes, depending on the depth of the filling. Keep the top nice and pale, covering loosely with foil if it shows signs of browning.

Remove from the oven when a skewer inserted in the middle of the cake emerges clean. Allow the cheesecake to cool completely before slicing.

For extra flavour and texture, you can add 50g (2oz) ground almonds to the pastry, replacing an equal quantity of flour, and add some ground spice, such as cardamom, or some finely grated lemon zest.

Tiramisu

My husband Tom told me that tiramisu first came to England on an Alitalia flight from Rome some years ago. It jumped off at Heathrow, made for the open fields, and has multiplied to the extent that it has been found on every Italian, neo-Italian and pseudo-Italian menu since then.

Note: this recipe contains raw eggs.

Serves 6 to 8

250g (¼lb) sponge fingers
150mls (¼ pint) strong black coffee or
    espresso
3 tablespoons cognac
250g (½lb) mascarpone or cream cheese
4 tablespoons thick yoghurt
100g (4oz) ricotta
100g (4oz) icing sugar
1 teaspoon pure vanilla essence
2–3 free-range egg whites
1 tablespoon grated plain chocolate
1 teaspoon finely ground coffee

Dip half the sponge fingers in the mixed coffee and cognac, and place in the bottom of a glass serving bowl. Blend the mascarpone, yoghurt, ricotta, sugar and vanilla essence until smooth. Whisk the egg whites until stiff, and fold into the creamy mixture. Spoon half of it into the glass bowl. Cover with the remaining sponge fingers, dipped in the coffee and cognac mixture, and then spoon on the rest of the cream, smoothing the surface. Sprinkle the surface with the chocolate and coffee, then cover, and refrigerate for several hours before serving.

Sutlac (Turkish rice pudding)

Note: this recipe contains raw eggs.

Serves 6

100g (4oz) pudding rice, soaked overnight
up to 750mls (25oz) milk
125g (generous 4oz) sugar
½ teaspoon mastic resin, in pieces (about 3)
    – optional
1 teaspoon cornflour
2 tablespoons double cream
1 lightly beaten free-range egg yolk

Rinse the rice. Pour three-quarters of the milk into a heavy saucepan, bring to the boil, and stir in the rice. Cover, and simmer on the lowest possible heat until the rice is tender and the milk absorbed. Add more milk if necessary and do not let the rice catch. It should be very soft. Stir in most of the sugar, keeping back a teaspoon or so.

Pound the mastic with the remaining sugar until you have a fine powder. Slake the cornflour in a tablespoon of milk, and stir it into the rice. Simmer it for a few minutes more to cook the cornflour.

Beat the egg and cream, and mix a little of the rice mixture into it; stir this back into the pudding, away from the heat. Stir the pulverized mastic into the pudding until well mixed, and then spoon the pudding into small dishes for serving.

Chill until required. The top of the pudding is traditionally browned under the grill. I also like to sprinkle on top some pistachios, ground in a mortar with a little cinnamon and sugar. Mastic, the resin of a shrub, can be bought in Middle Eastern and Turkish food shops.

Shahi tukra

Serves 2

600mls (1 pint) milk
pinch of saffron threads
sugar to taste
2 thick slices good-quality white bread
ghee or concentrated butter for frying
pinch of freshly ground cardamom
1 teaspoon blanched, lightly toasted almonds
1 teaspoon unsalted and shelled pistachios
edible gold or silver leaf – optional

Put the milk in a wide, shallow saucepan, bring to the boil, add the saffron threads, and simmer until reduced by two-thirds. Add the sugar, and simmer for a further ten minutes. In fact, the last time I made this I used skimmed milk, which, when reduced as directed, was quite sweet enough without any added sugar.

Remove the bread crust and cut out two rounds or four triangles, as you wish. Fry in the ghee over a medium heat until crisp and golden brown. Put the bread into the milk, and simmer for a few minutes. Transfer the bread to plates, pour the sauce around it, sprinkle with the cardamom and garnish with the crushed nuts and the gold or silver leaf, if you wish. This final decoration turns the dish into something quite spectacular, as indeed are its flavours.

In order to reduce the milk slowly so that it doesn't burn, I put it in an ordinary saucepan on the lowest heat, smallest burner, with a heat-diffusing mat between. It takes hours, which is fine if you are around to keep an eye on it, but if not, use the chef's method of reducing it in something like a clean, heavy frying pan. The milk resulting from either method may possibly remind you of evaporated milk. Which is exactly what it is. It is for you to decide whether you wish to take the short cut of opening a can.

Quince and apple fool

Serves 4 to 6

1 quince
3 or 4 well-flavoured apples, such as Russets or
    Coxes
150mls (¼ pint) mead or cider
2 or 3 cloves
honey to taste
300mls (½ pint) double cream, whipped, or
    homemade custard – see p. 27

Wipe the quince, core, and chop it. The apples take less time to cook and can be added later. Simmer the quince with the liquid and cloves until almost tender. Core and quarter the apples, and add to the pan. Cook until tender. Drain off any excess juice, keeping it for another dish, and rub the fruit pulp through a sieve. If you have used cider, add honey to sweeten. When the fruit is cold, fold in the cream or custard, and spoon into glasses. Serve with crisp, spicy biscuits.

The perfect crème brûlée

This luscious dessert has somewhat obscure origins, having evolved in England, but is probably of French inspiration.

Despite its French name, the recipe appears neither in *L'Art Culinaire Français* nor in *Le Répertoire de la Cuisine*, both comprehensive manuals of classic French cooking. It does not appear in either the homely *Tante Marie* or Pellaprat's *La Cuisine Familiale et Practique*, nor yet in *Larousse Gastronomique*. The nearest thing to it is crème anglaise, which is none other than a stirred, not baked, egg custard made by pouring scalded cream or milk over egg yolks beaten with sugar, which is then cooked further until it thickens, and then chilled, which thickens it even more.

On the other hand, this recipe and technique are to be found in numerous English recipe collections dating back to the Middle Ages. *The Ordinance of Pottage*, a fifteenth-century collection, has a recipe for Crème Boyled, which is essentially as described above, and flavoured with saffron. We find it, too, in the Elizabethan kitchen, and then fairly regularly from the eighteenth century onwards. Mrs Mary Eales, confectioner to Queen Anne, has recipes for ratafia cream and sack cream, which are the same flavoured custards, as does Hannah Glasse in 1717. The version with the crunchy caramelized topping is to be found as long ago as 1769, as Burn't Cream, in Elizabeth Raffald's *The Experienced English Housekeeper*.

Marcel Boulestin, who enjoyed the dessert many times at Trinity College, Cambridge, claims it was invented by Mr Hartmann, for many years the Swiss head chef at Trinity towards the end of the nineteenth century. The dish was then known as Crème Brûlée à la Trinity. But the plot thickens. Jane Grigson in *English Food*, and Florence White in *Good Things in England* some forty years earlier, describe how the recipe was brought to Trinity by a Scottish undergraduate in the 1860s. It was rejected by the kitchen, but when the undergraduate became a fellow in 1879, it quickly became part of Mr Hartmann's repertoire.

'Of French inspiration' is probably the best description. So many of our dishes have similar origins, which is scarcely surprising given the Norman Conquest, the influx of émigrés and their chefs after the French Revolution, and the nineteenth-century colonization of London's kitchens by Carême, Soyer and Escoffier, not to mention the twentieth-century Roux, Blancs and Bourdins.

YOU NEED, for 6 people, 600mls (1 pint) double cream, 1 vanilla pod, 6 free-range egg yolks, 50g (2oz) caster sugar, 100g (4oz) Demerara sugar.

METHOD Bring the cream and vanilla pod to the boil. In a bowl beat the egg yolks and caster sugar and pour the scalded cream on the mixture, beating continuously. Strain the mixture into a double boiler, or a bowl set over hot water. Scrape the vanilla seeds into the custard, and use the pod, once rinsed and dried, to flavour vanilla sugar. Heat the custard, stirring continuously, until it thickens. Remove from the heat and stir until cool. Pour into ramekins and chill until set. Sprinkle on an even layer of Demerara sugar and caramelize it under the grill or with a salamander. Chill again until required.

The perfect *panna cotta*

Essentially a cream jelly rather than cooked cream, this is an exquisitely silky, rich pudding.

YOU NEED, for 8 people, 4 sheets gelatine, or 4 teaspoons gelatine granules, 600mls (1 pint) double cream, 300mls (½ pint) full-cream milk and enough sugar to sweeten to taste.

METHOD Soften the gelatine in a little water, and then drain it. Heat the cream and milk to blood heat, then add the sugar, if you're using it, and drained gelatine. Stir until both have dissolved, and then allow to cool. Before the mixture begins to set, pour it into a wet pudding basin or jelly mould. Refrigerate overnight.

TO SERVE Loosen the pudding by holding a hot cloth to the mould, or by briefly dipping it in hot water, and carefully turn it out onto a shallow dish.

It can be decorated with mandarin segments macerated in orange juice, ruby-red pomegranate seeds if available, crystallized fruit, candied citrus peel or even angelica cut into appropriately decorative shapes. Or simply grate chocolate over the top.

Cakes and biscuits

As an alternative to the simnel cake, which is traditionally made for Mothering Sunday, I devised a recipe for a lemon tea loaf, a moist and delicious treat for afternoon tea. It is an easy recipe to adapt to other flavours. For example, take out a quarter of the cake batter, omit the lemon and add coffee essence and a coffee liqueur such as Toussaint, then swirl it lightly back into the batter as you spoon it into the loaf tin; this will give you a marbled coffee cake. A chocolate one can be made in the same way. Alternatively, add a handful or two of chopped crystallized orange peel and some grated zest, or some ground ginger and chopped crystallized ginger.

Lemon tea loaf

4 large free-range eggs, separated
175g (6oz) golden caster sugar
juice and zest of a lemon
225g (8oz) softened unsalted butter
200g (7oz) self-raising flour

Beat the egg yolks and sugar until pale and creamy. Add the lemon juice, zest, butter and a quarter of the flour, mixing well. Fold in the rest of the flour, then the stiffly whisked egg whites. Spoon into a greased, floured loaf tin and bake for about 30 minutes at 180°C/350°F/gas mark 4, or until a skewer inserted in the middle comes out clean.

Baker's note

Loaf tins do not come in standard sizes. I have three which purport to be 1kg (2lb) tins, but each has different dimensions. When choosing which one to use, add up the approximate weight of ingredients in the recipe, then transpose that into volume. Measure the same volume of water into a jug and pour it into your loaf tin. Ideally, the liquid should come to within no more than 2 to 3 centimetres (1 inch) of the rim, to allow for the cake to rise. And note that a large egg, minus the shell, weighs about 65 grams (3oz). *Home Measures* by Shirley Bond, published by Grub Street, is an extremely useful reference to sizes and measurements in the kitchen, as well as in the home generally, particularly as, despite those who hate it, we move towards full metrification.

I like to bake this next cake in an enamelled cast iron terrine of 1kg (2lb) size, in which I normally make fish and game terrines. It is long and narrow rather than broad, and gives small, neat slices, about twenty-five. Well grease and flour any cake tins before using them. And if you use a particularly rich mix, full of fruit and sugar, it is a good idea to line the tin first.

Lemon cake

Serves 6 to 8

250g (½lb) unrefined caster sugar
125g (5oz) unsalted butter
350g (12oz) plain flour sifted with a pinch of salt
grated zest of 2 lemons and juice of one
3 free-range eggs, lightly beaten
100mls (4oz) milk

Cream the butter and sugar, and gradually add the flour, lemon and eggs, before adding the milk. Pour the cake batter into a buttered and floured cake tin, about 22cm (9 inches) in diameter and about 7.5cms (3 inches) deep. Bake in the centre of a preheated oven at 180°C/350°F/ gas mark 4 for about an hour, or until a skewer inserted in the middle comes out clean. Remove from the tin and serve warm, but not hot or cold. To decorate, either dust with icing sugar, or spread with lemon marmalade and scatter toasted flaked almonds on top.

Passion cake with gold fruit

Serves 4 to 6

125g (4oz) caster sugar
4 free-range eggs, separated
grated zest of 1 orange
125g (4oz) self-raising flour, sifted

Preheat the oven to 180°C/350°F/gas mark 4. Prepare a heart-shaped cake tin, or, if you prefer, a round one, about 20cm (8–10 inches) diameter, 4cm (1½ inches) deep. Put half the sugar in a pudding basin set over a saucepan of hot water. Add the egg yolks, and whisk until thick and pale. This will take about 5 minutes, during which time you should also whisk in the orange zest. Whisk the egg whites, together with half the remaining sugar, until peaks form. Fold in the rest of the sugar, and whisk until firm and glossy. Fold the sifted flour into the egg yolk mixture, and then fold in the egg white mixture. Spoon into the tin, shaking to fill it evenly. Bake for 10 to 12 minutes, until just firm to the touch. Turn out onto a cake rack to cool.

filling

300mls (½ pint) double cream, physalis, Sharon fruit, kumquats, mango, passion-fruit, icing sugar for sifting

Whip the cream and, having halved the cake, spread one half with the cream. Whichever fruit you choose should be sliced

Chocolate

Any good restaurant worth its name will have at least one chocolate dessert, and perhaps a sampling plate of six or seven. From this single ingredient one can create a broad palette of flavours and textures, from an austerely elegant chocolate sorbet to the voluptuous terrine of three chocolates. Dense chocolate tarts and airy steamed puddings, old-fashioned mousses and hot soufflés, chocolate meringues and chocolate bavarois are just some of the desserts that you can make. Then come a whole army of cakes, biscuits and confectionery, and, fortunately, there are a few good books on the subject to offer guidance and inspiration.

Generally, I prefer my chocolate as plain as possible, with not too many added ingredients, so I would say yes to chocolate cake but no to chocolate tart filled with berries. Probably the world's favourite chocolate dessert is the warm chocolate cake. Served with the centre still slightly runny, making its own sauce, the creation of this cake is ascribed to various origins. It has since spawned many versions all over the world.

When cooking with chocolate, do not look for 'cooking chocolate', unless it is that sold as *couverture* and used by professional pastry cooks and confectioners. Look for a chocolate with a cocoa solids content of at least 70 per cent. And the higher the cocoa butter content the better, for a well-textured chocolate and the best flavour. Fortunately, supermarkets caught on some time ago to the reality of chocolate. I do not want to see tumblers of milk pouring into my bar of chocolate; I want to see cocoa beans tumbling into it.

I particularly like the Waitrose Continental plain chocolate, made in France, with a minimum of 72 per cent cocoa solids. Maison Blanc sells Michel Cluizel Grand Amer, which has a minimum of 85 per cent cocoa solids.

From Lakeland (tel: 015394 881 00) comes a 'new' product, imported from America, Pure Chocolate Extract; a couple of tablespoons of this will give tremendous class to your chocolate puddings and cakes. By infusing cocoa beans in alcohol in a process invented a hundred years ago, the volatile flavour 'top notes' of chocolate are captured in much the same way that perfume is captured in alcohol. For more about chocolate, see Chapter 4.

or halved as appropriate, piled on to the cream and the top half of the cake then replaced. Dust with icing sugar before serving. When using kumquats in the cake, I often halve them and poach them gently with passion–fruit pulp and sugar.

Prune, chocolate and Armagnac tipsy cake

250g (½lb) unsalted butter
200g (7oz) dark muscovado sugar
4 free-range eggs, lightly beaten
275g (9oz) self-raising flour
25g (1oz) cocoa powder
pinch of salt
200g (7oz) stoned prunes, finely chopped
100g (4oz) chopped pecans or walnuts
1 teaspoon pure vanilla essence
75mls (3oz) Armagnac or chocolate liqueur
milk

Cream the butter and sugar until light and fluffy. Sift the flour, salt and cocoa together. Beat the eggs and flour alternately into the creamed mixture. Stir in the rest of the ingredients except for half the spirit, and adding enough milk to give a soft dropping consistency to the mixture. Grease and line a loaf tin, and spoon in the mixture. Smooth the top, and bake for 2 hours in a preheated oven at 150°C/300°F/gas mark 2.

Remove from the oven and allow to cool in the tin. Pour the remaining spirit over the cake, having poked holes in it with a skewer. Cover the cake with foil, and allow to stand in a cool place until the spirit is absorbed. Then wrap the cake in greaseproof paper and foil. It will keep for several weeks, and if possible should be kept for at least three days before broaching, in order for the flavours to blend and develop.

Shortbread

Serves 8

175g (6oz) unsalted butter, at room temperature
75g (3oz) caster sugar, plus extra for finishing
200g (7oz) plain flour sifted with 25g (1oz)
    cornflour

Cream the butter and sugar, and then work in the dry ingredients. Knead lightly and briefly into a ball of smooth soft paste. Roll into a circle, shape in a shortbread mould, or press into a square or round sponge tin, first buttered and floured. Crimp the edges with a fork, prick all over and mark into rectangles, squares or traditional wedges.

Bake in a preheated oven at 150°C/300°F/gas mark 2 for about 45 minutes until pale gold in colour. Remove from the oven, and allow to cool slightly in the tin. Transfer to a wire rack to cool, and, while still hot, dredge with caster sugar.

This is particularly good made with concentrated butter, available in many supermarkets. You can use caster sugar in which a vanilla pod has been stored.

Five-spice almond crisps

Makes 24

125g (4oz) ground almonds
15g (½oz) rice flour
200g (7oz) caster sugar
1 teaspoon five-spice powder
2 free-range egg whites, lightly whisked

Line two baking sheets with rice paper. Mix together the dry ingredients, and then fold in the egg whites until thoroughly blended. The mixture can be piped or spooned on to the baking trays. Leave plenty of room for the mixture to spread.

Bake at 180°C/350°F/gas mark 4 for 20 minutes or until a pale golden brown. Cool on a wire rack. These are delicious served with ice creams, sorbets, mousses and custards, and indeed on their own with a cup of tea or coffee.

Forgotten almond crisps

To use up some of the egg whites left over from making custard and ice cream, try these meringue-like biscuits. You leave them in the oven overnight, hence their name. The biscuits keep well if stored in an airtight tin, but do not attempt to make any meringue-like dish in humid conditions. A weepy mess will result.

Makes about 6 dozen

4 free-range egg whites
300g (10oz) golden caster sugar
1 teaspoon pure almond essence or
    2 teaspoons almond liqueur
pinch of salt
350g (12oz) chopped almonds

Preheat the oven to 180°C/350°F/gas mark 4.

Line 4 baking sheets with baking parchment or foil. Beat the egg whites until they stiffen. Add the sugar slowly, a tablespoon at a time, and continue whisking. Add the liqueur and salt, and whisk until the meringue is stiff and glossy. Fold in the almonds

Drop the mixture, by teaspoons, onto the baking sheets, and place in the preheated oven. Turn off the oven and forget the biscuits until next morning.

Madeleines

Makes 24

100g (4oz) caster sugar
100g (4oz) self-raising flour
pinch of salt, about half a coffee spoon
2 free-range eggs, lightly beaten
150g (5oz) unsalted butter, melted

Preheat the oven to 230°C/450°F/gas mark 8. Butter and flour madeleine moulds or bun tins.

Sift together the dry ingredients. Beat in the eggs, and then mix in the melted butter. Pour the batter – and the mixture really is quite liquid – into the prepared moulds, and bake in the top half of the oven for 5 to 7 minutes.

Remove from the oven once the madeleines are golden, well risen, and with the characteristic 'bump' in the middle. The recipe multiplies well, certainly by up to ten; I learned the recipe using a kilo of flour.

If you wish, you can add, with the eggs, lemon zest, or some vanilla seeds. I have also used a little orange-flower water and grated orange zest. Alternatively, you can use vanilla sugar.

Madeleines are delicious when freshly baked and served still warm, with, for example, a vanilla ice cream and a fruit sauce, or for a subtle Proustian experience, try the following.

Make a strong infusion of tilleul (linden tea) in about 450mls (¾ pints) water, and when well steeped, dissolve in it at least half the volume of sugar and the juice of a lemon or, even better, a lime. When cool, freeze to granita or sorbet, as you prefer, and serve a scoop of it with a warm madeleine or two.

Alternatively, use real lime to flavour the madeleines, as in the next recipe.

Lemon and lime madeleines

Makes 24

100g (4oz) caster sugar
100g (4oz) self-raising flour
pinch of salt, about half a coffee spoon
2 free-range eggs, lightly beaten
130g (5oz) unsalted butter, melted
finely grated zest of a lime and a lemon

Preheat the oven to 230°C/450°F/gas mark 8. Butter and flour some madeleine moulds. These are very shallow, fluted and an elongated shell shape. If you use bun tins, the mixture will fill twelve, not twenty-four and you will not, of course, get the same shape as a madeleine.

The perfect tuile

Make miniature versions to serve as petits fours, or use the mixture to make crisp lacy baskets to hold ice creams, sorbets or mixed berries.

YOU NEED 100g (4oz) unsalted butter, melted, 150g (5oz) golden caster sugar, 40g (1½oz) plain flour, 40mls (1½oz) orange juice and 25g (1oz) softened butter for greasing the trays.

METHOD Heat the oven to 200°C/400°F/gas mark 6. Generously grease two baking sheets, or use non-stick mats. Mix the ingredients to a paste. Take a quarter of it, and with your fingers spread it into a circle about 15cm (6 inches) in diameter. Make another circle on the same baking sheet, and bake for 7 to 8 minutes until golden. Remove from the oven, and while still soft, shape each biscuit. Do the same with the second tuile. If it has become brittle, return the baking tray to the oven for a few seconds. Bake and shape the remaining two in the same way.

Sift together the dry ingredients. Beat in the eggs, and then mix in the melted butter and zest. Pour the batter into the prepared moulds, and bake in the top half of the oven for 5 to 7 minutes.

Remove from the oven once the madeleines are golden well risen.

Pralines

Makes 3 to 4 dozen

300g (10oz) caster sugar
150g (5oz) light muscovado sugar
300mls (½ pint) double cream
300g (10oz) pecans or almonds, coarsely
    chopped
2 tablespoons butter
pinch of salt
1 teaspoon pure vanilla essence

In a heavy saucepan or frying pan, cook the sugar and cream over medium heat, until the sugar has dissolved, stirring only enough to prevent sticking, and without scraping down the sides.

As soon as the mixture is boiling rapidly, add the nuts, butter and salt. Let the mixture reach 165°C/320°F on a sugar thermometer, remove from the heat, stir in the vanilla, and beat vigorously with a wooden spoon for 2 minutes.

When the mixture begins to thicken and cool, spoon it into rounds on greased wax paper, and leave to cool completely. Wrap each individually and store them in an airtight box or tin.

It's worth getting up very early to make these, if you do not like the idea of sweating over a hot stove on a summer's day.

Macarons

The next recipe is for the French *macarons*, delicate almond confections, and not at all like English macaroons.

Makes about 40

125g (generous 4oz) ground almonds
225g (8oz) icing sugar, plus 1 tablespoon
100 mls (4oz) egg white (from 4 or 5 free-range
    eggs)
1 teaspoon dried egg white – optional

Sift the ground almonds and measured sugar together. Whisk the egg whites and, as they firm up, sprinkle in the powdered egg white, if using it, and the tablespoon of sugar, whisking until the mixture is firm. Add some of the almond and sugar mixture to the egg white and fold in gently, and then gently fold in the remaining dry ingredients, which should finish with the consistency of soft paste.

Pipe into small mounds, about 2 to 3cm (1 inch) apart, on baking sheets lined with non-stick baking material. Let the *macarons* dry for about 20 minutes before baking at 150°C/300°F/gas mark 2 for four minutes. Turn the tray around and cook for another four minutes.

Allow to cool, then sandwich with butter cream (p. 31) or the filling of your choice.

Ices

Homemade vanilla ice cream

Note: this recipe contains raw eggs.

Serves 4 to 6

500mls (18oz) full-cream milk
1 vanilla pod
6 free-range egg yolks
100g (4oz) golden caster sugar
150mls (5oz) single, double, or whipping cream

Scald the milk with the vanilla pod, and pour it over the egg yolks, beaten first with the sugar. Beat the mixture continuously, strain it into a bowl set over, but not touching, simmering water. Add the cream, and stir until the custard thickens.

Rinse the vanilla pod, split it, and stir the seeds into the custard. Once cool, freeze the custard in an ice-cream maker, sorbetière, or the ice-making compartment of the freezer. If the latter method, you will need to stir it from time to time to ensure a smooth mixture.

Before entirely frozen, additions can be stirred in such as rum-soaked raisins, toasted flaked almonds, crushed crystallized roses, chopped crystallized fruit, or a measure or two of strong espresso.

Baked ice cream

Thomas Jefferson was not the first to bring ice cream to America, but his kitchen was doing fascinating things with it. Samuel Leatham Mitchell, after dinner at the White House in 1803, wrote, 'Among other things, ice creams were produced in the form of balls of frozen material, enclosed in covers of warm pastry, exhibiting a curious contrast, as if the ice had just been taken from the oven.' And this happened some sixty-four years before Seward's Folly, the sale of Alaska to the United States by Czar Alexander II, which was celebrated in New York by Delmonico's chef in the 'invention' of the Baked Alaska. Intriguing. Another twist in the 'hot ice cream' story. Irresistible. I had to try it. It works, if you use a very fine ice cream, made with the purest ingredients.

Serves 4 to 6

500mls (18oz) best ice cream – see next recipe
12 or 18 sheets filo pastry, about 15 x 15cm
melted butter
light muscovado sugar
golden icing sugar
beaten free-range egg yolk and milk glaze

Scoop the ice cream into four or six balls or quenelles, and freeze until hard. Take three sheets of filo for each ice cream, and layer them on top of each other, brushing each layer with butter and sprinkling with the muscovado sugar. Put the ice cream in the centre and enclose in the pastry, as either an envelope or a bundle, sealing the edges by brushing with the egg glaze. Brush more over the exterior, and bake in a very hot oven, 220–250°C/450–500°F/gas mark 7–9 for about 6 to 8 minutes, keeping as close an eye as possible on proceedings. Serve immediately, dusted with icing sugar. Very pretty on glass or dark plates.

Rice pudding ice cream

Serves 4 to 6

100g (4oz) pudding rice
1 vanilla pod
600mls (1 pint) full-cream milk
200g (7oz) caster sugar
300mls (½ pint) double cream

Cook the rice and vanilla pod in the milk until the grains are tender. Remove the vanilla pod, split it, and scrape the seeds into the pudding. Stir in the sugar while the mixture is still hot, and allow it to cool. Bear in mind that the sweetness will diminish in intensity when the mixture is frozen. Whip the cream, fold it into the rice, and freeze the mixture either in an ice-cream maker or a freezer container.

Verbena ice cream

Note: this contains raw eggs.

Makes 1 litre

good handful dried lemon verbena
250mls (8oz) sugar syrup, made with 250g
    (8oz) sugar and 250mls (8oz) water
375mls (13oz) full-cream milk
250mls (8oz) whipping cream
4 free-range egg yolks, lightly beaten in a bowl

Simmer the verbena in the syrup for 5 minutes, and leave to infuse until cool, removing the pan from the heat. Scald the milk in a separate saucepan, remove from the heat and stir in the verbena syrup. Leave again to infuse until cool and only then strain. Scald the cream and pour on the egg yolks, whisking all the time. Return the saucepan to a very gentle heat, and stir the custard continuously until it thickens slightly. Combine the custard with the flavoured mixture and when cool, freeze in the usual way.

Fresh fruit sorbet

Serves 2

200mls (7oz) freshly squeezed orange or
    grapefruit juice
100g (4oz) unrefined caster sugar dissolved in 1
    tablespoon water

Mix the juice and syrup, and freeze in the usual way. Less sugar will give a grainier, more crystalline sorbet, more of a granita, whereas more sugar will give a softer texture.

Lemon and lime sorbet

Serves 4

200mls (7oz) water
200g (7oz) granulated sugar
50mls (2oz) freshly squeezed lime juice

200mls (7oz) lemon juice
finely grated zest of one lime and 1 lemon

Make a syrup of the sugar and water and allow to cool. Mix the syrup, juice and a further 250mls (8oz) water, together with the citrus zest. Freeze in a sorbetière or ice-cream maker.

Linden and lemon sorbet with bitter chocolate galettes

Serves 2

1 lemon
2 tablespoons linden flowers (available from
    herbalists or shops that sell herb teas)
200mls (7oz) water, boiling
100g (4oz) granulated sugar, or more to taste
50g (2oz) dark chocolate, at least 70 per cent
    cocoa solids

Thinly peel off the lemon zest, and put it with the linden flowers in a jug.

Pour on the boiling water, and leave to infuse for 10 minutes. Stir in the lemon juice and sugar, and when this has dissolved, strain the infusion, cool, and freeze in a sorbetière, ice-cream maker or freezer container.

Break up the chocolate, and put it in a small heatproof glass jug. Stand it in very hot water until the chocolate has melted.

Pour the chocolate onto a sheet of greaseproof paper, a drop at a time, and allow it to spread to thin discs. When set, peel off the paper, and serve with the sorbet.

Lavender sorbet with blueberry soup

It makes a big difference using fresh lavender. The aromatic oils fade fairly quickly, and if you use dried lavender the flavour tends to be somewhat musty. This sorbet recipe is one I have been using for eighteen years, since the hot summer of 1982 when I raided my mother's lavender bush and started cooking with flowers for the first time.

Serves 6

Sorbet

600mls (1 pint) water
400g (14oz) granulated sugar
1 lemon
2 tablespoons fresh lavender flowers

Make a syrup of the water and sugar and bring to the boil. Thinly peel off the lemon zest, and put it with the lavender flowers in the boiling syrup. Leave to infuse for an hour or so.

Stir in the lemon juice, strain the infusion, cool and freeze. Using less sugar will give you a grainier sorbet, and more sugar makes it smoother.

Soup

    400g (14oz) blueberries
    100mls (4oz) red grape juice
    juice of half a lemon
    2 or 3 tablespoons sugar
    600mls (1 pint) chilled water

Put all but a handful of the blueberries, the grape juice, lemon juice, sugar and water in the blender, and blend until smooth.

Pour into chilled soup plates, and add a scoop or quenelle of the lavender sorbet. The whole blueberries are added for garnish; fresh lavender flowers or mint leaves can also be used.

Cherry soup with almond ice cream

Serves 8

Ice cream

    300mls (½ pint) milk
    300mls (½ pint) single cream
    250g (½lb) softened almond paste
    8 free-range egg yolks
    caster sugar, if required

Heat the milk, cream and almond paste in a saucepan. In a bowl, beat together the egg yolks and sugar. When warm, add a quarter of the cream mixture to the egg mixture, and thoroughly incorporate. When the cream mixture boils, pour it over the egg mixture, beating continuously.

Sieve the mixture into a clean saucepan, and cook gently until it will coat the back of a spoon. Cool, then freeze in an ice-cream maker or in a box in the freezer. An ice-cream maker will turn the mixture and make it smooth. You will need to stir it by hand or in a food processor during the freezing process for a really smooth ice cream if you freeze the mixture in a container.

Soup

    200mls (7oz) water
    200g (7oz) sugar

    200g (7oz) unsalted butter
    about 1kg (2lbs) stoned cherries
    1–2 tablespoons kirsch

Use a clean non-stick frying pan, and in it put the water, sugar and butter. Heat gently until the sugar has dissolved, and then cook the mixture until syrupy. Add the cherries and poach for 5 minutes, stirring in the kirsch right at the end. Pour the syrup into shallow soup plates or dishes together with a portion of cherries, and serve a scoop of the almond ice cream on top.

Dessert biscuits

    125g (generous 4oz) unsalted butter at room
        temperature
    175g (6oz) icing sugar
    125g (generous 4oz) plain flour, sifted
    5 or 6 free-range egg whites
    pure vanilla extract

Lightly cream together the butter and sugar, and then add the rest of the ingredients, mixing to a paste. Rest the mixture in the refrigerator for 15 to 20 minutes. Spread it as thin as possible in circles on a buttered baking sheet. Bake at 180°C/350°F/gas mark 4 for 8 to 10 minutes. As soon as you remove the sheet from the oven, you can roll up each biscuit while still warm, then shape them into tuiles (see p. 227) or leave flat. Transfer the biscuits to wire racks to cool. Make small or large ones, and add spices and flavourings, as you wish.

Spiced rhubarb sorbet with ginger ice cream and brandy snap wafers

Whereas I am not keen on *le grand dessert*, where a little bit of everything appears on the plate, I particularly like desserts created around a single fruit. Thus one might have a sliver of pear tart, a small pear poached in wine and a scoop of pear sorbet in a tuile basket. Or a fruit soup, really just a glorified fruit salad, might be served with a scoop of matching ice cream in the middle, accompanied by crisp biscuits or a tender madeleine. For an easy variation on this theme, you might bury a spoonful of lemon or passion-fruit curd under a blanket of cream in a tuile basket, lightly dredge with sugar, and caramelize the top, garnishing with a fruit crisp. This next recipe is based on the rhubarb and ginger theme.

GINGER

Early November, with its frosts, barely clothed trees and autumn bonfires, reminds me of childhood in Yorkshire, especially the warm smell of weekend baking and, most of all, the rich, inviting aromas of gingercake for Sunday tea.

Ginger has always been one of my favourite flavours. When I first started cooking, I could only buy sneeze boxes of ground ginger and could afford neither decorative jars of preserved ginger, nor wooden boxes of the crystallized kind. Now fresh ginger is available everywhere for use in sweet and savoury cooking. And I like to buy the thin, pink shavings of Japanese pickled ginger, for its sweet, hot flavour is excellent with fish, poultry and salad, as well as *sashimi* and sushi, its traditional partners. I have also used it in gingercake on several occasions, and it is an excellent substitute for preserved ginger.

When buying fresh ginger, look for the firmest specimens possible, with a tight satiny skin and few protuberances. If you find a very fresh piece with healthy looking shoots, break a couple off, and pot them in standard potting compost. You may be lucky enough that it will grow into a beautiful ornamental house plant. And, as a bonus, it will give you a new fresh rhizome, although you have to destroy the plant to get at it, of course.

In addition to fresh ginger, which keeps quite well in the salad drawer of the refrigerator, it is worth having a stock of the pickled ginger that I have described; cubes of crystallized ginger for baking, and a jar of preserved ginger in syrup for an instant enlivener of vanilla ice cream, crêpes and soufflés. You can, of course, preserve your own ginger. It is also useful to add flavour in the form of a ginger wine. To make this, I slice a good-size hand of ginger, and push it into a bottle of fino or Amontillado sherry. This is lovely for flavouring stir-fried vegetables, or steamed fish or chicken.

Traditional baking has always made much use of ginger, and not just in the British Isles in our parkin and gingernuts. We find it in the French *pain d'épices*, the German *Pfeffernüsse* and *Lebkuchen*, the Dutch *spekulaas*, the Polish *piernik*, and the Scandinavian 'pepper' cakes and biscuits, which are, in fact, made with ginger.

All of these baked goods, and others like them, are often associated with the festive season, particularly Advent and the gift-giving on Saint Nicholas day, 6 December. Think of gingerbread houses and hearts to be strung on the Christmas tree. This firm dough, mixed with honey and syrup, is often made a few days before required to allow the special flavours to be absorbed. In Sri Lanka ginger is used in what must be the world's richest Christmas cake, using twenty-five eggs and pounds of rich dried fruit. I imagine that the recipe has its origins in the Dutch or British culinary influence on Sri Lanka, rather than the Portuguese.

Whilst it is clear that the Portuguese and Spaniards took ginger to West Africa and the Caribbean in their colonizing missions, it is the spice-trading nations of Britain and the Netherlands, with their East India companies, which seem to make more use of it in their cooking. I have never been aware, visiting Spain and Portugal extensively, of much use of ginger in their own cooking.

Ginger came to Europe very early from China, and in the Middle Ages it often appeared on the table as a condiment. One of my favourite dishes, Hainan chicken, also uses ginger as a condiment, mixed with salt. It is a lovely, homely Chinese dish, and one I cannot recommend too highly (see p. 51).

A whole range of spice mixtures in many cuisines relies on a touch of ginger for a delightfully warming sensation – from our own pickling spice mixtures, to the French *quatre épices*, the Chinese five-spice mix and the many curry pastes and powder masalas of the subcontinent. In Morocco you will find ginger in *ras el hanout* and in the Ethopian *berebere*. In Baltimore one of our favourite dinners is crab. There the small blue crabs are boiled with handfuls of powerful Old Bay spice mixture, which includes ginger, and then, once drained, the whole pot of crabs is tipped onto the newspaper-covered table. You are handed a hammer to get at the succulent, sweet white flesh and, if you are sensible, you order pitchers of beer. A crab boil is not a dainty meal, but an enormously tasty one.

Ginger's role is much too important to confine to baking, and you will find many recipes throughout the book which require it. And it is indispensable in this refreshing and useful cordial.

Ginger cordial

Makes about 500mls (18oz)

75g (3oz) fresh ginger, peeled and thinly sliced
500mls (18oz) water
juice of a lemon
250g (½lb) granulated sugar

Put all the ingredients in a saucepan set over low heat. Let the sugar dissolve, and then bring to the boil. Simmer for a few minutes, then remove from the heat and let the ginger infuse for several hours, or overnight for a stronger cordial. Strain, bottle, and refrigerate. This makes an excellent flavouring for ice creams and custards.

Do not throw the ginger away, either, but chop it, and mix it into ice cream. Dilute the ginger syrup with chilled sparkling water for refreshing home-made ginger ale.

In China, a ginger tea is often served after game dishes to aid digestion and 'sweeten the mouth'. I like to make a strong infusion of ginger, allow it to cool and then freeze it to a granita, making a wonderfully sharp, clear palate cleanser.

Ginger tea and granita

Serves 8 to 10 in small cups, or 6 as a granita

600mls (1 pint) water
300g (10oz) sugar
5cm (1 inch) piece ginger, peeled and sliced
thinly pared zest of a lemon and its strained juice.

Put the water and sugar in a saucepan, and heat gently until the sugar has dissolved. Simmer gently for 3 minutes. Put in the ginger, lemon zest and juice, remove from the heat, and allow it to infuse for 10 to 20 minutes. Strain and serve. Alternatively, cool it, and then freeze.

Note: this ice cream recipe contains raw eggs.

Serves 10

Sorbet

500g (1lb) trimmed rhubarb
2 tablespoons water
500mls (18oz) sugar syrup, made with 500g (18oz) sugar and 500mls (18oz) water, flavoured with seeds of green cardamom, cinnamon sticks or cloves
juice of half a lemon

Prepare the rhubarb and cook it gently in the water (until tender). When cool, blend with the flavoured syrup and the lemon juice. Freeze in a sorbetière or ice-cream maker.

Ice cream

Makes 1 litre (1½ pints)

75g (3oz) fresh ginger, peeled and finely chopped
250mls (8oz) sugar syrup, as above, no flavourings
375mls (13oz) full-cream milk
5 free-range egg yolks
250mls (8oz) whipping cream

Simmer the ginger in the syrup for 5 minutes. Remove the pan from the heat. Scald the milk in a separate saucepan, remove from the heat and stir in the ginger syrup. Infuse for about an hour and do not strain at this stage.

Proceed with the ice-cream making in the usual way, reheating the milk and syrup mixture before pouring it on the beaten egg yolks to make the custard. Stir this over a very low heat until it thickens just enough to coat the back of a spoon, but without letting it curdle. The ginger is removed when the custard is strained before the addition of the cream, and the mixture is then frozen. For a more intense flavour, press the ginger through the sieve.

Once the ice cream is made, freeze it in a lined Swiss roll tray, which will give you rounds or rectangles for the brandy snap wafers.

Brandy snap wafers

Makes about 50

75g (3oz) each golden syrup, Demerara sugar, butter, plain flour
½ teaspoon ground ginger

1 tablespoon brandy

In a heavy saucepan combine syrup, sugar and butter and heat gently, stirring until the sugar has dissolved and the butter melted. Remove from the heat and cool slightly before stirring in the ginger and brandy and sifting in the flour.

Take teaspoons of the mixture and spread on prepared baking sheets. Bake for about 8 minutes in a preheated oven at 160°C/325°F/gas mark 3.

Trim into neat circles or rectangles and cool on wire trays. These will keep for up to 1 week in an airtight container.

Cut out the ice cream to the same shape as the brandy snaps and sandwich together. For each serving, place a quenelle or scoop of sorbet on the plate, together with an ice cream sandwich. Garnish with shredded preserved stem ginger, preserved angelica and frosted mint leaves.

Camomile sorbet with peach soup

Serves 6

Sorbet

1 lime
2 tablespoons dried camomile flowers
600mls (1 pint) water, boiling
200–300g (7–10oz) granulated sugar

Thinly peel off the lime zest, and put it with the camomile flowers in a jug. Pour on the boiling water, and leave to infuse for 10 minutes.

Stir in the lime juice and the sugar, and when it has dissolved, strain the infusion, cool and freeze.

Using the lesser amount of sugar will give you a grainier sorbet, and more sugar makes it smoother.

Soup

ripe peaches, peeled and roughly chopped
juice of half a lemon
2 tablespoons sugar
600mls (1 pint) chilled water

Put the peaches, lemon juice, sugar and water in the blender, and blend until smooth.

Pour into chilled soup plates, and add a scoop or quenelle of the sorbet. Very thin slices of peach can be added for garnish, as can fresh camomile flowers or mint leaves.

Recipes from here and there

Gâteau basque

This traditional Basque pastry is not a soft, moist sponge, but has a slightly crumbly, biscuity quality.

Serves 6

125g (generous 4oz) unsalted butter
100g (4oz) plain flour
40g (1½oz) ground almonds
1 coffee spoon fast-action yeast
3 medium-size free-range eggs
125g (generous 4oz) vanilla sugar, or caster
    sugar in which you store a vanilla pod
2 teaspoons rum

pastry cream

2 medium-size free-range egg yolks
50g (2oz) caster sugar
2 teaspoons cornflour, slaked in a little of the milk
200mls (7oz) milk

10 stoned, ready-to-eat prunes, cut into 4, or
    150g (5oz) preserved cherries, stoned and
    drained
free-range egg and milk for glaze

Melt three-quarters of the butter, and use the rest to butter a cake tin about 22cm (9 inches) in diameter and 7.5–10cm (3–4 inches) deep. Mix the flour, almonds and yeast in a bowl. Whisk the eggs in another bowl with the vanilla sugar until light and fluffy. Fold in the flour mixture, butter and rum.

Carefully mix, and let it rest for 15 minutes or so while you make the pastry cream. Beat the eggs and sugar, and then add the cornflour. Stir in well. Scald the milk, and pour it over the eggs, beating continuously. Transfer to a saucepan, and bring to the boil, stirring continuously. When the mixture thickens, remove the pan from the heat and allow to cool.

Divide the cake mix in two, and use half to line the cake tin. Smooth the surface, and spoon on the pastry cream to within 2.5cm (1 inch) of the edge.

Arrange the pieces of prune or cherries in the cream, and then carefully spoon or pipe the rest of the cake mixture over it to cover and seal in the cream. Brush with beaten egg and milk to glaze, and bake in a preheated oven at 200°C/400°F/gas mark 6 for 40 to 45 minutes. Remove from the oven, cool on a rack, and serve warm or cold.

Papos d'anjo (Angel throats)

This is a typical Portuguese dish, much easier to make than it might seem, rich and eggy, and first cooked for me by my friend in Lisbon, Teresa Grilo.

Makes 20 to 24

250g (½lb) caster sugar
150mls (5oz) water
½ vanilla pod
4 free-range egg yolks
1 free-range egg white

Butter and flour two bun tins.

Dissolve the sugar in the water, and cook it over a low heat with the vanilla pod. Meanwhile, beat the egg yolks until they are foamy and pale. Whisk the egg white until firm, and fold carefully into the egg yolks. Spoon the mixture into the bun tins – a scant tablespoon of the mixture in each should fill all 24 holes.

Cook in the top of a preheated oven at 220°C/450°F/gas mark 7 for about 5 minutes, or until just set.

Remove the little soufflés from the tins, and allow to cool slightly on wire racks. Dip them, with two forks, into the hot syrup, and arrange them in a shallow glass or china dish.

Pour the rest of the syrup over them, discarding the vanilla pod, cool, and chill until required.

Pudim de nozes (Walnut puddings)

This is another easy-to-make Portuguese dessert, perfect with a small espresso.

Serves 4 to 6

125g (4oz) shelled walnuts
¼ teaspoon ground cinnamon
3 free-range eggs
175g (6oz) caster sugar
whipped cream and extra walnuts for decorating

Grind the walnuts and cinnamon to a paste. Beat the eggs and sugar, and mix in the nuts. Butter some moulds, ramekins or a bun tin, and pour in the mixture. Place in a roasting tin with a little water, and cook until set in a pre-

heated oven at 220°C/425°F/gas mark 7. Timing will depend on the depth of the mixture, but bun tins will take about 5 minutes. When cold, turn the puddings out of the moulds, and decorate with the whipped cream and half-walnuts.

Toucinho do ceu (Egg and almond cake)

Although often described as a cake, this Portuguese dessert is perhaps more of a pudding in texture. A small piece makes the perfect mouthful to accompany a tiny cup of strong black coffee.

Serves 6 to 8

250g (½lb) granulated sugar
100mls (3½oz) water
125g (generous 4oz) blanched and halved or
    whole almonds
50g (2oz) unsalted butter
4 free-range egg yolks
1 whole free-range egg
1 scant tablespoon plain flour, sifted
½ free-range egg white lightly whisked with
    1 tablespoon caster sugar – for glaze
1–2 tablespoons granulated or preserving sugar

Dissolve the sugar in the water, bring to the boil, and cook for 4 to 5 minutes. Stir in the almonds, and remove from the heat. Allow to cool. Beat in the butter, eggs and flour, and pour the mixture into a well-buttered cake tin about 18–20cms (7–8 inches) square. Bake in the centre of a preheated oven at about 150°C/300°F/gas mark 3, for about 40 to 45 minutes. When the cake is cooked, a skewer poked into the middle will emerge clean. Cool the cake in the tin, and then turn onto a plate. Brush the top with the glaze, and when just tacky, sift on the coarser sugar.

Tarte de natas (Cream tart)

A very simple Portuguese dessert, ideal when accompanied by a compote of fresh or dried fruit.

Note: this recipe contains raw eggs.

Serves 8 to 10

500mls (18oz) milk
395g (14oz) can sweet condensed milk
4 sheets or 4 teaspoons gelatine

3 free-range egg whites
75g (3oz) shortbread or other fairly plain
    biscuits, finely crushed

Mix both milks together in a bowl. Soak the gelatine in 4 table-spoons of water, and then dissolve in a bain-marie. Add to the milk, giving a good stir to make a creamy texture. Whisk the egg whites to firm peaks, and gently fold into the milk. Place a greased flan ring on a baking sheet lined with greased silicone paper. Sprinkle the crushed biscuits to form an even base inside the flan ring, and then pour the mixture over it, filling the circle to the top, and leave in the refrigerator until set. When ready to serve, invert a flat plate over the flan ring and turn the pudding over. Remove the silicone paper and the flan ring. The biscuit crumbs will now be on top.

Pane di natale (An Italian Christmas Loaf)

Signora Lancellotti sat me down with a cappuccino, and gave me this *pane di natale* recipe, which she had learned in her mother-in-law's kitchen. Not nearly as rich as our own Christmas cakes and puddings, it is made with the ingredients that would be found in most larders in the village near Modena where she and her family live. Concentrated grape juice is not available here, so use prune juice or ordinary grape juice, enriching with a little of the thick, raisiny sweet Pedro Ximenez sherry.

Makes 4 loaves or cakes

approx. 1kg (2lbs) dried fruit and nuts, including
    walnuts, hazelnuts, almonds, pine nuts,
    raisins and figs
about 1 litre (32oz) carton red grape or prune
    juice
4 tablespoons Pedro Ximénez sherry
approx. 1kg (2lbs) strong plain flour
50g (2oz) yeast
4 tablespoons mincemeat – optional

Prepare the fruit and nuts the day before you bake. Chop the larger nuts and the figs, and put all the fruit and nuts in a bowl. Add enough juice to cover, and stir in the sherry. Leave for 24 hours, and stir the mixture occasionally.

The next day, mix the flour and yeast, and stir in the fruit and nuts and enough liquid to make a dough. Add the mincemeat, if using it. You can, if you wish, let it rise slowly, covered, for 24 hours in a cool place, or let it rise in a shorter time at a higher temperature. In other words, treat it as you would bread, and let it work to your timetable rather than the other way round. Shape into four loaves and place in greased and floured tins, or shape into round cakes about 12cms (5 inches) in diameter and place on baking sheets. Allow to prove for an hour or so, covered with a light, damp cloth. Bake at 180°C/350°F/gas mark 4 in a preheated oven for 20 minutes, then turn down the heat a couple of notches, and finish baking for a further 20 to 25 minutes until the loaves sound hollow when tapped. The crust will be very hard, and traditionally the cake is stored for eight days before eating, covered with a cloth moistened with *saba,* or thick grape juice, which 'feeds' and moistens the cake. Or you can do as was done in Camillo Lancellotti's mother's house, and brush the loaves with a goose feather dipped in the liquid. The cake would be stored in the larder.

Speculaas koekies (Dutch spice biscuits)

Makes about 60

200g (7oz) unsalted butter
300g (10oz) plain flour
1 teaspoon salt
1 teaspoon baking powder
4 teaspoons ground *speculaas* spice, or ground
    mixed spice
275g (9oz) dark muscovado sugar
1 large free-range egg

Cream the softened butter with the sugar until light and fluffy. Mix in the egg. Sieve the remaining ingredients together, and blend into the butter mixture. Leave to rest in the refrigerator overnight. Roll out half of the dough on a floured surface to the thickness of a pound coin, and cut into rectangles of about 3 x 4cms (1 x 1½ inches). Place on a buttered baking tray, and cook in a preheated oven at 150°C/300°F/gas mark 2 for 15 to 18 minutes. Remove, and let cool on wire racks. Continue with the rest of the dough.

The Crab Shack on Tybee Island off the Georgia coast near Savannah is one of those places you always hope to find when messing about by the sea. We knew nothing about it but just followed our noses to a bleached and weathered wooden shack on a quiet dock on Chimney Creek. A large square bar for the locals, tables under the trees for the tourists, and tables inside, cooled by an overhead fan and protected from bugs by mosquito-mesh panels for the serious eater.

The food is always worth taking seriously in these unprepossessing places by the sea. Fernando and Paco Hermosa's Bar Bigote in Sanlucar at the tip of Andalusia, Neptuno in Azenhas do Mar, west of Lisbon, Moran's on the Weir in County Galway, O Grove in Galicia, Il Re del Pesce in Malta, Sammy's in Mgarr on Gozo, Fernando's on Taipa Island, Macau, the lobster shacks in Maine – all will reward you with the freshest shellfish imaginable: sweet, salty, succulent and best eaten as simply as possible.

A few days later, having eaten a good portion of Georgia's shrimp harvest, we turned our attention to the oysters of the Florida panhandle. The coast road south of Tallahassee is lined with small oyster-fishing villages, and indeed, on closer inspection, the soft shoulder appears to be made of nothing but shards of oyster shell. Oyster shacks abound, or you can buy your own for a backyard barbecue. But we ate ours in Boss Oyster in Apalachicola, another of the world's great seafood destinations. On the half-shell, deep fried, barbecued and with every imaginable topping, we decided to make dinner an oyster feast, when it had been our intention only to share a beer and six oysters as an appetizer before going to one of the town's smart old inns for dinner. The seafood pizza was memorable – another idea to try at home. The pre-cooked base had lightly steamed seafood on top, the whole covered with a white, roasted garlic sauce finished under a hot grill.

But back to Captain Flanagan's Crab Shack. Only the blue crabs were in season when we were there, and those a little on the immature side. So we let someone else do the work and ordered devilled crab. This we followed with a local dish, Low Country Boil. Potatoes, sweetcorn, boiling sausage and plenty of shrimps were cooked together in a highly seasoned broth, and brought to the table in a large pot. A roll of paper towel was put on the table, and periodically we emptied the bowls of shells and

husks into a bin set in a well in the centre of the table. Ice-cold Jamaican Red Stripe beer or a frozen Margarita was the only possible accompaniment.

Casual, served from a central pot, eaten with your fingers, this is perfect food for easy entertaining, as are my other variations in the mixed seafood recipes.

No first course is needed, but I like to finish with melon in lime and ginger syrup, a watermelon drowned in vodka or some other cool, refreshing fruit salad.

Lobster and crab

Unless you have an excellent local fishmonger, to get the freshest, sweetest product you should cook the crustacea yourself, rather than buying ready-cooked. Lobster is an expensive ingredient, and it is worth eating it at its very best.

However, cooking it yourself means killing it yourself. There is, according to the RSPCA, no known way of killing lobsters absolutely humanely, and, if there is any uncertainty, the animal should have the benefit of the doubt.

Some people suggest electrically stunning them; others recommend putting the lobster into luke-warm salt water and very gradually raising the heat. The short, sharp blow through the nervous system has its advocates too. But in Canada and Maine, lobsters are plunged into an inch or two of fast-boiling water. 'Live crustaceans die in a few seconds,' we are told by a number of cookery experts. According to the RSPCA, it can take 2 to 3 minutes, rather than a few seconds, for a lobster to die in boiling water. If a large number of crustacea are being cooked in a big pot, then it can take much longer because the water will take much longer to come back to the boil.

Since lobsters live in very cold water, the RSPCA recommends, as the least inhumane way of killing them and the one most feasible for a domestic kitchen, chilling the creature in ice slurry or in the freezer for about 30 minutes, which reduces it to a state of torpor; it is then killed by piercing it through the cross-mark in the carapace with a heavy cleaver or kitchen knife, cutting right down to the chopping board. The lobster can then be boiled or steamed. If you wish, for steaming or grilling it can be split down the middle and opened out. All that needs removing are the feathery gills under the carapace, the stomach sac of gritty substance in the 'head' part of the lobster and the intestine, which runs down the centre of the tail and is quite visible when the lobster is split down the middle. Severing through the nerve system with a heavy knife or cleaver is indeed the fastest and most efficient way to kill a lobster, if you are deft with these implements. It is the method used by many chefs.

A crab has two nerve centres, and these should be destroyed before the creature is cooked. The RSPCA advice is to use an awl or something pointed of similar diameter. Turn the crab onto its back, lift the tail flap and you will see a small hole at the base of a distinct groove. Paralyse the crab by firmly piercing this nerve centre to a depth of at least 2cm (half an inch). Complete the process by pushing the awl or skewer between the moveable plates at the mouth, between the eyes. The crab can then be boiled or steamed. We would, I imagine, eat much less meat if we had to take on the responsibility for our own actions and appetites every time we wanted to eat chicken, or sausages or a hamburger.

Once the water has come back to the boil, allow 15 to 20 minutes for a 1–1.5kg (2–3lb) crab. Canadian and Maine lobsters have a thinner shell than the Scottish or European one. The usual size is about 600g (1¼lbs). Allow 12 minutes for a Canadian lobster and 15 for a European one, once the water has come back to the boil. The shell of a European lobster is a much more defined, dark blue colour, whereas the Canadian lobster shell is greeny-brown. Both, of course, turn bright red when cooked.

After experimenting with both kinds, I have come to the conclusion that, like most things, lobsters are a matter of taste. Whilst I found both Canadian and European, when bought live, to have a similarly good, firm, chewy texture when cooked, the flavour of true European lobster was more 'meaty' and subtle, and the Canadian one was more directly salty-sweet tasting.

If you decide to buy a lobster already cooked, make sure that its tail is tightly curled. A limp-tailed lobster indicates that it was dead and possibly deteriorating before it was cooked. A crab should feel heavy for its size, with no sound of liquid sloshing around inside.

Preparing crab

As an occasional Saturday treat, I sometimes prepare a fresh crab, having ordered it a couple of days in advance from the local fishmonger. They boil it for me in the morning and I collect it at lunchtime. Preparing it, that is, removing all the meat from the body and claws, takes a good hour or so, but the resulting supper – a casual do-it-yourself kind of meal – is well worth it.

The flavour and texture of a freshly boiled, sweet, juicy crab are incomparable, every bit as good as lobster at a fraction of the price. Order the largest crab you can get, over 2 kilos (4lbs) if possible. Larger crabs are easier to pick than smaller ones, as the body cavities are larger. The shells are usually harder, however, and you will need a solid cleaver and nutcracker to break open the heavy claws.

To deal with the crab and extract all the meat, first remove the claws and legs. Separate the shell from the body. Remove and discard the pale, feathery gills which are also known as 'dead men's fingers', and the stomach sac, like a tiny crumpled plastic bag. Scoop the pale, soft meat from the shell, and scrape off any sticking to the body part. Mix this with softened butter, finely chopped shallots or spring onions, mace, cayenne, salt, pepper and enough lemon juice to taste. Spoon this into the cleaned and shiny crab shell, or into a bowl. This creamy part is delicious as a filling for sandwiches, omelettes and baked potatoes.

To get at the white meat, bash open the legs, claws and honeycomb-like body with cleaver, hammer or nutcracker, and use a pick or narrow spoon handle to tease it out of the cavities. The meat can be lightly seasoned, and eked out if you wish, with mayonnaise, crème fraiche or whipped cream and chopped herbs.

For a crab supper, I put both the white and the dark meat on a platter, surrounded by boiled new potatoes and plenty of vegetables, perhaps small artichokes, broad beans, French beans, raw carrots and radishes – whatever is available. To go with it, I make a bowl of garlicky mayonnaise. I also shred some iceberg lettuce, make guacamole, warm up some tortillas and have a hot sauce and salsa available too. So I make up first a small plate of crab aioli, and then, as a second course, I roll the crab in a soft tortilla with traditional Tex-Mex accompaniments.

Any left-over crab can be transformed into a soufflé.

Crab soufflé

Serves 6

50g (2oz) butter
Parmesan or breadcrumbs – see recipe
600mls (1 pint) milk
salt
freshly ground black pepper
freshly grated nutmeg
7 free-range eggs, 5 of them separated
50g (2oz) plain flour, sifted
150–200g (5–7oz) white crab meat

Butter a soufflé dish or dishes, and dust with a little grated Parmesan or toasted fine breadcrumbs.

Put three-quarters of the milk in a saucepan with the seasoning and remaining butter. Bring to the boil.

Beat the two whole eggs with the 5 egg yolks, the flour and the remaining milk, and stir slowly into the boiling milk over a low heat. Stir continuously until the mixture thickens but does not curdle.

Remove from the heat. Whisk the egg whites until stiff. Stir the crab into the white sauce, and then fold in the egg white.

Pour into the prepared dish, or dishes, and bake in a preheated oven at 200°C/400°F/gas mark 6 for 12 to 22 minutes, depending on the size of the dishes.

Parmentier of crab

Serves 4

1kg (2lbs) potatoes, peeled, cut up and boiled
butter, milk or olive oil for mashing
seasoning
finely chopped spring onion or chive – optional
finely chopped chervil or tarragon
350g (12oz) white crab meat
4 tablespoons crème fraiche or mascarpone

Mash the potatoes, while still hot, with the butter. For a plainer mash, simply keep back a little of the cooking water from the potatoes. Season to taste, then add the chopped herbs if you wish. I would choose one or other flavouring, not both. Line a pie dish with half the potato. Mix the crab and cream and spoon into the lined dish. Cover with the rest of the mashed potato and bake in a preheated oven at 200°C/400°F/gas mark 6 for 15 minutes.

Crab, asparagus and new potato salad

Serves 8

1kg (2lbs) English new potatoes
1kg (2lbs) English asparagus
500g (1lb) white crab meat
300mls (½ pint) soured cream, Greek yoghurt,
    single cream or homemade mayonnaise
zest of 1 lemon
salt
pepper
fresh chives, chervil or dill, finely chopped
salad leaves

Scrub and steam or boil the potatoes until tender. Snap the asparagus stalks, discarding the woody or tough portion, and boil the tender part in plenty of lightly salted water. Skin or peel the potatoes, if you wish, and dice or slice them. Mix them with the asparagus. When somewhat cooler, mix them with the cream, yoghurt or mayonnaise. If using mayonnaise and the potatoes are too hot, this will cause the mayonnaise to split. Grate in the lemon zest, add seasoning and the herbs, and fold into the salad. Spoon the potato and asparagus onto the salad leaves, with a heap of fresh crab meat on top. Whole herbs can be used to garnish it.

West Indies

The city of Mobile, Alabama, has a world-class oyster bar, Wintzell's Oyster House, downtown on Dauphin Street, where oysters are 'fried, stewed, or nude' and served at the bar, where one counter-hand does nothing but open oysters as fast as the customers can eat them. The chef's wife comes in every morning to make 30 gallons of gumbo, a deep, dark, spicy fish stew or soup, served with rice. There you will also find an authentic Mobile speciality, a marinated crab salad called simply 'West Indies'. It is thought to have been introduced to Mobile about sixty years ago by a sea captain who used to fish the Caribbean waters. It is a light, summery dish, excellent as part of a buffet, and because it is sealed in a jar it could easily be transported to a picnic.

Serves 4 to 6

500g (1lb) fresh chunky white crabmeat
1 large sweet, mild onion, sliced
75mls (3oz) grapeseed oil
50mls (2oz) cider vinegar
½ teaspoon each salt and pepper
6 ice cubes, crushed
Cos or Little Gem lettuce leaves
paprika
chopped parsley or chervil – for garnish

In a 1 litre (2 pint) preserving jar, make several layers of crabmeat and onion. Whisk the oil, vinegar and seasoning together, and pour over the top. Cover the crabmeat with crushed ice, and seal the lid.

Refrigerate for 24 hours at least. Serve spooned onto Cos or Little Gem lettuce leaves, dust with the paprika, and decorate with the herbs. An alternative is 500g (1lb) cleaned and prepared squid, which can be poached for 5 minutes. When cool enough to handle, slice into rings and layer with the onion. Scallops, queen scallops and shrimps can be prepared in the same way.

Spicy crab cakes

Serves 2 to 3 as a main course, 4 to 6 as a first course

1 bunch spring onions, trimmed and thinly sliced
2 tablespoons olive oil
500g (1lb) white crabmeat
1 free-range egg yolk, and 1 whole egg, separated
2 heaped tablespoons fresh white breadcrumbs
2 tablespoons each chopped chives, basil, coriander, fennel, or tarragon and parsley
1–2 teaspoons Tabasco or Jalapeño sauce
1 teaspoon Worcester sauce
½ teaspoon Angostura Bitters
salt
pepper
2 tablespoons mayonnaise
olive oil for frying

Gently fry the spring onions in the 2 tablespoons olive oil, and then mix in the rest of the ingredients, except for the egg white and mayonnaise. Whisk the egg white to firm peaks, then fold, together with the mayonnaise, into the crab mixture. Shape into cakes, small, large or medium, depending on how you plan to serve them.

Shallow-fry in olive oil, or use a non-stick pan, until golden brown on both sides. This is a fragile mixture, and you may prefer to chill the cakes before frying.

Serve with a fresh tomato sauce, salsa or garlic mayonnaise, together with some salad leaves and herbs.

Steamed lobster, oriental style

Serves 4 as a starter

2 x 600–750g (1½–1¼ lbs) uncooked lobsters
flavourings for the lobster – see recipe
aromatics for the steam – see recipe

Having first chilled them as described on p. 237, chop each lobster quickly and cleanly down the centre, putting the point of a heavy knife or cleaver through the cross-mark on the carapace, right down to the chopping board. Open out, and remove the stomach sac in the 'head' and the intestine, which runs the length of the tail. Place the lobster halves on a plate, and set on a rack in a steamer. Put some aromatics in the water. I like to use a slice of fresh ginger, a long sliver of orange peel or a piece of dried orange peel, and a split stalk of lemon grass or a sprig of lime leaves.

To flavour the lobster, sparingly spread on a mixture of grated ginger, chopped spring onions and garlic, or garlic chives and some crushed fermented black beans, or a splash of soy sauce. All of these ingredients are available from oriental supermarkets. Cover and steam the lobster for 8 to 10 minutes, once the water comes to the boil. Transfer the lobster halves to dinner plates, and serve with a dipping sauce of toasted sesame oil, soy sauce, rice vinegar and, if you like, a little chopped chilli and grated ginger.

Spring rolls

A little fresh lobster meat will go a long way when mixed with blanched bean-sprouts, sliced and disgorged cucumber, crushed toasted peanuts, sliced dried mushrooms, chopped mint, basil and coriander, and wrapped in Vietnamese spring roll wrappers, *banh trang*, which are available from oriental supermarkets. The wrappers need to be dipped in cold water and left to soften for a couple of minutes. Eat the rolls on the day you make them, preferably within a few hours. Salad spring rolls of this kind make a lovely, light lunch. Small versions can be made for starters.

Flamed shrimps with *rouille* and herb and lemon rice

Serves 6

1.5kg (3lbs) raw shell-on prawns or shrimps
1 litre stock (1¾ pints) – see recipe
500g (1lb) basmati rice
1 lemon
4 tablespoons parsley, finely chopped
2 tablespoons olive oil
1 tablespoon butter
3 tablespoons Brandy de Jerez, Armagnac or
    other flavoursome spirit
salt and pepper
tablespoon of harissa
bowl of garlic mayonnaise

Remove the shells and heads from the prawns and make a litre (1¾ pints) of stock by boiling the debris in a litre or so of water. Strain it into a clean saucepan, and stir in the rice. Bring to the boil, cover and lower the heat to the merest simmer. Cook for 18 to 20 minutes until the rice is cooked and the liquid absorbed. Add the finely grated lemon zest, a dash of juice and the parsley. Fluff it up carefully with two forks, cover and leave while you cook the shellfish. This is quickly and simply done, heating the oil and butter in a large frying pan or wok, stirring in the prawns, and cooking them until they turn pink. Pour on the spirits, stand well back and light. Shake the pan, distributing the juices, and when the flames have disappeared, season lightly.

Mix the harissa and mayonnaise. If you cannot find this brick-red chilli-hot paste from Tunisia, improvise by mixing into the mayonnaise, little by little, to taste, some cayenne, plenty of paprika, some dried crumbled oregano leaves and a little tomato paste.

To serve, border a large platter with the rice and spoon the prawns and the rest of the lemon juice into the centre.

Shrimp tostadas

Serves 4

sunflower or grapeseed oil for shallow-frying
4 small tortillas
150g (5oz) crème fraiche or light cream cheese
6 spring onions or 1 shallot, peeled or trimmed,
    and finely chopped
3 tomatoes, seeded and diced
2 tablespoons fresh coriander, chopped
2 or 3 pickled jalapeño peppers, chopped
1 tablespoon lime juice and grated zest of half a
    lime
250g (½lb) peeled coldwater shrimps
salt
pepper
half an iceberg lettuce, shredded
1 ripe avocado, peeled and diced

Heat the oil in a frying pan, and in it fry the tortillas, one at a time, until crisp. This will take about 2 minutes each. When cool, spread each with the crème fraiche.

Gently mix, in the order given, the onions, tomato, coriander, jalapeño, lime, shrimps and seasoning. Cover each tostada with the shredded lettuce, heap the shrimp mixture on top, and spoon the diced avocado over it, finishing off with any remaining crème fraiche.

The perfect prawn cocktail

Some like their prawn cocktails made with jumbo shrimps from tropical waters, but for sweet, fresh juiciness Greenland prawns are hard to beat; shell them or buy them shell-off.

YOU NEED, for each person, some iceberg lettuce or some small peppery salad leaves, 2–3 heaped tablespoons shelled North Sea prawns, a little vodka, tomato juice, grated horseradish, freshly ground pepper, Tabasco, squeeze of lime, lime zest and a martini glass.

METHOD Shred the iceberg and put it or the other salad leaves in the bottom of the martini glass. Heap the prawns on top, draining the juice into a small jug. To it add the vodka, tomato juice, horseradish, pepper, Tabasco and lime juice to taste, whisk and pour over the prawns.

TO SERVE Garnish with a twist of lime and serve your prawn cocktail, or seafood martini, with a dash of pride and a hint of irony.

Colcannon with prawns

Serves 4 to 6 as a starter

500g (1lb) potatoes, peeled and diced
500g (1lb) leeks, trimmed, sliced and rinsed, or
    2 bunches of spring onions, prepared in the
    same way
150mls (¼ pint) milk
250g (½lb) shredded cabbage
handful of rocket or watercress, chopped
150g (5oz) butter
1 teaspoon lemon juice
freshly ground black pepper
200–300g (7–10oz) peeled prawns

Boil the potatoes in water until soft, and then drain.

Simmer the leeks or spring onions in the milk. Strain the milk into the potatoes and mash them, and then stir in the leeks.

Cook the cabbage in a little boiling salted water until just done, adding the rocket or watercress for the last minute or two. Drain and beat into the potato and leek mixture, with a little butter, if you like.

Melt the rest of the butter and add the lemon juice and a little pepper, and in it beat the prawns. Divide the colcannon between four plates, make a well in each heap, and spoon in the buttery prawns.

Cod with clams and parsley broth on a potato and cheese fondue

Almost by accident, I devised a recipe that is a little like a *fonduta*, a little like an *aligote*, but different from both. When I boil potatoes for mashing, I often keep the cooking liquor for soup. If the potatoes are particularly floury, the liquid separates with a thick potato layer at the bottom. I used this layer to add to a white sauce, into which I then beat grated cheese. The resulting potato and cheese 'fondue' was delicious. I spooned it into hot soup plates, placed a piece of cod fillet on top, and poured around it a moat of parsley and clam broth with a few very fresh steamed clams.

Serves 2

1 small to medium potato, peeled and diced
25g (1oz) butter
25g (1oz) plain flour

250mls (8oz) milk
50g (2oz) Parmesan cheese, grated
salt
pepper
pinch of nutmeg
2 x 200g (7oz) pieces of cod fillet, skinned
1 tablespoon extra-virgin olive oil
500g (1lb) fresh clams, well scrubbed
1–2 tablespoons parsley, very finely chopped, or
    pounded
100mls (4oz) each water and good dry white
    wine

Boil the potato in about 150mls (¼ pint) water and, when soft, mash to a pulp, without straining off the water.

Using the butter, flour and milk, make a white sauce (p. 26) in the usual way, and then beat in the cheese and the mashed potato. Season with salt, pepper and a little nutmeg. Keep it warm while you first cook the cod fillet in a frying pan with the olive oil, and cook the clams and parsley in the wine and water until the clams open.

Serve as described above.

Mussels can replace the clams. The cooking juices should be quite green with parsley, to provide a nice contrast. If you have a juicer, you can even add some parsley juice.

Mussel and quail egg salad

Serves 6

3kg (6lbs) mussels, scrubbed and rinsed
100mls (4oz) dry cider
1 shallot, peeled and chopped
a few parsley stalks or celery tops
4 leeks, split, rinsed and cut into julienne strips
2–3 teaspoons grain mustard
salt
pepper
1 tablespoon cider vinegar
4 Savoy cabbage leaves, rinsed, ribs removed,
    and shredded
5 tablespoons walnut oil
6 quail eggs

Tug the byssus, or beard, from the mussels and discard any that remain open. Put the mussels in a lidded saucepan, with the cider, shallot and parsley or celery for flavouring. Put the lid on and cook until the mussels open. This takes only a few minutes.

Strain the liquid through a very fine sieve and put to one side. Tip the mussels into a colander and shell them when cool enough to handle. Mix 2 tablespoons cooking liquor with one of walnut oil, and stir into the mussels to keep them moist. Boil down the rest of the cooking juices to 2–3 tablespoons. Mix with the rest of the walnut oil, the mustard, seasoning and cider vinegar.

Steam or stir-fry the greens, and spoon onto plates. Arrange the mussels on top. Heat a well-greased or non-stick frying pan, and in it fry the quail eggs, having first carefully cracked them and put them into a saucer or other shallow container, to transfer them to the frying pan. Top each salad with a lightly fried egg and spoon the dressing over the top. Alternatively you can poach or boil the quail eggs.

Spiced mussels in coconut milk

Serves 2 as a main course, 4 as a starter

1 onion, peeled and finely chopped
1 celery stalk, trimmed and finely chopped
1 tablespoon groundnut or sunflower oil
   or butter
2 tablespoons medium or hot curry paste, to
   taste
2kg (4lbs) mussels, scrubbed and bearded
300mls (½ pint) coconut milk or cream
1–2 tablespoons fresh coriander leaves,
   chopped

Fry the onion and celery in the fat until soft, and then stir in the curry paste, and cook for a further 5 minutes. Add the mussels, the coconut milk and coriander, cover with a tight-fitting lid, and steam for about 5 minutes to open all the mussels. Shake from time to time to make sure they are well coated with the spice mixture and coconut. Serve in soup bowls with plenty of bread.

Oyster cream stew

Serves 4 as a starter

600mls (1 pint) shucked oysters and their liquor
1 celery stalk, trimmed and thinly sliced
1 shallot, peeled and finely chopped
25g (1oz) butter
600mls (1 pint) single cream, or 300mls (½ pint)
   single cream and 300mls (½ pint) milk

The perfect moules marinière

When mussels are at their best, from autumn to Easter, enjoy this inexpensive treat in the classic French style. Served with plenty of bread and followed with a salad and cheese, it makes a meal in itself, especially when accompanied by a bottle of chilled, crisp Muscadet *sur lie*, the natural partner to moules marinière.

YOU NEED, for 2 servings, 2kg (4lbs) mussels, 2 shallots or one onion, peeled and finely chopped, glass of dry white wine, freshly ground black pepper, 2–3 tablespoons soft white breadcrumbs, 2–3 tablespoons finely chopped parsley, 2 tablespoons butter.

METHOD Scrub the mussels under cold running water, tug off the 'beard' or byssus and knock off any barnacles with the back of a knife. Rinse the mussels and discard any which remain open after this rough treatment – they are dead. Put the mussels in a lidded saucepan with the rest of the ingredients. Cover with a lid and cook on a high heat until the mussels are cooked, that is, when they all open. Holding the lid on firmly, shake the pan from time to time.

The whole thing takes longer to write about than to cook, and from putting them on the heat to tipping them into a heated tureen should take no more than about 5 minutes. So not only an inexpensive treat, but a quick one.

white pepper
salt
pinch of paprika

Strain the oyster liquor into a saucepan, and add the celery, shallot and butter. Cook gently until the vegetables are completely soft. Add the cream or cream mixture, and bring to the boil. Slide in the oysters, which will immediately reduce the heat. Bring back barely to simmering point, and season the stew with the salt, pepper and, for colour, a little paprika. This is traditionally served with a handful of oyster crackers, but other crisp biscuits or croutons will do.

Laver

Sometimes also known as laverbread, laver is not a bread at all but a seaweed, or rather one of two seaweeds, *Porphyra laciniata* (purple laver), or *Ulva latissima* (green laver). It clings to the rocks at low tide around the western coasts, and looks like bolts of brown satin. Rinsed thoroughly and cooked for hours if you gather it yourself, it is also available from good fishmongers and counters.

But who wants to eat seaweed? Well, the Japanese know laver too, as *nori*, which is used in soups and for making sushi rolls. One mouthful of laver tells you it's good for you. You can taste the mineral salts, the iodine and the tang of the sea. Like all edible seaweeds, it is rich in vitamins and minerals, such as calcium and iron.

This dense and richly flavoured dark green purée is a natural adjunct to fish and shellfish dishes. Try spreading a little on triangles of hot buttered toast and topping it with an oyster, raw or poached, shrimps, or a freshly steamed mussel. Stir a spoonful or two into fish or shellfish stock to make a flavoursome sauce. I mix it with mashed potatoes to serve with cod, and even better, mixed with left-over fish and mashed potatoes to make fish cakes. It is also good mixed into dough to make unusual bread rolls and into pasta dough to make flecked and flavoured lasagne or tagliatelle. Mixed with chopped scallops or prawns, it makes a wonderful filling for pasta.

Traditionally, however, it is used quite differently. In Wales laver is mixed with lamb or mutton stock, a little butter and the juice of a lemon or Seville orange, and served as a sauce to accompany roast lamb or mutton.

Ideally, of course, this will be the meat of sheep which have grazed on marshy salt meadows. This is the same neat culinary affinity that makes us want to serve rowan jelly with Scottish Highland lamb or venison, and thyme and rosemary with meat from animals that have fed on wild herb-strewn hillsides.

Laver, which has been eaten in Britain since Anglo-Saxon times, is the main ingredient in a classic breakfast dish from the time when we used to have fry-ups for breakfast. It is mixed with equal quantities of oatmeal, seasoned lightly, shaped into patties, rolled in fine oatmeal and fried in bacon fat. You could replace the bacon fat with olive oil and serve the laver bread with a piece of steamed undyed smoked haddock, for a lighter breakfast.

Oysters and leeks with a Guinness hollandaise

This next recipe is a very special dish for two – rather more time-consuming to make for more people, unless you have help in the kitchen.

Serves 2

12 fresh oysters
125g (generous 4oz) unsalted butter
2 leeks, trimmed, thinly sliced and well rinsed
4–5 tablespoons double cream
6 tablespoons Guinness
1 shallot, peeled and chopped
2 free-range egg yolks
1–2 teaspoons lemon juice

Carefully open the oysters, and strain their juice into a small saucepan. Put the oysters to one side, and keep the deep shells.

Take 25g (1oz) of the butter, in it sweat the leeks until soft, then stir in the cream and cook until somewhat reduced.

Cook the oyster juice, Guinness and shallot, and reduce to 2 tablespoons. Put this in a blender together with the egg yolks and lemon juice, then melt the remaining butter, and when very hot, gradually add it, with the motor switched on, to the egg yolks. Alternatively, mix the 'hollandaise' in the usual way.

To serve, spoon a little of the leek mixture into each shell, place an oyster on top, and coat with a little of the sauce. Brown lightly under a hot grill.

Alternatively, divide the oysters between two shallow dishes, first spread with leek; then finish off with sauce, and put under the grill for a few minutes.

Scallop and mango salad with hazelnut dressing

Hazelnut oil has a low smoke point and is not good for cooking; use it for salad dressings, as here, or to season hot vegetables.

Serves 4

8 or 12 scallops
a little grapeseed or groundnut oil
finely grated zest of a lime, and its juice
freshly ground black pepper
1 large mango, not too ripe
1 or 2 leeks, trimmed, halved, rinsed and cut in
    julienne strips
salad leaves
salt
about 4 tablespoons hazelnut oil
fresh chervil or coriander – for garnish

Brush the scallops with the grapeseed oil. Season them with the lime zest and pepper and grill or sear them in a hot pan for a minute or two, or until done to your liking. Put to one side. Peel and slice the mango. Blanch the leeks in boiling water, or, if you like, deep-fry them briefly until crisp. Heap the salad leaves on plates, arrange the mango slices and the leeks. Mix the hazelnut oil, a little salt and lime juice and pour over the salad. Put the herbs on top or around it and serve.

Spiced scallops in potato jackets with summer salsa

Serves 4 to 6

12 medium-size scallops
2 teaspoons ground cumin
½ teaspoon fine salt
½ teaspoon ground black pepper
2 or 3 very large potatoes, elongated rather than
    rounded, and peeled
a little plain flour or potato flour
1 onion, peeled and chopped
grapeseed or sunflower oil
1 or 2 red chillies
2 peaches
½ mango
lime juice and coriander leaves
oil for frying

Remove and discard the muscle pad and the intestine, which runs round the white part of the scallop. Cut off the orange part, and put to one side. Mix the seasoning, and use to season the scallop, both parts. Cut long thin slices from the whole potatoes, discarding the curved top and bottom slices. The slices should be not much more than the thickness of a twenty-pence piece. Fold one potato slice over each white scallop part, and one over each orange piece. Dab a little flour around the inner edges, and press together to seal, or secure with a cocktail stick. Chill until required.

To make the salsa, fry the onion in the grapeseed oil until soft, but not browned. Seed the chillies, slice into the onion mixture and cook for 2 to 3 minutes more. Spoon into a bowl. Dice the peaches and mango quite small, and mix with the onion and chilli. Season with lime juice to taste, and stir in chopped fresh coriander. Heat the oil to 170°C/325°F, and fry the wrapped scallops until crisp and golden; this will take no more than 2 to 3 minutes. Drain on paper towels, and while still hot transfer to plates and spoon a little salsa to the side. Fresh coriander leaves or watercress make a good edible garnish, as does a pile of jicama (yam bean) sliced and cut into julienne strips, lightly seasoned with lime juice and salt.

Scallop and bacon skewers

Serves 2

6 scallops, cleaned and trimmed
6 cap mushrooms, blanched
½ teaspoon each freshly ground black pepper,
    ground cumin and coriander
12 paper-thin rashers streaky bacon, rind
    removed

Make the sambal first, a few hours in advance, or the day before.

Season the scallops and mushrooms with the spice mixture before wrapping them in the bacon and threading onto two soaked wooden skewers. Put under a hot grill and cook for 4 to 5 minutes, less if you like your scallops translucent rather than opaque.

This is very good served with a relish made by squeezing all the water out of some grated cucumber, and mixing with a little chopped green chilli, plenty of fresh coriander, some lime juice and unrefined sugar, and a diced ripe avocado.

Skewers of scallops, mussels and oysters

Serves 8

8 rashers streaky bacon, rind removed
24 large Welsh mussels
8 or 16 rock oysters
8 Scottish diver scallops, cleaned and removed
    from the shell
75g (3oz) unsalted butter, melted
100g (4oz) soft breadcrumbs

Blanch the bacon in boiling water for 2 minutes. Steam the mussels until they're just open, and remove from the shells when cool enough to handle.

Remove the oysters from their shells. Cut each rasher of bacon into 3 or 4 pieces, and thread on 4 skewers with alternating mussels, oysters and scallops.

Roll the filled skewers in melted butter and breadcrumbs, and grill or deep-fry for 5 to 8 minutes, turning from time to time.

Serve the skewers alone, or on a bed of salad with a lemony vinaigrette.

Low country boil

For each person allow:

250g (½lb) (at least) raw, shell-on prawns or
    shrimps
water – see recipe
2 or 3 small potatoes
1 corn cob
1 boiling sausage – see recipe
about 2 teaspoons Bissell's Seafood Boiling
    Mixture – see below

Remove the heads from the prawns and with them make a stock by covering with 150–200mls (5–7oz) water per person and cooking for 30 minutes. Strain into a cooking pot large enough to hold all the ingredients you have calculated. Peel the potatoes or not, as you prefer. Small red potatoes are quite attractive just scrubbed and halved. Remove the husk and silk from the corn and chop each cob into two or three pieces. Slice the sausages into meaningful chunks.

Simmer the potatoes in the broth, to which you have also added sufficient of the Boiling Mixture, a heady blend of spices. When the potatoes are half done, add the sausages. Cook for five minutes, then add the shrimps and corn. Bring back to the boil, and simmer for about three minutes more until the shellfish is pink and the corn tender.

Serve and eat very hot. The dish should not be garnished or tarted up in any way.

Bissell's seafood boiling mixture

2 tablespoons freshly ground pepper,
1 tablespoon each ground ginger, allspice,
    cumin, dried thyme, dried oregano, fennel
    seeds, lemon grass, mustard seeds,
4 tablespoons sweet paprika.

Seafood gumbo

Serves 6

2 tablespoons lard
2 tablespoons plain flour
1 large onion, peeled and finely chopped
2 celery stalks, trimmed and finely chopped
1 green and 1 red capsicum, peeled, seeded
    and finely chopped
1 leek, peeled, sliced and thoroughly rinsed
2 cloves garlic, peeled, chopped and crushed
1.5 litres (2½ pints) fish, chicken or vegetable
    stock, boiling
12 oysters, shucked
6 squid cleaned and cut into rings
500g (1lb) peeled prawns
6 large prawns in the shell
1 tablespoon *filé* powder – see recipe

In a large heavy saucepan melt the lard, and sift in the flour. Cook to a deep golden brown, and add half of the onion, celery, capsicum, leek and garlic, and cook for 1 to 2 minutes.

Gradually pour on the boiling stock, stirring to keep the mixture smooth, and add the remaining half of the vegetables. Cook for 20 to 30 minutes, and then add the shellfish. Cook for 10 more minutes, and then bring to the boil; stir in the *filé* powder, and remove from the heat immediately.

Allow it to stand for at least 15 minutes for the flavours to mature. Serve over boiled rice.

If you cannot get *filé*, a fine green powder of dried sassafras leaves, add half a dozen or so okra pods, sliced, when you add the vegetables. These will add the necessary texture, which is more than just the thickening achieved with the roux – rather a smooth, almost gelatinous silky quality.

Shellfish in paper bags

Fish, and particularly something as delicate and fragrant as shellfish, lends itself especially well to paper-bag cookery. I love to cook scallops with a little soy sauce, sherry, fresh ginger and spring onions in a paper parcel for a fresh, oriental-flavoured dish.

For this next recipe I would use mussels, some scallops, the biggest, juiciest prawns I could find, even a crayfish or langoustine each, if possible. Use strong baking parchment for these parcels.

Serves 4

50g (2oz) butter
16 mussels in their shells
4–8 scallops, depending on size, or 16 queen
    scallops
8 prawns
4 crayfish or langoustines – optional
4 tablespoons parsley, chopped
seasoning
2 tablespoons good white wine or dry vermouth

Cut four rectangles from baking parchment, and fold each in half down the middle. Cut each piece of paper into a heart shape with the fold running down to the point. Liberally butter the paper hearts.

Scrub the mussels well, remove the beard and knock off any barnacles. Place 4 on one side of each paper heart. Add the scallops, prawns and langoustine or crayfish, if using them. Sprinkle on the parsley, and season lightly. Splash the wine over the shellfish. A 'good white wine', by the way, is a wine that you would be prepared to drink.

The parcels are now ready to seal. Fold over the other side of the heart. With the edges together, fold the paper over, making tight overlapping folds, or rolling the edges together to seal the parcel. Prepare the other parcels in the same way, and lay them on a baking tray. Place it in a preheated oven at 200°C/400°F/gas mark 6 for 8 minutes. Serve while hot, placing each parcel on an individual plate, and cutting them open at the table.

Cataplana

This next recipe, for a fish and shellfish casserole, is a classic of the Portuguese kitchen, and not at all difficult to prepare at home.

Unless you have a *cataplana*, I suggest a deep, lidded sauté pan that will fit in the oven. Choose fresh firm-textured fish, such as sea bream, red snapper, monkfish, John Dory and cod or haddock. Aim for at least 2 to 3 different kinds of fish, and a similar variety of fresh shellfish, such as clams, mussels, prawns, langoustines and lobsters. Allow 200g (7oz) fish and 100g (4oz) shellfish each, as this is a one-pot meal requiring nothing more than salad and bread, plus a little fruit for dessert.

The fish should be filleted, skinned, and cut into 5cm (2 inch) chunks, approximately. The shellfish should be scrubbed, trimmed and rinsed, as appropriate.

Prepare the base, or *fond,* first, as the fish only takes a little time to cook.

Serves 6 to 8

1 onion, peeled and thinly sliced
1 red and 1 green pepper, seeded and thinly
    sliced
2 or 3 garlic cloves, peeled and thinly sliced
1 bay leaf
extra-virgin olive oil
4 to 6 tomatoes, peeled, seeded and chopped
4 tablespoons good dry white wine
8 tablespoons fish stock
salt and pepper
fresh parsley
fresh coriander

Gently fry the onion, pepper and garlic in the oil, with the bay leaf, until the vegetables are soft. Add the tomatoes, wine and stock, and cook for 15 to 20 minutes until you have a flavoursome sauce.

Heat some more extra-virgin olive oil, and briefly fry the fish in it, but no longer than to just remove the raw look. Put the fish, shellfish and *fond* in the *cataplana* or pan, and put in a preheated oven at 220°C/425°F/gas mark 7 for 10 minutes. Remove the pan from the oven, add the seasoning and a handful of chopped parsley and coriander. Bring to the boil, and serve immediately.

BUFFET FOR SIX OR EIGHT

Skate, leek and watercress terrine

Quick chicken liver pâté

Hindle Wakes pie

Black pudding and leek cottage pie

Chilled orange and white chocolate rice pudding

Several of the recipes in this menu, some of them old favourites in new guises, can be prepared in advance, which makes this an ideal meal to serve as a weekend buffet when you are entertaining friends. In addition, the ingredients are neither expensive nor recherché, and so will not make too great a dent in the budget or require too much shopping time.

One more thing the dishes have in common is lots of flavour and interesting textures. I would add a basket of crudités, a bowl of green salad and a loaf or two of good bread, rather than serving extra potato or vegetable dishes. Real ale or real English cider could accompany these homely and rustic dishes just as well as your favourite wine. A luscious orange muscat wine is perfect with the unusual, creamy rice pudding, served in this instance chilled, with an elegant crisp crust of white chocolate.

Skate is generally served hot, often with a brown butter sauce spiked with vinegar, capers and perhaps deep-fried parsley. However, its firm, sweet flesh and rich sticky quality make it ideally suited to a terrine, and this one slices beautifully, with a marbled effect from the green vegetables. A simple vinaigrette, or a more elaborate mayonnaise-like sauce, will accompany the terrine very well. I particularly like one which I make by infusing some saffron in a little fish stock, adding extra-virgin olive oil, a dash of orange juice, some capers and finely chopped parsley. Or try a fresh tomato sauce made by blending fresh tomatoes, sieving them, and beating in extra-virgin olive oil and sherry vinegar.

Alternatively, a garlicky mayonnaise will go very well.

Another quite different terrine, or pâté, is the simple chicken liver pâté, one of the first things I used to cook when entertaining friends. It is as good now as it was then, and I always wonder why I do not make it more often. It keeps well, and is a good filling for sandwiches and topping for canapés, if you have any leftovers.

Next comes more offal. Yes, I like offal. It is used here in the cottage pie. This traditional Monday dish was originally devised to use up leftovers from the Sunday roast. However, since the Sunday joint is no longer as universal as it once was, cottage pie is now often made from scratch as it is such a good dish. In due season, I often make a haggis version, and here instead of minced beef I use crumbled black pudding, combined with leeks and topped with mashed potatoes, a robust and winning combination.

Individual cottage pies can be made in ramekins, and if you have metal ring moulds you can serve this as a very elegant version of cottage pie, as a stacked and plated main course. To do this, butter the rings, and place them on a greased baking sheet. Spoon leeks in the bottom, with black pudding on top. Press well down, and top with mashed potatoes. Bake in the usual way, and then slide the filled moulds off the tray and onto plates with a spatula. Remove the ring moulds. Spoon a little gravy around, and top with some flat-leaf parsley.

For those who do not like leeks as much as I do, may I suggest that you substitute tomatoes or spinach in the skate terrine, and fennel or mushrooms in the Hindle Wakes pie. This pie, which is good hot or cold and is exceptionally good picnic food, uses the traditional Hindle Wakes ingredients of chicken, prunes and leeks. Frequently served as a cold buffet dish, Hindle Wakes is a stuffed, often boned, chicken, glazed with mayonnaise and aspic. The prunes and leeks accompany the chicken just as well in a pie, which makes for a less fussy dish. It is best made with a freshly poached chicken, and then you can boil down the stock to make a good rich gravy. When cold, it will make a stiff jelly. Use an organic or a real free-range chicken, if you can get one.

The first two recipes can be made the day before required, and the rice pudding should be made early enough to allow it to chill completely before

the melted chocolate is poured over it, and it should then be allowed to chill again before serving.

Skate, leek and watercress terrine

Serves 8

12 thin leeks, or 3 larger ones, trimmed and
  rinsed
large bunch of watercress, leaves only
1kg (2lbs) skate wings
freshly ground white pepper
sea salt

Use the white part of the leeks, and split the larger ones lengthways into 4. Poach in water for 15 minutes or so until tender. Remove from the water and drain on paper towels.

Meanwhile, blanch the watercress. Season the skate, put into the vegetable cooking water, bring to just simmering point, put the lid on, and cook the fish for 5 to 8 minutes. Remove it from the heat. When cool enough to handle, take the fish out of the water and carefully remove the strands of flesh from the cartilage. Reduce the fish liquid and cool. Put a layer of fish in a loaf tin lined with clingfilm, then a layer of leeks, more fish, a layer of watercress, and finish with the rest of the fish, lightly seasoning each layer. Pour on about 200mls (7oz) reduced and cooled fish stock, and allow the whole thing to cool before covering and refrigerating until set. Turn out, slice carefully, and serve with some salad leaves and a sauce as described above.

Quick chicken liver pâté

Serves 8 to 10

750g (1½lbs) chicken livers
200mls (7oz) milk
2 shallots or 1 small onion, peeled and chopped
100–125g (4oz) butter
1 teaspoon crushed juniper berries
salt
pepper
2 tablespoons cognac
2 tablespoons port, Madeira or Amontillado
  sherry

Trim the chicken livers, and put them in a bowl with the milk for 15 to 20 minutes. Meanwhile, gently fry the shallots or onion in a little of the butter until soft. Drain and dry the chicken livers, and add to the frying pan. Fry on a relatively high heat for 8 minutes or so with the juniper berries.

The chicken livers are nice if removed from the heat while still faintly pink inside. Season, and stir in the cognac while the livers are still hot, and then add the fortified wine. The residual heat will evaporate the alcohol.

When the chicken livers are cool, put in a food processor with the remaining butter, and process until smooth. Pack into a pâté dish or individual ramekins. Chill until firm. Allow to come to room temperature before serving with hot toast.

Hindle Wakes pie

Serves 6 to 8

1.5kg (generous 3lbs) freshly poached chicken
2 litres (3½ pints) poaching liquid
12 baby leeks or 3 or 4 normal ones, cooked
  until tender
12 soaked stone-free prunes
250g (8oz) button mushrooms, blanched and
  dried
1 lemon
2 teaspoons tarragon, finely chopped
salt and pepper
250g (½lb) shortcrust pastry – see p. 29
200g (7oz) puff pastry
1 free-range egg, beaten with 2 tablespoons
  milk
cream

Remove the meat from the chicken. Discard the skin. Chop the bones, if you can, and put them back in the cooking liquid.

Simmer for 30 minutes. Then strain, and boil down the liquid to about 500mls (18oz).

Line a deep pie dish or cake tin with the short pastry. Layer the cool chicken meat, leeks, prunes and mushrooms, seasoning each layer very lightly, grating on a little lemon zest, sprinkling on a little lemon juice and a good pinch of tarragon.

Add several tablespoons reduced stock, and cover with a lid of puff pastry. Make a hole in the centre, and keep this open with a roll of stiff paper.

Brush the surface with the egg-and-milk glaze, and bake for 25 to 30 minutes at 190°C/375°F/gas mark 5. Remove from the oven.

If you want to serve the pie hot, mix the remaining egg glaze with 2–3 tablespoons cream and the same of stock.

Pour it carefully through the hole in the lid, and return it to the oven for 5 minutes.

If I want to serve the pie cold, I allow it to cool, pour in as much liquid stock as it will take to set, and then refrigerate before slicing.

Black pudding and leek cottage pie

Serves 6 to 8

500g (1 lb) black pudding
1.5kg (about 3 lbs) potatoes, peeled
750g (1½ lbs) leeks, trimmed, sliced and rinsed
2oz milk
freshly grated nutmeg
fresh ground black pepper

Cook the leeks in a little milk and drain them, reserving the milk.

Boil the potatoes until tender, drain, and mash with the reserved milk. Season the potatoes, using plenty of pepper and nutmeg.

Spread the leeks over the bottom of a buttered ovenproof dish. Remove the skin from the black pudding, dice or crumble it, and layer on top of the leeks. Cover with the mashed potatoes, smooth, and fork a pattern on the top, if you wish.

Bake for 35 to 40 minutes at 180°C/350°F/gas mark 4, raising the heat a notch or two for the last 10 minutes to brown the top.

As this is quite a dry dish, you might want to serve some gravy with it.

Chilled orange and white chocolate rice pudding

Serves 8

100g (4oz) pudding rice
6 cardamom pods, crushed
zest of two mandarins, and 3–4 tablespoons
    flesh
up to 1.25 litres (about 2 pints) full-cream milk
caster sugar, to taste
150mls (5oz) whipping cream
200g (7oz) white chocolate
50g (2oz) dark chocolate, at least 70 per cent
    cocoa solids

Cook the rice, cardamom pods and mandarin zest very slowly in the milk until the grains are tender. This can be done in a very low oven. Remove the cardamom.

Stir in the orange flesh and the sugar while the mixture is still hot, and allow it to cool. Whip the cream, fold it in, and spoon the mixture into a soufflé dish. Chill.

Melt the two chocolates separately and spread the white chocolate on top of the rice pudding. Swirl or feather in the dark chocolate and leave to set.

Big soups and simple dishes

Recently, a colleague commented to me that she thought ours would be the last generation of cookery writers to make stock. I hope she is wrong, and, much as I respect her, I do not think she is right to avoid recipes which require stock. Instead, substitutes are suggested: vegetable or tomato juice; water left over from boiling potatoes, soaking dried mushrooms or cooking fish; sherry, wine, soy sauce and miso.

All these do, of course, have a place in soup- and sauce-making, but if one were to do without stock altogether one's cooking would be the poorer for it. Stock-making does take time, but not your time. Once the ingredients are in the pot – and this need be nothing more than beef bones, a chicken carcass, a ham bone, or some fish bones, then a bay leaf, a celery top and some peppercorns – you need to be around only until the stock comes to the boil. You can skim the scum from the surface, but then you can disappear – a couple of hours or more for chicken stock, for the whole day if you're making beef or veal stock, but no more than 20 to 30 minutes for fish stock. Naturally, the usual safety precautions need to be taken.

Then, with the beautiful stock you have produced, the whole world of soup-making expands even further. I have no truck with the society hostess who would never serve soup to her guests, saying, 'You wouldn't build a house on a lake, would you?'

A few slices of Parma ham, a piece of pâté, some sardines in olive oil, a cucumber salad or other simple starter, a baked apple or rhubarb fool to finish, and a main course of soup make for an ideal casual supper.

My soup recipes come from different culinary cultures, some developed in my own kitchen, some collected on my travels. Several times, in and around Jimena de la Frontera, in Andalusia, I have eaten a very good soup called *sopa de puchero*. Made from broth, rice, pieces of ham and eggs, it is a good way of using up left-over stock and other bits and pieces. I like it very much as a supper dish.

Traditionally, the broth is made from chicken and beef. One or the other will do, as will pork, ham or veal stock, or a mixture.

Sopa de puchero

Serves 4

50g (2oz) rice, long or short grain
1.15 litres (2 pints) stock
4 free-range eggs
100g (4oz) diced or shredded ham
mint leaves

Cook the rice in the broth until tender.

Meanwhile, boil the eggs, no more than 3½ to 4 minutes. Cool the eggs under the running cold tap, and shell them.

Put one egg into each heated soup plate with a quarter of the ham. Pour the rice and broth over it, and serve immediately with a few fresh mint leaves stirred in.

You can roughly cut up the eggs in each bowl, or let everyone do it for themselves.

Tortilla soup

My recipe for tortilla soup is inspired by the many soothing bowls I sampled in Texas. It is, apparently, a favourite of those suffering from jet-lag. One of the best versions I tasted was in a tiny family-run Mexican restaurant in the suburbs of San Antonio. Although it sounds exotic, it is not at all difficult to make, and tortillas are increasingly available in supermarkets.

Serves 6

500g (1lb) free-range chicken breasts, raw
1.5 litres (2½ pints) chicken stock made from
     the carcass
1 onion, peeled and sliced
3 garlic cloves, peeled
1 teaspoon ground coriander
2 tablespoons sunflower oil, plus extra for frying
     the tortillas
400g (14oz) can tomatoes, drained
juice of a lime
2 fresh jalapeño, or other small hot green
     peppers, seeded and finely chopped

salt

pepper

6 small or medium corn tortillas, halved and cut
    into 1cm (⅓ inch) strips

fresh coriander, chopped

Simmer the chicken in the stock for 20 minutes or so, and let it cool in the liquid. Put the stock to one side, discard bones and skin from the chicken, and shred it finely.

Gently fry the onion and garlic in the oil until the onion is wilted. Add the coriander and tomatoes, and cook for 20 to 25 minutes.

Rub through a sieve, or blend. Stir in the lime juice and chillies, and season lightly.

Fry the tortilla strips in batches until crisp, and drain on crumpled paper towels. Add them, and the chicken, to the soup, bring to the boil for 2 to 3 minutes, and serve in deep soup bowls, garnished with the chopped coriander.

Fish *ajiaco*

In Colombia, *ajiaco* is a soupy stew in which the main ingredients are several kinds of potatoes, corn, *guascas* – a local herb – and *aji*, or hot sauce. Traditionally, chicken is added, but in the past I have made an entirely vegetable-based *ajiaco*, which is very good indeed. Now try it with fish; this is possibly the best variation of all. You cannot, I think, get guascas here, which is why I have always called my chicken version *ajiaco sin guascas* (p. 51), but you can use watercress, mizuna or rocket for a similar effect.

Serves 4 to 6

2 onions, peeled and sliced

2 tablespoons olive oil

2 large floury potatoes, peeled

1 litre (1¾ pints) chicken, or fish stock

4 medium waxy potatoes, peeled

500 g (1 lb) small potatoes

600 mls (1 pint) dry white wine

2 or 3 sweetcorn cobs

500 g (1 lb) undyed smoked haddock fillet, skinned

500 g (1 lb) haddock fillet, skinned

6 scallops, cleaned

bunch of watercress, trimmed and shredded,
    with a few sprigs left whole for garnish

In a pot gently fry the onion in the oil, and add the large potatoes, cut up into pieces. Add half the stock, and simmer for 20 minutes, before adding the waxy potatoes, sliced into thick collops, and the small potatoes.

Put in the white wine and the rest of the stock, and cook until the small potatoes are tender and the floury potatoes have collapsed to thicken the soup.

Cut the corn cobs into 2 or 3 pieces, and add to the pan, together with the fish, cut into good-size chunks, the scallops and watercress.

Bring gently back to just below boiling point, and let it barely simmer for 5 minutes. Serve in hot soup plates, with or without hot sauce, and with plenty of good fresh bread.

Minestrone

Minestrone soup is one of the first dishes I learned to cook as a child and it remains one of my favourites. Then, bacon rinds and trimmings provided the flavouring. Now I make my stock with a knuckle bone from a Parma ham. The soup is even better the next day and almost makes a meal in itself, so full of beans and other vegetables that a spoon will practically stand up in it; use haricot, cannellini or borlotti beans. If you wish, small soup pasta or broken-up spaghetti can be added. Alternatively, use just vegetable stock and make an entirely vegetarian version, or cook a ham bone with the vegetables if you prefer.

Make at least twice the amount you need, for the reheated version makes a very acceptable Tuscan-style *ribollito*. The best way to eat it is to put a piece of good, chunky, chewy bread, either a day or so old or lightly toasted, in the bottom of the soup bowl, anoint it liberally with extra-virgin olive oil, and pour the re-boiled soup over the sops.

Serves 6 to 8

250 g (½ lb) soaked cannellini beans

1.5 litres (2½ pints) stock

1 tablespoon olive oil

1 onion

1 carrot

1 stick celery

1 leek

1 small white turnip

6 ripe tomatoes

cloves of garlic, to taste

1 quarter cabbage, shredded

handful of green beans

2 courgettes, sliced

seasoning

pesto – optional

Place the soaked beans in a heavy saucepan with enough stock to cover them, and simmer while you prepare the rest of the vegetables.

Heat the olive oil in a frying pan. Excluding the cabbage, beans and courgettes, peel and finely chop all the vegetables, removing the seeds from the tomatoes. Turn these in the olive oil, and when lightly browned add them to the pot of beans, together with the rest of the stock. Bring to the boil, cover with the lid and cook in a low oven, 170°C/325°F/gas mark 3 for 2 to 3 hours, or on the hob on low heat.

About half an hour before the end, prepare then add the cabbage, beans and courgettes.

Season to taste, and allow to cook until the last 3 vegetables are just done.

To serve, stir in a little pesto, or a little more olive oil.

Spiced parsnip soup

After Christmas, or whenever you have a freezer full of stock, try my parsnip soup. It is not the same as Jane Grigson's excellent, and much copied, curried parsnip soup, but uses the subtle and warming 'English' spices – nutmeg, mace, clove and cinnamon. The soup is particularly good made with ham stock.

Serves 6

2 onions, peeled and sliced

25 g (1oz) butter or olive oil

3 large parsnips, peeled and diced

¼ – ½ teaspoon each of nutmeg, cinnamon,
    mace and cloves

1.5 litres (2½ pints) stock

salt

pepper

cream, chopped parsley or flat parsley leaves
    – for garnish

Gently fry the onion in the fat until golden. Stir in the parsnips, and add the spices. Cook for a few minutes before adding the stock, and then simmer until the vegetables are tender.

Sieve or blend until smooth. Put back in the saucepan, bring to the boil, and season to taste.

Pour into hot soup bowls, and decorate before serving. A dash of fresh orange juice and a little grated zest, added as you bring the soup back to the boil, make a nice touch.

Summer soups

To think of soups as suitable only for warming winter meals would be to miss out on some wonderfully refreshing delicate summer dishes. Think of a cool, silky vichyssoise, smooth with potato and with a gentle hint of leek. Think of it again, in a new guise, flavoured and lightly coloured with saffron. Imagine the bare hills and parched earth of an Andalusian summer, and then imagine a shady street in Cordoba, a dark doorway, a dim, cool interior, and a rough earthenware bowl full of chilled, piquant gazpacho.

Whilst there are hundreds, if not thousands, of soup recipes already in the international culinary repertoire, the imaginative cook can still produce a range of individual and exciting soups from a vast array of ingredients. One might almost say that there is no foodstuff which cannot be used in soup: fruit and vegetables certainly, fish, meat and poultry, of course, pasta, pulses, rice, cheese, even bread and eggs can be used in soups. As with most things, what you get out of it depends on what you put into it. You cannot make good soup from poor ingredients. By poor, I do not mean cheap. I mean old, stale, spoilt. Some of the best soups I have ever eaten have been made from the simplest of ingredients – fried garlic, day-old bread, water or broth, perhaps a handful of herbs and a fresh egg. Such are the soups of the Iberian peninsula, the Portuguese *sopa alentejana* and the Spanish *sopa de ajo*. My friend José Antonio Valdespino, chef/restaurateur at La Mesa Redonda in Jerez, makes a slightly more sophisticated version, a bread and tomato soup. It is the perfect soup for a cool summer evening, when you want something warming but not rich. Summer is also the right time to do it, as you have a better chance of finding sweet ripe tomatoes.

Another good source of ingredients for soups is the salad patch of your vegetable garden. Those bolted lettuces may be too far gone for the salad bowl, but you can use them to make a fine green soup, to serve hot or cold. I like soups with this versatility, for you never quite know if it is going to be warm enough to serve a chilled summer soup. One which I only plan on serving in the hottest weather is the cucumber, prawn and buttermilk soup, a lovely pale green, with pink prawns floating on top and a refreshing acidity from the buttermilk.

Over the years I have developed a range of fruit and vegetable soups, which I find very appealing. I long ago felt the need for summer soups other than the gazpachos, delightful though they are in their various guises. I have experimented with many combinations – carrot and apple, fennel and apple, tomato and redcurrant, courgette and melon. The most successful soups have been those where the fruit and vegetable are complementary rather than hugely contrasting in flavour. And, of course, the colours must be similar; otherwise, if you cross a green vegetable with a red fruit, you finish up with a very muddy-looking soup.

The best thing about these soups is that they are equally delicious hot or cold. Although they will need stirring before serving, they do not have a great tendency to separate. One or two points common to the preparation of all of them needs to be borne in mind. If you use a non-stick saucepan, there need be no oily surface to the soup, and that means fewer calories. A vegetable stock or a very light chicken stock can be used. I prefer the former, as it does not mask the fresh flavour of the soup, as a meat stock might. What is more, if the meat stock is too concentrated, a chilled soup may turn into a jellied one. Season the soup only lightly while hot, and then, if serving chilled, add more seasoning if you think it needs it.

Chilled soups can have a spoonful of cream or yoghurt whisked into them before serving. If you want to enrich a hot soup, break an egg into a small jug. Whisk into the egg a tablespoon of hot soup, and pour it through a sieve into the hot, but not boiling, soup, and stir thoroughly. Chilled soups look particularly good served in glass bowls which have stood in the freezer for half an hour or so, and they should definitely be served cold rather than tepid.

José Antonio's tomato soup

Serves 4

500g (1 lb) ripe tomatoes
1 large green pepper
1 small onion, peeled
1 garlic clove, peeled
150mls (¼ pint) extra-virgin olive oil

850mls (1½ pints) water
about 400g (14oz) good-quality bread, such as
   sourdough
salt
fresh mint leaves

Thinly slice the vegetables, and cook them in the olive oil in a large sauté pan over a gentle heat until they are tender. Transfer to a saucepan. Add the water and the bread, broken into chunks. Mix well, cover, and cook for 5 to 10 minutes until tomato and bread are amalgamated. Season with salt, and stir in some shredded mint leaves before serving. You can also divide the mixture between 4 ovenproof bowls, crack an egg into each, and finish cooking in the oven.

Prawn, cucumber and buttermilk soup

Serves 4

1 cucumber
600g (1 pint) buttermilk
300mls (½ pint) semi-skimmed milk
400g (14oz) peeled prawns
fresh dill, basil or coriander leaf

Simply put the peeled, seeded and roughly chopped cucumber in a blender or food processor with the buttermilk, semi-skimmed milk, half the prawns and a little fresh dill, basil or coriander leaf, and blend until smooth. Chill, season to taste, stir in the remaining whole peeled prawns and serve.

For an oriental version of this, use coconut milk, coriander, mint or basil, and a little grated fresh ginger and lime zest.

Summer vichyssoise

Serves 4 to 6

1 large potato, peeled and chopped
1 onion, peeled and chopped
1 tablespoon sunflower oil
750g (1½ lbs) leeks, white part only, sliced
1.15 litres (2 pints) vegetable or light chicken
   stock
good pinch of saffron threads, infused in some
   of the stock
salt
freshly ground black pepper
3–4 tablespoons yoghurt or single cream
   – optional

Fry the potato and onion gently in the oil for a few minutes without browning. Add the leeks and about 140 mls (¼ pint) of the stock, together with the saffron and its infusing liquid, and cook until the vegetables are soft. Allow to cool slightly, make a purée in a blender or food processor, sieve, and stir in the rest of the stock. Chill until ready to serve. Just before serving, season to taste, and, if using, stir in the yoghurt or single cream.

Charred plum tomato and plum soup

This is one of my favourite vegetable-and-fruit soup combinations and is best made at the end of the summer when tomatoes are at their sweetest and plums just coming into season.

Serves 4 to 6

12 ripe plum tomatoes
2 tablespoons olive oil
1 small onion, peeled and finely chopped
1 celery stalk, trimmed and finely chopped
850 mls (1½ pints) vegetable stock
3–4 pieces sun-dried tomato
6 ripe plums, stoned and chopped
basil
salt
freshly ground black pepper
4–6 tablespoons soured cream or thick yoghurt

Halve six of the plum tomatoes lengthways, and roughly chop the rest. Using a frying pan and a saucepan, put a tablespoon of olive oil in each. In the saucepan cook the chopped tomatoes and vegetables with the pieces of sun-dried tomato until soft, but without really browning them. Fry the halved tomatoes in the frying pan until the skin has turned dark brown, and then transfer them to the saucepan. Pour a little of the stock into the frying pan, and scrape up all the cooking residues, which will give you quite a dark golden-brown liquid. Pour it into the saucepan. This, and the charred tomato skins, give the soup an unusual depth of flavour.

Poach the plums in some of the remaining vegetable stock until just tender. When cool, put them in a blender or food processor with the soft vegetables and tomatoes, the remaining stock and some basil leaves. Blend until smooth, and sieve.

The soup can be served chilled or hot. Season to taste just before serving, and serve with some more fresh basil leaves, shredded just before use, and a swirl of soured cream or thick yoghurt.

Lettuce and mint soup

Serves 6

50 g (2oz) butter
1 onion, peeled and diced
1 large potato, peeled and diced
½ teaspoon salt
freshly ground white pepper
175 g (6oz) lettuce leaves, chopped
1.15 litres (2 pints) vegetable or light chicken
  stock
2 teaspoons finely chopped mint
1 tablespoon whipping cream – optional

Melt the butter in a heavy saucepan. When it foams, add the onion and potato, and turn them until well coated. Sprinkle with salt and pepper. Cover, and sweat on a gentle heat for 10 minutes. Add the chopped lettuce leaves and stock. Boil until just tender, but do not overcook or the lettuce will lose its colour and flavour. Make a purée in a blender or food processor, after cooling slightly first, and then sieve; add the mint, the cream, if using it, and more salt and pepper, if necessary. Bring back to the boil, and serve immediately. For extra glamour, you can serve the soup with a freshly poached, neatly trimmed quail egg floating in each bowl.

Summer garbure

The following recipe is not the thick, heavy rustic soup of the Pyrenees, but a much lighter version, based on one I tasted years ago, cooked by Firmin Arrambide at St Jean Pied de Port.

I use some of the goose fat I save from the Christmas goose, a little of the confit I usually make, some sliced spicy sausage such as chorizo or cabanos, and a few shreds of cured ham. I buy a knuckle end of Parma ham when I can, and use it in soups, scrambled eggs, quiches, and with pasta. If you do not have confit, you can use the fillets from duck or chicken breasts, and olive oil replaces goose fat very well; many people might find it preferable.

Serves 6

1 teaspoon goose or duck fat, or extra-virgin
  olive oil
1 onion, peeled and finely chopped
250 g (½ lb) young carrots peeled or scrubbed
  and sliced
250 g (½ lb) cabbage, shredded

1.5 litres (2½ pints) chicken or ham stock

150 g (5oz) flageolets, or cannellini beans,
    soaked and cooked

75 g (3oz) each shelled peas and broad beans

meat additions, such as spicy sausage, cured
    ham, chicken breasts, etc.

salt

pepper

paprika, or *piment d'Espelette*

Heat the fat in a large saucepan or casserole, and lightly brown the onion. Add the carrots, cabbage, stock and flageolets. Cook until those vegetables are tender, 25 to 30 minutes, add the peas, beans and meat. Simmer for 2 to 3 minutes, season to taste, and serve.

If you have vegetarian guests, you can replace the stock with vegetable stock and omit the goose fat and meat additions. Squares of fried or smoked tofu can be added.

Glamorous soups

Intensely flavoured soups served in coffee cups have become a favourite *amuse-bouche* in restaurants, and they do indeed act as an excellent appetizer when a large bowl of soup might be *de trop*. But I love soup, and sometimes like to experiment with more elaborate soups and garnishes.

Deriving inspiration from two Mediterranean dishes, gazpacho and *brandade de morue,* the next recipe can be prepared partially in advance. In fact the *brandade* needs to be made the day before to allow the juices to set and bind the fish, olive oil, garlic and milk to a creamy paste, which you can shape into quenelles with two dessertspoons.

Tomatoes are simply blended and sieved, seasoned with sea salt, extra-virgin olive oil, a dash of sherry vinegar, if you like, and some garlic. This thick fresh 'soup' is served chilled with minutely diced cucumber, red, yellow and green peppers spooned into the middle, and the *brandade*, which

I make from smoked haddock, on top. Whilst the soup vegetables can be peeled and diced in advance, the tomatoes are best prepared just before required, to retain their fragrance. This is a lovely dish, one to turn to again and again in the summer, especially as tomatoes get riper and sweeter. Where possible, until I can get good home-grown ones I buy Canary Islands tomatoes. Those from Fuerteventura, grown near the sea, are said to be the sweetest.

Chilled tomato soup with gazpacho garnish and *brandade* of smoked haddock

Serves 6 to 8

500 g (1 lb) undyed smoked haddock fillet

200 mls (7oz) milk

6–8 garlic cloves, peeled and blanched

4 tablespoons extra-virgin olive oil, hot

freshly ground black or white pepper

½ cucumber

1 each medium-size red, yellow and green
    pepper

1kg (2 lbs) very ripe tomatoes

1 tablespoon sherry vinegar

fresh basil

sea salt

freshly ground black pepper

chervil, dill or basil – for garnish

Put the fish and milk in a sauté pan, and poach until the fish is just done – 3 to 4 minutes will be sufficient, not much more.

Remove the fish and when cool enough to handle, discard the skin and any bones, and put the fish and garlic in the food processor. Process until the fish is quite broken up.

Gradually add the hot olive oil and enough of the milk to make a paste – of spreading, rather than liquid, consistency. Season with pepper. Scrape into a container, and once cool, refrigerate until required.

Discard the seeds of the cucumber. Peel it, slice lengthways, cut into thin strips and then tiny dice. With a potato peeler, peel the thin skin from the peppers as far as you can. Very firm, smooth, taut peppers can be peeled raw with a swivel peeler. You will probably not manage the top and bottom, which can be chopped off and used in another dish such as piperade, perhaps. Halve the peppers, remove the seeds, and cut into tiny dice. If pepper

The perfect tomato soup

Tomato soup is only worth making for the few weeks of summer when the sun has had a chance to give the fruit some flavour. Even then, tomato is so acid that you need to add other ingredients to temper this. Soup made only of tomatoes is not very good.

YOU NEED, for 4 people, an onion, a carrot, a medium potato and 1 or 2 celery stalks, olive oil, up to a kilo (2 lbs) of ripe, sweet tomatoes, salt and pepper, a generous handful of lovage, or, failing that, some sprigs of basil or tarragon, and milk.

METHOD Peel and dice the vegetables (not the tomatoes) and fry them gently in a tablespoon or so of olive oil until the onion is translucent and golden, and the rest of the vegetables soft. Add 2–3 tablespoons of water if necessary, to stop them burning. Add the tomatoes, roughly chopped, and simmer, covered, for 15 to 20 minutes. Season lightly and stir in the herbs. Add about 200mls (7oz) milk and blend the soup until smooth. Sieve and return it to the saucepan. Reheat and adjust the seasoning before serving.

ALTERNATIVE Instead of herbs, add cumin and cardamom, and replace the milk with coconut milk.

---

skin does not bother you, then do not bother to peel them first.

To prepare the tomatoes, put them in a blender or food processor with more oil, the vinegar, basil and seasoning, and blend until smooth. Sieve into a jug.

To assemble the dish, stir the tomato soup, and pour into soup plates. Spoon a flattened mound of vegetables in the middle, and place a quenelle of smoked haddock on top. Decorate with some fresh herbs, and serve immediately.

Chilled caviar vichyssoise

The soup recipe which follows provides the base for a number of festive variations, which I have also included. They are perfect recipes for Christmas and New Year parties.

Serves 4

4 or 5 large leeks
1 large potato
1 litre (32oz) vegetable or light chicken stock
200mls (7oz) double cream
2 tablespoons chopped chives
salt
pepper
25–30g (1oz) small can Sevruga caviar

Trim the leeks, slice, and rinse thoroughly.

Peel and chop the potato. Put both in a saucepan, cover with stock, and simmer until the vegetables are soft.

Blend with the remaining stock and the cream; sieve or not, as you prefer, although the sieved version is more elegant.

Stir in the chives, and season to taste. Chill until required, and check the seasoning before serving with a teaspoonful of caviar, carefully positioned on top of each serving.

Try these variations:

Hot vichyssoise with chilled smoked salmon cream

Process until smooth 100g (4oz) smoked salmon trimmings with 50g (2oz) unsalted butter or 4 tablespoons crème fraiche. Chill and then shape into quenelles to serve on the heated soup.

Vichyssoise with oysters

Carefully remove 4 or 8 oysters from their shells, and strain the juice into the soup. Put the oysters in a saucepan, cover with water, and heat gently to about 50°C/100°F. Hold at this point for 2 minutes, then remove the oysters with a slotted spoon.

Arrange on top of the soup, hot or cold, as you wish, with a feather or two of chervil for garnish.

Curried cream of cauliflower soup with mint and cucumber raita

Serves 4

1 onion, peeled and thinly sliced
1 tablespoon sunflower oil
1–2 tablespoons mild or medium curry paste
1 small cauliflower, separated into florets
2 tablespoons plain flour

600 ml (1 pint) vegetable or chicken stock

200 ml (7oz) coconut milk

salt

pepper

½ cucumber, roughly chopped

150 ml (5oz) thick Greek yoghurt

small green chilli, split and seeded – optional

small bunch mint, leaves only

Gently fry the onion in the oil until wilted and transparent. Stir in the curry paste and the cauliflower. When this is well coated, sprinkle with flour, stir until the flour is absorbed, and then add the stock. Bring to the boil and simmer until the vegetables are soft.

Remove from the heat, and put in a blender with the coconut milk. Blend until smooth, and return the soup to the pan. Reheat and add salt and pepper as necessary. Meanwhile, rinse the blender, and in it blend the remaining ingredients to make the cucumber raita.

Serve the soup with a swirl of cucumber raita, and hot naan or chapattis.

Onion soup

I make the best onion soup the day after I have roasted a joint of beef on the bone and served it with roasted onions. I make the broth using the onion skins, cooking juices and beef bone, and then proceed as follows:

Serves 4 to 6

4 large onions, peeled and thinly sliced

50 g (2oz) unsalted butter

pinch of mace

150 mls (¼ pint) good dry red wine

1.5 litres (2 pints) beef broth

seasoning

In a large heavy saucepan cook the onions very slowly in the butter to a soft translucency. It does not matter if they begin to turn golden; it is better that they do, since the sugar in the onions becomes more flavoursome as it caramelizes. However, they must not burn. And burnt onion skins should not be used, as they will add nothing but bitterness.

When the onions are soft, add the mace and red wine. Raise the heat, and let the wine almost evaporate. Stir in the beef broth, bring to the boil, season, and serve.

To dress it up, you can serve the soup French-style. Toast bread on one side, and then float a piece, toasted side down, on each bowl of soup, and heap with grated Gruyère or Comté cheese. Finish off under the grill or in the top of a hot oven. Sturdy, ovenproof soup bowls are essential in this recipe.

Tomato and quince soup

Serves 6 to 8

1 onion, peeled and finely chopped

1 carrot, leek and celery stalk, washed, trimmed and finely chopped

1 tablespoon sunflower or groundnut oil

1 quince, peeled, cored and grated

1 kg (2 lbs) ripe tomatoes

1 litre (1½ pints) vegetable or chicken stock

salt

pepper

crushed seeds of green cardamom pods

Cook the four vegetables in the oil until soft, and then add the quince and tomatoes, and cook until the quince is soft. Remove from the heat, and allow to cool before liquidizing with half the stock.

Sieve and return the mixture to the saucepan with the remaining stock. Add the cardamom seeds, bring to the boil, season to taste, and serve.

You can swirl in some soured cream or crème fraiche, but I think the soup needs nothing else. If you do not like crushed cardamom in the soup, add it with the vegetables and it will be sieved out.

Take five

Greens are good for you. And so are the yellows and oranges of the vegetable world. Vegetables are top of everyone's menu now that the nutritionists, health experts, growers, importers and marketers have had their way. We can expect to hear more and more about food that is good for us, instead of constantly being bidden not to eat certain foods. This makes eminently good sense, for if we eat plenty of vegetables and fruit we shall be too full to snack on cakes, biscuits and sweets, or to want large quantities of meat, cheese, rich sauces and puddings.

It is recommended that we eat five to eleven portions of fruit and vegetables a day. This sounds a lot but is easily reached: half a grapefruit or a plate of grilled mushrooms for breakfast, an apple or a glass of orange juice mid-morning, a bowl of vegetable soup and a piece of fruit for lunch, and for dinner, a tomato salad, a serving of carrots or broccoli, and a poached pear provide seven portions.

Vegetable juices

One way to increase your intake of raw vegetables is to make vegetable juices. Here are three of my favourites. Each of the recipes given will produce about 250mls (9oz) juice. A juicer is a worthwhile investment.

Terracotta

3 ripe tomatoes
3 scrubbed carrots
½ sweet red pepper, seeded
½ Bramley apple
2 or 3 leafy celery tops

Red harvest

3 ripe tomatoes
3 scrubbed carrots

¼ red pepper, seeded
1 or 2 beetroots
a handful of rocket or watercress leaves

Sunburst

½ yellow pepper, seeded
4 carrots
3 ripe tomatoes
half a peeled, stoned mango
juice of half a lemon

Vegetables as a first course

When we are entertaining friends, I try to get away from the feeling that I ought to serve a fish course before a meat course. But there is a good reason for planning meals this way, with fish followed by meat. Two good reasons, in fact – white burgundy followed by claret, or, occasionally, red burgundy. To Tom, my husband, it is not a proper occasion without the full works, and hang the expense; we can live on pasta and vegetables for the rest of the week.

I am conscious of this too in restaurants with a fixed price menu. Even the best restaurants seem to feel it is important to offer a substantial protein-rich starter, followed by a large helping of protein for the main course. Invariably, it is the generous host who feels he or she must give customers their money's worth.

But vegetables are not cheap second-class citizens of the culinary world. A serving of prime asparagus, a perfect globe artichoke, a salad of grilled aubergine and pepper, will cost as much as many fish courses. And, if I want a celebratory meal but do not want to serve meat or fish at all, I will make a colourful vegetable terrine, serve it with a comforting mix of grains and pulses, and follow it with hot mushroom pies and broccoli flans, for example.

There is such a huge range of possibilities for producing exquisite vegetable dishes that it is no hardship to serve them before a main course of meat, poultry or game. Consider a carefully composed vegetable salad, or a vegetable soup, chilled or hot, as the weather dictates. In season, freshly cooked English asparagus served with melted butter, enlivened with a spark of lime juice, with home-made mayonnaise or with a sauce mousseline, would be a perfect first course. Perhaps a salad of grilled vegetables? Or a Mediterranean vegetable tart?

Many of the recipes in this chapter make ideal first courses, either singly, or in the case of some of the salads, as part of a selection. You can also use the chapter, combined with the chapter on grains and pulses, to make up a variety of vegetarian menus.

Pressed grilled vegetable terrine

The following recipe can be used as a blueprint for similar terrines. Replace, for example, the aubergines with cooked and well-drained asparagus or green beans, and the peppers with cooked artichoke *fonds*.

Mushrooms, I've found, are difficult in terrines. However thoroughly they have been dried after cooking, when pressed and left they eventually release liquid and spoil the texture and appearance of the finished dish.

Serves 6 to 8

2 large aubergines
4 courgettes
4 red peppers
2 yellow peppers
extra-virgin olive oil
1 leaf of gelatine, softened in cold water
    and then dissolved in 140mls (½ pint)
    well-seasoned vegetable stock

Slice the aubergines and courgettes lengthways. Quarter the peppers, and remove the seeds and pith. Brush the vegetables lightly with oil, and bake in the oven until tender, or cook on a griddle or under a grill. The peppers should be charred, and then, when cool enough to handle, skinned. Layer the vegetables in a loaf tin or terrine. Pour on enough vegetable stock just to cover, and let the vegetables absorb it for 20 to 30 minutes. Then cover the terrine with cling-film, and drain off most of the excess liquid. Refrigerate overnight, turn out, slice, and serve with a herb vinaigrette, or a mint, yoghurt, shallot and cucumber sauce.

Hot mushroom pies

Makes 6 to 8

125g (¼ lb) button mushrooms, wiped and sliced
25g (1oz) unsalted butter
2 tablespoons dry Oloroso or Amontillado sherry
freshly ground pepper
salt
2 chopped pickled walnuts – optional
good pinch of mace
2 tablespoons soft white breadcrumbs
grated zest of ½ lemon, and a little juice
200g (7oz) flaky pastry – see p. 29
free-range egg yolk, for glaze – optional

Fry the mushrooms in the butter over a high heat, add the sherry and let it evaporate. Season, and mix with the walnuts, mace, breadcrumbs, lemon zest and juice. Roll out the pastry, and line some small tart tins. Place some of the mixture in each lined tart tin and top with a pastry lid. Brush with an egg yolk and water glaze if you wish, and bake in a preheated oven at 200°C/400°F/gas mark 6 for 15 to 20 minutes. Serve hot or warm.

Broccoli flans

You can serve these warm broccoli flans with a homemade tomato sauce or an anchovy and garlic sauce; or simply slice cooked baby beets, put them on the plate around each flan, and then add lemon juice, freshly ground black pepper and extra-virgin olive oil.

Serves 4

400g (14oz) broccoli stalks
few stalks of flat-leaf parsley
salt
pepper
2 medium-size free-range eggs, lightly beaten
3–4 tablespoons double cream
nutmeg

Chop the stalks into 4 or 5 pieces, and separate the florets. Drop them in a saucepan of boiling water with the parsley, keeping back a few leaves for garnish, if you wish.

When the stalks are just cooked, drain, and rub the broccoli through a sieve. Add seasoning, and stir in the eggs and cream, making sure all is thoroughly mixed.

Spoon into lightly oiled moulds, darioles, ramekins, or whatever you have. I use small heatproof French glass tumblers, which have the shape of a pudding basin.

Place the moulds in a bain-marie, a large saucepan or a roasting tin, with water two-thirds of the way up. Partially cover, and cook over a low heat for 15 to 20 minutes. You can also put them in the oven, preheated to about 180°C/350°F/gas mark 4.

When set, remove, and when cool enough to handle, turn out onto plates and garnish as you wish, adding some freshly grated nutmeg while the flans are still very warm. Although these can be served hot or cold, the flavour comes through best when just warm.

Spring vegetables

Asparagus and other luxuries

I always like to celebrate the English asparagus season. The flavour and texture of home-grown asparagus, with its satin-smooth green stems, its incomparable fresh, sweet, yet earthy flavour and its elegant simplicity, are most appealing, and it is one of those vegetables that is so agreeable to eat.

Like samphire, artichoke leaves and the old-fashioned way with pea pods, asparagus is best eaten in the fingers, dipped in melted butter or dressing, and then bitten off, the stalk drawn through the teeth to extract the soft flesh. The slender spears can also be dipped into homemade mayonnaise, an orange-flavoured sauce mousseline, or a soft-poached, boiled or fried egg. This last is a particular favourite, and I often stretch the dish

to a main course by adding some steamed Jersey Royals, in season at the same time. And tips of thin asparagus, or sprue, with a poached quail egg make a dainty miniature, as an appetizer, if you like such things. When I have finished eating it this way, almost to surfeit, I use asparagus in tarts, salads and pizzas.

Cold cooked asparagus makes a marvellous sandwich filling. I like it either with thin slices of home-roasted free-range chicken, liberally anointed with a good mayonnaise and sandwiched between slices of fresh wholemeal, or, alternatively, with a well-seasoned chopped-egg mayonnaise, also in wholemeal.

Asparagus risotto, asparagus in a thick creamy béchamel wrapped in a crêpe, topped with grated Parmesan and finished off under the grill, asparagus soup, asparagus in a casserole with new potatoes and baby artichokes, asparagus on a wholemeal pizza, and asparagus loaf are just some of the ways I like to cook this luxury spring vegetable. Try it too in a tart with English goat's cheese – the two combine beautifully, especially when partnered with a glass of dry, crisp Sauvignon blanc, so redolent of flowering-currant bushes, and, to me, the perfect spring white wine.

One might argue that if asparagus is so good, why not eat it all year round? We get it sent from Thailand, from Mexico, from Australia and Chile in the winter, and in early spring from Spain, at prices not much different from those we pay for English asparagus. But I prefer to argue for eating food in season. This is not just some romantic notion that we should live as our ancestors lived. Eating locally grown food in season not only supports the farming community, it also makes economic sense in that transport costs are less. It is also a much more pleasurable experience. There is the anticipation of this short season of exquisite food, and there is the knowledge that it has not taken days, or weeks, to reach our table, losing a lot of its flavour and nutrients on the way. Anyway, I do not want to eat strawberries and asparagus in winter. That's when I want to eat Jerusalem artichokes, pumpkin and celeriac.

Another way to cook asparagus

We are accustomed to cooking asparagus either in a special asparagus pan, where it cooks with its feet in water and its head in steam, or in a frying pan full of boiling water, with the spears lying flat, or in a steamer. The problem with this is that some of the flavour, and certainly some of the minerals, are left behind in the cooking water. This is definitely worth keeping for asparagus soup.

Applying direct dry heat to asparagus, however, retains all its qualities. Roast it, grill it, or fry it. Truly, you will be surprised at the results.

I have a ridged cast-iron griddle, which I brush with oil, and then cook the thicker asparagus spears on it. And white asparagus is excellent cooked this way, yielding a concentrated yet subtle flavour. The charred stripes make it appetizing to look at too, and I serve the spears with a sprinkling of coarse sea salt, a little more oil and a dash of lemon juice, or better still, sherry vinegar.

Roasted asparagus and new potatoes

Serves 4 to 6

olive oil
12–18 asparagus spears, trimmed
1kg (2lbs) new potatoes such as Jersey Royals, scrubbed
coarse sea salt
freshly ground black pepper

Pour some olive oil into a roasting tin, and in it roll the asparagus and potatoes.

Roast for an hour or so at 200°C/400°F/gas mark 6. Move the vegetables to a lower shelf if they show any signs of burning, although by the time they are served, they should be nicely browned in places. Season lightly before serving.

Roasted asparagus and goat's cheese tart

Serves 6

225g (½lb) shortcrust pastry – see p. 29
500g (1lb) fresh green English asparagus
olive oil or butter
coarse sea salt
225g (½lb) fresh English goat's cheese
125g (¼lb) curd cheese

Roll out the pastry, and line a loose-bottomed flan dish, about 20cm (8 inches) diameter or make a free-form rectangular case on a baking sheet, twisting up the corners to give some depth. Prick the base. Cover with greaseproof paper, and fill with pasta shells or baking beans and bake in a preheated oven at 200°C/400°F/gas mark 6 for 30 minutes. Allow to cool.

While the pastry is baking, cook the asparagus. Trim down to the tender parts, roll them in olive oil or melted butter, and place on a baking sheet. Roast until tender. Remove from the oven, and cool. Sprinkle with salt. The asparagus can also be fried or cooked on a cast-iron griddle. Beat the two cheeses together until smooth, and spread in the pastry case. Arrange the asparagus on top, and serve.

Herb wholemeal pizza with asparagus, baby leeks and mushrooms

Serves 2 to 4

Dough

250g (8oz) wholemeal plain flour
1 teaspoon fast-action yeast
1 teaspoon salt
1 tablespoon fresh herbs, finely chopped, such as basil, thyme and marjoram
about 150mls (¼ pint) warm water

Put the flour, yeast and salt in a food processor and blend together, then add the herbs and process briefly once more. Gradually add the water (you may, or may not, need it all) until you have a soft, springy dough that is not too wet, nor too firm. The dough should stick to itself, rather than to your hand. Let the dough rest in the food processor while you prepare the vegetables.

Topping

200g (7oz) each tender green asparagus, baby leeks and oyster mushrooms
2 tablespoons extra-virgin olive oil
garlic, crushed – optional
1 tablespoon finely chopped parsley
175g (6oz) mozzarella cheese
hard cheese for grating

Trim the asparagus and leeks, and steam or boil them for a minute or two, until not quite tender. If the oyster mushrooms are large, tear them into pieces, and fry them in half the olive oil. You can add crushed garlic, if you like, and the chopped parsley.

Knead the dough for 5 minutes, and roll it into a round or rectangle, depending on what you are baking the pizza in, or on. Brush with the remaining oil. Slice the mozzarella, and arrange the cheese, asparagus, leeks and mushrooms on the pizza.

Grate on some hard cheese, and bake in a preheated oven at 200°C/400°F/gas mark 6 for 20 minutes.

If you prefer, you can spread a tomato sauce on the pizza before adding the vegetables, but I rather think it is better without. Goat's cheese makes an excellent substitute for mozzarella; even if it does not have the same melting and stringy quality, the flavour is marvellous with asparagus.

Summer flavours

A vegetable patch in summer offers the best possible excuse for indulging in some home-cooked, home-grown vegetables. The vegetable patch that I have in mind is deep in the heart of the Missouri countryside. It is attached to a white clapboard house, which has a porch with a swing on one side and a barbecue on the other. Country music, with a plangent guitar and a yearning voice, drifts through the open windows.

Our hostess is vegetarian, but that does not stop her grilling bacon for those that want to add it to their tomato and lettuce sandwiches. Her tomatoes in summer reach an extraordinary size: one juicy red slice will overlap most bread, and the richness of flavour is incomparable. Salads, tarts, soups and stews are all enhanced by these magnificent scarlet beauties. Such vegetables need little adornment or seasoning in the way of dressings, oils and sauces.

Alongside peas and beans, for the first time, I picked okra from the vine. Pale green, satiny, small and elegant, these sweet pods, full of silky-coated seeds, were so fresh and tender that we ate them raw, dipping them in a little coarse salt. When shopping at home, even picking them out individually,

I have never found okra good enough to eat raw. I usually make a vegetable stew, combining it with aubergines, the best tomatoes that I can find, and a little chilli.

Next to the bacon on the barbecue, and perhaps some chicken, Elizabeth will also place some corn, which cooks perfectly in the fierce dry heat. Cooking time is about 15 minutes, and the corn is fresh and sweet enough to eat without even melted butter.

While the barbecue is heating up, we mix flour and cornmeal, add some chilli, and bake a batch of golden, crumbly cornbread. However much we make, we never make enough.

Herbs and lettuces are picked for a big salad bowl, and we decide against making a pudding. With huge sweet watermelons, golden peaches and perfect strawberries, we do not need any.

As it gets dark, the Missouri countryside sounds like jungle warfare; June bugs and fireflies hang in the velvety night, and around us echoes the din of all kinds of crickets and other night creatures. The barbecue embers smell smoky and evocative, and our fingers are sticky with juices from the corn, tomatoes, and everything else that we have been eating.

Fresh wholesome food, quickly and simply cooked, eaten in good company, is my idea of true relaxation. The next few recipes are inspired by Elizabeth's vegetable patch. They are ideal for entertaining and would be fine for a lunchtime or supper buffet. All the recipes are suitable for vegetarians, but you could add, as I suggest, some barbecued chicken. First a trio of salads, for which warm cornbread is an excellent accompaniment – see p. 15.

Broad bean and mint salad

Serves 6 to 8

1–1.5kg (2–3 lbs) broad beans

2–3 tablespoons extra-virgin olive oil

2 teaspoons lemon juice, plus finely grated
     lemon zest

5 tablespoons vegetable or chicken stock

salt

pepper

1 or 2 tablespoons cream, thick plain yoghurt or
     fromage frais

fresh mint
salad leaves

Shell the beans, boil until tender, and, if you have the patience, pop them out of their skins.

While still warm, dress them with the next six ingredients, well mixed first, then stir in the finely chopped fresh mint.

Serve warm on a bed of salad leaves.

Bread and tomato salad

Based on a dish I ate in Andalusia, this recipe is similar to the Italian *panzanella*.

Serves 6 to 8

400g (14oz) white or wholemeal bread, in one
   piece
4 tablespoons sherry vinegar
4 tablespoons iced water
750g (1½lbs) firm, sweet, ripe tomatoes,
   peeled, quartered and seeded
2–3 garlic cloves, peeled and crushed
½ teaspoon coarse sea salt
freshly ground black pepper
6 tablespoons extra-virgin olive oil
few spring onions, trimmed and sliced
flat-leaf parsley or basil leaves, shredded
   – to garnish

Tear the bread into bite-sized pieces, and spread on a baking sheet. Place in the oven at 150°C/300°F/gas mark 2 for a few minutes, or until slightly crisped.

Put the bread in a bowl with the vinegar, water, tomatoes and garlic. Mix well, and season with salt and pepper.

Stir in the oil, and leave to stand for 30 to 40 minutes to let the flavours develop.

Sprinkle with the onions, and garnish with the herbs before serving.

Summer salad of tomato, melon, mozzarella and cucumber with lime and nasturtium dressing

Serves 6 to 8

175g (6oz) each of yellow and red cherry or
   miniature plum tomatoes

2 or 3 kinds of melon
1 lime
1 teaspoon honey
1 tablespoon cider vinegar
2 tablespoons finely chopped chervil, basil or
   mint
3 tablespoons skimmed milk or soya milk
salt
pepper
300g (10oz) mozzarella, diced, or use the
   miniature mozzarella
1 cucumber
3 or 4 nasturtium leaves and flowers

Put the tomatoes in a bowl.

Using a melon baller, scoop out balls of melon flesh, having first removed the seeds, and add to the tomatoes.

Peel the cucumber, halve, discard the seeds and dice, or make into small balls with the appropriate utensil, and add to the bowl.

Grate the zest of the lime into a jug. Stir in the honey, lime juice, vinegar, herbs, milk, shredded nasturtium leaves and seasoning.

Spoon the salad onto plates, with or without salad leaves. Arrange the mozzarella on top, and spoon over the well-mixed dressing.

Garnish with nasturtium flowers.

Marinated cherry tomatoes

Serves 6 to 8

1 teaspoon fresh thyme or lemon-thyme leaves
½ teaspoon coarse sea salt
pinch of unrefined sugar
good pinch freshly ground black pepper
1 or 2 cloves garlic, peeled and chopped
1 teaspoon grated lemon zest
1 tablespoon lemon juice
100mls (4oz) extra-virgin olive oil
500g (1lb) cherry tomatoes, red and yellow, if
   available
fresh basil leaves

In a mortar pound together the dry ingredients, including the garlic and lemon zest. Gradually add the lemon juice and olive oil, and pour over the tomatoes in a bowl; the tomatoes should have their stalks removed.

Leave for a few hours, or overnight. Before serving, stir in some shredded basil.

Warm tomato and aubergine salad

This dish is so simple that it hardly needs a recipe. It is important to cook the aubergine thoroughly. There is no merit in al dente aubergine. It is like biting into thick felt.

For two people, slice a moderately sized aubergine, brush the slices with olive oil, and grill or fry them. Meanwhile, slice and season two or three tomatoes, and when the aubergine is soft, alternate slices of it with the sliced tomato. The heat of the aubergine warms the tomato slightly and enhances its flavour. Season with sherry vinegar and a little more olive oil, and add herbs for flavour, basil or mint for preference.

Roasted tomato and goat's cheese salad

For this, use individual goat's cheeses or two pieces from a larger cheese, fresh or drier, as you prefer.

Serves 2

4 firm, ripe tomatoes
2 slices wholemeal bread
2 x 50–75g (2–3oz) portions of goat's cheese
a couple of handfuls – 50g (2oz) – salad leaves
3 tablespoons pumpkin seed oil, or other
    favourite nut or seed oil
salt
pepper

Quarter the tomatoes, and scoop the seeds and 'jelly' into a sieve, set over a bowl. Roast or grill the tomato pieces, and remove the skin once it is loose enough to do so. With a pastry cutter, cut two rounds from the bread, and toast it under the grill. When you are toasting the second side, put the cheese on top, and let it heat through.

Heap the salad leaves on two plates, put the tomato pieces around them, and place the goat's cheese on toast on top. Rub the tomato residue through a sieve, and mix in the oil and a little seasoning. Pour over and around the salad and serve. This is particularly good with a mixture of watercress, rocket and mache, or lamb's lettuce.

Roasted fennel, red pepper and tomato salad

Quarter a fennel bulb, or cut into 8 wedges depending on size and shape, and brush with oil. Quarter a red pepper and discard the seeds. Prepare a couple of tomatoes as in the previous recipe. Grill or roast the vegetables and skin the peppers and tomatoes when cool enough to do so. Make a dressing with the tomato liquid and extra-virgin olive oil, together with the usual seasoning.

Sweetcorn

Although I have seen fields of it near Heathrow, most of the sweetcorn we buy in Britain is French and Spanish, and it reaches us tasting fresh and sweet. As a change from just munching it straight from the cob, dripping with butter, I have used it in several recipes, including a delicious golden gazpacho (p. 269).

Boiling is perhaps the simplest way to cook corn, but do not overdo it – no more than 3 to 4 minutes is sufficient. And do not add salt to the cooking water, as this will toughen the kernels when you want them to remain crisp.

To grill corn on the barbecue, carefully peel back the husk so that you can remove the silk, and then wrap the husk back around the ear, twisting, or tying, to secure it at the top.

Soak the ears in cold water for 10 minutes to stop them from drying out during cooking. Place the wrapped ears on the grill, about 10cms (4 inches) from the heat, and cook for 15 to 20 minutes, turning them occasionally.

You can, of course, also cook corn in the oven, wrapping it in foil, husks and silk removed, with a knob of butter, for 10 to 15 minutes or so.

Many recipes call for kernels cut from fresh ears of corn. You will need 6 ears to obtain about 250 grams (8oz).

I like to add the kernels to soups, salsas and scrambled eggs. Add them, too, to muffins, pancake batter and cornbread. Corn combines well with cooked diced potatoes and ham in a mustardy dressing for a substantial salad. Or you can do a cooked version, adding chopped onion, tomato and green pepper (skinned), topping it with a béchamel sauce (p. 26), grated cheese and breadcrumbs, and finishing it off in a hot oven.

Some of these same ingredients also make a very good chowder.

Corn chowder

Serves 4

2 tablespoons olive oil
1 onion, peeled and chopped
1 or 2 potatoes, peeled and diced
500mls (16oz) milk
1 bay leaf
kernels cut from 4 ears of corn
100g (4oz) diced cooked ham
1 tablespoon chopped flat-leaf parsley
seasoning

Heat the oil in a saucepan, and in it fry the onion until soft and golden brown. Stir in the potato, milk and bay leaf, cook for 15 minutes, and then add the corn and ham and cook for 5 minutes more. Add parsley, season to taste and serve.

If you like, you can thicken the soup by making a purée of a third of it, and stirring it back into the rest of the chowder.

Sweetcorn and yellow tomato salsa

In this next recipe, ripe red tomatoes can replace the yellow ones, and you will have an even more colourful salsa.

Serves 6

1 large mild onion, peeled and chopped
1 tablespoon sunflower oil
500g (1lb) yellow tomatoes, halved, seeded and
    chopped
1 or more green or red chillies, seeded and
    finely chopped
150mls (¼ pint) apple juice
salt
pepper
2–3 tablespoons fresh coriander, chopped
2 cobs sweetcorn
2 teaspoons cornflour

Gently fry the onion in the oil until soft, and then add the tomatoes and chilli; raise the heat, and add the apple juice.

Cook the vegetables until soft, and then add the seasoning, the coriander and the corn kernels, cut with a sharp knife from the cob. Slake the cornflour with a little cold water, and stir into the salsa until it thickens. Serve cold with grilled meats, fish or vegetables.

Golden gazpacho

Corn is also one of the ingredients in this unusual chilled soup.

Serves 4 to 6

2 cobs of sweetcorn
1 small melon
1 ripe mango
1 ripe papaya
2 shallots, or a small mild onion
1 litre (1¾ pints) vegetable stock
lightly toasted flaked almonds
seasoning

Boil the corn for 2 to 3 minutes. When cool enough to handle, cut the kernels from the cobs, put a handful or so aside, and put the rest in the food processor.

Peel and dice the melon, mango and papaya, put some aside for garnish, and put the rest in the food processor, together with the onion and vegetable stock. Process until smooth. Season to taste, and chill.

Serve in bowls or a tureen, garnished with the remaining corn, the diced fruit and the flaked almonds. If you wish, you can add yellow tomatoes, yellow pepper and some fresh chilli to the soup.

Aubergine, okra, corn and tomato stew

This rich vegetable stew has even more flavour if made the day before required and eaten cold, but not chilled, with hot pitta bread. If you like such things chilli-hot, then cook a small green or red chilli in the stew but carefully remove the seeds first.

Serves 6 to 8

1 medium onion, peeled and sliced
6 tablespoons extra-virgin olive oil
3 large aubergines or several smaller ones,
    trimmed and diced, not too small
6 garlic cloves, peeled and crushed
250g (8oz) okra
750g (1½ lbs) peeled tomatoes, fresh or canned
a few sprigs of thyme
kernels cut from 3 or 4 corn cobs
salt
freshly ground black pepper
chopped flat-leaf parsley, or coriander

Fry the onion gently in the olive oil, using a flameproof casserole or heavy saucepan.

Add the aubergines and fry all over, then add the garlic, okra, tomatoes and thyme. Bring to the boil, then turn down the heat and continue to cook, partly covered, until the vegetables are tender. Add the corn, bring back to the boil, and simmer for 2 to 3 minutes more.

Check the seasoning, scatter on the chopped parsley, or coriander, and serve.

Tomatoes and other Mediterranean flavours

What could be more summery than tomatoes at their best? The 'green' pungent scent as they are snapped from the vine, the tight, satiny skin, and the warm, sharp-sweet juice which bursts out as you bite into the fruit are, for me, some of the most evocative sensations.

Even our shop-bought summer tomatoes in Britain, picked relatively close to home and making a shorter trip from the grower to the supermarket and greengrocer, have something of these qualities, and as for home-grown tomatoes, they are a true feast.

I have decided to give up Dutch 'vine-ripened' tomatoes in winter, having, sadly, come to the conclusion that they are not worth eating. Only when the sun has begun to shine in the summer do they have any flavour. Even as late as May, I have found them bland and woolly-fleshed, although they have plenty of colour and juice. The vine-ripened tomatoes from southern Spain that I buy at the same time are entirely different, with sweet, juicy and flavoursome flesh. Holland gets no more sun than we do in Britain, so everything comes from hot-houses; however technologically advanced and electronically controlled, this surely cannot make up for lack of sunlight. So in July and August I have a surfeit of tomatoes until the end of their season. Quite often that will mean a tomato salad for lunch or as a first course for dinner. Basil and mint, but not together, are my favourite tomato salad herbs.

The only seasoning I use with them is coarse sea salt, freshly ground black pepper, and whatever is my current favourite extra-virgin olive oil. And those, generally, are the only condiments I use in any salad, supplemented by a good bottle of vinegar. This might be an old *balsamico*, made by my friends the Lancellottis in Modena, and I will add the merest drop of this elixir. Or it might be a bottle of A. R. Valdespino sherry vinegar, available in some supermarkets. Not long ago, I opened a bottle of one-hundred-year-old sherry vinegar given to me by Miguel Valdespino, which he drew from the family cask, and it was like no other sherry vinegar I have ever had, as dark and thick as old *balsamico*, with the concentrated nose of a rare Oloroso and a revelation on the palate; again, this is measured out by the drop.

Fresh tomato tart

This tart gives off one of the most appetizing smells imaginable. A more elaborate tart can be made with courgettes and aubergines, as in the subsequent recipe. Because both tarts are made with bread dough, they have little, if any, fat in them, unlike pastry dough, at least a third of which will be fat.

Serves 4 to 6

Dough

300g (10oz) strong plain flour
1 teaspoon fast-action easy-blend yeast
1 teaspoon salt
about 150 mls (¼ pint) hand-hot water
2 tablespoons olive oil – optional

Sift the dry ingredients together, and then stir in the water. You may not require it all, or you may need a little more, to produce a soft, but not sticky, dough.

Knead for 10 minutes on a floured worktop until you have a smooth, elastic dough.

Put the dough in an oiled bowl, cover with a damp cloth and put it somewhere to rise. When the dough has doubled in volume, knock it back, and knead it lightly once more. Working on a floured work surface, roll and stretch it to fit an oiled shallow tart tin about 25–30cm (10–12 inches) in diameter, pressing the dough up the sides as well to form a wall.

Topping

75mls (3oz) extra-virgin olive oil
6 cloves garlic, peeled and thinly sliced
   – optional
750g (1½lbs) firm, ripe tomatoes, sliced
salt
pepper

Brush the dough all over with some of the olive oil, and scatter slices of garlic on the bottom, if using it. Arrange the tomato slices on top, in overlapping circles, and brush with the remaining oil. Lightly season with salt and pepper, cover, and let the dough prove once more for about 45 minutes. Bake in the top half of a preheated oven at 200°C/400°F/gas mark 6, for 20 to 25 minutes.

This tastes best warm, or just cold, but not refrigerated.

Napoleon of tomato and aubergines

I first served this crunchy, flavoursome stack of bread and vegetables as an accompaniment to grilled lamb cutlets. It also makes an excellent first course, or, with the addition of more vegetables and sliced goat's cheese, a very good light main course; and, with the right kind of cheese, it is suitable for vegetarians.

Serves 4

2 aubergines
4 tomatoes
8 slices bread
extra-virgin olive oil
salt
pepper
4 sprigs of rosemary, about 7.5cm (3 inches)
   long

Choose aubergines and tomatoes of roughly the same diameter, about 5–7.5cms (2–3 inches). Slice the aubergines, and cut 2 or 3 slices from each tomato, keeping the end pieces and letting the seeds and liquid drip into a bowl.

Grill, roast or fry the aubergines, and then the tomatoes. Cut 8 circles from the bread, and fry them in olive oil. Between two circles of fried bread, layer the cooked tomato and aubergine, and secure the stack with a sprig of rosemary.

Rub the tomato residue through a sieve, and add olive oil and seasoning for a dressing to serve with the bread stack. The fried bread can also be spread with tapenade for an even more provençale flavour.

Mediterranean vegetables tossed with fennel juice

Serves 4 to 6

2 fennel bulbs
1 mild onion, peeled and sliced
4–5 tablespoons extra-virgin olive oil
150g (5oz) green beans, topped and tailed, and
   broken into pieces
4 courgettes, sliced
1 red pepper, grilled or roasted, and peeled
200g (7oz) spinach or Swiss Chard leaves,
   rinsed and dried
1 tablespoon sherry vinegar
2 tablespoons toasted pine nuts
2 tablespoons sultanas or raisins

Roughly chop one of the fennel bulbs, and juice it. If you do not have a juicer, blend or process with a little water and rub through a sieve to obtain fennel juice. Otherwise, grate the fennel over a bowl and sieve it to catch the juice. Slice the other into wedges.

Fry the onion in the olive oil, and then add the fennel, beans, courgettes and peppers. Cook, stirring until the vegetables are crisp and tender, about 6 to 8 minutes.

Stir in the fennel juice, raise the heat, and stir in the greens. Splash on the sherry vinegar, stir in the pine nuts and raisins, and serve immediately.

Mediterranean vegetable tart

Whilst you could use mushrooms and leeks in this tart, I usually make it with courgettes, red peppers and aubergines, together with the tomatoes, for an impressive tart full of bright Mediterranean colours and flavours. Fennel too would be a good addition. It should be quartered and blanched first until reas-onably tender; otherwise, it will not cook in the same time as the other ingredients. Courgettes I blanch whole, and then slice, unless they are no more than little-finger length, in which case I halve them lengthways.

Aubergines are best lightly cooked, grilled or roasted before using in the tart. Shredded mint or basil add the final touches.

Serves 6 to 8

300g (10oz) bread dough – see previous recipe

2 aubergines
3 or 4 large courgettes
4 large red peppers
8 large ripe tomatoes
olive oil
coarse sea salt
mint or basil, shredded

Prepare the dough and line the tart tin or baking sheet as above. You could also use a paella pan, roasting pan, Swiss roll tray, or any other broad, flat container that will go into the oven. A pizza tray or stone is, of course, ideal.

Slice and grill the aubergines until just beginning to soften. Parboil the courgettes, and peel the peppers. You can do this by holding them over a gas flame until charred, or quarter and roast them. Cut the core out of the tomatoes, and squeeze out the seeds. These can be sieved and the juice used for tomato vinaigrette.

Brush the dough with olive oil, and arrange the vegetables on it. Dribble on a little more olive oil, and sprinkle with coarse sea salt.

Bake in the centre of a preheated oven at 200°C/400°F/gas mark 6 for 45 to 50 minutes. Serve warm or hot.

Moroccan salads

Normally in the summer I would not think of cooking tomatoes, but when I visited Marrakesh I much enjoyed a salad in which the tomatoes are cooked very slowly. The traditional recipe recommends adding a little sugar for seasoning, and indeed, sugar is usually recommended to help along a tomato that might be lacking in zing. Even better, though, is a drop of maple syrup, which I find excellent as a seasoning. I always have a bottle of new season's New England syrup in the refrigerator. With tomatoes, the sharp fruitiness is not masked by sugar, and there seem to be flavour compounds in maple syrup which complement those of savoury foods.

To go with the tomato salad, I have suggested several other salads which would make a perfect first course to a Moroccan meal, followed by a plate of grills, a pile of steamed couscous and a spicy vegetable stew.

Tomato salad

Serves 4 to 6

1kg (2lbs) ripe, firm tomatoes
2 tablespoons extra-virgin olive oil
salt
pepper

Peel and quarter the tomatoes, and discard the seeds.

Put the oil in a sauté pan or shallow saucepan, and in it stew the tomatoes very gently, without breaking them up but until their liquid has all but evaporated.

Season near the beginning with just a little salt and pepper.

Cook the tomatoes for about an hour, and then allow to cool. Serve cold, adding more seasoning if necessary.

Sweet potato salad

Serves 4 to 6

1 mild onion, peeled and chopped
5 tablespoons olive oil
good pinch of powdered saffron
1 teaspoon grated fresh ginger, or ½ teaspoon powdered ginger
1 teaspoon each paprika and powdered cumin
1 teaspoon each chopped parsley and coriander
1 tablespoon grated lemon zest, or chopped pickled lemon
500g (1lb) sweet potatoes, peeled and diced
100mls (4oz) water
juice of half a lemon

Gently fry the onion in the oil until wilted with the spices, herbs and lemon zest, then add the sweet potatoes and enough water to half cover them.

Cook until the potatoes are done and the sauce reduced by half, and stir in the lemon juice before serving.

Aubergine salad

Serves 4 to 6

500g (1lb) small aubergines
1 garlic clove, peeled
salt
1 teaspoon each paprika and ground cumin
1 tablespoon each lemon juice and olive oil
2–3 tablespoons chopped parsley

Quarter the aubergines lengthways without removing the stalk. Put in a saucepan with the garlic, a good pinch of salt, and about 300mls (½ pint) water. Cook until tender. Drain and mix with the spices and remaining ingredients.

Beetroot salad

Serves 4 to 6

500g (1lb) beetroot, cooked
½ teaspoon each paprika, cinnamon and cumin
2 tablespoons orange flower-water
1 tablespoon lemon juice
1 to 2 teaspoons light muscovado sugar

If possible, use warm, freshly cooked beetroot.
Peel, slice thickly, and put in a bowl, well mixed with the rest of the ingredients.

Lettuce and orange salad

Serves 4 to 6

3 Little Gem lettuces
3 oranges
2 tablespoons lemon juice
1 tablespoon each orange-flower water, olive or groundnut oil, and light muscovado sugar

Cut the lettuces into wedges, and peel and slice two of the oranges.
Arrange these on a platter. Mix the juice of the third orange with the remaining ingredients, and spoon over the salad. Serve at once.

Okra in tomato and olive oil

As well as being part of a *meze* table, this is an excellent dish to serve with grilled lamb cutlets or lamb kebabs. And you can, of course, use fresh okra, in which case it will not need soaking first; simply trim it and add it with the garlic.

Serves 8

2 x 45g (2oz) packets dried baby okra (available from supermarkets and shops selling Mediterranean and Middle Eastern products – Cypressa brand)

1 medium onion, peeled and thinly sliced
6 tablespoons extra-virgin olive oil
1 or 2 garlic cloves, peeled and crushed
8 ripe tomatoes, peeled, seeded and chopped, or 1 x 400g (14oz) can chopped tomatoes
salt
pepper
fresh coriander

Rehydrate the okra according to the directions on the packet. Meanwhile, gently fry the onion in the olive oil until lightly browned. Stir in the garlic and add the drained okra. Cook for 5 minutes and stir in the tomato. Simmer gently for 20 minutes or so, season to taste, stir in some chopped coriander and add a few leaves on top just before serving.

Sweet pepper, tomato and chick pea salad

Serves 8

6 large red peppers
8 ripe tomatoes, peeled if you like, seeded and cut into strips or chopped
400g (14oz) cooked or canned chick-peas
1 level teaspoon cumin seeds
pinch of ground chilli
1 clove garlic, peeled and crushed – optional
2 tablespoons each extra-virgin olive oil and groundnut oil
1 tablespoon lemon juice
small bunch of flat-leaf parsley, finely chopped
salt

Grill or roast the peppers, and remove the skins and seeds. Dice or cut into strips, and mix well with the rest of the ingredients.

Autumn and winter vegetables

I once had the honour of being asked to open the annual show of the Haseley and District Horticultural Society near Oxford. It was a wonderful day out; there was not only a marquee full of horticultural exhibits, but medieval skittles, an Aunt Sally, a Punch and Judy show, a parade of vintage cars, and right at the end of the day, an auction of the produce left over. Some people went away with bunches of huge dahlias, others with marrows, cabbages and homemade jams and marmalades. I had my eye on class 39, 'a collection of four kinds of small vegetables suitable for nouveau cuisine (sic)', and exhibitors could choose to show baby turnips, Pink Fir Apple potatoes, baby beetroot, Zefa Fino fennel, Oregon Sugar Pod mangetouts, Super Roma tomatoes and other delicacies. This was an unusual display next to the thigh-length leeks and football-size prize onions, which I noticed the proud owners did not leave behind for auction.

The winner of class 39 took home Le Manoir Cup, offered by Raymond Blanc, who had opened the competition in a previous year. It was the Frenchman's bemusement at the size of the prize parsnips, leeks and onions that led him to this generous gesture, from which I benefited in the shape of a bag of exquisite fresh baby vegetables, which went into many good soups and salads in the days following.

As a cook, I recognize the great debt I owe to gardeners and horticulturalists, for it is from them that I get the raw materials that I love so much, such as freshly dug potatoes, crisp green beans, peppery young turnips, fragrant bunches of basil and rosemary, full, ripe, sweet tomatoes on the vine, and even flowers. But I have, over the years, noticed a singular ambivalence on the part of the gardener towards the cook. When I was a child, my parents had little time to garden, but my father grew tomatoes for many years. My mother and I would think up all kinds of recipes for them, but he felt we should simply admire them in their neat rows on the kitchen window-sill, where he had placed them after picking.

The relationship between cook and gardener must be one of the oldest in human society – as old, I think, as the somewhat competitive nature of the gardener. I have been reading Gerard's *Herbal*. John Gerard was born in Cheshire in 1545, and by 1596 he was a well-established gardener and had published his first work, a list of plants that he had cultivated in his own garden. Running to twenty-four pages, this was probably the first garden catalogue.

But throughout his *Herbal*, he cannot resist gloating little comments to the effect that although such and such a plant was particularly rare, expensive or difficult to grow, 'I do have some in my garden.' And of tomatoes, newly introduced to England and called apples of love, he says that 'they grow in Spain, Italy and such hot countries from whence myself have received seeds for my garden, where they do increase and prosper'. He writes of the herb hyssop, 'all kinds of hyssope do grow in my garden, and in some others too', and of potatoes, which were then described as Virginia potatoes, 'they grow and prosper in my garden as in their own native country'.

Harvest festival casserole, with feta, chilli and chive cobbler

Serves 4 to 6

2 or 3 corn cobs
4 cloves
1 onion, peeled and quartered
1 tablespoon olive oil
6 cloves garlic, peeled
350g (12oz) small or salad potatoes
6 green or yellow courgettes, or 3 of each
200g (7oz) green beans
150g (5oz) okra
6–8 small sweet tomatoes
bunch of spring onions
150mls (¼ pint) vegetable stock
150mls (¼ pint) white wine
salt
pepper

cobbler topping
1 or two red chillies, seeded, soaked in hot
    water, and drained
bunch of chives, trimmed and chopped
250g (8oz) self-raising flour

½ teaspoon baking powder

½ teaspoon salt

25g (1oz) butter, chilled and diced

50g (2oz) feta cheese, diced

about 150mls (¼ pint) buttermilk, or yoghurt and
water

Cut the kernels from the corn, and put to one side. Stick the cloves into the onion, and brown the pieces lightly in the oil in a casserole. Add the garlic, potatoes, courgettes, beans and okra, and the white wine.

Simmer for 10 to 15 minutes, and then add the rest of the vegetables and stock, together with seasoning, and cook for a further 5 to 10 minutes.

Meanwhile, make the cobbler by putting all the ingredients, except for the liquid, in a food processor, and process for 30 seconds or so. Add the liquid, and process just enough to lightly bind the dough.

For a lighter topping, this scone-type mix is even better made by hand, exactly as you would with scones. Lightly roll out, cut into rounds, and place these on top of the vegetables, around the edge of the casserole.

Put in a preheated oven at 200°C/400°F/gas mark 6, for about 10 minutes, until well risen and golden. Protect the vegetables by placing a circle of foil over them, but not the pastry.

Sweet fennel and onion confit with olives and sardines

Serves 8

3 large mild onions, peeled and thinly sliced

6 tablespoons extra-virgin olive oil

3 large round fennel bulbs, sliced

6 tablespoons white wine, water or vegetable
stock

1 teaspoon ground cumin

1 teaspoon ground coriander

salt

freshly ground black pepper

3 tablespoons sultanas or raisins

3 tablespoons toasted pine nuts or flaked
almonds

24 black olives

2 or 3 cans sardines in olive oil

Gently fry the onion in oil for 10 to 15 minutes, and then add the fennel, the liquid and cumin and coriander. Continue cooking for 15 to 20 minutes, stirring from time to time to prevent sticking. Season to taste with the salt and pepper, and stir in the fruit and nuts. Spoon the mixture onto plates, and serve hot, warm or cold, with a few olives and a couple of drained sardines on top of each. Use the feathery fennel tops for garnish.

For a more substantial first course, heap the mixture on top of hot pitta bread, and for a more elaborate dish, on rounds of pre-baked pastry enriched with egg yolk and made very short and crisp with plenty of butter or vegetable shortening.

Using some of the same ingredients, a very quick and refreshing starter can be made by thinly slicing round fennel bulbs, spreading them with olive paste, and topping with a spoonful of thick yoghurt.

Braised vegetables

Some vegetables taste as good cooked as raw, and, indeed, take on new flavours altogether, but it is important to choose the right method. Celery, fennel, chicory can be steamed, stir-fried or served raw, but I particularly like them braised in the oven, simply with a little stock, wine or meat juices. If I have a roast or casserole in the oven, then a dish of braised vegetables will often be served first, sometimes finished off at the last moment with a crisp golden topping of grated cheese, breadcrumbs and/or nuts. Leeks braise well, alone or with diced ham and a bay leaf for flavouring. Cabbage, too, can be braised, and it is particularly good as an autumn or winter vegetable. Stuffed cabbage parcels make an unusual first course.

Cabbage parcels

Use leftovers from the Sunday roast or from a ham, or nuts mixed with rice, couscous or other grains, herbs and seasoning to taste. Take the outer leaves of a Savoy cabbage for the wrappers, and blanch them. Shred the inner leaves and cook until tender, and then mix with the rest of the stuffing. One or two soaked dried ceps, finely chopped, will add a good flavour, or try it with dried tomatoes. Remove the tough part of the central rib from each cabbage leaf, and overlap the two halves. Spoon on the filling, and roll the leaf into a neat parcel. Place in an oiled ovenproof dish, and when full, sprinkle with extra-virgin olive oil, wine or stock, and bake for about 35 minutes at 180°C/350°F/gas mark 4.

Baked and roasted vegetables

Unless using an open fire, 'baking' is the more correct term for anything cooked in an enclosed oven. But we still refer to roast beef and roast potatoes, so here, by extension, are roast vegetables. However, the method of cooking quite removes them from the category of potatoes cooked around the joint and absorbing fat from it. It is a dish to try when you have the oven on for cooking a pot-roast bird, as these vegetables are marvellous with chicken. Root vegetables contain a good deal of starch, which in cooking turns to sugar, and most spectacularly when a high heat is applied to cut surfaces which then turn brown, caramelize, and seal to a crispness. Half an onion, browned and caramelized in the oven or under the grill, gives an excellent dark colour to stock for casseroles, sauces and, above all, French onion soup.

I use celeriac, parsnips, thick carrots, potatoes, swedes, turnips and sweet potatoes. Apart from the potatoes, I peel the vegetables, and brush the baking dish with olive oil. The vegetables should be cut into wedges to give a larger surface area to caramelize. Cook them for about an hour at 180–200°C (350–400°F)/gas mark 4–6. Sweet potatoes should be added about halfway through cooking, as they have a softer flesh. See Chapter 13 for potato and root recipes.

Boiled vegetables

Forget images of waterlogged carrots and soggy cabbage. Walls of cellulose are what hold vegetables together, and cooking breaks these down, but there is no need to reduce them to an unappetizing pulp.

Boiling is the fastest method for vegetables destined for mashing and purées, and it is one of the most efficient ways of cooking fibrous vegetables, such as cardoons and globe artichokes.

Winter salads

In winter I like to make a red coleslaw, using red cabbage, red onions, beetroot and dried cranberries or cherries, left over from winter baking. Raisins or currants can be substituted. Make a large bowlful of this with the dressing of your choice, and serve it with marinated herring pieces.

One of my favourite salads involves a fairly lengthy preparation time for the cucumber, so it is worth doing two or three cucumbers at once. They keep for a few days in the refrigerator and they can also be used to make an excellent stir-fry to accompany chicken or fish.

This next is a crisp yet delicate salad that can be given an Italian or oriental flavour, depending on the oils, vinegars and seasonings used. I usually use carrot as the other main vegetable, but you can also use *daikon* (mooli, or white radish), kohlrabi and jicama (yam bean), which are all crisp root vegetables.

Oriental cucumber and carrot salad

Serves 4, plus leftovers

3 cucumbers
2–3 teaspoons sea salt
6 medium carrots, scrubbed
thumb-size piece fresh ginger
1 or 2 lemon grass stalks
grated zest of a lime and 1–2 tablespoons juice
½ teaspoon sugar
½ teaspoon coarsely ground black pepper
2 teaspoons soy sauce
1 tablespoon toasted sesame oil
2 tablespoons crushed roasted peanuts

Halve the cucumbers, discard the watery core, and thinly slice. Put in a colander, sprinkle with the sea salt, and leave to drain for at least an hour if possible, and up to 4 hours.

Rinse the cucumber, and dry thoroughly in a clean towel. The cucumber will be soft and wilted but will have a good flavour and a surprisingly crisp texture. Make juice with two of the carrots, the ginger and the lemon grass. Stir in the lime zest, juice, sugar, pepper, soy sauce and sesame oil. Shave the remaining carrot into ribbons with a potato peeler and heap on to plates with the cucumber around it. Pour the dressing over the carrot, and scatter the peanuts over the salad.

To make an Italian version, leave out the oriental aromatics and use extra-virgin olive oil, wine vinegar or traditional balsamic vinegar, and a pinch of chopped mint or penny royal.

A few more from here and there

Ajiaco sin pollo

The first *ajiaco* recipe that I published in England after my return from a visit to Colombia in 1988, I had to call *ajiaco sin guascas* in the absence of the indispensable herb. It was quite clear that, although the versions I ate had chicken in them, potatoes were the main ingredient. There may well have been times in the early development of the dish when the native Americans had neither fish nor fowl to add to the pot and used only the roots, tubers and vegetables growing nearby, from which it is but a close step to a vegetarian or vegetable *ajiaco*, an *ajiaco sin pollo*. And, if potatoes are the main ingredient, it is the hot, sharp *aji* which gives the dish its name. I have dried *guascas*, the herb in question from Colombia, but you can also use watercress.

This is a good dish for a crowd, and leftovers can be blended to make a silky, soothing soup.

Serves 6 to 8

1 onion, peeled, quartered, and each quarter
    stuck with a clove

2 or 3 large floury potatoes, such as King
    Edward, peeled
1.5 litres (2½ pints) vegetable stock
750g (1½lbs) Maris Piper, or other similar
    all-purpose potatoes
750g (1½lbs) Charlotte, La Ratte, Pink Fir Apple
    or other waxy potatoes
1 or 2 orange-fleshed sweet potatoes
1 butternut squash, piece of pumpkin, kabocha
    or other squash
4 leeks, trimmed and rinsed thoroughly
1 bunch of watercress, washed and picked over
3 corn cobs, cut into 3 or 4
seasoning
fresh coriander

To make the *ajiaco*, put the onion in a large pot or casserole. Cut the floury potatoes into chunks, and add to the pot with the stock. Let it come to the boil, while you prepare the rest of the vegetables.

Scrub the all-purpose potatoes, and slice the waxy ones about 1cm (⅓ inch) thick; halve the other potatoes to make bite-sized pieces. Peel the sweet potato and squash, and cut into chunks. Slice the leeks, and finely chop most of the watercress, leaving a few sprigs to add with the coriander as garnish.

When the stock is boiling, add the rest of the vegetables, except the corn, and simmer until they are soft. By this time, the first batch of potatoes will have collapsed nicely to provide thickening for the stew. Bring to a rolling boil, add the corn, and boil for 2 to 3 minutes. Add a little seasoning, and then serve from the pot or ladle into large soup bowls, decorate with a little more greenery.

For accompaniments, put into separate ramekins some capers, some soured cream, some chopped watercress and some *aji*. Also slice 2 or 3 ripe avocados, sprinkle with lime juice, and arrange on small side plates for each serving.

Aji

Serves 6 to 8

2 leeks
1 or 2 green chillies, seeded and finely
    chopped
about 2 tablespoons fresh coriander leaves,
    chopped
3 tomatoes, halved, seeded and chopped
salt and pepper
juice of a lime

Shred the well-washed leeks, and mix with the chopped chilli, fresh coriander and tomatoes. Season to taste with the salt, pepper and lime juice.

Vegetables stuffed with mint and tabbouleh

Serves 6 to 8

24 small vegetables – about 50g (2oz) – such as tomatoes, courgettes, peppers, onions, aubergines
250g (8oz) tabbouleh
3 cloves garlic
1 heaped tablespoon finely chopped mint
sea salt
freshly ground black pepper
good pinch ground cumin
extra-virgin olive oil

Prepare the vegetables as appropriate. The tomatoes will not need blanching or parboiling, but cut a slice off the top, scoop out the seeds and juice. Rub these through a sieve, and reserve the juice. Sprinkle lightly with salt, and stand them upside down to drain.

The courgettes and aubergines should be parboiled, the courgettes for 3 to 4 minutes, the aubergines for 10 minutes. Rinse under cold water. Cut them in half horizontally, and scoop out some of the centre, leaving about 1cm (½ inch) flesh attached to the skin. Finely chop the flesh from the centre, and reserve.

Cut the top off the peppers, remove the seeds and pithy ribs from inside. Grill and peel them, or if you don't mind them with the skin on, parboil for 4 to 5 minutes and rinse under cold water. Peel the onions, parboil for 10 minutes, and remove the centre, leaving the outer two layers of skin for stuffing.

To make the stuffing, finely chop the centre pieces of onion, and mix with the tabbouleh, together with the sieved tomato juices, chopped courgette and aubergine. If you are only using tomatoes and peppers for stuffing, then use a larger amount of tabbouleh. Peel and crush the garlic and mix into the rest of the stuffing ingredients, together with the mint and spices, and season to taste.

Spoon the mixture into the vegetables, and place them in a lightly oiled roasting tin. Sprinkle a few drops of olive oil on top of each, and bake in a preheated oven at 180°C/350°F/gas mark 4 for 30 to 35 minutes, or until the vegetables are tender. Cooking time will depend, to a large extent, on how tender and fresh the vegetables were to begin with.

The perfect guacamole

Avocados are plentiful and relatively inexpensive. Buy them hard and perfectly unblemished, with the vestigial stalk still attached, and the fruit will ripen in the fruit bowl in a few days.

YOU NEED to feed 8 people, 4 large ripe avocados, salt, pepper and a fresh lime, six spring onions, trimmed and cleaned, fresh red or green chillies, depending on your tolerance, and a bunch of fresh coriander, rinsed and dried.

METHOD Peel and roughly chop the avocados, then mash with the salt and pepper, grated lime zest and a little lime juice. Finely chop the spring onions and seeded chillies and stir into the mashed avocado. Cover with clingfilm until required, but preferably serve immediately.

ALTERNATIVES For a smooth guacamole, put all the ingredients in the food processor and switch the 'pulse' button on and off until you have the texture you prefer.

Vegetable gumbo

If you can get powdered *filé*, so much the better. This dried and powdered sassafras is what gives the gumbo its distinctive texture, somewhat thick and shiny. Extra okra can be used in place of *filé*. The chilli can be left out, or increased to taste.

Serves 4 to 6

sea salt
1 large aubergine, about 400g (14oz)
1 large onion, peeled and cut into wedges
1–2 tablespoons olive oil
400g (14oz) chopped tomatoes – canned will do
500g (1lb) Maris Piper, Cara, or other small potatoes, which should be scrubbed
1.5 litres (2½ pints) vegetable stock
150g (5oz) okra
1 green or red chilli, seeded and chopped
500g (1lb) courgettes, trimmed and sliced

200g (7oz) green beans or runner beans,
    topped and tailed, sliced if using runner
    beans
kernels cut from 2 or 3 corn cobs
seasoning
1 teaspoon *filé* powder

Dice and lightly salt the aubergine, and leave it in a colander for half an hour or so, and then rinse and dry it thoroughly.

In a large casserole brown the aubergine and onion in the oil without burning them. Stir in the tomatoes, and cook until all the liquid has evaporated and they too begin to caramelize.

Add the potatoes and a third of the stock. Simmer for 15 minutes, and then add the rest of the stock, the okra left whole and the chilli. Simmer for 20 minutes, then add the courgettes and beans and simmer until the vegetables are tender.

Add the corn kernels and seasoning, boil for two minutes, and remove from the heat. Slake the *filé* in a tablespoon or two of water, and stir into the stew, which should not boil after the addition of the *filé*.

Serve from the pot, with steamed or baked basmati or Carolina rice, and a sweet and sour salsa.

Mango and avocado salsa

Here is a very easy and good recipe for salsa. It can be made in the food processor.

Peel and roughly chop a firm mango and an avocado. Chop, but do not blitz, in the food processor with a peeled onion, a little fresh ginger and some fresh coriander. Stir in grated lime or lemon zest and juice, salt and pepper to taste, and a little light muscovado sugar.

Index

Index

Index